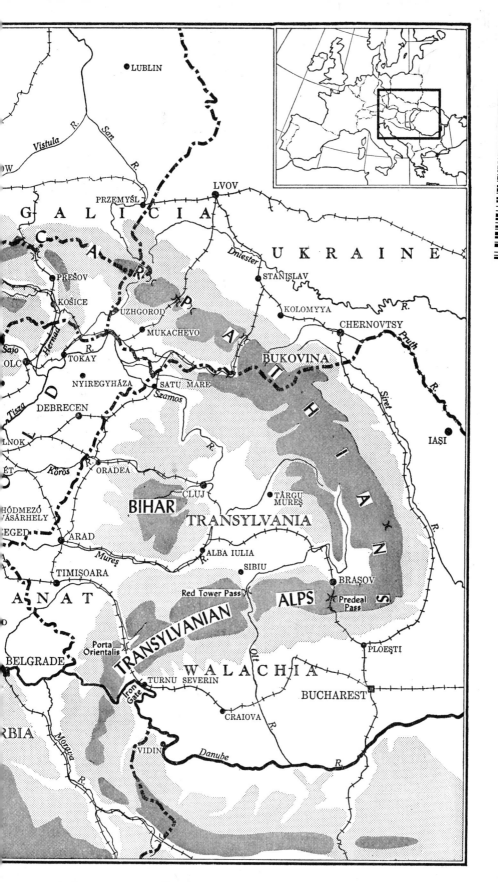

BORDERLAND *A Historical and Geographical Study of Burgenland, Austria*

A Historical and
Geographical Study
of Burgenland, Austria

BORDERLAND

Andrew F. Burghardt

MADISON: 1962

UNIVERSITY OF WISCONSIN PRESS

Published by The University of Wisconsin Press,
430 Sterling Court, Madison 6, Wisconsin

Copyright © 1962 by the Regents of the
University of Wisconsin

Printed in the United States of America
by the Vail-Ballou Press, Inc., Binghamton, New York

Library of Congress Catalog Card Number 62-15992

To Mary

PREFACE

The initial research for this study was carried on in Austria during the academic year 1956–57. I conducted my library research in Vienna and Eisenstadt and spent much time in Burgenland observing local conditions and speaking to the inhabitants. This research was supported by the Foreign Field Research Program conducted by the Division of Earth Sciences; National Academy of Sciences—National Research Council, and financed by the Geography Branch, Office of Naval Research. The study formed my doctoral dissertation, and my continued interest in the area prompted a more profound historical investigation which led to the writing of this book. Much of this new research has again been carried on in Austria; in this work I have been supported by a United States Government (Fulbright) Research Grant. A visit of Hungary in April–May, 1961, enabled me to corroborate some of my conclusions.

Anyone familiar with the area treated may wish to disagree with some of my name choices. Certainly several anachronisms occur in this study: e.g. the "Amber Road" has had other names through the centuries; the principal party of Austria is now not the "Christian party," but the "People's party"; Mattersburg was really Mattersdorf when the capital of Burgenland was being selected. These and others have been allowed because changes in nomenclature or frequent necessary explanations would succeed only in confusing the non-specialist. For the same reason I have chosen the German name, March, instead of the more frequently used Slavic name, Morava, for the river entering the Danube near Bratislava; unfortunately another Morava enters the Danube near Belgrade, and that Morava has no acceptable alternate name. Occasionally, for the sake of simplicity and clarity, I have coined names: e.g. I refer to the Porta Hungaria as the Carnuntum or

Hainburg Gap, since those cities are prominently treated in the text. Most of the place names are those in current usage, although a name formerly used may be given if the locality was important under the older name.

The notes are intended to be primarily informational. Generally, sources are cited only for quotations and to supply further information. I have tried to limit the number of notes, so as not to smother the reader with arid references. The exceptions to this policy are chapters 9 and 10, where the complicated and controversial nature of the material necessitates the use of many and long notes. The specialist will, I am sure, recognize most of the facts mentioned, at least in the first two parts of the book. In any case a full bibliography of the sources utilized follows the text.

When I first arrived in Burgenland I was totally unfamiliar with the area and would not have been able to commence, much less complete, my studies had it not been for the assistance of many persons. The Geographisches Institut of the University of Vienna helped greatly by introducing me to some of the primary sources. Herr Professor Bobek and Herr Anasiedler were especially helpful. I wish to thank the now retired director of the Burgenländische Landesbibliothek, Hofrat Dr. Homma, for supplying me with a letter of introduction which proved invaluable in my interviews with government officials, and also Herr Amtsrat Semmelweis, Dr. Sinowatz, and Dr. Ernst for their welcome assistance in my research in Eisenstadt. I am indebted to Herr Walter Dujmowitz for much personal information on Burgenland and for my introduction to the pertinent doctoral dissertations.

I owe special thanks to Professors Richard Hartshorne and Andrew Clark of the Department of Geography of the University of Wisconsin, who supervised my doctoral work and have kept in constant touch with me and my work; thanks are due also to Professor Michael Petrovich of the Department of History of the University of Wisconsin for urging me to pay increased attention to the position and role of the Croats within Burgenland, and to Professor Albert Tezla of the University of Minnesota, Duluth, for directing me to the principal Hungarian bibliographies. Above all others I wish to thank my wife, Mary, who has given editorial assistance to this study and has shared my enthusiasm for Burgenland.

Since so much of my information was gained from interviews, I feel obliged to indicate to the reader the sources of this personal information. The persons with whom I spoke included the following: a former chancellor of Austria; the Landeshauptmann of Burgenland; the Secretary and three other functionaries of the Socialist party of Burgenland; the Bezirkshauptmann of Neusiedl Bezirk; the Bezirkshauptmannstellvertreter of Eisenstadt Bezirk; the Oberamtmann of Oberwart; the two directors and two librarians of the Landesarchiv- und bibliothek, Eisenstadt; the Direktor of the Landesmuseum, Eisenstadt; employees of the provincial government, Eisenstadt; a Stadtrat of Rust; the editor of the *Grenzland Kurier*, Neusiedl; two border guards; the director (?) of the Catholic diocesan archive, Eisenstadt; Catholic priests in over a dozen villages; the Superintentur of the A. B. Evangelische Kirche (Lutheran), Eisenstadt; several Lutheran pastors or their wives; the wife of the Calvinist pastor in Oberwart; the principals of the Gymnasia in Eisenstadt and Mattersburg, and the Hauptschulen in Deutschkreutz and Stegersbach; teachers in numerous other villages; the founder, a past president, and the present president of the Croatian Culture Society; the secretary of the Croatian Publication Society; the Kroatische Schulinspektor, Eisenstadt; three professors of the University of Vienna; one nobleman; and many peasants in all parts of Burgenland.

Vienna, June, 1961

CONTENTS

Contents

ILLUSTRATIONS
following page 144

MAPS

PANNONIA

INTRODUCTION

In the center of Europe the great mass of the Alps halts in its eastward march and fronts the broad expanses of the Hungarian Plain. As if blunted by the steppe to the east, the upland splits, thrusting long ridges to the northeast and southeast to encompass the lowland before it. Smaller ridges extend briefly eastward before disappearing into the plain. Beyond the massive Alps lies the westernmost extension of the steppes which have long formed a grassland connection between Mongolia and central Europe. Here, where the Europe of small basins and valleys meets the expanses of Eurasia, the intensive farmer of small plots has often been accosted by the nomad. Huns, Avars, Magyars, Mongols, and Turks have entered this lowland and encamped there.

The elliptical ring formed by the Alps, the Carpathians, and the Balkan highlands has not formed the protective wall suggested by maps. Four significant gateways lead easily into this large basin, and all four have led invaders into its flat interior. To the northwest is the Vienna gateway allowing entry from Germany; to the southwest are the Julian (Slovenian) passes leading from northern Italy; to the northeast are the several passes which connect with the grasslands of the Ukraine; to the southeast is the river routeway leading southward from Belgrade to the Aegean and Turkey. Because of these gaps, the western portion of the Carpathian Basin [1] has long been one of the crossroads of Europe. The influences of Rome and of Byzantium, of Moscow and Karakorum have been felt in Budapest and Vienna.

Defense of this broad basin against outside forces has always been difficult. The defenders could never seal all the passes. Once the invader was within the bastion wall there were few further barriers to hinder his progress. Beyond the mountains there was only the plain. Not until he reached the Danube did the invader from the east meet a major obstacle, and only where the Danube cut a gorge through the Börzsöny-Bakony range was there a site that could support a national fortress center. It has often happened, therefore, that as soon as an outside force has gained a preponderance of power it has been able to breach the mountain wall and, once inside, has easily overrun the central area of the basin.

Yet, between A.D. 1000 and 1526 this was not part of a "Shatter Belt." [2] These plains at that time were the site of a strong, well integrated state. The Magyars, who had entered the basin as a marauding group, made the necessary transition from the nomadic to the Western style of organization. The entire lowland was unified into one state, and the plain became the home of a powerful political unit for the first time in known history. The Romans had organized the western and eastern portions of the basin but had avoided the central steppe; the Franks had integrated the western portions into the Carolingian marchlands but had avoided the flat openness beyond the Danube. The Magyars alone formed a core of power within the basin and remained to organize its full area.

The internal organization formed by the Magyars remained stronger than the forces surrounding it until it was overwhelmed by the Turks, advancing from the southeast, in 1526. With the destruction of the Hungarian power, the Turks occupied the central plain. Habsburg Austria occupied the western portions of the basin, while in the eastern portions, where the mountains formed a natural fortress, a virtually independent Transylvania carefully tended the seeds of a Hungarian rebirth.

After 1683 the control of the area of the basin was simplified into a contest between one external power, Austria, and the reborn internal power, Hungary, which was gradually regaining its strength. In 1867 this contest was finally won by the Hungarian power, which regained virtually full control of the entire basin area. In 1918, however, this internal organization of the basin was shattered again, and once more the rims of the plain were annexed by outside powers. These powers differed from all previous intruding forces in that they were numerous and small, and that none of them had in themselves effected the expansion into the basin. They extended their control beyond the valleys and smaller basins of Bohemia, Walachia, Serbia, and German Austria onto the great plain. Only the core of the basin was left to the Magyars.

The interior, Magyar force again began to try to regain control of the entire basin, and reached the mountain wall of the Carpathians to the northeast between 1939 and 1945. But again outside forces swamped the internal core of power. At present the Soviet Union has crossed the northeastern passes to annex a small portion of the plain, and controls the entire basin except for the western and southern margins. The will of the internal force has not been crushed, but now the Magyars must concern themselves not with organizing the whole basin, but, simply and dramatically, with regaining their basic national freedom.

Burgenland forms the western fringe of the Carpathian Basin. The last blunted hills of the Alps and the first reaches of the plain form its topographic base. Within the narrow limits of Burgenland one leaves the Alpine ranges and enters the steppe. Here is the divide between upland pasture and steppe pasture.

This eastern rim of the Alpine lands has long served as a protective borderland for Western Europe. The Avars, the Magyars, the Mongols, the Turks, and now the Russians have come this far and stopped. Here ended the grass highway from the center of Eurasia. The mountain mass has stood as a barrier rebuffing invasions further westward, but in the course of these invasions, these first slopes and their broad valleys have often been ravaged.

Burgenland is a borderland between East and West. The historic boundary of the marchlands of the Holy Roman Empire forms its western limits; the "Iron Curtain" now forms its eastern limits. This was the fringe of Hungary and is now the fringe of Austria. Until recent years the division between industrial and manorial Europe occurred along its western boundary. In this transitional borderland a manorial culture and system of landholding has since 1922 been integrated into a Western economy. Beyond the latest occupation boundary to the east, large landholdings are being perpetuated by those governments which have substituted bureaucrats for the former nobility.

The people of Burgenland have long learned to look to the east to see what new riders are advancing toward them. It is only since 1955 that the Soviet occupation forces have retired eastward out of this westernmost borderland of the Hungarian plains.

Although it is customary for some historians to assume that human beings have performed their actions upon a featureless landscape, these actions have always had, in reality, a geographic component. All the acts of man are performed upon a topographic stage, and often these acts cannot be understood properly without an appreciation of their topographic framework. It is true that man can ignore the differences between place and place on the surface of the earth, but, except in extreme cases, he has not; differences in fertility of the soil or in ease of transit have always been considered important. While terrain in itself cannot predetermine what man does or where he does it, nevertheless the human preference for a direct road over a meandering road, for fertile soil over sterile sands and rocks, and for dry land over marsh, has made the diversity of topography highly significant in the history of Europe. It is the object of this study to anchor the major movements of over two thousand years of human activity firmly in the terrain upon which they occurred.

This is, therefore, a historical geography or, perhaps, a geographical history. Special attention will be paid to those phenomena which seem to bear a direct relationship to variations in topography: the trade routes, invasions, boundaries, and, particularly, those focal centers of human activity, the cities. Attention will be focused also upon the vital geo-political ideas which moved men in their organizations of the Pannonian lands.

Since the narrow strip now known as Burgenland cannot be understood within merely its own narrow frame, the scope of this analysis has been extended to include all of that land between the north-south Danube and the Wienerwald (Vienna Woods), that land that was known to the Romans as Pannonia. Within this area lie the cities which through the centuries have attested to both the crossroads position and the frontier function of this meeting zone of East and West: Carnuntum, Savaria, Székesfehérvár, Vienna, Pozsony, and Budapest.

This study will examine this area from the beginnings of history to the present day. Through the earlier chapters the focus will be broad enough to include all of northern Pannonia, and often the heart of the basin and the Alps. Later the areal viewpoint will be narrowed to the confines of Burgenland, that border contact strip which expresses in modern terms the historicogeographical essence of this borderland.

2

THE SETTING

Within the area of Roman Pannonia the Alpine massif fractures into a number of ridges which extend as forested fingers into the broad lowlands to the north and east.[1] The Alpine system is composed of three principal parallel bands: a central, rugged, crystalline mass, flanked by limestone formations. The southern flank lies mostly in Italy (the Dolomites) and Jugoslavia, but the crystallines and their northern flank of limestones, and sandstones beyond, front the Pannonian lowlands. In places the contrast between mountain and plain is severe and dramatic, but elsewhere sloping surfaces, composed of the gravelly materials washed down from the mountains by millennia of streams, form a softened transition between the two unlike zones.

In Pannonia the general trend of the terrain is from the southwest to the northeast. The fingered ridges stretch from the main massif towards the great ring of the Carpathians just beyond the Danube; the Carpathians in turn form a continuation of the Alpine system towards the east. The streams of Pannonia also flow towards the northeast where they join the master stream, the Danube. Even those streams which begin by flowing southeastward from the southern flank of the crystalline mass gradually turn, first toward the east and then the northeast, to join the prevailing alignment of the topography.

The ridges fanning out from the Alps enclose increasingly larger segments of the flatlands, until beyond the last, detached wall of the Bakony extends the vastness of the heart of the plain, the Great

Alföld. The basins formed by these ridges are in turn divided by marshes and lakes which have formed in the bottoms, and by the many-branched streams flowing toward the Danube. Though much of the marsh has been drained and the braiding streams bridged, this alternation of forested uplands and marshy lowlands has had a great impact on the lives of the inhabitants of Pannonia. Separate cells of dense population have resulted, and the many boundaries drawn in this area have generally passed through the wet or upland barrier belts between these cells. Since the ridges are not, this far east, icy and glaciated, the wet lands have been the greatest barriers and the most frequent bearers of boundaries. The major routeways—prehistoric tracks, Roman roads, imperial highways, and railroads—have consistently chosen the same paths, that is, those pathways that best avoid mountain and marsh. The fortresses and cities have developed at those key points which control these routeways, and hence control the flow of trade, armies, and migrating hordes which have moved through the centuries from cell to cell to the lands beyond.

Flowing from west to east, and then sharply south, is the majestic Danube. This primary stream of central Europe cuts across the prevailing southwest to northeast alignment of the terrain features to unite and to separate, to be a highway and a barrier. Where it cuts through the upland spurs, the river has offered men an easy routeway between the cells; but where it crosses the flat basins it has spread itself widely, splitting into myriad arms encompassing large, variable, marshy islands. Crossing the Danube has not been easy in the flat country, and the key crossing points have developed where the river issues from the constriction of a gorge. In these western portions of the Carpathian Basin the Danube has been the greatest of all the topographic barriers to movement. It was to be expected that the Romans, advancing from the southwest, would establish their border along this river.

Through much of its path across Austria the Danube flows along the northern edge of a lowland corridor between the Alps to the south and the granitic massif of the Bohemian Forest (Böhmerwald) to the north. Fifty miles west of Vienna the river veers sharply northward for ten miles across the southeastern corner of the Bohemian Forest. This gorge, the Wachau, is one of the most picturesque portions of Austria, and resembles the "heroic" part of the Rhine. Ruins of medieval castles crown the tops of the hills, whose slopes are covered with vineyards and apricot trees. One castle, Dürnstein, gained undying fame as the prison of Richard the Lionhearted, and the scene of his legendary discovery by his minstrel, Blondel. Just beyond the fortress crags of Dürnstein, at the city of Krems, the Danube surges out of the constrictions of the granite gorge and spreads broadly over the Tullner Feld, the first and smallest of the series of basins. This narrow lowland, roughly thirty miles long and fifteen wide, in turn ends at the Wienerwald.

The Wienerwald (Vienna Woods) is the only Alpine range that reaches the Danube unbroken. It is the northeastern extension of the *Flysch* (sandstone) zone which flanks the northern limestone belt. The Danube cuts through this ridge; the resulting narrow valley has been of geo-political [2] significance since the dawn of history. Towering almost nine hundred feet above the Danube is the Leopoldsberg, the "Acropolis of Vienna," the first seat of power of the Austrian dukes in the Vienna Basin. Across the Danube the ridge continues briefly as the Bisamberg, then gradually descends to blend into the rolling country of the Weinviertel.

South of Vienna the line of contact between the Alpine spur and the lowland before it is sharp and dramatic. Limestone cliffs border the western edge of the basin and give evidence of the geologic subsidence that has caused this lowland. At the base of the uplands lies a continuous belt of vineyards, producing some of the finest wines of Austria, and a number of thermal springs that have been used at least since the time of the Romans.

To the east of the Wienerwald is the second of this series of basins. Once again the Danube spreads horizontally as it leaves the constriction of the gorge. Channels alternate with marshy islands, and until the river was regulated eighty years ago the threat of floods and of sudden erratic shifts of the river bed hung over the area. At the point where the braiding begins stands Vienna, the metropolis of the Danube lands.

The three-mile wide belt of wet land lying adjacent to the Danube effectively divides this basin into two unequal parts. The southern portion is the Vienna Basin, the northern the Marchfeld (March lowland).[3] The contrast between the two portions is striking. South of the Danube over 80 per cent of the population is engaged in nonagricultural pursuits; north of the Danube over 60 per cent is engaged in agriculture. The greatest urbanized area of the Danube lands fills the western rim of the Vienna Basin, but this urban concentration stops at the river; the Marchfeld is rural South of the Danube gravel terraces have raised the surface well above the level of the marshes, and both towns and roads crowd close to the river; north of the Danube the land is low and flat, and the towns and routes have been kept well back from the dangerous waterway.

Both halves of this lowland bear concentrations of routeways pointing toward the city at the gap in the Wienerwald. The Vienna Basin penetrates southward forty miles to the base of the central range of the Alps, thus allowing the southbound highways and railroads to by-pass the limestone ridges which, further west, guard the entrances to the crystalline core. The Marchfeld, in turn, penetrates one hundred miles to the north, where it leads to the Moravian Gate, that broad gap joining the Danubian lands with the North European Plain. This basin has been a major focal area of routeways since the dawn of history, and great cities have developed at those favored points where the Danube can be crossed easily.

Each portion of this basin contains a major stream; in the Vienna Basin it is the Leitha, in the Marchfeld, the March. Because of the broad depositions of gravel and sand by the streams of Tertiary times, these two rivers have been shoved toward the eastern side of the low-land. In the eleventh and twelfth centuries broad swamps accompanied the courses of both the Leitha and the March, and it was along these marshy watercourses that the medieval border between Austria and Hungary was placed.

Thirty miles east of Vienna another Alpine spur is crossed by the Danube in a shorter gorge. This spur, or rather series of short ridges, is a continuation of the central crystalline portion of the Alps and forms the principal connecting link between the Alps and the Carpathians. North of the Danube the Little Carpathians (Malé Karpathy) rise at the river edge and continue unbroken toward the northeast. The significant location at the end of the gap is occupied by Bratislava (Pozsony, Pressburg). South of the river the upland consists of three separate hill clumps. Forming the southern flank of the gorge are the Hainburg Hills, and guarding the river gap is the old fortress city of Hainburg, adjacent to the ruins of Roman Carnuntum. South of this clump of hills is the ten-mile wide Bruck Gateway, guarded by the fortress city of Bruck (see Map 9). This broad gap is utilized by the Leitha River, and by the principal routeways between Vienna and Budapest; through this gate have surged many of the great invasions from the east. Forming the principal separations between the Vienna Basin and the greater lowland to the east are the twenty-five-mile long Leitha Range and its lesser companion, the Rust Ridge. These are in turn separated from the main crystalline massif by the funnel-shaped Sopron Gateway. Whereas at the western end of the Vienna Basin only one gap pierces the upland rim, at the eastern end three gateways lead from the Vienna Basin to the Little Alföld.

Beyond the Little Carpathians the Danube enters the third low-land, and the first one that is considered to be a portion of the greater Carpathian Basin. This is the Kis ("Little") Alföld (in Magyar Alföld means "low world," hence lowland or basin). It is several times larger than the Vienna-Marchfeld basin, stretching eighty miles east-west and almost 150 miles north-south. Again the Danube spreads as it leaves its rock walls, only now the flood plain is wider, the islands larger and more numerous.

The lowest surface of the Little Alföld occurs close to its western margin and well south of the Danube. Twelve hundred feet below the crest of the Leitha Range, and separated from the Danube by a series of gravel terraces, Lake Neusiedl (Neusiedler See) rests upon the surface.[4] Extending eastward from the southern end of this shallow steppe lake is a broad area of marsh known as the Hanság. This belt of marsh, reaching to the braided Danube, separates a small triangular lowland from the remainder of the Little Alföld. For centuries these marshes formed a linguistic divide between German and Magyar, and they now bear a portion of the Austro-Hungarian border. It was through these swamps that the majority of the refugees fled from Hungary in the winter of 1956-57.

Both north and south of the Danube the Little Alföld is divided in two by a central stream. North of the Danube this is the Váh (Waag); south of the Danube the Rába (Raab). Though neither is accompanied by extensive marshes, both have had military significance in the past. Fortress cities guard their junctions with the Danube, Komárno on the Váh, Győr on the Rába.

Framing the Little Alföld on the southeast is the crystalline, partly volcanic hill chain, the Bakony. This too is broken into separate hill clumps, and a fifty-mile extent of forested gravel terrace joins its western end to the closest spur of the Alps. In western Hungary these hills clad in beech and oaks have long been important as a source of timber; fine vineyards cover the south-facing slopes. The Danube cuts across a continuation of this range, the Börzsöny, in a significant curving gorge just upstream from Budapest. The old fortress city of Buda is located on the southernmost clump of hills along the Danube, where the river once again begins to braid upon the plain.

Below the southern slopes of the Bakony lies Lake Balaton, the largest lake of Europe. Like its counterpart, Lake Neusiedl, it is shallow and variable. South of Lake Balaton and west of the Danube there are still a few hill clumps, but beyond the Danube spreads the Nagy Alföld or Great Alföld,[5] the lowland heart of the Carpathian Basin. Occasional sand dunes and tiny lakes in wind-blown depressions dot the surface, but otherwise it is a broad area of high fertility. Only the houses, the long-handled wells, and the planted trees break the level skyline; only the meandering rivers flowing sluggishly towards the Danube interrupt the unbroken spread of space. This was the home of tribe after tribe of nomadic peoples who had followed the belt of steppe from Iran and Turkistan past the Ukraine and through the Carpathians. This has been the westernmost home of the nomad in Europe, and it remained so until one of the nomadic peoples themselves transformed it into a granary for Europe.[6]

Burgenland occupies the western fringe of the Little Alföld. Within its borders the central crystalline massif of the Alps meets the plains of the Carpathian Basin. Here on its broadest front is the transition from the forested heights of Austria to the tilled plains of Hungary. The firs and spruces of the Alpine slopes yield gradually to the beech and oaks of lower elevations; near the foot of the slopes a line, sharply drawn by centuries of peasant labor, separates the forest from the vineyards and fruit trees, the wheat and the rye. In Burgenland almost every peasant owns a tiny forest plot on the adjacent slope, and its timber supplies him with fuel for the winter as well as material for tools and building.

West of Burgenland, on the borders of Styria and Lower Austria, the crystalline mass reaches the zone of perpetual snow for the last time at the Schneeberg (6,800 feet), which towers above the approaches to the Semmering Pass. The Semmering saddle at 3,200 feet is by far the heaviest travelled route between the Vienna Basin and northern Italy. Extending eastward from the Semmering to the borders of Hungary is a triangular-shaped crystalline plateau, the Bucklige Welt (the buckled or humpbacked world). The upland surface of this area, with an elevation of two to three thousand feet, is gently rounded and covered with farms, while the stream valleys are narrow, forested, and flanked by steep sides. On the upland, peasants have lived in relative isolation for centuries. The canyon-like valleys cut the Bucklige Welt into separated units, though these valleys do lead eventually to the cities on the plains beyond. In the spring, traces of snow remain for weeks here after they have vanished from the adjacent Vienna Basin, and the stream bottoms are often marshy. Until buses began to thread their way over the slopes a few decades ago, these peasants lived a way of life based on local self-sufficiency, and they developed dialects and folkways uniquely their own.

The Bucklige Welt is split in two by the broad furrow of the Pitten valley which leads upstream from the Vienna Basin to the Wechsel Pass. In the eleventh and twelfth centuries the Wechsel Pass was the principal link between the Vienna Basin and the Mediterranean world, and the Bucklige Welt was established as a separate border marchland to protect and extend the German frontier. But since those centuries this area has been left aside by traffic moving over the Semmering Pass further west.

The Bucklige Welt extends briefly into Burgenland, its surface gradually lowering toward the east. Two oval-shaped prongs continue the upland barrier beyond the present Hungarian border. The Sopron Range extends to within five miles of the southern end of Lake Neusiedl; the Köszeg Range attains an elevation of 2,900 feet before descending into the plain at the border city of Köszeg. Fringing these spurs are roughly dissected gravel terraces which, in effect, extend the upland areas into the lowland embayment between the two ranges. One of these terraces extends east of Köszeg; the Roman road to Carnuntum moved around this surface rather than across it.

South of the Wechsel Pass the rim of the crystalline massif turns to the southwest, rising above the medieval road from Hartberg to Graz. Issuing from the Alpine flank is a sequence of gravel terraces which descend in elevation towards the east. Numerous small streams flowing from the mountain crest cut these sloping terraces into narrow parallel bands. These stream valleys and the gravelly uplands between them form a semicircular pattern as they gradually turn from the southeast to the east where they join the northeastward flowing Rába. The streams have had little resistance in cutting into the gravelly materials, so that the valleys tend to be broad and flat bottomed. Many of the valley bottoms are over a mile wide where the streams leave Austria.

This alternation of broad valleys and forested terraces constitutes the whole of eastern Styria and southern Burgenland and extends briefly into Hungary beyond. The contrast between the bottoms and the terraces rising above the valleys is sharp. The terraces are mostly forested with but occasional cleared plots; the bottoms are completely cleared and the fertile soil is intensively tilled. The danger of flooding is still a threat in the spring; therefore, most of the villages are located on the margin of the floodplain, at the foot of the bluff. Each valley contains a ribbon of population, with the villages joined into a chain (or two chains) by the roads at the foot of the bluffs. Each valley tends to form an economic and social unit, and until the advent of the paved road and the bus, contact between the different valleys was, at best, infrequent. The valley roads lead eventually to the cities on the plain, and since these valleys open into Hungary, the cities are Hungarian cities; prior to 1922 most of the traffic of southern Burgenland moved naturally along the valley roads to Köszeg, Szombathely, Körmend, and Szent Gotthárd, all of which served as the connecting links between the separated valley realms and Vienna and Budapest.

North of the crystalline massif there is a relative absence of the terraces that dominate the southern flank. Terraces do exist, but the drop from the crest to the lowland is very sharp. Only twenty miles separates the Rosalien Range (which forms the edge of the Bucklige Welt) and Lake Neusiedl, the lowest portion of the Little Alföld. One of the terraces acts as a partly wooded connection, across the Sopron Gateway, between the Bucklige Welt and the Leitha Range.

The Leitha Range is the principal divide between the Vienna Basin and the Little Alföld. This ridge, as well as the smaller Rust Ridge nearby, is a crystalline feature flanked by outcrops of limestone. Because of the presence of limestone these two ridges are a major source of building material for Vienna. Large quarries flank the ridges, and many of the buildings on the Ring in Vienna were constructed of the stone quarried at St. Margarethen and Mannersdorf.

The Leitha Range is most impressive from the east where it rises over a thousand feet above the Wulka and the lake. The beech and oak forests that cover its upper surfaces not only have supplied the timber needs of local peasants, but also have served as hunting grounds for the Eszterházy princes, whose palace dominates the small city of Eisenstadt. Furthermore, the lower slopes of the Leitha Range as well as the eastern slopes of the Rust Ridge form enormous continuous vineyards. For forty miles along the Leitha Range and a terrace edge northeast of the lake, the vineyards are virtually unbroken, and for centuries wine has been the main export item. Sopron and Wiener Neustadt were great wine trading cities in medieval times, and Eisenstadt and tiny Rust purchased their rights as free cities with the proceeds of the wine trade.

North of Lake Neusiedl is the oval-shaped Parndorf Heath (Parndorfer Heide). This is another terrace, but deposits of loess (windblown silt) have laid a fertile covering over the sterile gravel. The flat, exposed surface of the Heath is the driest and most wind-swept portion of this border area. Villages huddle below the edge to escape the fierce north winds and to utilize the slopes so excellent for the vine. The flat Heath surface remained one of the last parts of Pannonia to come under the plow, and until the early nineteenth-century steppe-like sheep pasturing was the principal use made of the area. Only 150 years ago did the noble large landholders bring the surface under cultivation by constructing work camps, planting trees for protection from the wind, and digging deep wells to procure precious water.

Below the edge of this terrace, stretching to the south and east, lies the flatness of the Little Alföld. No hills frame the skyline.

Villages are large and far apart. Long-handled wells draw the fresh water from far below the surface. Near the lake, small brackish ponds, locally known as *Zickseen,* fill the depressions that have formed from the action of the wind. Toward the southeastern end of the lake the surface of the land descends imperceptibly to the level of the ground water. Here is the Hanság, the broad belt of marshland which man has avoided throughout history by moving through Sopron or Győr. Numerous canals cut the surface to drain the land for crops; sugar beets, suited to heavy, wet, but rich soil, are the most important source of revenue. These canals are rarely bridged, since men have never wished to cross the wet lands; but in 1956 people in flight did wish to cross here, and the canals became cruel barriers.

Formerly this was an area of large manorial holdings; only the lords, working on a large scale, were able to put these lands, so often devastated by the Turks, back into production quickly. Even today many of the old manorial work camps, each known as a *Hof* or *puszta,*[7] dot the countryside, though the large landholdings are gradually being subdivided within Austria and have been replaced by large state-organized holdings in Hungary.

Few natural phenomena have intrigued European geographers as much as has Lake Neusiedl. Between 1919 and 1949 almost two hundred published works dealt specifically with this body of water. Most intriguing to scientists have been the questions concerning its source and its marked and unpredictable fluctuations in water level. The lake has no basin of its own, but literally lies on the surface. Consequently, it is very shallow; although twenty-two miles long, it is nowhere over four feet deep. The volume of water in the lake has fluctuated in cycles of indefinite and unpredictable duration. Neolithic artifacts have been found on the lake bed, and according to a local legend the present lake area was at one time the site of five villages (which are actually named).[8] After attaining a high level in 1677, the lake shrank slowly until, in 1740, it had virtually dried out. By 1786 it had extended to its greatest area in recorded history, 198 square miles. (Its present area is approximately 120 square miles.) Between 1831 and 1840 it was again at a low stage, but returned to 137 square miles in 1850. In 1868 it had disappeared except for a few pools, and the salty, lacustrine bottom was divided among the surrounding villages, with the peasants trying to farm the lake bed. The water soon returned however, and by 1883 had attained a maximum depth of eight feet. Its most recent minimum was in 1934 when its greatest depth was only sixteen inches; that year the water heated, in summer, to a temperature of 93 degrees, and in winter was frozen solid.

Only one stream, the Wulka, empties into the lake. It has been estimated that the water added to the lake by streams and precipitation on its surface does not equal half the amount evaporated from the surface. Therefore, the lake must also be fed by ground water, which here, in the lowest portion of the Little Alföld, forms a standing lake.

The lake need not dry out to lose most of its water. At times, a strong persistent wind from the north has pushed the water into the southern end of the lake bed, thus flooding the reeds in Hungary and leaving the northern end dry.

Drainage of the lake has long been considered. The Roman emperor Galerius is reported to have cut a canal from the southeastern end of the lake to the Rabnitz (Répce), but how successful this drainage attempt was is not reported. Between 1873 and 1895 the Hungarian government constructed the Einser Kanal from the lake to the Danube. Unfortunately, the difference in elevation between the lake surface and the level of the Danube is so slight that in times of high water the river has fed water back into the lake. With the drawing of the international boundary across the lake the possibility of permanent drainage of the lake bed ceased. The lake mouth of this canal is now plugged with silt and reeds.

The presence of tall reeds around the lake has made this one of the finest game preserves of Europe. The reeds form a belt, averaging a mile and a quarter in width, which almost surrounds the lake. This belt is absent only at the northeastern shore and reaches its greatest width at the southwestern end. Bird life is remarkably profuse in this wet land, and the storks of Rust have become famous throughout Austria and Hungary.

Despite its great interest to students and writers, the lake has been until recently of little economic value to the people living around it. The waters were formerly used for the production of saltpeter, and the dense stands of reeds are still utilized by local craftsmen in the making of baskets. Fishing is obviously poor and hunting is discouraged in the interests of preservation of the rarer species of birds.

Within the last few years "baths" have been established at several points along the lake shore. Although swimming is out of the question in such shallow water, the lake has become a favorite beach area for the Viennese; it is within an hour's drive, there is much sunshine, and the cost is low. The villages along the shore have attempted to increase tourism by holding flower festivals, and in Mörbisch an outdoor theatre has been built. The *puszta* look is being emphasized more and more, and the Mörbisch theatre has presented operettas with a Hungarian setting. Every September crowds of Viennese come to the lake shore to sample the famous "Ruster" wine, or its Mörbisch or Oggau counterpart. Very few of these "tourists," however, stay overnight within Burgenland; few even order a large meal at one of the village *Gasthäuser*. The lake still contributes relatively little to the economy of the surrounding villages.[9]

The inhabitants of Burgenland, in themselves, attest to their position along a frontier. Elements from the west, east, and south have been mingled to form a people and a way of life that is unique. Most of the Burgenlanders are of German stock, though their ancestors immigrated from several parts of the medieval empire. But interspersed in the German area are clusters of Croats who came from the south and Magyars who entered from the east, and spread over the hillsides are the huts of that most singular of all the nomadic peoples, the gypsies. Family names also suggest the intermixture of peoples; many of the "Germans" have names that are notably Croatian or Magyar in origin.

Though Burgenland is predominantly German-speaking, its appearance is distinctively Hungarian. The language came from the west, but the clothing and the house and village types came from the east. In marked contrast to the constrictions of Alpine terrain, space is abundantly available, and villages sprawl as they do nowhere else in Austria. Large, rectangular open spaces form the centers of most of the villages on the Little Alföld. Houses are low and long with the narrow end toward the road; strips of garden land stretch back from the road. Only the church spire rises above the uniform level of the roofs. Formerly these roofs were of thatch, but now most have been tiled. Usually the houses are whitewashed, but occasionally, as in the village of Luising, painting of the front face makes each house distinctive from its neighbors.

Though in the north some of the "Hungarian look" extends into the Vienna Basin and Marchfeld, further south the line of contrast between the village types suggestive of the steppe and those of the mountain is sharply drawn along the line that for over nine hundred years separated Austria and Hungary. West of this boundary is the world of the Alps, with those sturdy houses in tightly compressed villages that seem in such deep accord with their mountain backdrops. To the man of the mountains the world of the steppe has always seemed alien. Even the Viennese feel this. Though the traces of the steppe penetrate to the vicinity of their city, the Viennese feel themselves a part of the mountain world. To them the windy, dusty plains, the low sprawling villages, the flocks of geese, the heavy boots and black clothing are not only quaint but also somewhat distasteful. Vienna is an outpost of the West, and though Burgenland, the border-land, is now within Austria, it still seems to be a part of the East.

~~~~~~~~
~~~~~~~~
~~~~~~~~

3

~~~~~~~~
~~~~~~~~
~~~~~~~~

PANNONIA

Precisely when human settlement of Pannonia began cannot be ascertained, but it is clear that the flanks of the ridges have borne a dense population for several millennia. Remains dating back to approximately 5000 B.C. have been unearthed from the soils of Burgenland.

For Neolithic man (10,000–3000 B.C.) this was an ideal locale for settlement. The slopes and tops of the ridges were densely forested and in the valley bottoms the land was wet, but on the rolling ground between the two, conditions were excellent for agriculture. Thick deposits of loess formed the base of a rich, easily-worked soil which, because of its porosity, was often not covered with trees. The adjacent forests supplied wood for fuel and tools, as well as streams of precious clear water; within the wooded darkness lay also the possibilities of refuge and defense. The gaps between the forested ridges allowed for the development of trade.

Within the Carpathian Basin settlements occurred principally in narrow belts at the foot of the ridges but above the marshy bottoms. Beyond to the east lay the terrifying vastness of the Alföld, defenseless and waterless. Settlement on the great plains was scarce and limited to the vicinity of the rivers, which supplied water and marshy refuge. The majority of archeological discoveries in Burgenland have been in the area of the Sopron Gateway, an area which offered primitive man an ideal combination of loess soil, defense, and the possibilities of active trade.

Even in Neolithic times the interchange of goods, ideas, and techniques between various parts of Europe must have been active. The remains of this age show little variation between the Carpathian Basin and the settlements along the Rhine or along the Baltic and Black seas. It is evident that Neolithic man was engaged more in agriculture than in hunting. A type of shifting agriculture with intensive working of small plots seems to have been predominant. Crops included barley, emmer wheat, peas, beans, lentils, and flax; only small herds of stock were kept. In the Bronze Age (2000–1000 B.C.) a metal technology developed in Central Europe, and one of the more notable mining centers occupied the eastern slopes of the Köszeg Range. Antimony from these mines was used as a substitute for tin in the manufacture of bronze.

In the Hallstatt Period (The Early Iron Age, *ca.* 1000–400 B.C.) trade routes were well developed in Pannonia, though it is difficult to ascertain exactly where they were located. Our best indication is the Roman network, since Roman roads and towns were often based on their pre-existing counterparts.[1] During the first millennium B.C., trade became very active in the Mediterranean as Phoenician and Greek mariners established trading posts around the full peripheries of the Mediterranean and Black seas. Penetration of the Carpathian Basin from the east was possible up the Danube and through the Carpathian passes. Trade connections between the Greek cities on the Black Sea and the populated fringes of the basin were established early, and flourished after the sixth century B.C.

Of even greater significance to Pannonia was its proximity to the head of the Adriatic, the northernmost extension of the Mediterranean. The low Julian passes allowed easy access from the plains to the sea and have been used since the beginnings of human movement in central Europe. By 500 B.C. northeastern Italy had become a center of industrial and commercial life, and from this economic hub two major routeways penetrated the Carpathian Basin. One road followed the line of the Sava River along the southern margin of the plain to Dacia (Transylvania), which was a major mining area, and to the Black Sea beyond; the other turned northward, skirting the eastern edges of the Alps.

The latter north-south road has become famous historically as the Amber Road.[2] The shipments of amber were collected at the mouth of the Vistula near the present city of Gdansk (Danzig), whence the road ran southward to the headwaters of the Oder. In the earlier centuries the road seems not to have utilized the Moravian Gate but rather passed through the Glatz Pass slightly further west. (The broad Moravian Gate was blocked by a vast marsh.) After this easy crossing of the Sudeten Hills the road followed the March River to its confluence with the Danube. The route probably ran along the eastern bank of the March, since the surface was higher and drier, and the streams narrower, there than on the western bank; furthermore, the adjacent Little Carpathians offered sites for protective fortresses.[3]

Another alternate routeway may have been used between the Oder and the Danube. A branch of the Amber Road probably crossed the Carpathians through the Jablunka Pass and then followed the southeastern flank of the uplands to the Danube. Since the southeastern slope faced the sun and was ideal for settlement, this branch road may have passed through a zone of relatively dense population.

The Amber Road was the shortest and easiest routeway between the middle Mediterranean and the Baltic, and much more than amber moved along its path. In return for the raw materials shipped southward, cargoes of manufactured goods moved northward. Metallic vases, manufactured in northern Italy, have been found in southern Poland and near the mouth of the Oder.

Both branches of the Amber Road met the Danube where the river is constricted between the Little Carpathians and the Hainburg Hills. The principal commercial settlement developed on the south bank at this key crossing site. Traces of an important Hallstatt settlement have been found on the Braunsberg, which rises seven hundred feet sharply above the confluence of the March and the Danube.[4] Carnuntum, the city that developed just to the southwest of this site, is thought to be of Illyrian origin and to date from the Hallstatt period. Because of the position of the Amber Road and the scarcity of good crossing points over the Danube, it is almost certain that all the traffic north-south, as well as movement along the Danube, passed through this pre-Roman Carnuntum.

The movement of peoples into the Carpathian Basin from the east and the west first becomes clearly discernible in Hallstatt times. The Illyrian peoples themselves may have been an invading group which had conquered a previously resident population, and it is possible that nomadic groups have sparsely occupied the Alföld for millennia. The first of the devastating incursions from the east of which we are certain was that of the Scythians around 700 B.C. These Iranian riders from the steppes entered the basin from both the northeast and southeast and destroyed the Dacian state, which had enjoyed a notable cultural development. Like all of the steppe riders that were to follow, the Scythians were loosely organized into tribal units which rarely worked together. They settled in the northern reaches of the Alföld and in southern Transylvania, though they penetrated to the furthest reaches of the basin and to the lands beyond. Their constant plunderings impoverished the pre-existing agricultural economy, but also steadily lessened their numbers; in time they were probably assimilated by the peasants, upon whom they had depended for their basic needs.

Around 400 B.C. the Celts entered the basin from the west, and their arrival marked the beginning of the La Tène period in Pannonia. The penetrations of the Celts followed the established routes and the bands of dense population; the heart of the Alföld was probably avoided, as they expanded along the Carpathian and Sava flanks of the great lowland. The Celts first conquered and then mingled with the Illyrians, finally producing the Pannonians encountered by the Romans.

Approximately two centuries later these Pannonians began to feel the influence of Rome. By the end of the third century B.C. Roman power was established at the head of the Adriatic, and, with the acquisition of the great port and manufacturing center of Aquileia in 181 B.C., the Adriatic entrances into the Carpathian Basin were firmly in Roman hands. Roman merchants, craftsmen, engineers, and mintners penetrated Pannonia long before the Roman army; during the second century B.C. Latin gradually became both the commercial and the diplomatic language of Pannonia. Even the Celtic coins of the time show Latin inscriptions. The subsequent Roman invasions of Pannonia were to secure militarily what had largely been secured economically long before.

Prior to the Roman wars which led to the annexation of Pannonia, an attempt was made to unite the basin from within. Dacia, centered within the natural fastness of Transylvania, had once again developed into a powerful state. Between 76 and 44 B.C. Burebista, king of the Dacians, conquered an empire. He entered Pannonia and decimated its Celtic inhabitants. The plains east of Lake Neusiedl that had been settled by the Boii tribe were so devastated that they remained the *Deserta Boiiorum* until Roman settlement repopulated the area a century later. These conquests put the Dacians in control of both of the arterial highways of the Carpathian Basin, and in the position to threaten northern Italy. The Dacian Empire was short-lived, however; it did not survive its founder. Nor does it seem that the Dacians gained effective control of the center of the basin; their armies probably skirted its open vastness to follow the belts of population and communications. For when the Romans entered Pannonia in force, the Yazyges, another nomadic people, occupied the Alföld.

The Romans had long realized that the Alps were at best but a poor defensive boundary against the barbarians from the north. Incursions or threats of incursions had been frequent, and Burebista's forces had stood on the threshhold of northern Italy. In 16 B.C. marauding bands from Noricum and Pannonia pillaged the plains at the head of the Adriatic; the subsequent Roman retaliation not only subdued the marauders but also moved the imperial boundary from the mountains to the Danube beyond. This marked advance northward was not accomplished with ease; two and a half decades of bloodshed were required before Pannonia was subdued.

Noricum was promptly annexed in 15 B.C., but the tribes of Pannonia offered fierce resistance. Under the command of Emperor Tiberius the Roman forces advanced along the two principal routes from Aquileia into the Carpathian Basin. A southern force occupied the tongue of land between the Sava and the Drava, while a northern force moved along the Amber Road to Carnuntum, which was then the last Norican town towards the east. The area between the Drava and the Danube was not occupied militarily.

As Tiberius moved to attack the Marcomani in Bohemia in A.D. 6, a great insurrection broke out in Pannonia and Dalmatia. This war became "the most severe which Rome had to sustain against an external foe since that of Hannibal." [5] An army of 120,000 men, the largest body of troops under one command to be assembled in the Augustan period, marched on the Pannonians. Finally, by A.D. 9 all resistance had been crushed, and in the following year Pannonia was incorporated into the Roman Empire.

During the first century A.D. the boundary of the Empire followed the Danube along almost its entire course from southwestern Germany to the Black Sea. Except for a subsequent advance into Transylvania (Dacia), the Roman limes, the imperial boundary, remained on the Danubius (Danuvius) for almost four centuries in fact, and for a millennium in theory. The longevity of this boundary is perhaps partially attributable to the fact that east of Vienna the river may have marked the border of the steppe, and within the steppe the Roman legions of massed men would have been at a serious disadvantage against the mobile nomadic warriors. But possibly the principal reason for the continuance of this boundary was that nowhere else in central Europe was there a physical feature that could so well serve the defensive needs of the Empire. The Danube was an unbroken line accompanied by broad marshes along most of its course. Barbarian raiding parties had been able to move virtually unnoticed through the Alpine valleys, but a crossing of the broad river was difficult for a barbarian people to effect in force, and even more difficult to conceal. The Danube was also a military highway of great potentialities. The Romans quickly established a Danubian fleet which not only kept watch along the full length of the river but also moved supplies and reinforcements to any threatened area. Though the Romans later established armed posts north of the Danube in present Moravia and Slovakia, the borders of the Empire remained on the river.

At the time of the Roman annexations, the boundary between the kingdoms of Noricum and Pannonia ran along the Leitha or the ridges separating the Vienna Basin from the Little Alföld, roughly the western boundary of Burgenland. Shortly thereafter the Romans shifted the boundary westward to the Wienerwald, ostensibly because Illyrian troops were to be stationed in Carnuntum, and Pannonia was part of Illyricum whereas Noricum was not.[6] Yet, more than this, the move represents an obvious adaptation to the problems of communications at the time, and the change was never rescinded. The Semmering Pass was not yet used, so that the principal connections between Rome and the Vienna Basin were along the Amber Road. The unbroken Wienerwald was the major divisive barrier south of the Danube. Whereas Noricum was a union of Alpine valleys, the Vienna Basin was the antechamber of the Pannonian plains.

For one hundred years Pannonia remained one province, and the capital was located at the central road junction, Savaria. As long as the threat of insurrection remained, the administrative center was Savaria, but with the complete Latinization of the province and the increase in Danubian traffic, the capital was moved to the frontier. Early in the second century Pannonia was divided into two portions, Superior and Inferior, which were, in effect, the northern and the eastern littorals of the Pannonian Danube. The two capitals were located at key military-trading posts in the Danubian gaps, Carnuntum and Aquincum (Buda).

The impact of the Romans on Pannonia was great and manifold. Order and organization came to the frontier. What had been an area of separate tribal units became a part of a vast civilized state. Trade could move freely and openly from Pannonia to Rome, Constantinople, and the Rhine. The productivity of Pannonia was increased many times as the empty Little Alföld was repopulated and an intensive method of agriculture replaced the previous primitive methods of land utilization. Paved highways were constructed along the historic tracks and trails, and, most significant for the purposes of this study, cities arose. Trading centers had existed previously, but now these became true cities.

The principal highway of Pannonia remained the Amber Road.

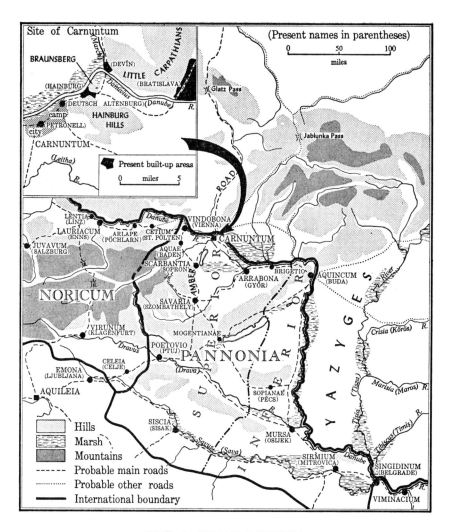

Site of Carnuntum

BRAUNSBERG

(DEVÍN)

LITTLE CARPATHIANS

(HAINBURG)

(BRATISLAVA)

(DEUTSCH ALTENBURG) (Danube) R.

camp

(PETRONELL) HAINBURG HILLS

city

CARNUNTUM

(Leitha)

R.

Present built-up areas

0   miles   5

(Present names in parentheses)

0   50   100

miles

Glatz Pass

Jablunka Pass

ROAD

LENTIA (LINZ)

Danube

VINDOBONA (VIENNA)

CARNUNTUM

LAURIACUM (ENNS)

ARLAPE (PÖCHLARN)

CETIUM (ST. PÖLTEN)

JUVAVUM (SALZBURG)

AQUAE (BADEN)

SCARBANTIA (SOPRON)

BRIGETIO

ARRABONA (GYŐR)

AQUINCUM (BUDA)

River

NORICUM

SAVARIA (SZOMBATHELY)

S U P E R I O R

A M B E R

VIRUNUM (KLAGENFURT)

MOGENTIANAE

Crisia (Körös) R.

Dravus

POETOVIO (PTUJ)

PANNONIA

Y A Z Y G E S

CELEIA (CELJE)

(Drava)

EMONA (LJUBLJANA)

I N F E R I O R

Marisia (Maros) R.

AQUILEIA

SOPIANAE (PÉCS)

Hills

Marsh

Mountains

Probable main roads

Probable other roads

International boundary

SISCIA (SISAK)

MURSA (OSIJEK)

Savus

(Sava)

SIRMIUM (MITROVICA)

Danube

Tibiscus (Timis)

SINGIDINUM (BELGRADE)

VIMINACIUM

MAP 1. ROMAN PANNONIA

25

This ran along the familiar path from Aquileia through Emona (Ljubljana, Laibach) on the Sava, Poetovio (Ptuj, Pettau), Savaria, and Scarbantia to Carnuntum. East of Poetovio another road left this axial highway and skirted the productive southern flank of the Bakony to Aquincum. From Scarbantia a road extended through the Sopron Gateway to Vindobona.

Connections with Constantinople were funneled through Sirmium on the Sava. This was the junction for the routes along the lower Danube and the Morava to the southeast, and along the Sava and into Pannonia to the northwest (see Map 1). From Sirmium important roads ran northward along the Danube to Aquincum, and northwestward, skirting the western end of Lake Balaton, to Savaria.

Tying together the furthest ends of the highway system was the road along the Danube. West of Carnuntum this road had great economic and military significance, since it was the only trans-Alpine highway joining Pannonia with the Rhine and Gaul. Within Pannonia, however, the shortest route from Carnuntum to Constantinople did not follow the Danube, but cut across the great bend by passing through Savaria.

The Mediterranean civilization was uniquely a city civilization. The city-state was the basic cell of political society, and the Roman Empire may be thought of as a union of city-states under the control of one greatest city. Each city had administrative, military, economic, religious, and cultural control of its own clearly defined territory. Within Pannonia a few cities dominated the life of the province; probably the most important of these were Carnuntum, Savaria, Aquincum, Scarbantia, and Vindobona. These centers deserve special analysis.[7]

Carnuntum

Carnuntum[8] was the largest of these cities, and for two and a half centuries the military and administrative center of Pannonia Superior. It was located immediately to the west of the Hainburg gap of the Danube, on the site of the present villages of Petronell and Deutsch Altenburg. The name of the city is thought to have been derived from *karn*, the Illyrian word for stone, and may have meant, "the city by the rocks." The Celtic-Illyrian town from which the Roman camp and city acquired its name was probably situated between the steep flank of the Hainburg Hills and the Danube, on or near the site of the present Hainburg.

This ancient site, though closer to the actual river gap and crossing, seems to have been too constricted for the Romans. Space was needed for the camp and the city, as well as for the plots of land which were allotted to the soldiers of the resident garrison. The pass between the Braunsberg and the main group of the Hainburg Hills was also too narrow and exposed for the rapid movement of large masses of troops, whereas just to the south of the hills was the broad Bruck Gateway, the northern portion of which came to be known as the Porta Carnuntiana. The Roman military camp was therefore located near the present site of Deutsch Altenburg, where the westernmost spur of the hills approached the Danube. This was a good defensive position and yet adjacent to the flat land. The urban area was just to the west of the camp and extended along the Danube for approximately two miles.

Carnuntum is now a rich archeological site. The remains of Roman times are evident in several places. Since Carnuntum was not rebuilt after its destruction by the barbarians, the ruins have not been altered by later construction, though many of the stones have been used in the building of the nearby villages and palaces. The foundations, mosaics, and heating systems of many of the homes are still evident. The two amphitheaters (one of which could seat 13,000) that have been uncovered indicate how closely the frontier city was integrated into the Roman way of life. A large arch, the Heidentor, now standing alone in the fields south of Petronell, hints at both the size and grandeur of Carnuntum.

Carnuntum's greatness had two dimensions, economic and military, and both of these were dependent upon the same topographic relationships. The highways that focused on the city were the avenues of both trade and armed movement. The limes road to the west led into the Vienna Basin and along the Danube to the Rhine and Gaul. The limes road to the east led into the Little Alföld and to Aquincum in the next river gap. The highway to the south led to both Rome and Constantinople. To the north ran the tracks leading through the lands of barbarian tribes (some of which were closely tied to the Empire) to the shores of the Baltic. The Danube was a prime water highway from the west, and Carnuntum was the port city at which soldiers, merchants, and goods left the river to continue along the Pannonian roads. The overland road from Constantinople and Asia Minor to the Rhine and the western Danube passed directly through Carnuntum. The city became, consequently, a major harbor of the Danubian fleet.

Although east-west traffic was of great significance, the principal reason for the greatness of Carnuntum was its key position in relation to north-south movement. Across the river was the long chain of the Carpathians which now separates Slovakia from Moravia. This attenuated ridge flanked all movement southward by any invading force. Passes such as the Jablunka do exist but an army had to remain on one side or the other of the ridge or be divided into two relatively ineffectual halves. The principal roads followed the flanks of the Little Carpathians to reach the river at the only good crossing point, the Carnuntum (Hainburg) gap. The legion stationed at Carnuntum was in the position to face a crossing force moving southward along either the eastern or the western flank of the dividing range. And should two large forces have moved southward, the Romans could have attempted to dispose of them one at a time, since coöperation between the two would have been difficult. Since the garrison stationed at Carnuntum could meet all invasions from the north, and could also move rapidly into either the Vienna Basin or the Little Alföld, the city was usually the headquarters of the emperors who confronted or revenged barbarian incursions into Pannonia. Tiberius, Marcus Aurelius, and Valentinian based their campaigns on this site. Diocletian convened the famous council of the four emperors here in 308.

The key location astride the principal routeways of central Europe was an advantage only as long as Carnuntum was protected by Roman power. When this power decreased along the frontier, barbarian hordes swept across the boundary and through the gateway city. During the many invasions Carnuntum suffered grievously and was destroyed at least twice. After its final desolation it never rose again. When order and organization returned to the area at the beginning of the eleventh century the patterns of routeways and the political boundaries had changed greatly. The topographic features remained the same, but the location had lost its former significance. The site of the once great city is now only partially covered by two small villages.

Vindobona (Vienna)

Although statistics are not available, it is possible that Vindobona was the smallest of these five cities. Though it was located at the first crossing point west of Carnuntum, Vindobona was well off to the side of the principal line of traffic flow. Only a branch of the Amber Road came to Vindobona, and the mouth of the March was thirty miles to the east. In contrast to Carnuntum, whose hinterland included both the Vienna Basin and the Little Alföld, Vindobona's hinterland was severely limited by the forested wall of the Wienerwald behind it. The crossing did make Vindobona a place of some military significance, and it was here that Marcus Aurelius died in A.D. 180, but otherwise Vindobona was completely overshadowed by Carnuntum.

The city had one special locational asset; it was at the Vienna gap of the Danube, so that all movement east-west, whether by river or by limes road, passed through the city. It could not be by-passed, because of the unbroken character of the Wienerwald range. Unfortunately this command of the river traffic was not of major significance, since the traffic generally moved on to the much larger Carnuntum, and only that traffic destined for the western part of the Vienna Basin left the river at Vindobona; for all other traffic the ideal place to transfer or distribute goods was Carnuntum. Similarly, the garrison at Vindobona could protect little more than the one crossing and one small corner of Pannonia.

The very insignificance of this crossing site became an asset in the period of troubles which followed the breakdown of Roman power in this area in the fourth century. Vindobona was tucked away between the many-channeled marsh of the Danube and the steep ridge of the Wienerwald; it was in a safer position, and was a less attractive prize, than Carnuntum. Whereas the larger center to the east was destroyed, Vindobona may have managed to survive the centuries of invasions.

Aquincum (Buda)

Early in the second century Aquincum became the capital of Pannonia Inferior, but it is doubtful if the city ever approached Carnuntum or even Savaria in size and importance. Aquincum was the terminus of another tributary of the Amber Road and was at another Danube gap and crossing point. It was, however, well off the north-south trade routes, at the extremity of a salient of Roman territory. The shortest land route from Carnuntum to the eastern half of the Empire cut across this salient formed by the big bend of the Danube, and thus by-passed Aquincum.

Aquincum became significant following the annexation of Dacia (Transylvania). Because of the sharp turn of the Danube towards the south, the river route between the upper Danube and Dacia was very circuitous; by far the shortest path was across the Alföld from Aquincum. Traffic between Pannonia and Dacia therefore probably left the river at Aquincum and moved across the plain, which was loosely controlled by the Yazyges.

Roman relations with the Yazyges were always somewhat uncertain; during the Dacian wars of 84–90 the Yazyges had assisted the Dacians. Hence Aquincum was not only a trading station but also an important military post guarding Pannonia against future invasions by the steppe nomads. Between 166 and 175 the Yazyges supported the Marcomani and Quadi in their devastating sweep into Pannonia, but they were then subdued by the Romans. Subsequently the Yazyges were submissive, but Rome lost Dacia to new invaders during the middle of the third century.

What happened to Aquincum at the time of the barbarian incursions is not fully known, but certainly it suffered the usual fate of the Roman frontier cities. Because of its exposed position, and because the fall of Dacia had partially diminished its significance, it is doubtful that the Romans made any strenuous efforts to maintain their control of Aquincum. The city and its name vanished under the hoofs of the riders of the steppe.

Scarbantia (Sopron)

As soon as Pannonia had been settled and roads established, Scarbantia was almost certain to become an important trading center. Here, at the southern end of Lake Neusiedl, the Alps in the Sopron Range come down to the lake shore. The Rust Ridge, which parallels the west shore of the lake, is separated from the Sopron Range by only a narrow gap. Because of the extension of the marshlands east from Lake Neusiedl, all traffic and all movement of armies from southern Pannonia to the Vienna Basin and Carnuntum was forced to move through this narrow gap. From earliest times this pass has supported a fortress city; Sopron has been a uniquely rich source of Hallstatt remains.

For the Romans this city became an important way station on the road northward to Carnuntum; from Scarbantia the roads funneled out into the Vienna Basin. It remained an important trading center, but, since it was now within the province rather than on the frontier, Scarbantia lost much of its military function. When Pannonia fell to the barbarians, Scarbantia suffered grievously; the movements of people along the Amber Road southward towards the enticing riches of Italy inevitably poured through the city in the gap. Yet, despite the devastations of the centuries of warfare that followed, the site never lost its commercial significance completely; except for the years of Avar occupation, it probably always was an important market center.

Savaria (Szombathely)

Probably second only to Carnuntum in importance was Savaria (Sabaria). Though not at a river crossing, nor in a narrow pass, this city was at the most strategic position in the interior of Pannonia. While Pannonia remained undivided its capital was Savaria.

A coincidence of a number of topographic relationships helped make this city the principal road junction within the province. Since the city was just to the southeast of the Köszeg Range, the first road westward, south of Carnuntum, here ran along the southern flank of the crystalline Alps. The broad Pinka valley also formed a westward extension of the lowlands into the Alpine flank. Because of the east-west extent of Lake Balaton, the highway from Sirmium (and Constantinople) to Carnuntum was deflected to Savaria where it joined the Amber Road. Also, because of the northeastward path of the Rába River, the road to Arrabona (Győr) left the Amber Road at Savaria and followed the stream to this important junction center.[9]

While the dangers to Pannonia were beyond the imperial borders, Carnuntum and Aquincum were the logical centers of military power, but once the frontier defenses had been breached Savaria became the ideal military headquarters. From this junction point roads led to all parts of the province; at this point the two highways from both capitals of the Empire met, and here was the first center south of the frontier which had access to the Alpine valleys. In the fourth century Roman attempts at the re-establishment of the old frontier were centered in Savaria.[10]

Though Savaria was to vanish as a city during the barbarian invasions, one of its sons helped to maintain its memory through the centuries. Saint Martin of Tours, the first person who was not a martyr to be canonized in the West, was a native of Savaria. On this embattled frontier he became a soldier before leaving for Gaul and the city with which his name has since been associated. The influence of the young soldier who divided his cloak with a beggar has remained strong in this borderland. Both the first monastery established by King Stephen in the new Kingdom of Hungary, and also the old cathedral in Bratislava (Pozsony, Pressburg), were dedicated to St. Martin. Within Burgenland today two cities and three villages bear the name of the Bishop of Tours, and less than a decade ago St. Martin was selected as the patron saint of Burgenland.

The period of Roman Pannonia's prosperity was relatively short. The evident strength of Rome after the conquest of the warlike Dacians seemed to guarantee peace on the frontier, and for the first sixty years of the second century the flat plains blossomed and the cities grew. But the pressure of the barbarians from the north gradually increased. The Marcomani and Quadi, settled in the lowlands of present-day Czechoslovakia, began to move across the Danube, only to be deported northward by the frontier guards. Suddenly, in the year 166, the barbarians, assisted by the Yazyges of the Alföld, burst into both Pannonias and Noricum. Most of the legions had been moved to the Armenian frontier, and the barbarian sweep was not halted until it entered northern Italy. Large numbers of the Romanized inhabitants were taken captive and the prosperous plains were plundered. Six years later Marcus Aurelius began his counter campaign. The barbarian raiding hordes were no match for the compact, disciplined Roman forces, and for eight years the Romans moved through the country of the folk beyond the Danube until the Yazyges and Quadi had been subjugated and the Marcomani almost exterminated.

Fifty-five years of peace followed these fourteen years of devastation. The cities were rebuilt, but the flat Little Alföld was probably not completely repopulated. Soon Pannonia was embroiled in the civil wars which did so much to weaken the strength of the Empire. Many of the aspirants for the imperial throne were from Pannonia or Illyricum, and the frontier country suffered serious damage from the incessant campaigns. By the middle of the third century, the plains of northern Pannonia again resembled the *Deserta Boiiorum*, and Emperor Gallienus allowed the Marcomani to settle these areas.

Between 270 and 375, though still Roman territory, Pannonia was increasingly exposed to invasions by the Quadi, the Vandals and the Sarmatians. The Germanic tribes from the north and the nomadic riders from the east combined forces to eradicate the Roman holdings on the Danube. In 370 Valentinian I made the last strong effort to secure the borders, but the fortifications built then could not hold back a Quadi raid in 374. In the following year the death of Valentinian at the hands of the Quadi ended the Roman rule of Pannonia.

With the collapse of this Roman rule, the history of the eastern rim of the Alps fades into obscurity. Only events of vast scope, such as the movements of tribes, can be accurately established. Whether or not remnant groups of Romans remained in Pannonia is not known. The Romans did withdraw their citizens from the defenseless area, but it is doubtful that all the inhabitants left. Possibly those clusters in the valleys close to places of refuge and away from the travelled routeways remained. Certainly, most of the cities were devastated; they were on the routeways and were especially liable to looting. Of the five principal cities of northern Pannonia only Vindobona seems to have survived, though each of the other key trading sites may have attracted a rudimentary kind of commerce as soon as each tribal unit became established in the area. Ruined or not, Carnuntum was still the ideal place to cross the Danube.

Despite the possibility of a remnant survival of Vindobona through the dark centuries, and the probability of some trading activity at the other urban sites, the great invasions, which did not cease until the establishment of Hungary in A.D. 1000, wiped the area clean of urban developments. When trade and urban life began again at the turn of the millennium, boundaries and cities were established anew on the basis of entirely new geo-political conditions.

4

THE MIGRATIONS
OF THE NATIONS

For six centuries Germanic, Slavic, and Asiatic peoples moved in waves through the Carpathian Basin. All settlement seemed ephemeral; tribal units occupied the choice lowlands only to move on to newer areas as other groups pressed upon them. One nomadic people, the Avars, ruled the entire basin for over two centuries, and yet vanished almost without a trace. Germans and Slavs attempted to establish empires only to have them collapse before the onslaughts of new invaders.

Throughout these "dark ages" of human movement the Empire tried to maintain control of Pannonia. The collapse of Roman power along the Danube did not mean the end of Roman claims to the historic frontier. The emperor at Constantinople continued to consider Pannonia as a part of the Empire, and the barbarian chieftains seem to have accepted this claim, though they disregarded its implications in practice. The unity and the extent of the Empire remained a powerful tradition and a potent political concept throughout these six centuries.

Because of the extent of the weakening Empire, and the transfer of its capital to Constantinople, many attempts were made to split the Empire into two parts for administrative purposes. In the famous division of 395 Pannonia was placed under the jurisdiction of Rome, but this arrangement was of comparatively short duration. In 427 the boundary between the eastern and western halves of the Empire was moved to the crest of the Wienerwald ridge, and Pannonia was placed under the rule of Constantinople. The principal connecting link to the capital no longer was Aquileia but rather Sirmium, and Vindomana (as Vindobona was now known) became an outpost of Byzantine rule and diplomacy.

The transfer of Pannonia from Rome to Constantinople was probably a result of the shift from road to river transportation within the Carpathian Basin.[1] The barbarian incursions had caused a widespread deterioration of the famed road system, and the highways that remained in good condition were, at best, poorly policed against robbers. Carnuntum and Aquincum may have been abandoned completely by A.D. 376. In contrast to the roads, the river route was more than a match for the barbarians; tribal groups could cross the river, but they could not control the stream itself.[2] Whereas communications between Vindomana and Aquileia became dangerous and unreliable, those by river between Vindomana and Sirmium remained open. Thus along the Danube a string of residual towns formed the basis of the Empire's hold on Pannonia, and though the province behind the river was repeatedly overrun, the thread of imperial control, running through the river stations of Sirmium, Mursa, Vindomana, Arlape, and Lauriacum, remained intact.

However, despite this hold on the Danube, the Empire did have to adjust its policies to the fact that the barbarians almost completely controlled Pannonia. By the end of the fourth century any attempt to keep the invaders out of Pannonia was virtually impossible. Yet the new arrivals seemed willing to accept the legal claim of Byzantium to Pannonia. They had no desire to overthrow the Empire; rather they wished to share in its riches. Byzantine diplomacy met this situation by concluding a series of treaties which allowed each of the invading tribes in turn to become *foederati* ("federates") of the Empire, and guarantors of the frontier. In this manner, though the power relationships within the Carpathian Basin were constantly changing, the political heritage of Rome remained alive in Pannonia throughout the time of the movements of the nations.

The principal cause of the wave of migrations that engulfed the Roman limes at the start of the fifth century was the westward movement of the dreaded steppe warriors, the Huns. Though their origin is still a mystery, it is thought that they originated in northern China, whence they were driven by a kindred people, the Avars, in the middle of the fourth century. The first facts about the Huns that are known with certainty are that they were by 370 in the grasslands south of the mouth of the Don, east of the Kerch Straits. It was not until the turn of the fifth century that the Huns moved into the Carpathian Basin in great force, although their raiding units had penetrated into the basin earlier. Their movement westward caused a mass flight of peoples, who swamped the Rhine frontier further west. By 380 Emperor Gratian had granted land in Pannonia to groups of the Ostrogoths and the Alans. In 401 the Vandals passed through Pannonia on their flight to Gaul. Between 409 and 433 Pannonia was again under Roman control, but the Huns occupied the Alföld beyond the Danube, so that the imperial hold on the area was somewhat precarious. Finally, in 433 the Roman general Aetius surrendered Pannonia to the Huns.

Until the introduction of gunpowder, the armies of Europe were helpless before the invasions of these steppe riders. The initial onslaught of every one of these groups, Scythians, Huns, Avars, Magyars, and Mongols, was devastating and uncontrollable; each group spread terror throughout Europe. Each group depended for its success upon the speed and mobility of a superior cavalry. The basic advantage the steppe warrior had over the European was simply that he was a nomad, while the other was a sedentary agriculturist. The nomad was forced by his way of life to roam widely in order to feed his flocks, and to live in the most meager fashion for weeks at a time. He was virtually inseparable from his horse, for without it he could not live upon the steppe. His horses were not bred for plowing, but rather for speed and mobility in the herding of sheep; the warfare of the nomad was but an extension of his manner of life.

On the other hand, the European has always been outstanding for his infantry, for he was always close to the soil. He had cavalry too, but the cavalry was not his way of life as it was with the nomad, and it was generally thought of as an adjunct to the infantry. The idea of the massed attack, which had been perfected by the Roman legions, was utilized by the European cavalry also; armored riders charged in one massive body against the lines of the enemy. Furthermore, within Europe small bits of terrain had great tactical value, whereas on the steppe no one locality had overwhelming importance. European warfare was concerned with highways, key towns, passes, and bridgeheads; steppe warfare dealt with expanses of space. The nomad could be stopped by a fortified position or by a broad river, but if he had space in which to maneuver he was almost unbeatable.

The European system of warfare depending on massed weight was no match for the nomads' astounding speed of maneuver, their sudden ferocious charges, their unpredictable retreats and flanking movements, and their clouds of arrows fired at top speed with what seemed like incredible accuracy. The steppe cavalry attacked the infantry of Europe in much the same way the American Indians attacked the wagon trains on the plains; they rode howling round and round the helpless and often shattered forces, sending waves of arrows in upon the surrounded group. The American plainsman had the rifle to offset the advantage of the wild cavalry, but the Roman did not. The Huns also possessed a bow stronger than that of the European peoples, so that they could ride beyond the effective range of their opponents' weapons. Finally, the nomad warriors possessed in their very appearance a great psychological advantage. The Europeans have always depicted them as living devils, as the people of Gog and Magog. Their facial appearance was uniquely hideous to the Europeans, and since they rarely, if ever, changed clothing, their attire consisted of tattered skins. The panic engendered by their "inhuman" appearance and by their fantastic speed of movement was undoubtedly an important factor in their military success.

Yet, though the Huns and their followers were looked upon as the mortal enemies of European civilization, this did not prevent Europeans from attempting to make use of their military prowess. Most of the initial incursions of the steppe warriors into central and western Europe were at the invitation of Europeans. The nomad has never had to seek out the Carpathian passes; there was always a European more than willing to show him the way. As early as 388 a Hun unit was used by Emperor Theodosius I to defeat the army of the usurper Maximus at Poetovio. The first Hun appearance along the Rhine was at the invitation of Aetius, Roman commander of the West, for whom they shattered the Burgundians. Repeatedly units of the Huns were used by the Romans in their internal squabbles or in their conflicts with the Germanic tribes.

When the Huns entered the Carpathian Basin at the beginning of the fifth century, they were not yet a united people. Rather they were a loose confederation of tribal units, each of which numbered about twelve hundred men. These tribes often acted in complete independence of each other, so that it was possible for Huns to appear as mercenaries on both sides of a battle.

They were originally a sheep-herding people and therefore had been widely dispersed over the grasslands. But their way of life and their political structure changed radically as soon as they entered the Carpathian Basin. With the conquest of the Goths and of the various

Germanic peoples settled within the basin, the Huns acquired as subjects an agricultural population. For the first time their basic food
needs could be met without the need of widespread grazing, and
quickly the Huns changed from sheep herders to straight plunderers;
no longer did the individual tribes have to wander far from each other.
Also, the Carpathian Basin supplied them with a base from which they
could easily reach the wealth of the Empire. The riches that had attracted the Germanic tribes into the Empire, now enticed the Huns
to raid the Empire.

During their occupancy of the basin the Huns were primarily a
raiding force. They raided not only to secure the specialty products,
including weapons, which they and their subject peoples could not
produce for themselves, but also to gain ostentatious wealth. With the
gradual rise in the "standard of living" of the Huns, the tribal chieftains demanded increasingly greater amounts of wealth to raise themselves above the ordinary members of the tribe. This desire for
ostentation was virtually insatiable, and despite peace treaties the raids
never ceased.

The Huns soon came to realize that this vast storehouse of riches,
so close at hand, could best be tapped if they themselves were united.
Raids were more successful if attacks were organized, and the wealth
could best be distributed by a central authority. The tribal units became a kingdom. At first there were two leaders, the brothers Bleda
and Attila, but in 445 Attila murdered Bleda and thereafter ruled
alone. His rule depended upon his ability to satisfy the demands of
the tribal leaders for wealth.

The Huns oppressed but did not annihilate the peoples they conquered. The first onrush of steppe warriors generally devastated an
area and decimated its population, since the nomads tended to take
what they wished and to destroy the remainder. However, once they
had settled in an area, they used the resident inhabitants as slaves to
produce food and clothing. Furthermore, the Huns did not necessarily
eradicate all the cities of the Empire. They as a people realized the
importance of trade. Many of their needs and desires could not be
met from their own production or from raiding, and trading centers
prospered along the peripheries of the Carpathian Basin.[3] However,
if the Huns were involved in actual warfare with the Empire, then
the border cities suffered horribly. In the war of 441 Viminacium,
Margum, and Singidinum (Belgrade), the three cities guarding the
junction of the Danube and the Morava, were all razed to the ground.
In the invasion of northern Italy in 452, Aquileia, which had never
previously been taken, was demolished; it never rose again as a city.
On the other hand, the cities of Pannonia were not involved in the

warfare between the Huns and the Empire, and probably simply stagnated. Vindomana more than likely continued to exist as a lesser trading post, linking the Carpathian Basin with the lands further west.

Though the kingdom of the Huns extended far beyond the Carpathian wall to include most of what is now Poland, the Ukraine, and Romania, the core of the kingdom was within the Carpathian Basin, the ideal location for the Huns. Here was the familiar grassland, with a resident supply of slave labor, and with direct access to the wealthy lands of the Empire. Though the exact location is not known, the main camp of Attila was probably along the middle Tisza.[4] From this position connections were easy with the trans-Carpathian portions of the kingdom, through the northeastern passes. Southward, the plains east of the Tisza extended unbrokenly to the Porta Orientalis, leading to the plains of the lower Danube, and to the mouth of the Morava, the gateway to Byzantium. The wealthiest portion of the Empire by far was the Byzantine half, and most of the raiding activities of the Huns were directed towards Constantinople. On the basis of a visit of Priscus to the headquarters of Attila in 449, some historians have felt that the camp was located east of the Tisza and north of the Körös, perhaps near the present Szolnok.

The constant raiding, which was such an essential part of the Hunnish way of life, eventually sealed the doom of the rule of the Huns. They gained their successes with an extremely small number of fighters in comparison to the numbers of their opponents, and the constant fighting gradually depleted these relatively few warriors. The populations of the Empire and of the Germanic tribes were large enough to absorb the heavy loss of life and property, but the Huns could not long suffer the continuing drain on their manpower. The effects of this depletion were soon evident. The first sign was in 447 when the Huns could only with great difficulty defeat a Byzantine army near Vidin on the Danube. This battle was the last victory that the Huns were able to gain over an imperial army, and it is evident that they never recovered from their losses in this battle. In 451 the Huns made their famous march into Gaul and were checked near Troyes on the Catalaunian Plains. Though beaten, they escaped to the Carpathian Basin. The following year Attila led his tribes into northern Italy, and although he succeeded in devastating the Po plains, he never crossed the Po River. It was near Peschiera, east of Milan, that the embassy of Pope Leo met the Huns and persuaded them to leave Italy.

In 453 Attila died suddenly, after a night of drinking. Because of the division of his kingdom among his many sons, concerted military action became impossible. Almost immediately the power of the Huns, so feared by Europe, collapsed. It collapsed in the way that the power of the steppe rulers of the Carpathian Basin has usually fallen. It was not crushed from without but from within. Though we are not certain of events, it seems probable that, after a period of raiding, the Scythians were conquered by the Dacians, whom they had enslaved, and the Scythians disappeared from history. Later the Yazyges, who had ruled the Alföld, were (*ca.* 334) overthrown by their subject peoples. Similarly, after the death of Attila the enslaved peoples of the Huns began to rebel. Almost immediately the Ostrogoths, dwelling somewhere in the Tisza valley, gained their independence. Shortly thereafter the other peoples revolted under the leadership of Ardaric, the king of the Gepids. In 455 the Gepids, together with the Sciri, Rugi, Suebi, and Heruls, completely defeated the Huns. Though isolated groups of the Huns may have remained within the basin, most of them fled across the Carpathians and vanished from the history of mankind.[5]

Following the destruction of the Hun kingdom the victorious Germanic tribes divided the more attractive portions of the Carpathian Basin among themselves. The Rugi occupied the Marchfeld, north of the Danube; the Ostrogoths settled in Pannonia as the new *foederati* of the Empire; the Sciri and Heruls were further east, and the Gepids occupied Transylvania. The central vastness of the Alföld probably remained unoccupied.

The influence of Constantinople was again felt along the frontier. The Danube was open to traffic, and it is probable that the Danubian fleet operated up the river, from its base at Sirmium to the northwestern outpost of Vindomina, as Vindobona was now officially called; however trade was probably minimal. The outstanding person along the frontier during the time of the Ostrogoths was not a merchant, administrator, or soldier, but a saint. The thirty years of St. Severin, "the Apostle of Noricum," form an interlude of light in the centuries of darkness.

Saint Severin traveled up the Danube in 454, the year following the death of Attila. He settled in Favianus, which may have been located at the present site of Heiligenstadt, a vineyard suburb of Vienna.[6] Favianus-Vindomina was not only the northwestern outpost of Byzantine influence, but also the eastern entrance to the Norican stretch of the Danube. The "man of God" moved frequently up and down the river between Favianus and Batava (Passau), establishing churches and bringing order and peace to the unruly peoples. The barbarians were awed by his power, bred of faith and fearlessness, and his walking

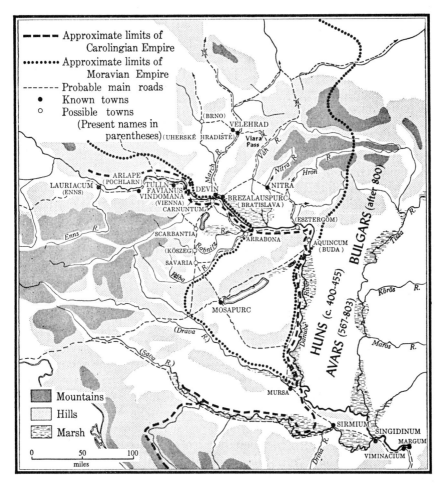

Approximate limits of
Carolingian Empire
Approximate limits of
Moravian Empire
Probable main roads
● Known towns
○ Possible towns
(Present names in
parentheses)

MAP 2. PANNONIA IN THE DARK AGES (*ca.* 400–900)

barefoot on the frozen Danube gained legendary fame. The spiritual power of this one man was of greater import in bringing stability to the limes than any kind of armed might could have been. Severin died in 482 and was buried in Favianus.

In 488, at the invitation of Emperor Zeno, the Ostrogoths left Pannonia for Italy, and bearing the remains of Severin, they moved southward along the ancient Amber Road. In 489, Theodoric, leader of the Ostrogoths, overthrew Odoacer and ruled Italy as the deputy governor of the Byzantine emperor. The other Germanic tribes, except the Gepids, seem to have left the Carpathian Basin also. Since most of the Roman citizens had accompanied Theodoric, a more complete darkness now descended on Pannonia.

The area that had been deserted by the mass evacuation was soon occupied by another Germanic group, the Lombards. They seem to have moved southward from the vicinity of the Elbe, through the Moravian corridor, to Pannonia.[7] Though the Lombards became the new *foederati* of the Empire, little is known of the eighty years of their occupation of Pannonia. Byzantine influence along the Danube probably remained significant, since this was the time of the great emperor Justinian. In 550 Vindomina was mentioned for the last time in an ancient text, when the Ostrogoth historian Jordanes referred to Sirmium and Vindomina as the two anchors of the Pannonian limes. Some Byzantine forces were probably stationed at the Vienna gap, and the Danube fleet may have moved freely along the river.

The time of the Lombards is notable, however, as the period when the Slavs began to move in appreciable numbers southward from their ancestral homes north of the Carpathians, although small Slavic groups may previously have entered the Balkans as early as the second century. By the middle of the sixth century the Slavs had sparsely occupied the present Bohemia, Moravia, and Slovakia, as well as the eastern portions of Pannonia. They settled in Pannonia with little political organization, if any at all, and are unique in Pannonian history in that they did not attempt to conquer the area or to set up new kingdoms of their own. They were not involved in any serious clashes with either the Lombards or the Gepids.

In the middle of the sixth century fighting broke out between the two ruling groups of the Carpathian Basin, the Lombards in Pannonia, and the Gepids in Transylvania. The Lombards turned to a newly arrived nomadic group, the Avars, for assistance. The two forces completely crushed the Gepid kingdom in 567, but for the Lombards the victory had been purchased at a great price. The Avars were now within the Carpathian Basin. In the following year, 568, the Lombards abandoned Pannonia to the new riders of the steppe, and moved south-ward along the Amber Road into Italy.

The Avars were a group of Turkic peoples whose ancestral home had been in the vicinity of the Altai mountains, to the north of Mongolia. Supposedly they were not true Avars, but a group of Turkic tribes who had assumed the name and become known as "new Avars." The name Avar has become, however, uniquely their own in European history. To the European they strongly resembled the Huns in appearance, fierceness, and way of life. Late in the sixth century their westward movement carried them across the Volga to the northern flank of the Carpathians; as early as 561 their raiding parties had come into contact with the Franks along the Elbe. The first mention of them within the Carpathian Basin is in connection with the campaign against the Gepids, though it is possible that small units had penetrated the mountain wall in the decade before.

Like the Huns, the Avars were fearsome warriors for several decades, even though the Byzantine armies scored local victories against them around 600. Like the warriors of Attila, the Avars were primarily predatory raiders. They had been united under one leader, their khagan, and their power was recognized well beyond the limits of the Carpathian Basin, though their headquarters were, like those of the Huns, east of the Danube in the Alföld. They focused their attention principally on the wealthy eastern half of the Empire, and their raids ravaged the Balkans and often threatened the imperial capital of Constantinople.

Associated with this extent of Avar terror was a remarkable expansion of the Slavs. Before entering the Carpathian Basin, the Avars had been located north of the Carpathians and had made the Slavs of that area their subjects. When they entered the basin the Slavs accompanied them and assumed the role of food producers for the nomad riders. Some Slavs had previously dwelt within the basin in any case, and it is probable that from the very beginning of Avar control of the basin the Slavs outnumbered the Avars. Perhaps because units of the Slavs usually accompanied the Avars on their raids, the movements of the Slavs were not restricted. As a result, while the Huns had stifled the expansion of the Germanic tribes within the basin and the Balkans, the Avars stimulated the movements of the Slavs.

The Avars further aided the Slavic expansion into the Balkans by not only destroying the border fortifications of the Empire, but also, because of their ravaging, clearing the land of previous settlement. By the end of the sixth century Slavic units had penetrated into southern Greece. The first advances were probably made by small groups, but by the close of the two centuries of Avar power in central Europe most of the Balkans had become largely Slavic. The Slavs sustained the barbarian control of areas that the Avars had only occasionally visited.

The inundation of Pannonia and Illyria under the waves of pagan Avars and Slavs had great consequences for Europe; for over two centuries the land bridge between the eastern and western halves of the old Empire was shattered. Signifying this break was the destruction of Sirmium, on the Danube, and Salonae, on the Adriatic coast. During these same centuries Moslem sea power expanded throughout the Mediterranean, and Constantinople and Rome came to be virtually isolated from each other.

Much has been made of the linguistic difference between the two halves of the Empire, but this disparity had existed for seven centuries without any serious disunity. Language differences alone cannot explain the political and ecclesiastical division that rent Europe between the sixth and tenth centuries. As long as adequate communications between the two halves had existed, a measure of unity was possible; Zeno could replace Odoacer with Theodoric, and Justinian could reconquer much of Italy. But with the severance of communications by land and sea, the two halves of the old Empire became isolated from each other and developed cultures increasingly at variance with and antagonistic to each other.[8]

The first revolt against the Avars came from within their territory, approximately fifty years after they had entered the basin. The revolt arose among the subject people, the Slavs, but was led by a Frankish merchant, Samo, who became the ruler of the political unit that resulted. The uprising broke out in the area of present Bohemia or Moravia, on the periphery of the Avar holdings, in the year 623, at the time when the Avars were engaged in an unsuccessful assault on Constantinople. The rebellion was immediately successful, evidently without much bloodshed, perhaps because the Avars were at a disadvantage in an area of hills and forests. It is probable also that the Avars were not too much concerned about what happened along the northwestern fringes of their domains; precise boundaries were not part of the steppe riders' outlook, and the Avars were interested primarily in the wealth of Byzantium, not in a barbarian frontier zone.

The capital of Samo's "state" is thought to have been at or near Vienna.[9] Certainly this was a logical point from which to govern the "state," whose area may have extended from Bohemia to present Slovenia.

Samo's "empire" withstood threats from both the steppe and the west. In 631 the Slavs successfully resisted the attempts of the Franks to annex their territory. The Franks were much stronger in number than the Slavs, but the core of Frankish power was far removed from the contested area, and serious barriers of upland and forest blocked the Franks in their advances on Bohemia, Moravia, or Vienna. As long as Samo lived, his state also existed.

It was at this same time that important events in the history of the Balkans took place; at the beginning of the seventh century the Croats and Serbs migrated to their present homelands in Jugoslavia. Both groups lived north of the Carpathians; the Croats, in "White Croatia," were immediately north of the Moravian Gate; the Serbs, in "White Serbia," were further west, in the area of the present Saxony. It is probable that each group consisted of a mingling of two unlike elements. The basic agricultural component was made up of Slavs who were still one in speech and culture, but overruling these people may have been Iranian riders who gave the groups their names and leadership. Thus both the Croats and the Serbs may at this time have been similar to the Huns and the Avars in that their population consisted of a servile agricultural group ruled by a privileged warrior class. In warfare the Iranians formed the cavalry, the Slavs the infantry. Probably it was the presence of this Iranian cavalry which enabled the Croats to defend themselves successfully against the Avars, Bulgars, and Magyars, all of whom practiced the methods of steppe warfare.[10]

In 626 the Avars once again attacked Constantinople. At this time Emperor Heraclius was also engaged in a war with Persia, and so approached the Croats to form an alliance against the Avars. The Croats accepted the offered alliance, and attacked the Avars from the rear. They moved southward along the ancient Amber Road through the domains of Samo to the southwestern corner of the Carpathian Basin.[11] After expelling the Avars from this northwestern corner of the Balkans, they received (*ca.* 640) the area, including Dalmatia and Bosnia, as their new homeland. The Serbs moved southward at approximately the same time, and were settled east of the Drina River in the "Theme of Thessalonika." With these new *foederati*, the Empire strengthened its northwestern frontier against the incursions of the Avars, but at the same time facilitated the expansion of the Slavs in the Balkans.

At this time the Slavs do not seem to have been capable of producing effective political leaders. The focus of their life seems to have been close to the soil, close to the family, and the powers of statehood were left in the hands of others. Thus though the Slavs undoubtedly were in the majority among the inhabitants of the Carpathian Basin at this time, they were ruled by Franks, Avars, Iranians, or Byzantines. As a consequence, when Samo died, *ca.* 658, his "empire" was divided among his sons and disintegrated. No great battle seems to have crushed the "state"; certainly there was no internal revolution. No one arose to take the place of the dead leader, and soon Avar rule again extended westward to the mouth of the Enns.

Though Avar rule became progressively weaker during the eighth century, and their kingdom could probably have been shattered with relative ease, there was no final revolt. The Slavs accepted Avar rule and made no attempt to contest it. With the passage of several decades a safe, unmolested border developed along the Enns, between the Avar kingdom and the neighboring Bavarian state. Bavarian settlers and missionaries began to move east of the Enns, even into the Tullner Feld. The threat of raids was always present, but the devastation of these raids had been much lessened by two centuries of bloodshed. Only a strong hand was needed to free Pannonia from the control of the Avar khagan.

Toward the end of the eighth century a new force was felt within the Carpathian Basin. For the first time since the Celtic invasion over a millennium before, a strong political power entered the basin from the west, along the line of the upper Danube. Previously Pannonia had been an outpost of Rome, when the basin was entered through the Julian gaps, or of Byzantium, when it was entered from the lower Danube; now it became an outpost of the Western, Carolingian Europe. The Frankish state was the theoretical successor of the Western Roman Empire, but its advent meant a completely new arrangement of political organization.

In 787 Charlemagne firmly integrated Bavaria into the Carolingian domains. Whereas before, the Bavarians and Avars had been at peace with each other in a transitional zone, now the Avars faced the full, massed might of Western Europe. A number of Avar incursions were easily crushed in 788 and 789 by the new masters of Noricum. For Charlemagne the riders of the steppe were not only a threat to his new eastern frontier, but also a criminal element in Christian Europe. They had perpetrated grave injustices against Christendom and the Church and deserved to be crushed. The Avars in turn helped to instigate a conflict by claiming the Enns as the boundary of their domains, while for the Franks, imbued still with the areal traditions of the Romans, the boundary was along the historic line between Noricum and Pannonia, the Vienna ridge.

In April, 791, two mighty Frankish columns moved eastward against the Avars. One column, under the direct command of Charlemagne, advanced along the southern bank of the Danube; the second column moved through Bohemia and reached the northern bank of the river near Krems. The Danube was the supply artery of the two armies; a fleet manned by the Bavarians accompanied the columns eastward. The two forces advanced simultaneously through the Tullner Feld and easily destroyed the Avar Rings (encampments) north and south of the river. Within the narrow confines of the Tulln basin, the badly outnumbered nomads could not withstand the charge of Western Europe. The two columns then combined and advanced along the ancient limes road as far as the site of Arrabona (Győr), the junction of the Rába and the Danube. Everywhere the Franks wasted the countryside, while the Avars fled before them. However, at the mouth of the Rába the pursuit ended, for it was now the end of summer and the Carolingian forces had suffered serious losses of their horses in the marshlands which meet at Arrabona. Confronting the army was the Little Alföld, within which was the enemy, difficult to locate and almost impossible to attack. After a short rest the army retired westward. One column returned directly along the Danube; the other turned southwestward, followed the ancient road along the Rába to the site of Savaria, and then turned northward along the Amber Road to reach the Danube at Carnuntum.

This campaign had badly defeated the Avars but had not completely crushed them. Beyond the Rába they still roamed the plain, possible threats to the new frontier of the Empire. A few years later, however, another attack by the Franks ended the last semblance of their power. In mid-winter 796, Frankish columns attacked swiftly, both along the Danube and eastward from the Julian passes. The two forces advanced across the Danube and stormed the principal Avar Ring, the ultimate center of the Avar kingdom. Untold wealth was discovered; the ostentatious accumulation of two and a half centuries of predatory raids lay heaped on the steppe between the Danube and the Tisza. All of this treasure was shipped westward, and much of it passed through the hands of Charlemagne, who dispensed it lavishly. The Carolingian realm, which had been relatively devoid of money, became sudsuddenly wealthy, and the resultant inflation is reported to have caused a 33 per cent rise in prices within one decade.

Though their power was thoroughly destroyed, the Avars did not cease all resistance until 803. Small groups then fled eastward or hid themselves in the more remote areas of Pannonia.[12] Perhaps the majority of them surrendered to the Franks and were settled in the empty lands of the Little Alföld, "between Carnuntum and Savaria," but this remnant of the former rulers of central Europe vanished with astounding rapidity. The last mention of them occurred in documents in 822, and in 828 King Ludwig dissolved their province.[13] Undoubtedly, very few Avars were left by 803; perhaps these were decimated by disease, or by the Slavs who could now repay their former masters for two centuries of servitude. In 858 the area was again referred to as a *Deserta*, and King Karlmann considered how to resettle its empty spaces. Like the Huns before them, the Avars vanished from history.

After the destruction of the Avar kingdom, Pannonia was incorporated into the Carolingian Empire. A new pseudo-Roman empire had gained control of Pannonia, and the Danube was again the frontier, but the core of power now was not in Rome or Constantinople, but in the vicinity of the Rhine. For four centuries ties with the Empire had meant ties with Constantinople; now they meant ties with Aachen or Regensburg. Western Europe had developed independently for two centuries and had succeeded in divorcing the concept of Roman rule from the city which supplanted Rome, Constantinople. A barbarian king from the northwestern fringe of Europe had laid claim to the Roman title and heritage and had advanced to the Pannonian frontier. The line between East and West was drawn anew along the line of the division of 395, but only because Frankish power exceeded Byzantine power and could separate Pannonia from Byzantium.

The central Alföld was not claimed by either empire. The Avars had vanished, but a new steppe people, the Bulgars, now dominated the grasslands. At this time the Bulgars were powerful enough to battle both empires and had carved themselves a new kingdom along the southern shore of the Danube in the area that still bears their name. Frontier battles with the Franks were ended by the treaty of 845, in which the Bulgars retained control of the Alföld plus the border areas around Sirmium and Singidinum. Since these two sites were key junction points on the routeways connecting the Carpathian Basin and Constantinople, a wedge of nomad and Slav still separated the Eastern and Western empires.

In the initial Carolingian organization of northern Pannonia, the boundary of the Ostmark was set at the Fischa River. The Fischa is a minor stream flowing northward through the middle of the Vienna Basin to the Danube. The Mark extended westward to the Enns, and was organized from Tulln, at the eastern end of the Tullner Feld. The flatlands east of the Fischa, extending to the Rába, were granted to the Avars. Beyond the Rába, the land was but poorly organized and sparsely settled by groups of Slavs.

In 828 King Ludwig, threatened by the Bulgars from the steppe, reorganized Pannonia completely. The Ostmark was now limited on the east by the Wienerwald, which became once again an administrative boundary. East of the Vienna ridge were two new Pannonian marks. The more important of these two was Upper Pannonia, extending from the Wienerwald to the general vicinity of Buda, though its extent east of the Rába was somewhat vague. Lower Pannonia was larger but was well to the south, and thus remote from the principal line of east-west communications.

Cities were probably non-existent in Pannonia at this time. If any of the ancient centers did survive the centuries of Avar domination, they were no more than primitive remnants. Chronicles of the time do mention Carnuntum and Savaria, but since the Roman names are used it is impossible to ascertain whether actual settlements, or only known sites, are referred to. A Salzburg chronicle of 881 does mention a "Weniam" which is thought to be the Carolingian forerunner of Vienna. Conditions in Pannonia were simply not conducive to the development of cities at this time. The land was but sparsely populated, by primitive peoples, mostly Slovene, who had not yet developed an extensive trade. This was only the wasted, empty, pioneer fringe of both eastern and western cultures. A feudal system of land-holdings was superimposed upon the conquered land, and the manor, not the city, became the focal point of wealth and power.

The latter half of the ninth century, the Carolingian century, saw the rise of the first genuine Slavic kingdom within the Danubian lands. This "state," known under the grandiose title of the "Moravian Empire," developed within those lands along the Danube that were considered by the Franks to be within their sphere of influence. Just as the Romans had penetrated north of the Danube, so too the Franks, especially the missionaries, penetrated north of the great river. Through most of its existence, the Moravian Empire was a "client state" of the Carolingian Empire,[14] but for a score of years between 874 and 894 it was a great power within central Europe and managed to unite most of the Slavs along the Frankish frontier.

In the vicinity of Pannonia the Moravian state consisted of three separate portions which were forcibly united into one by the strongest of the three. The core of the state was within the broad March valley. This has been, through the millennia, the corridor between the Danube and the North European Plain, and it became for the Moravians the organizational center of their state. The precise location of the capital is not known, but it appears to have been in the vicinity of the present town of Uherské Hradiště.[15] Here the March lowland was restricted between the flank of the Carpathians to the east and a dense forest just to the west. From this site on the March a road still runs over a low saddle, the Vlara Pass, in the Carpathians into present Slovakia and the valleys of the Váh and the Nitra. North of this site the roads fan out into Bohemia, Silesia, and Poland. This capital could be protected from an assault by the Franks from the south, and yet it had excellent means of communications to all areas north of the Danube.

An important outpost of power was at the critical Carnuntum (Hainburg) crossing of the Danube. Here two fortress cities, one on each flank of the Carpathians, guarded the crossing. At Devín, the fortress of Rastislav (the second great ruler of Moravia) was perched upon a steep rock overlooking the confluence of the March and the Danube. A few miles to the east, Brezalauspurc (Bratislava) guarded the eastern flank of the uplands.

The first expansion of the Moravian state (*ca.* 835) was eastward across the Carpathians into what is now the western half of Slovakia. This area had been organized by Pribina as a separate Slav province, a protectorate of the Franks. The organizational center of this area was at Nitra, located on the river of that name, the middle of the three rivers that flow from the western Carpathians into the Danube. Because of the swampy nature of the lowlands along the Danube, the principal road of Pribina's realm ran along the slopes of the foothills. Near Nitra this road met the road from Uherské Hradiště; north of Nitra roads probably penetrated the valleys of the Váh, the Nitra, and the Hron; east of Nitra the road ran to the important gap of the Danube above Buda. Nitra had been a Roman camp during the campaigns of Marcus Aurelius and was also the site of the first Frankish church built in the northern Little Alföld.

The third portion of the Moravian Empire, the last one to be added to the state, formed the eastern part of Pannonia. Since this area had but poor connections with the March lowland and was within the Carolingian boundaries, it was not obtained by Moravia until the Franks had been decisively defeated, in 874. Its western boundaries are not known, but it is thought that they may have been along the Rába River.[16] To the south, Moravian penetration may have extended beyond the Drava to the Sava.

East and south of the Rába the population of Pannonia was overwhelmingly Slavic at this time. Bavarian colonization had pushed eastward during the ninth century, but most of this settlement was further west in the valleys and foothills of the Alps. After he was driven out of Nitra by Mojmir (the founder of the Moravian state), Pribina was awarded by the Franks most of eastern Pannonia as a personal holding. Pribina established his center, and constructed his fortress, on a hill in the midst of the swamps at the western end of Lake Balaton. This fortress center was named Mosapurc (or Moosburg), "swamp fortress." Its Slavic name, Blatengrad, became the root of both the German and the Magyar names for the adjacent lake: Platten See, Balaton-tava.

Mosapurc was one of the most important settlements within Pannonia during the Carolingian century. It had considerable strategic significance. The long line of the lake, flanked by the Bakony Hills, divided Pannonia along a northeast to southwest line. Unless they entered through one of the passes east of the lake, the nomads of the steppe were forced to move around the western end of the lake. Similarly, the ancient direct road from Sirmium to Carnuntum had passed by the western end of this lake barrier. The passageway southwest of Lake Balaton was in turn limited to a width of thirty miles by the broad, marshy Drava valley to the south; Mosapurc guarded this passage between the lake and the Drava. During the ninth century the principal threat to the eastern frontiers of the Frankish realm came from the Bulgars, who were concentrated in the southern portions of the Alföld, and along the lower Danube. Any Bulgar attack into Pannonia was almost certain to pass by Mosapurc.

This key location had been utilized by the Romans, and was highly valued by King Arnulf of the East Franks; on at least three occasions he visited the frontier fortress. For Pribina it was not only a border bastion, but also the ideal location from which to govern his holdings; from there he could control his territories both to the north and to the south of the lake barrier. An impressive church was built here in the middle of the ninth century; its ruins are still visible at Zalavár, the Magyar successor to Mosapurc.[17]

By 874 Moravia extended into Pannonia, and northward into portions of present Bohemia, Saxony, Silesia, and southern Poland. However, the death of Sviatopluk in 894 ended the greatness of this ephemeral state. By 907 Greater Moravia had vanished completely.

Though Greater Moravia was very short-lived, its existence was of considerable significance to the history of Eastern Europe; Moravia was the setting for the work of Saints Cyril and Methodius. Because of the threat of a Frank-Bulgar alliance, the Moravians turned for assistance to Constantinople, in 862. Since among the Franks political and ecclesiastical penetration worked hand in hand, the Moravians requested from the Byzantines not only military help but also Slavic-speaking missionaries. Emperor Michael III agreed to this, happy to gain an ally against the Bulgars. The resultant military alliance allowed Moravia to survive, and the missionary activity made a permanent impress on the history of Europe. In 863 the two brothers, Constantine (Cyril) and Methodius, natives of Thessalonika who had learned Slavic in their youth, travelled up the ancient route to the Pannonian frontier. They seem to have moved from Sirmium through the lands of Kocel, the son of Pribina, to the center of the Moravian Empire. At Velehrad, about five miles west of Uherské Hradiště, they established their monastery and made their historic translation of the scriptures into Slavonic.

Because these activities were being carried on in territories which the bishops of Salzburg and Passau considered to be their own, the opposition of the Frankish clergy was severe. Coöperation seems to have been impossible because of the close alignment of missionary activity and political motives; Kocel soon drove the Frankish missionaries out of his realm. However, in contrast to the opposition of the archbishops of Salzburg, the popes of the time were strongly in favor of the new missionary efforts. They were not only happy to see the Slavs converted to Christianity, but they were also pleased to have the arrogant Frankish bishops limited in their attempts to increase their power. In order to separate completely the Moravian lands from Salzburg and Passau, Pope Hadrian II re-established the ancient Metropolitan See of Sirmium, and placed all of the Moravian lands, including Pannonia, under its spiritual jurisdiction.

The two decades of missionary activity had many far-reaching implications. Once again Pannonia had come within the sphere of Byzantine influence, and, as in the days of St. Severin, the military power of the Germans was overcome by a spiritual power from the east. The spiritual coöperation of Rome and Constantinople was one of the last symbols of the historic east-west unity of the Empire, and the earliest forerunner of the Uniat churches. Rome had spoken as the guardian of a Christian liturgy based on Byzantine tradition and using a Slavic tongue. Probably of greatest significance was the invention of the alphabet by the young linguist, Cyril, and the adaptation of the liturgy to this alphabet. This script, now known as the Glagolitic, was the ancestor of the Cyrillic alphabet still used in most Slavic lands. Following the death of Methodius in 884 (Cyril had died in Rome in 869), the Slavonic leaders were driven out of Moravia, but their efforts found fruitful soil among the Bulgars.

The Moravian Empire had been oriented toward the East; had it survived for several centuries, instead of several decades, the permanent division between the two Europes based on the Latin tradition and on the Greek-Slavonic could well have become fixed along the ancient divide of the Vienna ridge. It is possible too that Bohemia and Moravia would have developed separate cultures and become as different as the Croats and Serbs are today. On the other hand, the continuance of a Slavic state based in the Moravian corridor could have resulted in a permanent union of the western Slavs. Following the destruction of Moravia, the centers of power were shifted westward to Bohemia, and northeast to Poland, neither of which could control the other. Only Moravia was in the geographic position to organize all the lands of the western Slavs.

The ninth century was but an interlude in the era of the great migrations. A measure of order and organization had been introduced along the fringes of the Carpathian Basin, but this organization implied the absence of the rider of the Alföld; when the raider returned, the carefully constructed edifices of the Germans and the Slavs crumbled. The bold empires built along the fringes of the Alps and Carpathians fell under the hoofs of the next raiders of the steppe, the Magyars. Yet, though shattered, these two empires remained living memories within Pannonia. Charlemagne became the historic basis of all pro-German propaganda in 1918, just as the empire of Sviatopluk was recalled by the proponents of the Slavic corridor.

By this time the seeds of the state system of Europe had been sown within the Carpathian Basin. The two achievements yet required before these seeds could be brought to fruition were the subjection of the wild Alföld and the final eradication of the idea of the Roman limes along the Danube. These tasks the Magyars accomplished in that century of raiding which brought to a close the migrations of the nations.

DUNÁNTÚL

5

THE ARRIVAL
OF THE MAGYARS

None of the onslaughts of the steppe folk from the east had as devastating an effect on Europe as did the arrival of the Magyars.[1] For over a score of years European armies fled before them, and defensive forces hid themselves while the savage raiders rode by. The Huns and the Mongols gained reputations as ruthless plunderers, but their times of power were shorter, and neither of these groups penetrated as widely into western Europe as did the Magyars. Similarly the Avars rarely assaulted western Europe. During the first half of the tenth century the Magyars ravaged all but the utmost extensions of the continent.

The fantastic range and power of the Magyar raids was due not only to their military might, but also to the weakness of Europe, for during the early tenth century Europe was at her nadir. Moslem fleets and pirates controlled the Mediterranean, while the Norsemen ravaged the northern coastlines and islands. The Eastern Roman Empire was hard pressed to control a vigorous Bulgar kingdom, while the Carolingian Empire had fallen apart in the century after Charlemagne. The East Frankish Kingdom, which faced the new nomads directly, was ruled by a child king for several years during this critical time. This was the darkest of all the "Dark Ages" that Europe had to endure.

Within the Carpathian Basin the Germans and Slavs had been fighting with each other for over half a century, and the Magyars had, in fact, been led into the basin to assist in these wars. Pannonia had been wasted and largely depopulated even before the full fury of the Magyar storm swept over the borderland. In 894, the year before the Magyars moved as a body through the Carpathians, Sviatopluk had died, and the Moravian Empire had ceased to be a powerful state. Though the Germans and the Moravians joined forces briefly to confront the new raiders, the decade preceding the catastrophes of 904–7 was characterized principally by the attempts of the Germans to divide the former domains of Sviatopluk. Though it should have been obvious that their turn would be next, the Germans made no efforts to assist the Moravians in their struggle with the Magyars.

As Macartney has shown in his excellent analysis of the origins of the Magyars,[2] they were probably a union of two strains of people, one Turkic and the other Finnish. The joining of these two unlike groups probably occurred in the vicinity of the Urals, where the boreal forest meets the steppe. The union was mutually advantageous, since the Turks needed food and the Finns protection. The Magyars may then have been attacked by one of the numerous groups moving across the grasslands, as they seem to have split into two portions, one of which moved to the middle Volga, and the other to the mouth of the Don. It was this latter group which later moved into the Carpathian Basin. Around 830 they were attacked by another steppe people, the Circassians, and as a consequence moved across the Don, where their new home came to be known as Etelköz, the legendary ancestral home of the Magyars. Here they came under the suzerainty of the Khazars, a union of three Turkic tribes, one of which, the Kavars, joined the Magyars to become the warrior elite of the new combination. Around 889 yet another steppe people, the Petchenegs, attacked the Magyars and forced them to leave Etelköz; in 890 the latter group is known to have crossed the Dnieper south of Kiev.

The arrival of a new group of steppe nomads in the vicinity of the Carpathians tempted the European rulers to make use once more of this unexcelled cavalry in their own struggles. As early as 862 a Magyar unit raided the frontiers of the East Frankish Kingdom; this clash seems to have occurred in Pannonia, at the invitation of the Moravians. Thirty years later the Magyar units were employed by the Germans against the Moravians; at that time the East Frankish king, Arnulph, gained lasting opprobrium for inviting the Magyars into the Carpathian Basin. His contemporaries accused him of having thus "broken down the Great Wall of Gog and Magog and letting the imprisoned nations loose upon civilization." [3] Certain it is that the Magyars did not have to seek out the Carpathian passes. In these border wars the

Magyars ravaged Pannonia and soon learned about the wealth of Western Europe.

The events which led directly to the migration of this entire people into the Carpathian Basin were also a result of military activities carried on for a European state. In 893 the Byzantine emperor, whose state was being sorely pressed by the Bulgars, made an alliance with the Magyars to attack the Bulgars in the rear. Two-front warfare was favored by the rulers of Constantinople and had often been used successfully, but this time the astute Bulgar monarch made use of the same kind of tactics. After the Bulgars had been defeated by the Magyar onslaught, King Symeon began extended peace deliberations with Byzantium; meanwhile, however, he made a pact with the Petchenegs to attack the Magyars from the rear. In 895 the combined forces of the Bulgars and Petchenegs crushed the Magyars between them. Late that year the main mass of the Magyars moved through the passes of the northeastern Carpathians (according to legend, near Mukachevo) and entered the Alföld.

The center of Magyar power, under the leadership of Árpád, moved slowly southwestward along the northern fringe of the Alföld.[4] From this migrating "capital" nomadic units moved in all directions to subdue the indistinct tribal holdings which seem to have occupied Transylvania and the margins of the grassland. The Magyars soon struck against the two organized forces occupying the western portions of the basin, and by 899 the Moravians had purchased a brief peace from the Magyars. Since it was evident that the chief opposition to the Magyar advance lay to the west, Árpád established his center of power at Esztergom, in the gap of the Danube. Here he could face any countermove from the west, and from this position his warriors could freely move both to the north and to the south of the Danube.

In 900 the Magyars moved into eastern Pannonia, which soon became a popular settlement area for the sedentary Finnish portion of the population. The Rába, which had been the Franks' second line of defense against the east, now became for a brief period the frontier of Western Europe, although Magyar raiders crossed it freely. The first long raid seems to have occurred in 899, when the Magyars penetrated into northern Italy. In 900 they first swept through the Ostmark and followed the Danube westward into Bavaria. In the following years they focused their attention on their immediate neighbors to the northwest, the Moravians, and in a series of ravages between 904 and 906 they completely shattered the remains of Sviatopluk's empire. Only Bohemia escaped destruction, and the Moravian core of the former kingdom was utterly wasted, later becoming a large-scale glacis between the Magyars and the Holy Roman Empire.

In March, 907, the main horde of Magyar fighting forces crossed
the Rába. Since this threatened to become a full-scale assault on the
Ostmark, the margrave Liutbold of Bavaria assembled a large armed
force to defend the marchland. This army advanced to the frontier,
and on June 28th met the Magyars in the decisive Battle of Pressburg.
The precise location of this battle is not known, but it is said to have
occurred within sight of the fortress of Brezalauspurc (Pressburg,
Bratislava). Since the Magyars had been south of the Danube, and the
main route of the Bavarian advance would have been along the south
bank road, the battle probably took place in the vicinity of Kittsee,
the northernmost village of Burgenland.[5] This was an obvious place
for the Bavarians to make their stand, since it placed them in front of
the Hainburg and Bruck gaps in the hill chain separating the Vienna
Basin from the Little Alföld. However, this battlefield was ideal for
the tactics of the steppe riders; on the open ground they had sufficient
room for their devastating maneuvers. The Magyars soon surrounded
the slow-moving German army, rode around it howling fiercely,
and shot in their arrows with deadly accuracy. The desperate defenders were splintered into ineffective groups by the sudden cavalry
charges and then were mowed down as they tried to escape. At the
end of that day the margrave Liutbold, the Archbishop of Salzburg,
the bishops of Freising and Seben, numerous Bavarian counts, and
most of the Bavarian army lay dead upon the field. It was a disaster
for Western Europe. Immediately, the Magyar force rode westward
to dispose of a smaller force that had been left behind at the Enns.
This latter army, under Prince Ludwig, fled from the fortress of
Ennsburg, which had been built only six years previously specifically
to stop the Magyars. By the end of June, 907, the Ostmark had
vanished, and the entire Bavarian frontier lay completely open to the
attacks of the nomads.

Following the catastrophe of Pressburg, the Magyar raiders surged
unchecked across the lands of Western Europe. For over a score of
years Europe was in a state of panic. In 908 the margrave Burchard of
Saxony attempted to stop one of the raids but was unsuccessful and
lost his life in the battle; except for this encounter, the Magyars were
allowed to move about at will, for no one dared face them. Horrifying
tales helped to destroy the will of the West. The Magyars were
described as being akin to beasts, were said to consume human flesh
and blood and to kill all whom they found, except young women, who
were taken back with them into the Carpathian Basin. They were supposed to believe that every person a warrior killed would be his slave
after he himself had died; the assumption of this belief gave an appar-

ent purpose to their slaughtering, a driving force beyond the usual tendency of steppe folk to destroy what they could not carry away.

Even to us now, the range and extent of the Magyar raids seem almost unbelievable. They reached Flanders, Lorraine, and the Rhone Valley; they destroyed Basel and burned Bremen. Their forces appeared before Rome and swept to the "heel" of the Italian peninsula. Several times they were under the gates of Constantinople. Only the furthermost extensions of Europe—Iberia, Britain, and Scandinavia—seemed to be free from the threat of the Magyars.

At first the German princes attempted to buy off the raiders, and in this way Bavaria and Saxony obtained truces. But after more experience in withstanding the Magyar type of attack, and with a slow decline in Magyar numbers, the German rulers began to offer some resistance to the predators from the east. In 933 Henry the Fowler inflicted the first defeat on the Magyars. It was not a serious defeat, but it marked the turning point in the situation between the West and the nomad. Gradually resistance stiffened as the Germans came to realize that the Magyars were almost helpless against strong fortifications and were at a disadvantage in wooded, hilly terrain. The raids continued, but the steady drain of Magyar manpower was at last beginning to be felt; in 938 they were again repulsed in Saxony, and in 950 in Bavaria.

In 955 the Magyars raided the West in force; the riders moved through the lands of Bavaria and Swabia. The main horde remained in the Lechfeld and besieged the wealthy trading center of Augsburg, while raiding parties swept outward in various directions and penetrated well into France. King Otto assembled a large army and marched to the relief of Augsburg. As his forces arrived, the Magyars lifted the siege and gathered their forces along the east bank of the Lech River to face the oncoming Germans and Slavs. On August 10, 955, was fought one of the most significant battles in European history.

King Otto and his soldiers approached the battle against these "human devils" as a fight for Christendom, and the army moved into the conflict under the banner of Michael the Archangel. The Germans and Slavs had learned much in the fifty years since Pressburg. The army, now widely deployed, stressed cavalry rather than infantry, and had learned not to panic at the sweeping maneuvers of the nomads. During the night a Magyar unit had secretly crossed the Lech and in the morning sprang upon the supply wagons of the Bohemians from the rear. This was a favorite tactic of the nomads and was to be used devastatingly later by the Mongols against the Magyars. It usually insured victory, but this time the Duke of Lorraine attacked the surprising force and drove it off. Following this initial victory, the main army surged across the Lech and totally shattered the army of the Magyars. For the remainder of the day remnants of the Magyar army were hunted down and annihilated. According to Magyar legend, only seven of the warriors returned to Pannonia to bring the news of the disaster.

This victory made a profound impression on the people of Europe and formed part of the foundation upon which Otto and his successors built the Holy Roman Empire. Though it was undoubtedly a magnificent achievement, it must be kept in mind that this victory of Emperor Otto came when the Magyars had obviously been declining as an effective fighting force. One can even formulate a time rate for this weakening of a nomad force when in contact with Europeans: the Huns were just fifty-three years in the Carpathian Basin before their collapse, the Avars fifty years before the revolt of Samo, and the Magyars sixty years before the catastrophe on the Lechfeld. A half century of depletion caused by incessant raids made all the nomadic groups vulnerable to the organized attacks of the sedentary Europeans.

The victory on the Lechfeld was a turning point in the history of Europe. The six centuries of the migrations of the nations had been brought to a close. After this time, no new nations established themselves permanently within central or western Europe.

The Magyar storm was the final cauterization that cleared the soil of Europe for the development of a new civilization. Memories of the boundaries of the Roman Empire, as well as traces of tribal kingdoms, were swept aside and burnt away in the half century of holocaust. In the fifty years that followed the victory at Augsburg, the fundamental geo-political units of modern Europe were born. The medieval German empire, the Duchy of Austria, and the kingdoms of Bohemia, Poland, and Hungary all came into being during this half century. All of these states owed their existence not only to the defeat of the Magyars, but also to the eradication by the Magyars of what had existed before. Perhaps by coincidence, the beginnings of the kingdom of France, the unification of England, the first great advances in the reconquest of Iberia, the conquest of the Mediterranean Sea by the Italian city-states, and the final separation of the eastern and western Churches, all occurred within about a century of the Battle of the Lechfeld. Europe, as we now know it, began to take shape about 1000 A.D. What we erroneously call "medieval" was not the middle ages of anything; it was the youth of Europe, and all the childlike love of color, the unsophistication and crudeness, the chivalry and cruelty, the idealism that flamed into the Crusades, were manifestations of that lusty, romantic youth.

After the disaster on the Lechfeld, the Turkic warriors of the Magyar combination were but a remnant of their former numbers. With strong leadership the sedentary Finnish people could easily have overthrown the Kavar horsemen. However such a revolution did not occur among the Magyars, as it had among the Huns and Avars, because of the unique union of the two unlike elements. Whereas the Huns and the Avars had dominated the residents of the Carpathian Basin, the Turkic warriors and Finnish agriculturists had united to become the Magyars long before they had entered the basin. Hence there was no dissatisfied, subjected minority seeking an opportunity to revolt. The agricultural element of the Magyar population may also help to explain partly the bloodthirstiness of the Magyars in their raids. The Magyar horsemen neither needed nor desire an enslaved agricultural population, as the Huns had in the past. For the Magyars, the people they overpowered in their raids or conquests had no special usefulness; possibly only the young women were spared and enslaved. Consequently, the Magyar storm may have swept the basin clear of any previous settlement except in the more remote, forested areas west of the Danube.[6]

Although the Finnish element did not actually rebel against the Turkic horsemen, it did in fact supplant them. This is evident from the language of the present day Magyars, which is closer to Finnish than to Turkish. The ascendancy of the sedentary people over the horsemen seems mainly attributable to the gradual depletion of the warrior population while the agricultural population was increasing to the point where it formed the overwhelming majority of the total. During the crucial half century following the Lechfeld, it was this superiority in numbers among the settled folk that made the formation of the Hungarian kingdom possible.

With the increasing pressure from the outside nations, the descendants of Árpád came to realize that the entire people could be saved from the same extinction that had befallen their steppe predecessors only by forming a unified state comparable to the European states of the time. Only through unity could the survival of the nation be assured, and that unity had to be founded upon the sedentary majority, since the nomads were still imbued with the spirit of nomadic freedom. It was the singular genius of the Árpád leader Géza, and more particularly his son Stephen, that carried through this shift of the base of power from the warrior to the settled element. In effect, a Kavar chieftain founded his kingdom upon the strength of this lower level of society.

The Turkic element was not extinguished however. The Magyars remained a blend of the two peoples, and although the Finnish group gave the nation its language the Turkic element gave it much of its national character. Those Magyar traits of "military wildness, passionateness, fearlessness, and a tendency towards melancholy and sorrow which all steppe peoples have brought with them out of their limitless spaces," [7] were the contribution of the Turkic warriors. Because of continued intermarriage among the highest noble families, especially in Transylvania, some Magyars still possess the brownish skin, black hair, and somewhat slanted eyes of the original nomadic horsemen.

As was customary among the steppe nomads, the Magyars had originally been united in a loose confederation of tribes (a legendary seven). Around the year 890, when the Magyars were just to the east of the Carpathians, one of the tribal chieftains, Álmos, was chosen to be the leader among equals. This very idea of having a leader illustrated not only the influence of the surrounding kingdoms on the Magyars, but also their desire to tap the nearby sources of wealth. A unified command could most effectively face the European armies, supervise the raids, and distribute the spoils. It was the son of Álmos, Árpád, who, as a Magyar Moses, led his people into the Carpathian Basin and gave his name to the first royal dynasty of his nation.

After 955 the empires to the west and southeast once again began to advance toward their former holdings in Pannonia. By 1000 the Byzantines had regained the Balkans to the Sava River, the southern limit of the Carpathian Basin, while in the west the limits of the Holy Roman Empire had been advanced beyond the Wienerwald. As a result of these outside pressures, the Kingdom of Hungary was created, and a tribal confederation was transformed into a European state.

Such a transformation required more than just the power of a strong leader. Samo and Sviatopluk had formed unified states from tribal units, but these states had collapsed after the death of the leader. If a tribal confederation was to be successfully transformed into an organized state modelled on the states of Western Europe, the system of beliefs, the faith of Western Europe, was a necessary prerequisite to make the transformation permanent. A code of values that stressed loyalty to the tribe had to be replaced by a system of belief that extended this loyalty to the entire community of the nation, and which through a hierarchy of values erected a hierarchy of order. Whereas it was political pressure which had made the creation of the kingdom necessary, it was Christianity that supplied the vital organizing force.

Christianity had been introduced early among the Magyars. Most of their prisoners were Christians, and thus the new faith was quickly brought into the Magyar households. Furthermore, some of the Moravian religious centers may have survived the Magyar storm; thus, as Dvornik feels, the first proselytizing of the Magyars may have come from a Slavonic monastery at Esztergom.[8] The influence of Christianity increased greatly after 955, perhaps because of the tendency of pagans to associate success and failure with specific gods. German missionaries entered from the west and Greek missionaries from the southeast. In the decade after the Lechfeld two tribal rulers of the east were baptized by Byzantine monks, and a Greek monastery was established at Csanád, on the lower Maros River. Sarolth, the Christian daughter of one of these chieftains, became the wife of the Árpád leader, Géza, and so by 970 Christianity had entered the court. In 972 their son Vajt was baptized and given the name Stephen. Since St. Stephen the martyr was the patron saint of the Bishopric of Passau, some historians have felt that missionaries from Passau were probably active at the court in Esztergom. Géza may have been baptized at the same time; if so, he was the first Christian leader of the Magyars.

Stephen was raised as a Christian and may have come under the influence of St. Adalbert, the great missionary of the eastern frontiers of Europe. In 995 Stephen married Gisela, the sister of Henry II, later Holy Roman Emperor, and succeeded his father as leader of the Magyars. This marriage gave him, even if only temporarily, the support of the Western Empire in his campaign to unify and Christianize the Magyars. Later, when German influence in the kingdom seemed to be becoming dangerously intense, Italian monks largely supplanted the Germans. The odd spellings of the Hungarian language are thought to be the results of the attempts of Venetian monks to cope with the unique sounds of Magyar. Stephen was a genuinely religious man. He did not use Christianity merely as a means to unify his state; rather he pressed the conversion of the Magyars with an apostolic fervor. He had a deep devotion to the Virgin Mary; he dedicated his kingdom to her and was crowned on the feast of her Assumption.

On August 15, 1000, Stephen was crowned the first king of Hungary with the crown bestowed on him by Pope Sylvester II. With this gift, the spiritual head of Christendom had recognized the royal rights of a descendant of the predatory nomads. The granting of the crown represented the recognition by Europe that the entire area of the Carpathian Basin had become for the first time an organized state, and that the Alföld had, in a symbolic sense, been transferred from Asia to Europe. Hungary had been accepted as a kingdom within the European system of kingdoms, a Christian state within the European system of states, and the Magyars had been recognized as a nation within the European family of nations.

With this coronation the Roman limes, that for one thousand years had formed the underlying geo-political idea within the Carpathian

Basin, was replaced by an entirely new idea. "Pannonia" vanished; even as a local areal designation it was replaced by the Magyar term *Dunántúl* (Transdanubia). Throughout the six centuries of the migrations, Pannonia had always emerged after the ebbing of a barbarian flood, and the boundary had always returned to the Danube; but with the coronation of Stephen, the ghost of imperial Rome had finally been exorcised. A European state had replaced a Roman province, and the Danube had been changed from a frontier to an internal artery. Approximately a century later the Byzantine emperor presented another crown to the Hungarian king. This was combined with the papal crown to form the still-existing Holy Crown of King St. Stephen, which thus symbolizes the ancient ties of the basin with both Rome and Constantinople.

Over the centuries the crown has become the symbol of the Magyar individuality as well as the Hungarian state. The Magyars were keenly aware of the fact that they differed from the nations around them, and they always felt the pressure, even if not consciously applied, of the surrounding nations. The crown was the foundation stone of their state, and symbolized the freedom of the Magyars from the demands of both of the empires which had claimed Pannonia. The crown has, therefore, been more than an ornament to set upon the head of a monarch. To the Hungarians it has been even more important than the monarch; it has symbolized the nation. The Crown of King Stephen has also become the symbol of the Christian character of the Magyar people, and under this sign the Magyars stood as the bulwark of Christian Europe against the nomads of the steppe and the Moslem Turks.

In the contest for power which occupied the first decade of the reign of Stephen, his strength was based (with some German help) on the settled, agricultural majority which was heavily concentrated in the Dunántúl. Here, west of the Danube, the terrain was gently rolling, and precious water was available. Here too the soil had been cultivated for centuries; the incoming Magyars inherited the lands that had been carefully worked by the Slavs and Germans, and centuries earlier by the Romans, Celts, and Illyrians. The Dunántúl was not only the productive core of the new kingdom, it was also the land bridge joining Hungary to the Western Empire; consequently the kingdom was organized and governed from the Dunántúl.

The Hungarian kingdom was subdivided basically into a series of provinces or comitats.[9] In Magyar a comitat was known as a *vármegye*, which meant literally all the territory which was to be under the jurisdiction of a *vár*, a central fortress-city. In time these comitats came to be known simply as *megyek*. In the initial organization by Stephen, the country was divided into 45 megyek. As the empty lands became populated the number of megyek increased to 72, but these had been consolidated into 63 by the nineteenth century. Nevertheless, the area of each comitat remained remarkably constant, at least until the cutting up of the kingdom in 1919. Though at first the megye was just a necessary administrative division, during the centuries of Turkish and Austrian occupation it was the local vitality of these comitats which sustained the identity of Hungary.

The border strips of territory, including especially the westernmost portions now comprising Burgenland, were kept unpopulated for over a century. This was the *gyepű*, a glacis or empty zone along the frontier; only small fighting forces were allowed to live within this glacis. Medieval armies, almost of necessity, lived off the country across which they moved; therefore a belt of land ten to thirty miles wide, empty of population and hence of production, was a significant barrier against the invading force. As long as threats from the west seemed serious this border area was kept a wasteland, but by the twelfth century Hungary felt secure against Austria and promoted the settlement of the *gyepű*. Four fortress towns faced the western frontier and became the centers for the administrative organization of the border area. North of the Danube, Pozsony (Bratislava, Pressburg) guarded the important meeting of the Little Carpathians and the Danube. South of the Danube were Moson (Wieselburg), in the wet land at the junction of the Leitha and the Danube; Sopron (Ödenburg) on the site of the ancient fortress city, Scarbantia; and Vasvár (Eisenburg) on the bluffs overlooking the broad Rába valley.

The absence of Szombathely (Savaria, Steinamanger) is interesting. For the Romans, Savaria had been an excellent communications center, but for the Hungarians it was merely a site near the frontier, of little military significance. Vasvár, on the other hand, was in a position to command all the entrances into Hungary from south of the crystalline Alpine massif, that is from Styria. Vasvár was beyond the confluence of all the major streams of eastern Styria and southern Burgenland, the Rába, Feistritz, Lafnitz, Strem, and Pinka, at the turn where the broad Rába valley curves from its former west-east course to one south-north. At this point, therefore, all the routes from Styria left the valley and climbed onto the terrace surface to continue eastward into the core of the kingdom. Here too the successor of the historic

Carnuntum-Savaria-Sirmium road crossed the Rába. Not until the construction of the railroads in the nineteenth century did Szombathely regain some of the importance of ancient Savaria.

In addition to the administrative units, the megyek, the kingdom was divided into ecclesiastical units or bishoprics. In 1001 the pope established the Archbishopric of Esztergom at the court of the new king; he thus both completed and guaranteed the independence of Hungary by placing her territory permanently beyond the reach of Salzburg and Sirmium. Five years later a second archbishopric was established at Kalocsa on the east bank of the Danube, with jurisdiction over the churches of the eastern and southeastern portions of the kingdom. In 1009, five bishoprics were established within the Archbishopric of Esztergom: at Vác, in the middle of the Danube gorge; at Győr, the junction of the Rába and Danube; at Veszprém, near the eastern end of Lake Balaton; at Pécs, in the southernmost corner of the Dunántúl; and at Eger. Only the last named was to the east of the Danube valley. Then in 1034 the Bishopric of Nitra was added to serve the areas north of the Danube. The location of these ecclesiastical sees shows the dominance of the northeastern quarter of the Dunántúl within the kingdom. The earliest important monasteries were located in the same general area. Pannonhalma, dedicated to St. Martin, was established on a hill spur southeast of Győr, and Zirc in the middle of the Bakony. Later in the eleventh century the Archbishopric of Kalocsa was subdivided into three bishoprics, and had added to it Zagreb in the newly acquired Croatia.

Székesfehérvár

Shortly after his coronation King Stephen moved his capital from Esztergom to a carefully chosen new site, which, as far as we can tell, was not occupied by any town or even village at the time. This city, one of the earliest examples of a created capital, has been associated with the memory of Stephen ever since its founding. Its name reveals its royal character: Székes-fehér-vár, and its precise German equivalent Stuhlweissenburg, mean literally, throne (chair)-white-city (fortress), the white city of the throne, or better yet, the royal white city. The Latin name, Alba Regia, also refers to the royal character of the city.

We cannot know exactly why Stephen chose this particular site, but we can deduce some of the reasons why it was a good location for his capital. The preferable location of the new capital was somewhere in the Dunántúl (Pannonia), in the productive heart of Hungary, west of the Danube. This was also a settled area, safe from the

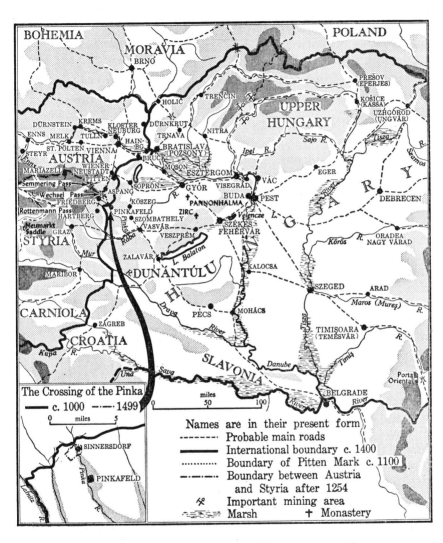

MAP 3. THE MIDDLE AGES (*ca.* 1000–1500)

threatened revolts of the tribal chieftains of the Alföld. Also, since the
new state was in close contact with the West, and since the first military threats to its borders came from the German-held areas, it was
advisable for the capital to be west of the Danube, within controlling
distance of the critical frontier. However, the capital could not be too
far west lest it lose contact with the tribes of the Alföld and of
Transylvania beyond. Therefore the ideal place for the capital was in
the eastern Dunántúl near the Bakony, since the Bakony hills separated
the westward-oriented Little Alföld from the tribal Great Alföld. The
first capital of the Árpáds had been where the Danube cuts through
the Börzsöny-Bakony range, but Esztergom faced west and was too far
removed from the Alföld. In later years, as the Alföld became highly
productive, the economic and political center of the kingdom moved
to the southwestern end of the Danube-Bakony gorge, to the Buda
crossing. For Stephen, however, Buda was already on the fringe of the
main productive area.

Along the southeastern flank of the Bakony a belt of water and
marsh extends from Zalavár almost to the Danube, a distance of one
hundred miles. Twenty-two of these miles separate Lake Balaton from
the much smaller Lake Velencze. The passageway between these two
lakes is almost a continuous belt of marshland, which was undrained
in the days of Stephen. For the soldier marshes have always been, next
to cliffs and icy ridges, the greatest of all barriers to movement, and,
before the days of artillery, fortresses on a hill surrounded by open
marsh were very effective strongholds. Székesfehérvár was established
on a bit of hilly ground in the middle of this marsh belt.

But Stephen did not choose this site merely because it could be
easily defended. He could very well have remained in the magnificent
natural fortress of Esztergom, on a hill overlooking the Danube. To be
effective, a capital must have rapid communications with all parts of
the country; Székesfehérvár was chosen evidently because it was an
important crossroads junction and therefore a location from which the
king and his emissaries could reach all parts of the realm quickly.

Just northwest of the city the Bakony breaks, and a broad low gap
separates the main mass of the hills to the west from the hill clumps
overlooking the Danube. This low gap was then and still is the easiest
route through the Bakony barrier between the Alps and Budapest.
More important yet than the ease of the passway was its alignment. As
can be seen on Map 3, an almost perfectly straight routeway runs from
Vienna through Székesfehérvár to the Danube. This line passes without detours the barriers of the Leitha Range, the Hanság marshes, and
the Bakony hills; it passes through the Bruck Gateway, the Győr
crossing, Székesfehérvár, and reaches the Danube at Paks, opposite
Kalocsa. This line undoubtedly explains much of the early organiza-

tion of Hungary. The road must have been much used to by-pass the broad curves of the Danube; the soldiers of the first Crusade are known to have followed this route. Its course may explain the selection of the otherwise inconspicuous site of Kalocsa for the second archbishopric of Hungary. Opposite Kalocsa the road from the royal city reached the Danube and hence there, on the east bank of the river, was established the see which governed most of the Alföld and Transylvania.

Crossing this vital road at Székesfehérvár was the ancient routeway along the southern edge of the Bakony. To the northeast this route ran to the Buda crossing, beyond which roads must have run along the southern edge of the Carpathians to Eger, and across the northern Alföld. To the southwest this route and its branches led into Styria, Croatia, and Italy.

King Stephen greatly enriched his city. With the treasure he had confiscated from two of the rebel chieftains he constructed a famous basilica to the Virgin Mary. In this city every king was crowned until 1527, and most of the kings of Hungary were buried here. Here too the kings held court with their nobles, and the Golden Bull of 1222 (the Hungarian Magna Carta) was proclaimed. One of the provisions of the Golden Bull was that the king was committed to the calling of an annual sitting of the nobility in Székesfehérvár. The final time of glory for the royal city came in the late fifteenth century, when the great king, Matthias Corvinus, rebuilt and enriched its palaces, churches, and monuments.

By the fourteenth century the city had begun to lose its predominance within Hungary. As the Alföld became the most productive portion of the kingdom, the major center of the nation moved to the city at the crossing of the Danube. Buda gradually increased in importance, though Székesfehérvár remained the traditional center of the arts. After the death of Matthias the city crumbled with the state. Emperor Maximilian occupied and looted the church in 1490, and in 1543 the Turks first entered its gates. The city suffered grievously during the Turkish wars; all its relics were looted and scattered and all its fine buildings burnt and demolished. Though Székesfehérvár has developed anew since 1688, only the foundations of the royal buildings and the memory of Stephen remain as reminders of its past glory.

The state idea [10] bequeathed to his nation by King Stephen was at that time unique in Europe, in that it dealt with a territorially completed state. In terms of area, the Kingdom of Hungary was fully grown when it was born. In other countries, such as England and France, the idea of the state originated within one vital area, within a kernel; centuries of germination and growth were required before that idea could be extended to the frontiers we now consider to be "natural" to those states. In Hungary no growth from a central, vital core was necessary. The kingdom had been established within an area eminently suitable to the creation of one state; in fact, if Hungary had not occupied the entire basin, she could scarcely have begun at all, since previous organization of the marginal portions had meant control from outside the basin. The great contribution of the Magyars to Europe was the organization of the Carpathian Basin, and this was possible as an entirety, or not at all. From the very first, therefore, the Carpathians and the eastern edges of the Alps bore the national frontiers. In the southwestern corner the boundary originally followed the broad, marshy Drava, but within a century the union of Hungary and Croatia had moved the borders into the mountains beyond the Sava.

Because the location of the boundaries was an inherent part of the state idea, the borders gained a surprising importance in the thinking of the Magyars. A Hungary without the centuries-old mountain frontier came to seem impossible. Hungary never had any other boundaries, even though temporary advances extended Hungarian dominion over parts of Austria, Galicia, Walachia, and Serbia. The Crown of King Stephen became not only the symbol of the nation and the kingdom, but also the symbol of the limits of that nation-kingdom. To the Hungarians these boundaries were sacred; to their neighbors they were clear and unmistakable. Until the nineteenth century they were not questioned, either within or without the state.

To the people living along the frontiers, the boundary was a sharp dividing line between nations with entirely different histories, and often between different ways of life. Even today, forty years after the dismemberment of the old kingdom, the sharpest contrasts in Central Europe occur along the remains of the frontiers of King Stephen. The contrasts between Croatia and Serbia, Transylvania and Walachia, Slovakia and Moravia, are still greater than the contrasts between many countries.

The portion of this frontier along the front fringes of the Alps separated Hungary from the medieval German empire and, later, from the independent Austria. Though often fought over, this portion has remained remarkably stable in the nine and one-half centuries since the coronation of Stephen. Changes have occurred south of the Danube in the broad gaps joining the Little Alföld and the Vienna Basin, but these changes have been relatively minor. Although in the dismemberment of Hungary the international frontier was moved eastward, the historic border is still extant; since 1921 it has served as the provincial boundary between Burgenland and the older provinces of Austria. Now, divorced from the tensions usually associated with boundaries, this linear heritage of the days of the birth of Europe can be studied freely. Such a study is of great historical and geographical value, since it leads to an understanding of the geo-political thinking of the early eleventh century and helps us to see how the men of that time looked upon the features of terrain with which they had to reckon.

The most striking historical fact about the Alpine portion of this boundary is that it bears no notable resemblance to any of the boundaries which preceded it. Since before the birth of Christ the principal Pannonian boundary had run along the Danube; now a line was delimited which ran at right angles to the great river. The new line did not even coincide with the ancient political divide along the Vienna ridge. In fact, both the Danube and the Weinerwald lost their importance, even for internal boundaries. None of the Austrian provinces utilized either the Danube or the Wienerwald as a limiting border, and several of the Hungarian megyek straddle the Danube. Instead, the new frontier ran along the broken spurs joining the Alps and the Carpathians. Now entirely new geo-political ideas resulted in completely new boundary delimitations.

For the first time the critical crossing point of the Danube was determined by the position of the arcing Carpathian chain. For the Hungarians the Carpathians were the national frontier belt, and the Wienerwald, though the most striking ridge south of the Danube, had no connection with the Carpathian chain. Thus the boundary crossed the Danube at the Carnuntum gap and followed along the Hainburg and Leitha spurs to the northeastern extension of the Bucklige Welt (the central crystalline massif of the Alps). This displacement from the Vienna gap to the Carnuntum gap was also, of course, a result of the steady Bavarian advance eastward. In 991 they had occupied the site of Vienna, so that by the time of the coronation of Stephen, the Germans controlled much of the Vienna Basin. The boundary was not established along the crests of the uplands; instead it used the more prominent rivers in the area, so that the border was placed not in the Little Carpathians and Leitha Range but along the March and Leitha rivers just to the west of the ridges. This illustrates one basic principle of early medieval boundary locations: the rule that, as much as possible, the borders were set along water courses, along rivers, streams, rivulets, or even ravines and gullies. The two principal reasons for this preference for streams were their ease of defense and their precision.

Obviously defense of the state is a major factor to be considered in the location of a boundary. This was especially true along the frontier between Austria and Hungary, since the land was devoid of settlement and production at the time. The ideal medieval boundary ran not only along a river, but preferably, along a river which flowed through a broad flood plain. In A.D. 1000, before settlement and drainage, the bottomlands were broad areas of marsh, and this belt of swamp and muck constituted a barrier of the greatest magnitude to movement of any kind. Such marshes were often barren of trees, so that the approach of a foe could be easily observed, and entrenchment was virtually impossible. Most serious of all was the virtual impossibility of moving armed knights, supply wagons, and, later, artillery across the marshy terrain. Before the days of the airplane and long-range artillery nothing (except of course an icy ridge) was a better defensive zone than a broad belt of marsh. Another considerable barrier to movement was a forest, even more serious than a hill, unless the slope was unusually high and continuous. Since in Hungary and eastern Austria a wooded ridge is usually referred to as a forest (*Wald, erdő*), rather than a ridge, it is evident that the forest was considered to be a stronger barrier than simply a difference in elevation. Within a forest, just as within a marsh, movement was limited to but a few roads. Hence the ideal boundary was one that followed a river which ran in a flat-bottomed, marshy valley, in front of a heavily forested ridge. This was the case with the Austro-Hungarian frontier along the March, Leitha, and Lafnitz rivers. In all these cases, the location of the frontier was clearly to the advantage of the Hungarians, who were for the most part stronger than the Austrians before 1526.

The second reason for the preference given to streams as boundaries was their comparative exactness. This seems strange to contemporary geographers, since rivers in flat country are infamous for their shifting channels and changing meanders. Since medieval times men have devised far more exact ways of determining position, but then these means were not available, and as the border area was unpopulated in any case, slight changes in the position of the river had no significance. No known property lines existed at the time; if the boundary makers wished to have some sort of precision, they were forced to rely upon clearly recognizable natural features. The only features of the terrain that are clearly recognizable, linear, and relatively narrow are streams. As a result, medieval boundaries in central Europe consistently favored streams, and minor creeks and gullies gained an importance out of all proportion to their size or separating power. If a river could not be used, then a series of portions of streams was utilized, but, wherever possible, the boundary was fixed upon the indisputable fact of a stream course. Thus in the portion of the boundary between the Leitha and the Lafnitz (where no one stream could be utilized), the border made use of over twenty different streams and rivulets. Even at the top of the Wechsel Pass, between Lower Austria and Styria, the boundary was not fixed at the crest but along a minor stream just to the south of the crest.

South of the Danube the Leitha carried the boundary for approximately forty miles between the Danube and the edge of the crystalline Bucklige Welt at Wiener Neustadt. For most of this distance the river flowed just to the west of the wooded Leitha Range, and along the edge of a broad marshy area known as the Ebenfurther Moor, which occupied much of the eastern half of the Vienna Basin. Since this portion of the boundary cut across the Bruck and Sopron gateways, which bore the principal roads connecting Austria and Hungary, the Leitha became the symbol of the entire boundary. In the days of the Dual Monarchy the two halves of the Habsburg Empire were often referred to as Cis-Leitha and Trans-Leitha.

If the Leitha continued northeastward to a confluence with the Danube, it would empty into the Danube almost opposite the mouth of the March; this would have been ideal for the delimitation of the boundary. Instead, however, the Leitha is deflected eastward by one of the gravel terraces and does not enter one of the arms of the Danube until forty miles further downstream, at the fortress cities of Moson and Magyaróvár. This swerve of the Leitha necessitated a fixing of the boundary across the terrace surface between the Danube and the curve of the Leitha. The most logical position for this line seemed to be where the two rivers were the closest to each other, between Rohrau and Petronell, where they are less than four miles apart (see Map 9). This would have placed the Hainburg Hills entirely within Hungary, and thus not only would have located the boundary in front of wooded hills (to the advantage of the Hungarians) but also would have given the Hungarians control of both sides of the historic Carnuntum gap.

This location may have been the first one chosen for the boundary. Hainburg, in the gap, was an early Magyar fortress, and King Stephen built a church at the present Deutsch Altenburg. Very shortly afterwards, however, this hill area came under Austrian control. The boundary was moved eastward about ten miles and Hainburg was through most of medieval times a major frontier fortress of the Austrians. Perhaps the Austrians (Bavarians) effected this advance because their center of power, in the Vienna gap, was closer to the disputed frontier than was the Magyar center of power, at Székesfehérvár; or perhaps it was because the Germans were far more effective in utilizing the Danube, which, for them, flowed toward the contested area. In any case, in this advance the Germans gained control of the site of ancient Carnuntum. It is interesting to note that with the absence of a river to the west of the hill clump, the Hainburg Hills early lost their border barrier function for the Hungarians. The Hungarians did not readily accept this alteration of the boundary, however, and Hainburg was one of the most beleaguered cities of the border area. At the present time it is one of the most fascinating of the old fortress cities of Central Europe.

For some fifty miles the boundary curved across the spurs of the crystalline massif between the Leitha and the Lafnitz. In many ways this is the most interesting and informative portion of the old boundary, since in this section it could not be placed on a main stream. To some geographers, this portion has seemed to lack a strong physical basis for its location; the most prominent of Austrian political geographers, Robert Sieger, considered this long, irregular arc to be a "solidified, unfinished" boundary.[11] Yet, this line remained virtually unaltered for almost a millennium; this fact suggests that something more than accidentals determined its location.

The primary physical differentiation of importance near this part of the border is the transition from the crystalline Bucklige Welt on the west, to the level extensions of the Carpathian Basin to the east. The Bucklige Welt is an area of gently rolling uplands cut by steep-sided narrow valleys; the tops are often cleared, while the valleys are forested. The extensions of the Carpathian Basin, on the contrary, have cleared lowlands or flat valley bottoms with narrower, forested uplands. This contrast is significant when one considers the characteristics of the two opposing forces at the time the boundary was demarcated. The Magyars, from the east, were horsemen and plainsmen; the Germans, from the west, were mountaineers, Alpinists in this part of Europe. The Germans advanced their settlements along the upland pastures, whereas the Magyars advanced theirs along the lowland plains.

The patterns of boundary delimitation between the two groups may be summarized under six points:

1. All the lowland areas east of the Alpine uplands were occupied by the Magyars.

2. The Magyars advanced up the stream valleys as far as the valley bottom allowed them, that is, as far as the point where the lowlands became cramped into a V-shaped valley. This is noticeable at the four principal stream crossings in this portion of the boundary. Along the Schwarzbach, for example, the Lower Austrian village of Schwarzenbach is pressed, in serpentine fashion, between the stream and the

steep slope, whereas the next village downstream, Oberpetersdorf, Burgenland, is already in a broad valley.

3. The Magyars pushed their domains onto the edge of the Bucklige Welt, to the crest of the upland surface overlooking the lowlands. The entire boundary, in this portion, runs in upland areas.

4. Where historic roads, by climbing onto the uplands, crossed from the lowlands into Austria, the Magyars moved their control beyond the first crest of the upland, to include portions of the Bucklige Welt within their kingdom. This occurred in three localities which are still notable for their medieval fortresses: Forchtenstein, Landsee, and Bernstein.

5. The line was drawn along minor streams wherever possible; this was especially apparent at critical points, that is, where the boundary crossed a major stream valley.

6. Between the utilized sections of stream courses, the position of the boundary was not determined until after the area had become fully settled. Precise surveying was not possible, and variations of a few hundred yards were not considered generally important. After the border area was settled, the precise location of the line appears to have been determined by the relative rates of growth of adjacent villages on opposite sides of the border.

The crossing of the Pinka, the principal river encountered in this part of the boundary, illustrates some of these points well. Just north of the village of Sinnersdorf the Pinka flows through a narrow, wooded valley; Sinnersdorf is located just at the point where the valley widens enough to allow room for a village and some cultivation (see the inset of Map 3). The old boundary crossed the valley in the middle of this gap. The line coming in from the east followed a brook to its junction with the Pinka. On the opposite bank of the river, however, was not another tributary but a headland. The line therefore jogged southward for a quarter of a mile along the Pinka to the mouth of the first available tributary on the west bank, and then followed that brook up out of the valley.

After having curved steadily westward along the flanks of the Bucklige Welt, the boundary resumed its southward trend along the course of the Lafnitz. The Lafnitz is not a large stream, but it flows in a broad, formerly marshy valley between two of the gravel terraces so common to the southeastern flank of the crystalline Alps. The eastern margin of the valley is surmounted by an unbroken, forested escarpment 300 to 500 feet high. This line of bluffs has always been a serious barrier to local movement, and no significant road has crossed it. Eastern Styria and southwestern Burgenland are cut by many valleys similar to the Lafnitz, and though other troughs may not have as sharp local relief, they often contain wider streams. The Lafnitz was selected for the boundary probably because of its position. It is the only valley in the vicinity that served well the north-south alignment of the frontier. The other, often larger, streams tend to run diagonally to the prevailing trend of the border. Thus the Pinka would have brought the boundary into the Carpathian Basin, and the Feistritz would have extended a Hungarian salient far westward along the flank of the crystalline massif. The Lafnitz gave the simplest alignment, left the mountains to Styria and yet offered the Hungarians an admirable defensive position.

Where the Lafnitz turns sharply eastward the boundary left the river and traversed the interfluvial uplands for approximately thirteen air miles before reaching the headwaters of the Kutschenitza, which then carried the boundary southward to the Mur River.[12] In the middle of this stretch the border crossed the Rába, the principal river of the Dunántúl. The site of this crossing does not coincide with any constriction of the valley floor. The broad valley of the Rába continues westward for a score of miles into the heart of Styria, so that a crossing at the point where the bottom land ceased would have extended the line, in a marked salient, to the vicinity of Graz. Like the Danube further north and the Mur and Sava further south, the boundary had to cut across a broad flood plain, and in doing so it jogged for a mile and a half along the Rába in order to make use of minor streams entering the river from the north and south.[13] The position of the crossing seems to have been determined by the paths of the Lafnitz and the Kutschenitza, much as the crossing at Carnuntum-Hainburg was initially determined by the paths of the March and the Leitha.

This border between Austria and Hungary remained essentially unchanged, even though the Austrian dukes often utilized the internal troubles of Hungary to gain temporary control over the border megyek, and the Hungarians on two occasions became the rulers of entire Austrian provinces. These actual fluctuations of the frontier did not change the position of the frontier in theory. The Habsburg acquisitions beyond the Leitha were treated as Habsburg holdings within Hungary, not as extensions of Austria. Even after 1526, when the Habsburg emperor became also the king of western Hungary, the separation of the two countries was maintained, and until 1850 a tariff was collected on all goods crossing this border.

However, late in the 15th century a few alterations were made in the boundary. Hungary was very weak just prior to the Turkish engulfment, and in the Treaty of Pressburg, in 1491, the Habsburg monarch gained control over much of the western frontier of Hungary. Though these acquisitions did not at first alter the boundary in theory, the continuing control of them by Austria eventually led to their inclusion into Austria. In the *Ausgleich* of 1867, the Hungarians somewhat reluctantly accepted these alterations.

The changes which were effected in the western boundary between 1491 and 1702 were based on the local boundaries in the area, principally the limits of the manorial estates, the *Herrschaften*. In the interval since A.D. 1000 the border area had been completely settled and in effect had been surveyed. Local boundaries were available for use, so that the new boundary makers did not have to rely upon streams for a precise demarcation. Four of these shifts in the frontier were made, and though none was significant, they formed rather odd-shaped breaks in the formerly smooth line. The northernmost change comprised the village of Edelstal, which the lords of Kittsee occupied by force in 1590. Two of the alterations occurred along the Leitha. The northern of these coincided with the limits of the Herrschaft of Mannersdorf-Scharfeneck between the Leitha River and the center of the Leitha Range. The southern consisted of the wasted Herrschaft of Liechtenwörth, which was awarded to the adjacent Wiener Neustadt in compensation for the great damage the city had suffered in the border warfare. Though each of these two deviations from the Leitha River line was the result of a separate historical action, both changes illustrate the shift of the effective border barrier from the marsh to the wooded upland. In the five centuries since the original boundary had been established, the broad Ebenfurther Moor had been drained and settled; what had once been an empty moat became instead a belt of dense population. In contrast, the uplands were still forested, and during the period 1491–1702 the boundary was drawn through this effective barrier position along the Leitha Range and the crest of the divide between the Leitha and Wulka rivers. It must be noted, however, that when the boundary was again finally stabilized, the Hungarians had maintained their hold on the Leitha River at every important crossing point.

Only one slight variation marked the border south of Wiener Neustadt. This occurred at Sinnersdorf, where the border crossed the Pinka valley. The Herrschaft of Bernstein had come under Habsburg control in 1491. In 1499 the emperor separated the village of Sinnersdorf (see inset, Map 3) from the Herrschaft and awarded it to the Styrian lord of Thalberg Herrschaft in return for his contribution of thirteen hundredweights of gunpowder at the siege of Güns (Köszeg).[14]

Sharp contrasts are still visible along almost the full length of this old boundary. Burgenland, east of the boundary, has a clearly Hungarian, non-Austrian appearance, while the older Austrian provinces seem a part of Alpine Europe. At times the contrast is astoundingly sharp. The village of Landsee, the highest village of Burgenland, is located on the upland surface of the Bucklige Welt, immediately adjacent to the boundary. One road runs through the village; to the west it leads across the upland surface to Wiesmath, Lower Austria, and to the east it plunges a thousand feet into the lowlands of middle Burgenland. The locale and the topography here might lead one to expect a bit of upland Austria within the old frontier, but instead Landsee is a typical Burgenland village, with house types more similar to those in a village of the Alföld than to the dwellings in Wiesmath.

The contrasts along the boundary are less marked in the Lafnitz valley, where because of the unbroken escarpment east of the river the villages below turned toward Styria, and in those areas along the Leitha and near Hainburg which were at times in both countries. Yet, even when the differences are not visually obvious, differences in attitude remain. Potzneusiedl (Burgenland) and Deutsch Haslau (Lower Austria) are across the narrow Leitha from each other and have a combined population of less than one thousand; yet, the villagers have little to do with each other, insist on having their own churches, and support different political parties. The idea of "The Thousand Years' Boundary" affects the outlook of the people more than does mere proximity.

Along this line Hungary faced Western Europe for nine centuries. Across this line passed most of the trade of the kingdom, and though the movement of goods, merchants, Crusaders, and armies was brisk, the line remained a divide separating two distinct entities: the German empire to the west, and the true marchland of Europe to the east. The line separated the ideals and atmosphere of the plain from those of the mountains, and this marked difference was manifested in all the many facets of the ways of life of the border dwellers. Despite the inevitable influences felt across the border, the village types, architecture, music, costumes, and folklore reflected two different worlds, one of the mountains and the other of the plains.

6

THE BIRTH OF AUSTRIA

After the victory on the Lechfeld in 955, the forces of the Holy Roman Empire advanced steadily towards the east. With the defeat of the Magyars, the Bavarians, the archbishop of Salzburg, and the bishops of Freising, Passau, and Regensburg all wished to regain the holdings that they had lost in the Magyar onrush. They felt that they were following in the footsteps of Charlemagne, who had extended the western empire to the ancient limits of Pannonia. However, the Empire was still weak and was beset by internal difficulties; the rate of advance was slow, even if fairly constant. The Magyars could hardly have been present in any appreciable numbers west of the Tullner Feld, and yet it was a score of years before the Bavarians had moved from the Enns past the Wachau gorge.

In 972 the Bavarian forces captured St. Pölten, and in 976 they successfully stormed Melk, the Magyar stronghold at the western end of the Wachau. By 987 the Tullner Feld had been occupied as far as the western slopes of the Wienerwald. The major barrier of the Wienerwald was quickly crossed by the Germans, perhaps because the Magyars were not as adept as were their foes at making use of slopes and forests for military purposes, or of the Danube for transport and communications.[1] In 991 Vienna was taken, and with it fell much of the Vienna Basin as well. However, with the accession of King Stephen to the Hungarian throne the German progress ceased. An attempt to advance further was checked by the Hungarians, and in 1031 the boundary reverted from the Leitha to the Fischa. Then, following the death of Stephen, when Hungary was weakened by severe tribal rebellions, the Bavarians succeeded in shifting the border back to the Leitha, where it remained.

This slow, steady drive to the east added new territories to Bavaria, and a series of marchlands was established along the eastern flank of the Alps. Though initially there were many small marks, within two centuries they had been fused into four: the Ostmark along the Danube, Steiermark (Styria) along the upper Mur, Carinthia along the upper Drava, and Carniola along the upper Sava. By far the most important of these was the Ostmark, which became the core of the future Österreich (Austria) and eventually absorbed the other three marks. The Ostmark and Styria first appear in records about 970, but their establishment is generally taken to have been in 976, when the Ostmark was placed under the control of the Babenbergers, the first of the two Austrian dynasties. Extant documents first mention the "Ostarrichi" in 996.

Just as the Ostmark had been initiated from the fortress city of Enns, so Styria began from the fortress of Steyr, only ten miles south of Enns, on the Enns River. From Steyr it was possible to move through the central, crystalline Alps by way of the Pyhrn and Rottenmann passes (which had carried an important Roman road) into the valley of the upper Mur. The center of the new march came to be in the Mur valley, and in time Styria lost the area north of the Pyhrn Pass, including the city which had given it its name, Steyr. Perhaps because it lay generally south of the central Alps, Styria was at first united to Carinthia.

The present boundary between Lower Austria and Styria along the Semmering-Wechsel crest was not established until the middle of the thirteenth century. In 1043 the southern reaches of the Vienna Basin, from the Alpine crest to just north of Wiener Neustadt, were organized as a new marchland, the Pitten Mark. This occurred at a time when the Hungarians were beset by internal struggles, and the Pitten March was intended by the Germans to become the base for a penetration south of Lake Neusiedl into the Little Alföld. This abortive marchland coincided roughly with the Bucklige Welt; it was centered on the fortress of Pitten at the entrance to the deep, scenic Pitten valley, which bears the road leading from the Vienna Basin to the Wechsel Pass.

Although located entirely north of the main crest of the Alps, the Pitten March was initially united with Styria rather than with the Ostmark. Styria was separated from Carinthia in 1122, and in 1158 Styria annexed the Pitten March. Whatever the historical factors leading to this event may have been, the union does indicate that the eastern Alps were not considered to be a serious hindrance to the internal organization of a province. Evidently the Germans were adept at crossing mountain barriers and utilizing upland terrain. By noting the settlement patterns of the time we can perhaps understand the topographic basis of this union. Most of the Pitten March consisted of the Bucklige Welt, which is far more similar to Styria than to Lower Austria. Furthermore, because much of the southern Vienna Basin is an infertile gravel plain (the Steinfeld), the major break in settlement occurred not at the Wechsel crest but in the lowland around present-day Wiener Neustadt.

In 1154 the Ostmark was separated from Bavaria and became a duchy, and around 1192 the Ostmark and Styria were united into one marchland, called Österreich (Austria), with the boundary between the two halves of the new mark remaining as before. In 1194 the Babenberger duke of Austria completed a new fortress city at the western end of the Sopron Gateway, just north of the entrances to the Wechsel and Semmering passes. This city, called Neustadt or Nova Civitas, rapidly became a major trading center because of its control of routeways. It was not yet called Wiener Neustadt (Viennese new city) because it was still within Styria. The boundary between Styria and Lower Austria was not moved from the Steinfeld to its present location until 1254, when the Hungarians and Bohemians divided Austria between themselves and placed their border on the Semmering-Wechsel divide.

Though the limits of the Ostmark were moved steadily towards the east in the tenth century, its capital remained well back of the frontier. The first Babenberger had stormed Melk in 976, and there the capital remained for over a century, in a fine defensive position at the western end of the Wachau gorge of the Danube. At this point the ancient short cut through St. Pölten left the Danube, and from the vicinity of Melk the ruler could also reach Styria by way of an old, tortuous road through Mariazell. Nevertheless, Melk was far from the critical eastern frontier; probably fear of the Magyars was the main reason for the prolonged utilization of Melk as the capital.

As the Ostmark became stronger and the fear of Magyar invasions decreased, the capital was moved forward. Around 1100 Duke St. Leopold moved the capital to Tulln, just west of the Vienna range and hence still protected, and in 1118 to the Leopoldsberg overlooking Vienna. This hill forms the last summit of the Wienerwald south of the Danube and has been referred to as "the Acropolis of Vienna." The Leopoldsberg rises sharply almost nine hundred feet above the river and forms a natural fortress facing the east.[2]

The Leopoldsberg afforded an admirable defensive position but was awkward as a capital. States do not usually place their centers of national organization on the top of a mountain. The actual working capital of the Ostmark seems to have been located just behind the Leopoldsberg at Klosterneuburg, on the Danube in a hollow between two spurs of the Wienerwald. Although the capital was being gradually moved forward, defense was evidently still an overruling consideration. However, although Klosterneuburg was safe behind the Leopoldsberg, it was not an adequate center of communications. Sometime before the middle of the twelfth century the capital was moved to Vienna,[3] and when the separate Duchy of Austria was proclaimed in 1156 Vienna was clearly the capital.

VIENNA

Although Celtic villages were scattered throughout the triangular lowland now occupied by the metropolis of Vienna, the first settlement on the site of the present center of the city was begun by the Romans. The Celtic village from which the name Vindobona was adopted appears to have been outside the present Ringstrasse, south of the city core. We can assume that the Romans chose the particular site carefully, though we can only surmise what the reasons for the selection were. Since the present core of Vienna coincides with the position of the Roman camp, it is evident that they chose well.

As was mentioned previously, the Romans were interested in the Vienna gap because at that particular place was the only easy crossing of the Danube between Carnuntum to the east and Krems, forty miles to the west. The many islands and broad marshes along the river precluded any effective military or commercial crossing between the eastern and western limits of the Vienna Basin.[4] Vindobona was therefore at a critical place along the limes, a position protecting the imperial lands from invasions from the north.

The logical location for the military camp should thus have been at the crossing point. This was just outside the gorge, at the place where the Danube began to widen, roughly at Nussdorf. There the stream was still unobstructed by islands, but the current was less swift than in the gorge, and from the earliest known days of antiquity a ferry had crossed the Danube at this point. According to legend, in times of low water the Danube could be forded at Nussdorf. However, the Roman camp was not established at this crossing point; rather it was placed four miles further downstream, where the river had already braided widely. Four miles is not a great distance, and could be covered rapidly by a defending force; nevertheless it is clear

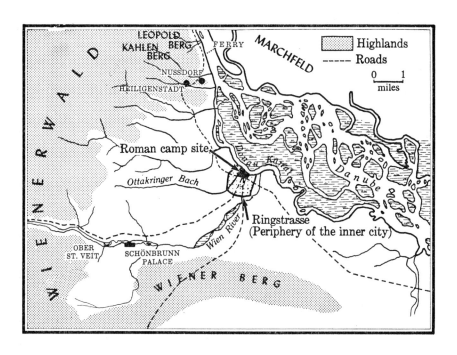

MAP 4. ORIGINAL SITE OF VIENNA

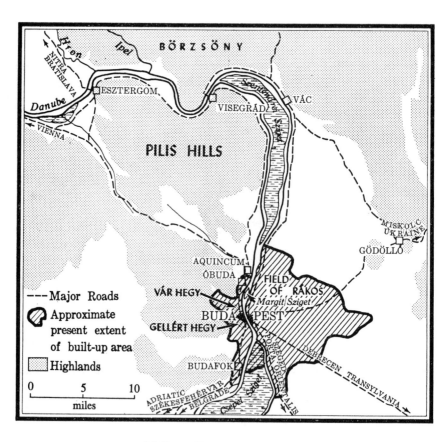

MAP 5. SITE OF BUDAPEST

that factors other than the site of the crossing must have determined the location of the camp.

Two reasons, space and defense, are generally given for the move away from the ferry; the land adjacent to the crossing was too hemmed in by the hills to allow sufficient room for expansion of the camp or for raising food. The food requirements of the border garrison had to be met either by local peasants or, later, by the troops themselves. The position chosen for the camp not only was in the midst of flat land, but was also suitable for defense, for it was on a low bluff overlooking the broad Danubian marshes. The Donaukanal (Danube arm), with its gentle current, was ideal for the mooring of small craft, and the marshy islands beyond made an excellent defense girdle. The camp was set down between two tiny ravines (now bearing the Rotenturm Strasse and the Tiefer Graben) which helped protect its flanks. Yet, these factors clearly do not explain fully the choice of the location four miles from the ferry. The combination of flat land and the possibilities of defense could be found much closer to Nussdorf, for example at the base of the hills. The decisive factor must have been not the need for flat land but the position of the major roads which served as the life lines of communication for the limes.

Vienna occupies a triangular lowland of about twelve miles on each side, forming the northwestern corner of the Vienna Basin (see Map 4). This small lowland is flanked on the northeast by the arms of the Danube, on the west by the Wienerwald range of the Alps, and on the south by a low ridge called the Wiener Berg. It is the latter which separates this subbasin from the remainder of the Vienna Basin. The Wiener Berg slopes from the front of the Wienerwald down towards the Danube; in its western half the ridge is moderately high, but further east it is easy to surmount, though a climb is necessary on both flanks. At the Danube it disappears entirely, and there, along the river bank, is the easiest access to Vienna from the east.

The triangular lowland is made up of a number of the gravel terraces which are so characteristic of the eastern flank of the Alps. These terraces have had considerable influence on the patterns of development of the metropolis and have been studied in great detail by European geographers. The most significant effect of these terraces, however, has been to raise the south bank of the Danube well above flood level. In contrast to the northern bank, which has always been subject to devastating inundations, the southern bank of the river rests secure some forty feet above the mean level of the river.

Only one river flows into the triangular lowland, and this river probably had great bearing on the precise location of the Roman camp. This Wien River rises well to the west of the center of the

Wienerwald range and flows eastward into the lowland; its valley forms the only notable break in the steep front of the range. After paralleling the Wiener Berg, the Wien River turns northeastward and joins the Danube arm toward the center of the small lowland. Before it was placed underground in the nineteenth century, the Wien River spread out over the level terrace surface near the Danube, forming a small belt of marsh. Since the easiest entry into the present urban area was from the east, this bit of marsh was of defensive importance and was utilized as part of the glacis in front of the medieval walls of the city. The central part of Vienna developed just to the northwest of the confluence of the Wien River and the Danube arm, northwest of this belt of wet ground.

The primary significance of the Wien River was not in terms of defense, however; of far more importance was the valley it had cut through the sharp face of the Wienerwald. A road could follow the river course westward out of the urban lowland and, beyond the headwaters of the Wien River, could descend the western slopes of the Wienerwald along another valley with relative ease. Hence this valley provided an east-west routeway through the otherwise un-broken Wienerwald, and through most of known history the road through the Wiental has been more important than the road through the Danube gap.[5] The road along the valley of the Wien River was less subject to natural disaster than was the road through the Danube gap. The Wien valley is not a gorge; its slopes are therefore less dramatic and hence less dangerous than are those of the Danube gap. Even more important were the fear of floods and the problem of wet ground encountered along the gorge road. Within the Danube gorge, in times of flood the water could rise suddenly and overflow the road hugging the southern bank. To the west of the gorge, the river road had to traverse the Tullner Feld, whose flat surface was often marshy in the spring, while, in contrast, the road along the Wien valley was relatively dry.

Perhaps of greatest significance was the fact that the road through the Wiental was far more direct than the road along the Danube. The Danube does not flow directly west to east but bends in numerous wide curves, and traffic has, in consequence, generally utilized straight short cuts across the curving stretches. Only rarely do important rail-roads and highways follow the river bank or utilize the water gaps carved by the Danube.[6] Within Lower Austria the Danube moves northward in the Wachau and then southward in the Wienerwald. Melk and Vienna are almost due west-east of each other, but the Danube flows in a curve to the north of them. The shortest route between Melk (and Linz, etc., beyond) and Vienna is a line some ten miles south of the river. This direct route follows the Wien River valley into the triangular lowland; it follows the northern bank of the stream and reaches the Danube and the river road, including the road to the key ferry, just to the west of the confluence of the Wien River and the Danube.[7]

Another road that has always been significant is one which runs along the western edge of the Vienna Basin. In Roman times this was a branch road that left the Amber Road at Scarbantia; in later times it was the road to the Wechsel and Semmering passes. Since the Roman conquest this road has passed through a belt of flourishing vineyards and has carried the trade of the western half of the Vienna Basin to Vindobona-Vienna. Coming from the south, this road crossed the Wiener Berg in its lower, eastern half and joined the other highways at the confluence of the Wien River and the Danube.

The Roman camp was established, therefore, near the ferrying site, at the junction point of the main roads, at the point where the arterial highway westward probably left the banks of the Danube. Here, whether southbound or westbound, traffic left the river; here, therefore, was the logical location for a Danubian port. Vindobona was more than the guardian of a minor crossing; it was the communications node linking the Vienna Basin, and hence Pannonia, with Noricum and the Rhine frontier.

As the barbarian tribes surged across the Roman limes, the network of land communications deteriorated seriously. In the intervals between the invasions, the forces of the Empire were re-established along the river boundary, but the roads that had been allowed to decay were not often repaired. With the collapse of effective Roman rule early in the fourth century, the highways were no longer adequately maintained, and travel along the unguarded routes was dangerous. Imperial control came to depend on the Danube fleet, so that only the road along the river bank remained generally under the control of Constantinople. The road through the Wien River valley appears to have lost much of its importance during the following centuries; what little traffic there was moved on or alongside the Danube.

This shift of traffic from the Wien valley to the Danube may have caused a change in the importance of local sites as well. Though a remnant Vindobona perhaps remained, clustered around its Christian church, the village had been shorn of much of its importance as a communications node. Since traffic east-west moved principally through the Danube gap, the more significant site was now at the crossing of the Danube. Heiligenstadt, adjacent to the Nussdorf ferrying point, seems to have become a local administrative center in the late fifth century. Here St. Severin may have established his monastery.[8]

Heiligenstadt (Favianus?) was in the favorable position of being located not only at the Danube crossing, but also in the belt of highest productivity, and amidst the greatest remaining concentration of Romanized, and hence Christianized, population. Following the conquest of Pannonia and Noricum by the Romans, the east-facing slopes of the Wienerwald became important for the production of wine, and so they have remained until the present day. (Emperor Domitian prohibited wine production in Pannonia in favor of the vintners of Istria, but it is doubtful that this prohibition was effective for long.) The incoming barbarians may well have expropriated the fruits of the vineyards, but it is doubtful that they laid waste the slopes as much as they ravaged the flat basin floor. The rudimentary agriculture of the Germanic tribes and the Asiatic nomads could not for some time meet the standards of the intricate care required by viniculture. Consequently, the vineyards probably remained intact, and the vine-clad slopes possibly continued to harbor a Christianized population amidst the largely pagan tribes. St. Severin felt that his primary task was to maintain the spark of the faith among the Christians of the area, and he may have placed his monastery among them. For a time then, Heiligenstadt perhaps replaced Vindobona as the communications, administrative, and ecclesiastical center of the western Vienna Basin.

Little is known concerning the Vienna Basin during the Carolingian century. The Danube remained the artery of communications, but it is not clear whether or not any one village was more important than the others. Klosterneuburg was established as a "new fortress" (*Neuburg*) at this time, and the Salzburg annals refer to a battle against the Magyars "ad Weniam" (Vienna?) in 881. Whether Vienna existed at this time, and, if it did, whether it survived the Magyar storm, is not important however, since it could have been no more than a hamlet when the Germans recaptured the site in 991.[9] For all practical purposes, the Vienna Basin was devoid of urban development in A.D. 1000, and it was the inhabitants of the new Ostmark who were to develop new cities in the area.

In their progress eastward during the second half of the tenth century the Austrians (Bavarians) advanced principally along the Danube River, and the moving of the capital from one river town to another illustrates the importance of the river at this time. The path along the Wien River valley existed but was relatively unimportant, except for military purposes, as long as the border area was considered to be unsafe. Even though the site of Vienna was regained by the

German forces in 991, the mention of the city as a settlement does not appear in extant records before 1030, and not as a place of importance before the middle of the twelfth century.

It was Duke St. Leopold who brought stability to the Vienna Basin and moved the capital to the crest of the Wienerwald. The population of the area must have increased markedly at this time; with peace, travel along the old roads was resumed. The factors which had influenced the Romans seem to have influenced the German settlers and merchants a millennium later. The basic road network was extended in the same directions, and along the same paths as the Romans had used: along the Danube, westward along the Wien River valley, and southward along the front edge of the Vienna range. As in the days of Tiberius these roads met not at the ferrying point but just to the west of the confluence of the Wien River and the Danube arm. Furthermore, just as the Romans had, so the Austrians found here also a safe, protected harbor for fishermen and for the small Danube boats. The Austrian city grew on precisely the same site as had the Roman camp, and this was not because of the survival of a village on the site of Vindobona, but because men in different centuries had laid their highways along the same topographic lines of least resistance.

Once again therefore, the direct road to the west was probably decisive in the location of the urban center. This fact has been manifested in various ways in the life and growth of the city. Although the second (?) Austrian duke in Vienna, Heinrich Jasimirgott, had his castle built on the northwestern side of the settlement (toward the Danube gap), by the mid-thirteenth century this fortress (Der Burg) had been moved around the periphery to a position facing the vital road from the west, in later centuries known as "die alte Reichsstrasse," and there the Burg has remained. The direction of the most rapid and widespread growth from the center of the city has been westward, along the Wien River road, and the principal shopping street of the Viennese has been that road, the Mariahilfer Strasse. In the seventeenth and eighteenth centuries the Habsburgs constructed their summer palace, the Schönbrunn, just off this trade artery, and the archbishop of Vienna built his summer home in the hills of Ober St. Veit, where the Wien River issues from the front face of the range. At the present day the dominance of this route is obvious; both the principal highway and the major railroad to the west utilize the valley of the Wien, whereas the south bank of the Danube, west of Vienna, is not followed by any important road.

Though in terms of location Vienna is an exact successor to Roman Vindobona, in terms of magnitude it is vastly different from its forerunner. In Roman times Vindobona was insignificant compared to

Carnuntum thirty miles to the east. In contrast to the tremendous growth of Vienna, the site of Carnuntum has not known a successor city (except the minor Hainburg which has fewer than 10,000 inhabitants), and is now of interest primarily as an archeological site. The major trade and administrative center of the Alpine-steppe contact zone was shifted from the eastern to the western river gap of the Vienna Basin, from Carnuntum to Vienna.

There were two principal reasons for this radical shift. The most important one was undoubtedly the location of the new boundary between Hungary and Austria. While both Carnuntum and Vindobona had been on the Roman limes, only Carnuntum was on the new border. The latter was now in the most embattled portion of the frontier zone, and armies often swept over its site. Just across the Danube were the Hungarian fortress cities of Devín and Pozsony (Bratislava); only five miles to the south, across the Leitha, was Hungary again. Carnuntum was in an Austrian salient, subject to constant military threat and to the curtailment of any possible trade by the encircling border. The Amber Road, which had been the commercial artery of Carnuntum, was cut twice within ten miles by the boundary, and the Hungarian fortress cities controlled both crossings of the Danube. The ancient highway atrophied. Alone of all the major highways of northern Pannonia, this, the most important of all, has not been reconstructed in later centuries. Carnuntum had grown with this highway and its branches, and just as the Amber Road never revived, neither did the Roman city it had served.

The second reason for the shift to Vienna was the change in the direction of traffic. Carnuntum, though an important river port, had owed much of its greatness to its control of north-south military and trade movement. However, with the creation of Austria and Hungary the primary direction of traffic turned from north-south to east-west, and the Danube became the artery of trade. Whether by the river, or by the roads paralleling its general course, all communications between the Ostmark and the remainder of the Holy Roman Empire met at Vienna, which thus gained complete control over east-west traffic. Carnuntum could not exercise a similar control, since the gaps at Sopron and Bruck afforded other entrances into Hungary. Then, because of its command of the vital east-west movement, Vienna came to control the north-south traffic as well, but only after new routeways to replace the old Amber Road had been developed.

Of prime importance was the development of a new route to the Adriatic. The Amber Road had been destroyed by the new boundary, and so the connection to the Mediterranean could no longer follow the easy path around the front spurs of the Alps. As could be expected, the first routeway which was developed utilized the first pass west of the new boundary, that is, the closest possible path to the ancient road. The new road ran southward along the western fringes of the Vienna Basin (to pass through the wealthy vineyard belt and to avoid both marsh and Magyar), through present Wiener Neustadt, and up the Pitten valley to the Wechsel Pass. Beyond the 3,230 foot Wechsel Pass the road followed the southeastern base of the crystalline range to the Mur valley at Graz. Along this road were such early fortress towns as Pitten, Aspang, Friedberg, and Hartberg. From Graz the road followed the broad Mur lowland southward to the Carniolan (Slovenian) portion of the Amber Road, which it followed through the Julian passes into northeastern Italy.

This Wechsel road had several disadvantages. It was a very indirect route; it moved southwest by the tedious method of first going south, then west, then south, and then west again. It was also a very tiring route, for between the Wechsel and the Mur the road crossed the many streams issuing from the Alpine flank. The road was forever climbing out of one valley only to descend into the next one. But, probably the most serious disadvantage was its proximity to the Hungarian border. Between Friedberg and Hartberg the road came virtually within arrow shot of the boundary along the Lafnitz. In the eleventh century Hungarian raiding parties were often active at the Wechsel summit; robber bands could attack merchant groups and then escape to the safety of Hungarian territory.

To avoid the constant Magyar threat, another higher path was often used. This route crossed the crest halfway between the Wechsel and the Semmering, at an elevation of approximately 4,500 feet. The road climbed to the utmost headwaters of the Pitten River and descended the headwaters of the Feistritz in Styria. This road was popular for a time and came to be known as the "Weinweg" (wine road), but it was even more arduous than the Wechsel, and also ran to Graz, so that the distance to Italy was not shortened.

The Semmering Pass does not seem to have been used much, if at all, by primitive man. The Romans made no use of it; they used the Amber Road to the east, as well as the Wechsel slightly, and the Pyhrn-Rottenmann passes to the west. The climb to the summit of the Semmering is especially steep on the north side, so that the 3,231 foot pass may for long have been unknown to dwellers of the Vienna Basin. The summit area was heavily forested and reportedly subject to sudden and severe storms. Early travelers feared the pass, for the dark summit was a favorite haunt for robbers.

The first moves toward the development of the Semmering Pass seem to have resulted from the union of the Pitten Mark and Styria in 1158, since Styria wished to establish more adequate connections with its transmontane addition. On the Styrian side the ascent to the Semmering crest is remarkably gradual and easy, so that it is clear why the pass was opened from the south rather than from the north. In 1160 a hospice was opened near the summit, and this event is generally taken to represent the beginnings of the use of the pass, although traffic over it did not become heavy until after the turn of the following century. Mürzzuschlag, at the Styrian foot of the pass, first appeared in records in 1236. By the middle of the thirteenth century the Semmering route dominated north-south traffic. As soon as the threat of thieves had been removed, the Semmering became *the* through route between the Danube and the Adriatic. The westward position of the pass placed it beyond the threat of Hungarian bands, but its greatest advantage was its directness. For seventy miles across Styria the new route followed the straight line of the Mur and Mürz valleys; in fact the path came as close to a straight line as seems possible for a road passing through mountainous terrain. Despite the steep climb up the north face of the Semmering, it was also a far less tedious route than the Wechsel. By following the main courses of the Mur and Mürz the traveler could avoid the tiring ascents and descents into small but steep valleys which were so characteristic of the Wechsel road. On the present highway there is, except at the Neumarkt Saddle, no grade of any consequence all the way from the Semmering crest to Venice.[10]

To complete their trading connections, the merchants of Vienna also sought a road to the north. The Amber Road had followed the flanks of the Little Carpathians, but since this range was now completely within Hungary, the old routeway was not open to the Austrians. Yet, the problem here was not as difficult as it was in the south, for the Marchfeld and most of Moravia are relatively flat. A new routeway northward was quickly developed. The new road to the north was built at some distance from the March River, because the area along the river bank not only was subject to flood (and often marshy) but, more important, was immediately adjacent to Hungarian territory. To avoid the twin threats of marsh and Magyar the road ran almost due north from Vienna to Brno, the administrative and commercial center of Moravia.[11] From Brno roads fanned out in various directions: northwestward toward Prague, northward to Breslau, and northeastward to Cracow.

As a result of the development of these new routes south and north of Vienna, the shortest road between the Baltic and the Mediterranean no longer followed the front edges of the Alps and Carpathians; the Brno-Vienna-Semmering road had replaced the Amber Road. Just as the Wienerwald range gave Vienna control over all trade with the west, so the Semmering gave the city control over all trade between Bohemia-Moravia and northern Italy. Vienna virtually monopolized the connections between East Central Europe [12] and the Mediterranean.[13]

Vienna became great because of the imposition of the works of man upon the details of the existing terrain. It was men who created the new routeways through the city, though the pre-existing topography laid the basis of the various possible routeways.

The supremacy of Vienna within East Central Europe was due as much to the power of the Austrian rulers as to its crossroads position. Had a strong military power not been based at the Vienna gap, the city might well have been torn away from the Western Empire. By maintaining the boundary along the Leitha and the March, the Babenbergers, and later the Habsburgs, made possible the tremendous growth of Vienna. Just as it was the new boundary that prevented the rebirth of Carnuntum, so a boundary along the Wienerwald could have destroyed Vienna. Had the Hungarians, in fact, been able to locate the boundary along the crest of the Vienna range instead of along the Leitha River, then the March valley would probably have remained the principal routeway to the north, and the Amber Road the main road to the southwest. In such a situation a new Carnuntum would perhaps have become the trading center and Vienna would have been merely a border outpost.

The very closeness of the boundary to the city assisted Vienna. Vienna became not only the crossroads site but also the customs post par excellence. Moravian and Hungarian merchants were forced to bring their products to this point and there place them into the hands of the Viennese merchants. In return the foreign tradesmen made their purchases there and took them across the border. Had the city been far from the boundary, both north and east, this direct trade with the merchants from the neighboring states would have been impossible.

The Austrian dukes came to Vienna because of its obvious advantages for communications. From this point the arm of the dukes could reach into all their domains; from this point the eyes of the dukes could watch all the passes leading into Austria from Hungary. Eventually, by their mere presence the dukes enhanced the importance of the city. Where the dukes were, there also were the political officials, the financiers, the churchmen, and many of the nobles. Wealth was concentrated in the capital, and this wealth created new markets for trade and new possibilities of controlling trade. The rulers favored their capital city; partly through favor, and partly through the desire for direct financial control of traffic, the dukes were instrumental in forcing foreign merchants to leave their wares in the hands of the Viennese middlemen. Foreign merchants could not move their products through Vienna; their goods entered by one gate and left by another, and between the two gates lay the beginnings of Viennese crafts and industry, the wealth of the merchants, and the power of the dukes.

Though trade east-west commenced as soon the the border area had become stabilized, the rapid growth of Vienna began with the Crusades. Portions of the first three Crusades used the Danube routeway towards Constantinople; in 1096 the Christian forces under Gottfried of Bouillon passed through Vienna, in 1147 both Conrad and Louis VII of France followed, and in 1189 Frederick Barbarossa moved along the Danube through Austria and Hungary. For all three of these Crusades Vienna was an important organizational center. The city was the last station within the Holy Roman Empire, and was therefore the last assembling and outfitting point for the Christian forces before they reached Constantinople. Just as the Danube had joined Pannonia and Constantinople, so now the great river served as the overland connection between Asia Minor and the German empire. The Crusaders had in effect reopened the ancient highway to the Straits, and traffic began to move along the river course. When King Richard the Lionhearted returned from the Third Crusade, although he had gone east by ship, he returned by the Danube road through Vienna.

The first mention of Vienna as a "civitas" appeared in 1137, and a hundred years later it had gained the full rights of a free city. It has been estimated that by the beginning of the thirteenth century, Vienna was second only to Cologne in population and wealth among German cities. By the middle of that century the city had reached the limits of the present inner city, and the walls that were to last for seven centuries were constructed by the Bohemian king, Ottokar II. The thirteenth century was a troubled time for both Hungary and Austria, but during the next century peace and great prosperity reigned along the Danube. The Anjou kings of Hungary (1308–87) brought stability to their kingdom; much of the Alföld became productive, and a heavy traffic of agricultural produce moved westward through Vienna.

Vienna stood as the intermediary between several areas of contrasting production. To the west were the German valleys and small basins, specializing in the fine handwork of craftsmen; to the southwest were the Alps, which yielded minerals, timber, and dairy products; and to the east was the Alföld, the home of horses and meat animals. At some distance, though in direct contact with the city, were the textiles of Flanders, the specialties and riches of the Mediterranean lands, as well as the furs and fish of the north. Vienna became the trading mart for the exchange of products among these differing productive regions.[14]

Because of its control of communications Vienna also possessed great potentialities for the organization of the Danube lands. The earliest expansion from Vienna was toward the south, as Austria incorporated the other border marchlands that had been established along the eastern edge of the Alps. In 1335 both Carinthia and Carniola were added to the lands of the Habsburgs; thus Austrian territory was extended to the vicinity of Trieste. Expansion to the north and east had to wait, however, until the powers there had been weakened. Following the shattering of the Kingdom of Hungary in 1526, the ruler of Vienna was for four centuries able to make full use of the city's advantaged position to unite the Danubian lands.

~~~~~~
~~~~~~
~~~~~~

7

~~~~~~
~~~~~~

THE FIVE
CENTURIES OF GREATNESS

Although modern man commonly associates times of European greatness with either ancient history (the Mediterranean) or with post-Renaissance history (northwestern Europe), it was the half millennium between 1000 and 1500 that saw the "golden age" of East Central Europe. In contrast, the eighteenth century of Vienna was but an interval of glory during centuries of disorder, and for only one city in an area of confusion. Hungary, Bohemia, Poland, Austria all were strong, prosperous states during four of these five centuries. Kings of Hungary and Bohemia could seek the crown of the Holy Roman Empire, and towards the end of this era, the rulers of Austria became the emperors and the most powerful rulers of Europe. The last Crusades, to Nikopol and Belgrade, were led by Hungarians. In the folklore of most of the states of East Central Europe, the memory of national grandeur focuses on these centuries, just as the memory of catastrophe dates from the troubled times toward their end.

It was a fortuitous blending of historical developments and geographic facts that favored the early rise to power of the states of East Central Europe. The topography of western Europe is characterized by many small basins and valleys, each of which has tended to develop its own distinctive traits. As soon as the overruling power of the Roman Empire had decayed and the Roman network of communications had deteriorated, these individual topographic units tended towards autonomy. The resultant fragmentation was probably aided by the tribal character of the Germanic invaders and the destructive quality of the nomadic raids. Though the ideal of a unity based on the memory of Rome, an ideal given new vitality by the Church, somewhat loosely held the separate units together, local autonomy was by the tenth century the rule rather than the exception. In many ways the Holy Roman Empire was more of a federation than a united imperial state.

In contrast, the topography of eastern Europe is characterized by large basins and broad plains which could, at the time, be united and effectively organized far more easily than could a comparable area of western Europe. Thus, in terms of area, the Kingdom of Hungary began as a completed state; from the first years of her existence Hungary incorporated the entire Carpathian Basin. The Kingdom of Bohemia also commenced virtually full-grown within the forested ramparts of the surrounding uplands, and soon added adjacent Moravia and Silesia. Whereas the states of Western Europe were forced by geo-historical conditions to begin from kernel areas and through a long process of growth to amalgamate the diverse surrounding regions, the states of Eastern Europe quickly attained their maximum extent; in consequence they were for several centuries more powerful than the embryonic Western states.

From the eleventh until the sixteenth centuries, East Central Europe was far from being a "Shatter Belt." On the contrary, Poland and Hungary were probably the most powerful single states of Europe and effectively shielded Europe against all invaders from the east and southeast. If there was a "Shatter Belt" at the time, it existed along the zone of ebb and flow where Christian and Moslem faced each other, not where German and Slav faced each other. The "Shatter Belt" of those centuries lay in the southern Balkans, in southern Italy, and in Spain.

The basic misfortune for Hungary and Bohemia was the fact that the terrain had given them too precise a state area. The ellipse of the Carpathian chain drew a treacherous girdle around Hungary; the mountains were enough of a barrier to make any extension of Hungarian control beyond them tenuous and temporary, and yet they were but a poor defense against the enemies of the kingdom. Bohemia too could only with difficulty expand beyond the walls of the Ore Mountains and the Bohemian Forest. Expansion to the east into Moravia and through the Sudetens northward into Silesia was possible and quickly achieved, but beyond those limits Bohemia could not easily expand.

While Bohemia and Hungary remained essentially confined within their historic borders, the states to the east and west gradually but steadily increased in both area and power. By the late fifteenth century Hungary and Bohemia had substantially lost their positions of relative power. Between the sixteenth and twentieth centuries two of the states that had developed gradually from small, kernel areas, Austria and Turkey, were able to overcome the static kingdoms and divide southeastern Europe between themselves. It was the recognition of this fundamental vital danger to his kingdom that, late in the fifteenth century, led Matthias Corvinus, perhaps the greatest king of Hungary, to spend the resources of his kingdom in a prolonged attempt to break the bounds of the Alps and Carpathians and to add to his threatened state the resources of areas beyond the mountain wall.

Far different from the ready-formed Kingdom of Hungary was the steadily growing state of Austria. Initially the Ostmark had included little more than the south bank of the Danube between the Enns and Carnuntum. Between 1000 and 1500 expansion northward or eastward was impossible because of the strength of the Hungarians and Bohemians. Instead, Austria expanded into and along the corridors of the Alpine valleys and basins, and by the end of the fifteenth century she had reached the Adriatic and her present westernmost borders. Though still smaller in area than Hungary, Austria was by 1500 at least of equal strength, since she possessed in Vienna the key center of wealth and communications, and she had the power of the Empire behind her, while Hungary on the other hand was engaged in a continual struggle with the Turks.

Just as the close of the fifteenth century witnessed the decline in the relative power of Hungary, it also saw the end of much of her commercial importance. Hungary lay astride the land routes between Constantinople (and hence the Orient) and Western Europe, and the trade initiated by the Crusaders traversed the kingdom. The voyages of Columbus and Vasco da Gama turned the traders of Europe from the eastern Mediterranean to the broad ocean to the west. Much has been written about the effect on the Italian city states of this shift of the routeways, but it probably hurt Hungary even more, since the discoveries in the west, added to the advance of the Turks, put an end to practically all through traffic. The devastating effects of a century and a half of alien occupation, combined with the fundamental shift in the trading patterns of Europe resulted in economic stagnation for Hungary in later centuries.[1]

From A.D. 1000 to 1500, however, East Central Europe was generally characterized by peace, order, and prosperity. The division between East and West which is now the most notable feature of this zone had no counterpart at that time. One Christian faith bound together all Europeans from the Atlantic to at least the frontiers of the Orthodox world. New ideas and techniques were carried freely throughout Catholic Europe by the growing class of craftsmen and artists. The first universities east of France and north of Italy were not along the Rhine but much further east, in Prague (1348), Cracow (1364), Vienna (1365), and Pécs (1367).[2] The forms and styles of art associated with Western Europe were also widespread in the east; Székesfehérvár was noted for its Romanesque and Gothic structures. In the time of Matthias Corvinus, Hungary shared in the artistic and intellectual activities associated with the early Renaissance.

Though the half millennium was (with the exception of the disturbed thirteenth century) a "golden age" compared to the years preceding and following it, each individual century had its distinct characteristics. The first century, the eleventh, was a time of stabilization. Along the Danube, a new order had been superimposed upon a pre-existent chaos, and a century was required before this new order could be firmly established. During these hundred years the boundaries were demarcated and the various states completed the organization of their territories. Perhaps as a result of the survival of the influences of steppe tribal life, Hungary was beset by several wars of succession, and was torn by a major revolt of the pagan tribes of the east against the Christian central government of the Árpáds. By the end of the eleventh century, however, Hungary had become stabilized under King St. Ladislaus (Lászlo) I, Austria under her duke, St. Leopold III, and Bohemia had become a kingdom under Wladislas II.[3]

Following this century of stabilization came one of prosperity. Wars and revolts were infrequent, dynastic successions were unbroken, and the international borders were universally accepted. Christian Europe turned its gaze and its propensities for fighting towards the Holy Land. The Crusaders marched to the east, and once again traffic flowed steadily through Vienna and across Pannonia. A time of settlement followed the establishment of peace, and the empty lands of Hungary and Austria became populated. Routeways were developed in all directions. The Wechsel and the Semmering passes became the arteries joining the Danubian lands with the Adriatic. The transfer of ideas and techniques now became feasible on a large scale; monasteries, which were then the technological centers of much of Europe, spread with startling rapidity. During the twelfth century at least fourteen major monasteries were established by the French abbeys of Clairvaux and Morimand within western Hungary, eastern Austria, and Bohemia. Wherever routeways converged new towns arose, and most of the important towns had received their charters as free cities before the middle of the following century. The largest by far of all the local centers, Vienna became the greatest city of East Central Europe.

The twelfth century of order and prosperity was followed by a century of catastrophe. Both Hungary and Austria underwent trials that tested their very existence. Some historians have maintained that the thirteenth century was the greatest of medieval centuries, and one, at least, has said that it was the greatest of all centuries. Such an evaluation reflects, however, a myopic limitation of European history to France and Italy. For most of the countries east of the Rhine the thirteenth was a century of horrors, and it is treated as such in the folklore of the East. The Kievan state was completely destroyed by the Mongols, and for centuries thereafter the Russian peoples lived under the domination of the Tatars. The Byzantine Empire was temporarily destroyed when Crusaders captured and looted Constantinople in 1204. Poland, Bohemia, Hungary, and the eastern parts of the Holy Roman Empire all suffered severely from the invasions of the Mongols.

With the exception of the Crusader rape of Constantinople, most of the crises of the thirteenth century can be attributed to the Mongol invasion. For the first time since the Magyar storm over three centuries previously, Europe faced an incursion by nomads, and the results were again disastrous. Like all their predecessors from the steppes, the Mongols, with their fantastic speed and maneuverability, their lack of fear and their hideous appearance, overwhelmed the armies of Europe. In the three centuries since the Lechfeld, Europe had forgotten how to combat the wild riders; even the Magyars now fought in typical European fashion. It is a remarkable sign of the continuity of steppe practice that the Mongols used the same battle plan against the Hungarians that the Magyars had used against the imperial forces on the Lechfeld. No European army defeated the Mongols, and if the thirteenth century was a time of greatness in France and Italy, it was only because the states to the east bore the impact of the onrush from the steppe.

From their base around Karakorum in what is now Outer Mongolia, the Mongols (or Tatars) had by 1230 conquered China and the entire steppe belt of Asia. Their raids had carried them to the fringes of the Kievan state, and in a great council in 1235 they decided to invade Europe. Their first moves westward brought them against the Russia of Kiev, and in a series of campaigns between 1238 and 1240 the Mongols completely destroyed the Kievan state.

In March of 1241, as the snows melted, the Mongols were encamped on the plains between Kiev and the present Lvov, just to the north of the northeastern passes leading into the Carpathian Basin. From this camp they were free to move westward north of the Carpathians, or through the mountain passes into Hungary, and in the devastating campaigns of the following month and a half they advanced in both directions. The major force of the army moved westward and shattered a Polish army on March 18, and then with startling rapidity they swept through southern Poland. Cracow was taken and burned. (The story of the bugler of Cracow dates from this event.) Moving through Silesia the Mongol horde met and almost annihilated an army of Germans and Poles at Liegnitz on April 9. German historians have credited the imperial army with inflicting such heavy casualties on the victorious nomads that they turned southward rather than continue further westward. Whether or not the Mongols suffered heavy losses at Liegnitz, their move southward appears to have fitted in well with their over-all plan; the force that turned southward was not fleeing, but rather was advancing to help dispose of Hungary, the remaining bastion to the east.

Following their success at Liegnitz the Tatars ravaged Silesia and Moravia and then rode down the March valley to the Danube. Since the wide Danube was a major barrier to the horsemen, they followed the north bank eastward to join the army units that had passed through the Carpathians into eastern Hungary. Still in April, on the Plain of Mohi by the Sajo River (near present Miskolc), the great battle was fought. The Hungarian force was shattered, and King Béla barely escaped capture or death. For the remainder of 1241 the victorious Mongols swept over the Alföld and Transylvania, and that winter they crossed the frozen Danube and ravaged the Dunántúl core of Hungary. King Béla was pursued to the Adriatic coast by the nomads, who swept all before them. Their raiding parties penetrated into Austria, but on the whole that state was spared. Then, as suddenly as they had come, the Mongols left.[4] Their leader Ogotai had died, and the Mongols retired into Asia to elect a new chieftain; they never again seriously threatened the Carpathian lands. The invasion of 1241–42 marked the last time until 1849 that the basin was invaded through the northeastern passes.

Hungary had been completely shattered and despoiled. Two centuries of careful settlement and development had been nullified in one year. The organization of the state had been destroyed, and as had been the case two centuries earlier, the kingdom again had to cope with rebellious tribes. In 1239 the Hungarian king had granted Cumans fleeing from the Mongols permission to settle in Hungary.[5]

With the collapse of the central authority these new pagan tribes became a grave source of unrest.

That the Hungarian state continued to exist at all is evidence of the acceptance of the idea of the lands of the Crown of King Stephen by all the Hungarian people, and of their continued consciousness of unity. In the year of devastation the Magyars of the plains had suffered far more grievously than had the Slavic peoples of the hill lands, and yet no separatist tendencies seem to have been manifested. Transylvania and Croatia do not seem to have sought any degree of separation. Though complete recovery was not to be achieved for almost a century, the willingness of the Hungarian people to work together towards this recovery symbolized and strengthened the unity of the nation. Hungary had survived a great crisis.

This crisis of Hungary led immediately to the crisis of Austria. Manifesting the typical tendency of European leaders to take advantage of the troubles of their neighbors, Duke Frederick II of Austria attempted to turn the weakness of Hungary to his own advantage. At the very time of the Mongol devastation, Frederick forced King Béla to yield to him the three western megyek of Hungary, Moson, Sopron, and Vasvár. The Hungarians were understandably bitter about this, and as soon as the Mongols had left, a series of skirmishes broke out in the frontier zones. In 1246, in a battle near Wiener Neustadt, Frederick was defeated and killed. Frederick left no son, and Austria was suddenly without a ruler.

The succession to the throne of the Babenbergers was contested by three parties: the Holy Roman Emperor, who claimed ultimate jurisdiction over the marchland, King Ottokar II of Bohemia, and King Béla IV of Hungary. In this contest, then, the site of Vienna was sought by German, Slav, and Magyar. Bohemia was at this time stronger than Hungary, and Ottokar soon had gained control over most of Austria. The Peace of Buda (Ofen), 1254, set the boundary for the first time along the Semmering-Wechsel crest of the Alps, with Ottokar obtaining Lower Austria, and Béla being given Styria. However, the Styrian lords refused to accept the rule of Hungary and called upon Ottokar for help.[6] In 1260 Ottokar obtained control of Styria, and in consequence controlled a significant belt of territory from Silesia through Styria.

This occupation of Austria by Ottokar was the last time that the northern Slavs gained control of the significant corridor of the Danube through the Alpine-Carpathian ridges. Samo may have briefly controlled Pannonia, Moravia, and the Vienna Basin; the Moravian state of Sviatopluk had extended for a few decades into Pannonia and Slovakia. Now, Ottokar united Bohemia, Moravia, Silesia, Austria, and Styria. These Slavic penetrations into the Danube corridor were possible only when the powers to the east and west were unusually weak. As soon as the neighboring states had regained strength, the Slavic hold on the Danube deteriorated. The control of Austria by Bohemia was almost certain to remain tenuous, in any case. An advance into the Vienna Basin was feasible from Moravia, but the center of the state was in Prague, far from the plains along the Danube. Since at least the year 1000, the axis of communications and of power in the vicinity of Vienna had run west to east, and Prague was too far removed from this axis of power.

Ottokar seems to have been aware of the weakness of his hold on Austria. He evidently realized that he could maintain his power over the Danube corridor only by gaining the official support of the Holy Roman Empire, since both Bohemia and Austria were within the Empire. The electors of the Empire did not, however, select Ottokar as the legal ruler of Austria; instead, in 1273, they chose as the new duke of Austria, Rudolph of Habsburg, the count of a small Swiss holding. In addition to the imperial sanction, Rudolph gained the support of the Hungarian king, Ladislaus V. Near Dürnkrut, on the west bank of the March, the decisive battle for the control of Austria was fought in 1278; the Bohemian armies were defeated and Ottokar died in the battle.[7] For the first time, a Habsburg had become the unquestioned ruler of Austria.

The Battle of Dürnkrut ended the time of crises. After three decades of turmoil and devastation, Hungary, Austria, and Bohemia were, in terms of area, exactly the same as they had been before the Mongol onslaught. However, another period of stabilization was required before complete peace and order could come to the region. King Ladislaus was killed by Cuman rebels in 1290, and in 1301 the last Árpád died. A short interregnum in which the local lords ruled almost autonomously was ended with the selection of the first Anjou king of Hungary in 1308. In somewhat the same way Bohemia experienced a change of dynasty at the start of the fourteenth century. Thus, the century of troubles ended with three new royal families, the Habsburg in Austria, the Anjou in Hungary, and the Luxemburg in Bohemia, stabilizing and reorganizing their states.

Once again peace and well-being characterized the lands of East Central Europe. The fourteenth century was another time of great prosperity. During these hundred years free of invasions and major threats from outside the area, the lands along the middle Danube knew their greatest order. Significant technological advances were made, and Upper Hungary (Slovakia) became one of the wealthiest mining areas of Europe. Universities were founded in Hungary, Austria,

Bohemia, and Poland. Cities grew rapidly, and Buda became a major cattle and wine market. Perhaps for the first time the Alföld was fully settled,[8] and Hungary became a major source of food and hides for Western Europe. This prosperity did not cease with the end of the fourteenth century, but by 1400 Hungary had had to face the Turks in a major conflict.

Although mining, crafts-manufacturing, and commerce could yield greater profits than agriculture, the land was the firm basis on which medieval economy was laid. Yet, though each agricultural unit tried to raise its own food, complete local self-sufficiency was not the goal of the farmer. The rapid growth of towns gave the lord of the manor and the free peasant an expanding market for agricultural surpluses. So conscious were the peasants of market possibilities that those who were in a position to do so generally raised high value, specialty products such as wine, rather than food for their own use.

The familar contrast between an agricultural Eastern Europe and an industrial Western Europe seems to have existed by the twelfth century. By the time the Magyars were settling the Alföld, Flanders, the Rhine Valley, and northern Italy had already become heavily populated manufacturing regions, and Danubian traffic consisted principally of westbound agricultural produce and eastbound manufactured items. By the fourteenth century this trade was highly developed and the tariff was a major source of governmental revenue.

Western Hungary, including present Burgenland, was oriented commercially towards Vienna; caches of coins discovered in the border area are proof of this point. At Zemendorf, west of Sopron, a cache that was buried in 1233 included, of a total of 1,891 coins, 1,860 of Viennese and only 5 of Hungarian origin. In nearby Purbach a find of over 18,000 silver coins dating from *ca.* 1452 contained over 15,000 Austrian coins. This large amount of money in an agricultural community suggests an intense and prolonged trade with Vienna.

The exports of Hungary to Austria consisted principally of animals. In the fourteenth century approximately 70 per cent of Hungarian shipments to Vienna were of cattle and horses, for whose growth Hungary was eminently suitable. These animals were shipped first to the border cities, principally Pozsony (Bratislava) north of the Danube, and Sopron south of the Danube, and these cities dealt directly with the great emporium of Central Europe, Vienna. From Vienna the animals were shipped to all portions of Central and

Western Europe. In return, manufactured items moved from Vienna, through the custom cities into Hungary. In 1458 approximately 80 per cent of the imports into Hungary through Pozsony were of textiles, and another 11 per cent were of metal wares, principally knives.

Governmental decrees constituted one of the major restrictions to a free flow of trade. The Austrian dukes attempted to protect home producers by banning the importation of competing products from Hungary. This ban exerted a great hardship on Hungarian artisans and vintners, since their products could not enter Vienna even for transit to areas beyond Austria. In the case of wine an exception was made for the wine produced on lands owned in Hungary by Austrian cities or citizens. The burghers of Wiener Neustadt possessed extensive vineyards on the hill slopes overlooking Lake Neusiedl. These wines evidently entered Austria in vast quantities and made Neustadt one of the principal wine centers of Central Europe.[9]

Because of this repressive domination of Hungarian trade by Vienna, the Hungarian kings sought ways to circumvent the city. Most of the ultimate customers for Hungarian products were beyond Vienna, so that alternate routeways seemed necessary and feasible. For the wine merchants new routeways were essential. Vineyards covered the southeastern slopes of the Leitha Range and the Little Carpathians, adjacent to the Austrian border, but the wine was destined for northern Europe, principally Poland and Silesia. Hence, new routeways were developed both to the north and the south.

The path to the north crossed the Danube either in the Carnuntum gap, at Pozsony, or in the vicinity of the Buda gap. Both of these routes moved along the Carpathian spurs and they met near Trnava. From Trnava two paths were available: one led northward up the Váh valley to the Jablunka Pass, which carried traffic into Poland and Silesia; the other moved across a saddle in the Little Carpathians to the border town of Holič, and then on to Brno, whence the roads fanned out in several directions. The latter road seems to have been the more important, and Brno became a major distributing center for both Viennese and Hungarian trade with the areas further north. These routeways circumventing Vienna were favored by the states involved; in 1335 the kings of Hungary, Bohemia, and Poland signed the Compact of Visegrád,[10] which guaranteed the protection of the merchants of all three states, and lowered the tariffs along the Holič road. The wines of west Hungary, notably the "Ruster," became famous in northern Europe because of these roads.

Hungary attempted to develop an alternate routeway to the south as well as to the north, but such a routeway could not compete with the Vienna-Semmering road. Venice dominated the Adriatic trade, and Vienna dominated the connections with Venice. From the center of Hungary traffic wishing to avoid Vienna was forced to climb over the Karst near the Adriatic, and then travel by ship to Venice. Despite all restrictions placed on trade with Vienna by the Anjou kings, the great city continued to dominate the foreign trade of Hungary.

For the first century and a half after the establishment of the Kingdom of Hungary, the area that is now included within Burgenland was virtually devoid of population. The border megyek were under the personal jurisdiction of the king, whose principal task was to defend the borders of the kingdom. This *gyepű*, or glacis of unproductivity, served as a moat protecting Hungary against incursions from Austria. German nationalists have maintained that some Carolingian settlements in this area must have survived the Magyar storm, but considering the nature and purpose of the glacis, this seems improbable. Though some names of possible Carolingian origin still remain: Peinicachu (Pinkafeld), and Kundpoldersdorf (Kobersdorf), the settlements themselves had more than likely been depopulated.[11]

Only a few groups of people whose loyalty was certain were settled within this empty border zone. Since the enemy across the boundary was German, these frontier watchmen were never German; they were Magyars or people akin to the Magyars. Two of these areas of Magyar settlement are still observable: the larger one, around Oberwart, guarded the frontier just south of the Wechsel Pass; the smaller one, around Oberpullendorf, protected the westward embayment of the lowland between the Sopron and Kőszeg ranges. The Petchenegs, another nomadic people, were also settled along the frontier. Two locations in the Sopron Gateway are thought to have been their camps, and the syllables *lövő*, which appear in many of the place names of west Hungary, are considered to refer to them.[12] With the exception of Devín and Pozsony at the Carnuntum gap (Porta Hungaria), all the border fortresses were well back of the boundary. Moson, Sopron, and Vasvár guarded the western gaps, but they were all ten to thirty miles east of the Leitha-Lafnitz boundary.

By the middle of the twelfth century the western boundary of Hungary seemed secure. The Árpád dynasty was at the height of its power and Hungary was, in most clashes, more than the equal of Austria. Trade was flourishing, and the idea of maintaining a part of the kingdom as an unpopulated border zone was no longer appealing.

The kings of Hungary decided therefore to populate this valuable territory and allow it to add to the wealth of the nation.

The settling of the area was accomplished in a fashion typically medieval. The territory was divided into manorial units, and the new lords were given the responsibility of populating their lands. Géza II gave land generously, and the great noble holdings of Burgenland had their origins at this time. Since the holdings adjacent to the border were expected to meet the initial onslaught of an invasion, they were larger than the units further east, and their castles were of necessity fortresses. In the middle of the Leitha Range was the castle, Scharfeneck, and below it in the valley lay its commercial center, Mannersdorf. Overlooking the Sopron Gateway on the northern slope stood Hornstein and on the southern slope, Forchtenstein. Hornstein is today a mass of ruins, but Forchtenstein is probably the finest fortress castle in Austria. Each fortress had its commercial center; for Forchtenstein this was Mattersdorf, and for Hornstein it was Eisenstadt, in the midst of a wealthy belt of vineyards. (Around 1365 Eisenstadt was separated from Hornstein and became another *Herrschaft*.)

Three fortresses guarded the perimeter of the lowland embayment between the Sopron and Köszeg ranges. In the northwest corner was Kobersdorf, in the southwest corner, Lockenhaus, and high above the western rim, Landsee. At the eastern ends of the Sopron and Köszeg ranges were the fortress cities of Sopron and Köszeg. Along the south flank of the Köszeg Range was Schlaining and to the west, on the upland surface of the Bucklige Welt, Bernstein. Still further south, on a volcanic plug rising sharply above the surrounding marshes, stood Güssing, the master throughout medieval times of much of present southern Burgenland. Since these border holdings were larger than the average holding within Hungary, the border lords exerted considerable power. Güssing and Forchtenstein at times made use of Austro-Hungarian conflicts to further their own policies; they acted as petty kingdoms in the interregnum between the Árpád and the Anjou kings.

The majority of the new settlers in this border area were Germans from neighboring Austria. The Magyars were still far from completing their occupation of the Alföld, whereas the Germans had already crowded the Alpine valleys. After 1150 the German peasants entered western Hungary and rapidly filled the former vacuum. Some of the newly settled areas suffered seriously from the Mongol invasion, but these territories had been resettled by 1250. Whereas any descendant of the original Magyars was considered to be of noble blood, most of the immigrant Germans were regarded as peasants. Consequently feudalism was stronger along the western periphery of the kingdom than in the Magyar interior.

The Hungarian kings not only made no attempt to hamper German immigration, rather they encouraged it. Germans had often been used by Hungarian monarchs in their struggles with the dissident tribes of the east; and too, the Germans were considered to be valuable additions to the country, since they had developed industrial and commercial techniques generally more advanced than those in use in Hungary. The kings followed the famous precept of King Stephen, that all foreign persons were to be treated as "guests," in the belief that a state whose citizens spoke many languages was certain to be stronger than one in which only one language was spoken. Some of the new nobility was of German background; members of Styrian families were granted lands by Géza II in 1157.

In the Middle Ages nationalism, inasmuch as it existed, was not equated with language. The practice of judging persons by the language they speak had not yet become widespread. The idea of a nation depended on a national "ownership" of a certain territorial extent, on a union of space and tradition, rather than of space and language. The state idea of the Kingdom of Hungary was, therefore, not predicated on the Magyar language. Through the natural process of assimilation Magyar came to be the predominant language, but the Hungarian Crown was not vitally concerned with language. The Kingdom of Hungary was a concrete medieval fact, and even had the majority of the population by the fifteenth century come to speak Slavic, the existence and the name of the state would not have been altered.[13]

Germans not only occupied the former glacis, they also settled in the cities. The increasing national prosperity fostered the growth of commerce and towns, and the Magyars were at the time not as capable of developing these as were the Germans from the west. Hence Germans were freely invited into Hungary to establish or expand the commercial life, and the second half of the twelfth century saw either the beginnings or the first rapid growth of the towns of Hungary.

The Germans became Magyarized very slowly, and, until Magyarization was urged in the late nineteenth century, they maintained their language and customs even though surrounded by people speaking other languages. This persistent clinging to their own national language and customs was fostered by the special status of the Germans within Hungary, and by their compact areas of settlement. They had been invited in as desirable colonists and had been granted special privileges. These privileges had in effect freed them from control by the local jurisdictional powers; they had their own nobility and clergy, and the right of direct appeal to the throne.

Within the kingdom the German townsmen were generally on a higher social level than that of the neighboring agriculturists. The Germans were the merchants, artisans, craftsmen, and technicians. The productive mines of Upper Hungary (Slovakia) were developed and maintained by German technicians. The cities were principally German speaking, so that most of the older cities of Hungary have both a Magyar and a German name: Buda (Ofen), Székesfehérvár (Stuhlweissenburg), Pozsony (Pressburg), Moson (Wieselburg), Magyaróvár (Ungarische Altenburg), Győr (Raab), Esztergom (Gran), Sopron (Ödenburg), Szombathely (Steinamanger), Kőszeg (Güns), Vasvár (Eisenburg), and Pécs (Fünfkirchen). Within these cities the Germans formed autonomous communities, and the preservation of their original tongue was assisted by the feeling of cultural superiority which they held towards the tillers of the soil. The Germans considered themselves to be a part of the cultural West and often treated Magyar as a barbarian tongue. Commonly a young man could not even enter a guild unless he could speak German, and marriage between members of unlike social and linguistic strata was rare.

The German peasants along the western border were, of course, not on a higher social plane than the Magyars. In fact the border nobility quickly became Magyarized, since its ties were principally with the Magyar nobility. German and Magyar peasants intermarried, and areas in which both languages were originally spoken soon came to use the speech of the local majority. Since the immigrants from Austria had formed compact areas of settlement, the German language became increasingly dominant along the western border. No attempt was made to force a new language upon the non-Magyars, and because the lives of the peasants were often circumscribed by the neighboring villages and market towns, German remained predominant. Gradually the Petcheneg and some of the Magyar groups were absorbed into the German-speaking majority. Only at Oberwart and Oberpullendorf did the Magyars maintain their language; here they formed compact groups and felt a deep sense of pride as defenders of the nation.

The fifteenth century was a time of deterioration of the strength of Hungary. Wars again became customary, and during these hundred years Hungary served as the bastion of Europe against the Turks. The country enjoyed prosperity and a burst of glory late in the century, but over all lay the shadow of the Turk. The kingdom also had to endure repeated struggles of succession to the throne. Late in the fourteenth century the second Anjou king had died without an heir;

the Luxemburg dynasty which followed died out in turn in 1437, and the interregnum was not brought to a close until the election of Matthias Corvinus in 1458, who also died without an heir, in 1490. When King Louis died at Mohács in 1526, he too left no heir.

The reign of Matthias (Mátyás, the son of Hunyádi János, the great hero of the Turkish wars) was the last period of glory for Hungary. Matthias brought the kingdom back to a position of glory and power after a period of weakness, and in a long series of wars he extended his dominion well into Central Europe. Since Stephen, he was the first Hungarian king to capture Vienna. In 1463 he forced Emperor Frederick III to renounce his claims to the throne of Hungary. (Frederick had been the candidate of the border nobility.) In 1471 Matthias obtained control of Bohemia-Moravia-Silesia,[14] and in 1480 he was elected Duke of Austria by the Diet of Lower Austria.

The conquests of Matthias produced another time of extreme crisis for Austria. Though the territorial unit named Austria continued to exist, it had been bound to its greater eastern neighbor, and for the first time, Austria, Bohemia, and Hungary were joined into one royal holding. The emperor had been forced to retire to Linz, and the border of Hungarian rule extended to the old limit of steppe power, the Enns River. In 1490 Matthias died, and with his death his conquests were lost. Again Hungary had not been able to incorporate permanently areas lying beyond her mountain borders; again Austria had survived a crisis.

Matthias has been criticized in retrospect; historians have felt that he squandered the wealth and strength of his nation in futile wars of conquest at a time when the enemy to the southeast required full attention. When the results are considered the charge is probably warranted, but Matthias, the son of the greatest of the Hungarian battlers against the Turk, knew well what faced Hungary to the southeast. For over a century Hungary had confronted the Turks, and the Turks had steadily gained in strength. By herself Hungary could not long hope to withstand the full force of an empire in control of the Balkans, Asia Minor, and the Levant. Continued successful resistance could be assured only by Western help in the life struggles of Hungary, but voluntary assistance could rarely be expected from the Holy Roman Empire. European rulers have always been willing to use alien forces against fellow Europeans, and the Turks may well have been for the Empire a welcome power along the frontiers of Hungary.

The acquisition of Bohemia and Austria was important not only because of the resources of these two countries, but also because they both were stepping stones to the position of Holy Roman Emperor. Hungary was not within the Empire, but Austria and Bohemia were.

With his control of these two states, Matthias became eligible for election as emperor and became, in fact, one of the strongest rulers within the Empire. His policy failed, however; the electors could hardly be expected to choose an invading Magyar as emperor, even if he stressed that the defense of the frontiers of Europe made this essential. In addition, Matthias may have been considered something of a usurper; he was not of royal blood and hence not a "legitimate" king of Hungary. In 1486 Maximilian was elected Holy Roman Emperor.

Matthias failed, therefore, to save Hungary and may even have hastened her downfall, but he did give the old kingdom a final time of great glory. The age of Mátyás appears in the folklore of Hungary as a short but brilliant era, and the king himself has become to all the peoples who lived within the historic Kingdom of Hungary, Magyar, Croat, German, and Slovak, the legendary personification of the mighty, just king.

THE TURKISH OCCUPATION

Just as the modern application of the term "Shatter Belt" to East Central Europe has caused many to forget the relative strength, stability, and prosperity of this zone between A.D. 1000 and 1500, so the Turkish occupation of Hungary has caused many to forget the one hundred and forty years during which Hungary was the bastion of Europe.

All the land routes between the Aegean heart of the Ottoman Empire and the European centers of population and wealth ran through Hungary. The roads from Constantinople, Salonika, and the Danube mouth converged on Belgrade, passed through the Dunántúl part of Hungary, and converged again on Vienna. Once the Turks had shattered Serbia, only Hungary stood between them and Central Europe. In 1389 on the Field of Kosovo the Serbian armies were crushed, and for 137 years Hungary had to face the Turks almost alone. So conscious were the Turks of the position and strength of the Hungarians that they termed the Battle of Kosovo a victory "won from the Hungarians"; [1] after the victory at Mohács, Suleiman hesitated to advance into Hungary because he could not believe that he had met the full power of the kingdom.

The Turkish invasion may be considered as the last advance of Asiatic nomads into the Carpathian lowland. The Ottoman Turks originated in Asia Minor as typical nomadic herdsmen, and their armies emphasized horsemanship during their time of superiority.

Though they quickly adopted Byzantine methods of organization, the Turks remained at heart a steppe people. At the Battle of Nicopolis in 1396 it was noted that their cavalry used lighter, more mobile horses than did the cavalry of their Western opponents. At least until the seventeenth century Turkish raids were a recurrent danger along the frontiers, and every advancing Ottoman army was accompanied by raiding units which ravaged the surrounding countryside for scores of miles in all directions. Throughout the five centuries of their occupation of the Balkans the Turks never turned to agriculture; the horse remained the symbol of caste and authority.

However, though the Turks were, like the Scythians, Yazyges, Huns, Avars, and Mongols, originally tribesmen from the grasslands of Central Asia, they differed from these groups in two important respects: in their faith and in their organization. Like the other steppe peoples the Turks were at first pagan, but evidently just before 1300 they accepted the Moslem religion. This newly acquired faith gave them their great zeal, and perhaps even inspired them with their basic idea of statehood. The propagation of Islam became for them the driving purpose behind the existence of their army and their empire. So too in their conquests religion was a decisive factor; all who embraced Islam were treated as citizens and brothers, all who did not were merely tolerated as aliens and subjects. The new faith was practiced ardently; as at least one author [2] has maintained, at the Battle of Nicopolis the Turks were better disciplined, they were freer from those curses of army morale, wine, women, and gambling, and were more pious than their "crusading" adversaries.

The Turks also differed from the other steppe invaders in their powers of organization. They learned much from the Byzantine Empire; in fact it has been said that the Ottoman Turks had no history before they came in contact with Byzantium. From the first days of the Ottoman Turks, their actions affected and were affected by the diplomacy of Constantinople. They served as warrior allies of various Byzantine factions, and it is evident that many of their ideas and techniques of statecraft were derived from the Eastern Empire, which they supplanted. The Turkish skill of organization was tragic for Hungary. Mohács was no worse a defeat than Sajo, but the Turks remained, whereas the Mongols had left within a year.

The geographic fact that the Turks entered Europe through Byzantium was therefore fundamental to their pattern of political development. All the other nomadic tribes had entered Europe from the steppes of the present Ukraine, and had descended upon Europe little better than wild predators; in contrast, the Ottomans advanced over the terrain of Byzantium, and entered Europe equipped with the

Byzantine techniques of organization. Just as Hungary was born of the union of the Magyar raiders and the ideas and techniques of Western Europe, so the Ottoman Empire was formed from the synthesis of the Turkish raiders with both the faith of Asia Minor and the techniques of the Eastern Empire.

The ancestors of the Ottoman Turks are thought to have fled from Central Asia to escape the Mongols, and they seem to have entered the northwestern corner of Asia Minor in the thirteenth century. There they settled in a fertile pocket near the eastern end of the Sea of Marmora. The escarpment edge of the Anatolian Plateau protected them from the tribes to the south and turned them toward adjacent Constantinople. Their first known chief, Estrogul, lived peaceably. His son Osman (or Ottman) began the policy of expansion by attacking and conquering the immediately neighboring tribes. The Ottoman holdings were still very small; it is thought that Osman had only about 400 fighting men at his disposal when he began his series of conquests. However, no nearby force was capable of effective resistance. During the Crusader occupation of Constantinople, 1204–61, the Byzantine Empire had been almost completely destroyed and its holdings partitioned. Though the "Empire" was reborn in 1261, it included only bits of territory in addition to the capital city. In 1326 Osman captured Brussa, which became the original capital of the Ottoman Turks, and a few years later his son, Orkhan, gained control of the important cities of Nicomedia and Nicea. The Turks were, like most nomads, relatively helpless before walled cities; it is probable therefore that these cities, which could not look anywhere for assistance, simply submitted to the obviously rising new power.

Byzantium was so weak that, despite the mounting danger from the Ottomans, the rulers of Constantinople repeatedly called upon them for armed assistance. In 1345 the sultan was rewarded for his help with the hand of the emperor's daughter, and shortly thereafter he was granted land on the European side of the Straits. Rapidly the Turks overran the southern Balkans, and in 1366 Sultan Murad moved his capital to Adrianople (Edirne).

By 1400 the Turks had completed the occupation of most of the Balkans. Gathering in the fragments of the Greek empire was not difficult, and the Turkish state was soon much larger and more powerful than either Bulgaria or Serbia. In 1379 Bulgaria was reduced to the status of a vassal state, and Serbia was destroyed in 1389. During the fourteenth century the advances of the Turks had been made almost entirely within the Balkans, and it was not until the conquest of the Balkans had been completed that they turned their strength against

Asia Minor. By 1400 only Constantinople and its distant satellite city, Salonika, were the remnants of the ancient Eastern Empire.[3]

The Turkish occupation of the Balkans had serious effects on the political development of those states for centuries to come. Though oppressed peasants may in some places have welcomed the overthrowing of their feudal masters, it can hardly be said that they welcomed the imposition of Turkish rule. The Turks brought with them an entirely different culture, a culture that was far more at variance with the values of the Christian world than is communism today. ". . . the Ottoman Empire, completely alien to its European subjects in origin, tradition, and religion, far from integrating them into a new type of culture, brought them nothing but a degrading foreign domination which interrupted for approximately four hundred years their participation in European history." [4] "Coexistence" between European and Turk became possible only when the Turk had ceased to be a threat (after 1700). In the areas occupied by the Turks political development practically ceased. The fact that the Carpathian Basin and the Balkans have in recent centuries formed a "powder keg" can be attributed largely to the stifling Turkish occupation.

In the mid-fifteenth century the seemingly irresistible advance of the Turks was checked by the greatest of the European fighters against them, John Hunyádi.[5] His first victory was gained near Sibiu in Transylvania, where a Turkish force was crushed in 1442. In the following year Hunyádi won an astounding series of successes and drove the Ottomans almost back to their capital, Adrianople. The Hungarian forces pushed the Turks southward from the Sava frontier up the Morava valley, defeated them at Niš, captured Sofia, and beat them again in the Maritza valley. The Peace of Szeged, signed in 1444, concluded the campaign and guaranteed ten years of peace.

Unfortunately, however, the peace was not maintained, but was broken treacherously by the Christians. At the instigation of the Papal Legate, Cardinal Cesarini, and the Byzantine emperor, King Ladislaus of Hungary was persuaded to break the truce and resume the assault on the Turks. The Ottomans retaliated quickly by bribing the Genoese fleet to transport the Turkish troops to Varna, where they inflicted a crushing defeat on the Western armies; King Ladislaus and Cardinal Cesarini both died in the battle. This disaster undoubtedly hastened the fall of Constantinople; the Turk was again free to concentrate on this vital bit of Greek territory remaining in the midst of the Ottoman Empire. With the aid of newly developed artillery the Turks conquered the imperial city in 1453.

Following the fall of Constantinople the Turks again were a serious threat along the Sava frontier. Yet Hunyádi was still defending Hungary; his troops won a series of clashes along the Danube, and in 1456 he led a Christian force in defense of the critical city of Belgrade. In a great battle the Turks were routed and the city was saved. Unfortunately, this was Hunyádi's last battle; he died that same year.

Two years after the death of Hunyádi János, his son Mátyás became king of Hungary.[6] As long as Matthias Corvinus remained on the throne the Turks scored no new major advances in Europe. In 1473 and 1475 they penetrated through Croatia into Carinthia and Carniola, but in 1477 they were defeated by Matthias. However, the death of Matthias in 1490 brought to a close this time of effective Hungarian power; the ensuing struggles for the throne seriously weakened Hungary, and no man of stature appeared to replace the Hunyádi father and son. In 1521 the Turks captured Belgrade, the southern key to the Carpathian Basin. Five years later Suleiman the Magnificent led a great army into Hungary, and on August 28, 1526, at Mohács, the small Hungarian army attempting to defend the kingdom was almost annihilated.[7]

King Louis died in the battle and Hungary was without a ruler, just when her southern boundaries had been shattered by the Turk. Once again the problem of succession troubled Hungary, but this time it was resolved in the presence of the Turkish conquerer. John Zápolya was elected king by the eastern nobles and, by the grace of the sultan, was given possession of two-thirds of the kingdom. Ferdinand of Austria was elected by the western nobles who saw in him their only remaining hope. Upon the death of Zápolya in 1540 the Alföld center of Hungary was occupied by the Turks. For a century and a half thereafter Hungary was divided into three portions: the central core was under direct Turkish control, and minarets sprouted in Buda; the eastern bastion, Transylvania, remained virtually independent as an autonomous, nationalistic Magyar state; the northwestern strip was under the control of the Habsburgs. The three units acted independently of each other; in fact, the Magyar distrust of the Habsburgs became increasingly evident at this time, for the Transylvanians and the Austrians more often fought each other than coöperated against their supposed common enemy.

To a citizen of the twentieth century it may be surprising that Hungary did not disappear entirely. Although three monarchs ruled simultaneously, in theory at least the old kingdom remained intact. The western strips acquired by the Habsburgs were treated not as annexations to the pre-existing Austrian state, but as portions of a separate state. The additions were referred to as Habsburg Hungary, and the boundary of King Stephen remained; tariffs were collected along the border, and the Austrians continued their restrictions on Hungarian imports. Meanwhile, the princes of Transylvania were very conscious of the existence of a Hungary, and were willing to fight Vienna continually in order to maintain the Hungarian character of the Habsburg-held portion. Repeatedly Transylvanian armies moved through the valleys of present Slovakia to uphold the Hungarian constitution against the Habsburgs.

The continuance of the concept of the Kingdom of Hungary, when to all appearances the state had been dissolved, depended ultimately on the belief that an objective truth governed the social order. Despite the subjectivity of daily actions and events, there was an objective final truth; there was an established, often hierarchical, order in heaven and on earth. Despite disputes, rivalries, and wars, order provided the framework of medieval life and thinking. Within this ordered world, except for the ideal of an empire, the kingdom was the highest and final geo-political unit. Kingdoms were treated as established units and were not to be partitioned. Border rectifications were, of course, possible, but even a changed border required the passage of at least a century before it could be accepted as part of the fundamental areal order. Rulers of one state could gain control of another state, but even then the units remained individual and distinct.

The Kingdom of Hungary was an outstanding example of such an accepted unit. Since she had begun full-grown in terms of area, no one could question her territorial extent. The granting of the Crown of St. Stephen had guaranteed the separateness, the sovereignty of Hungary, and even when the state organization ceased to exist, the state idea, and hence the nation, continued to exist. Though the Turks were in Hungary for almost two centuries, it was always recognized that they were *in Hungary;* similarly, after 1526 the Habsburg emperor was not *Emperor* of Hungary, he was *King* of Hungary. In later years this was defined in those familiar initials, K. u. K., which adorned all of the Habsburg ordinances, *Kaiser und König*, Emperor of Austria *and* King of Hungary.

For a century and a half what is now Burgenland was part of the fighting frontier between the Habsburg and the Sultan. In times of peace the Turks were fifty to one hundred miles distant; in times of war they frequently swept over this borderland. Even in peaceful times the threat of raids from the east was constant. No topographic barrier of any significance separated the borderland villages from the plains of the Carpathian Basin, so that defense of the frontier was difficult; the horsemen from the east had the advantages of surprise and unhampered movement. For five centuries these border holdings had faced west to protect Hungary from Austrian attacks; now they were forced to face a danger from the rear. They no longer were guardians only of an international boundary, but now were on the front line of Europe, facing the newest invader from the east.

During these decades the old fortresses were strengthened, but they served no important military function except as places of refuge. For the Turks a fortress was not worthwhile storming unless it sheltered a city. The raiders sought booty and slaves, and they simply rode by the medieval fortresses perched atop their steep rock spurs. Thus walled cities were invested, but Forchtenstein, Bernstein, Güssing, and Schlaining escaped unscathed.

For the peasant of the plains the fortresses were often too far distant to be reached in time. Local defense was necessary against the sudden terror of a raid, and as a result many villages were built compactly, like miniature fortress towns. A fine surviving example is Purbach, west of Lake Neusiedl. In the center of the village are the church, administrative offices, and stores; around this small central core are the homes, and facing outward, forming the periphery, are the stone barns, whose connected walls form a continuous fortification around the village. During the time of the Turkish invasions the village could be entered only from the west, and there only by passing through two low arches, which could be barred. In Purbach one legend of Turkish days has been perpetuated in stone; a comical statue of a Turk sits atop a chimney and is supposed to represent a Turk who was baked while attempting to enter a house. The Burgenland churches which date from the sixteenth century are obviously designed to serve not only as places of worship but also as emergency refuges. An interesting tower in the center of Breitenbrunn (a village north of Purbach) is said to have served this purpose.

In times of mass invasion, the peasants fled as best they could. No village could hope to withstand a Turkish assault, and the Turks were known to be ruthless in their treatment of the inhabitants once the attack had succeeded. To this day the people of Hainburg are more than willing to show the visitor the height to which the blood is said to have risen during the mass extermination by the Turks in 1683. Villages had little hope of escaping destruction, but on the other hand, the walled cities offered not only defense against the invaders but also the possibility of negotiation. A city such as Sopron or Eisenstadt could purchase its freedom, whereas a village such as Purbach was in no position to do so.

During the Turkish occupation of Hungary the position of the border was not static. It was more a fluctuating frontier than a precise boundary, a frontier which followed the line of the Bakony hills and Lake Balaton. All the areas to the south and east were continually under Turkish control until after 1683, so that despite numerous Austrian campaigns, Buda and Székesfehérvár [8] remained Turkish. To the northwest of the hill chain, a second line of defense ran along the Rába River. Except in times of invasions or raids all the territory west of the Rába was in the hands of the Habsburgs. Between Lake Balaton and the Rába River was a broad no man's land. Cities in this area changed hands frequently and ceased to exist as cities, becoming finally nothing more than key road junctions. The belt of the Bakony hills was devoid of population, and became in effect a glacis between the two forces. The wasted character of this belt is obvious from all the language maps of Central Europe, on which the Bakony appears as a German-speaking zone flanked by Magyars. In the eighteenth century Germans were brought in to repopulate the empty lands. The Danube formed the only clearly defined, unvarying boundary in western Hungary. Whereas the frontier moved back and forth in the Dunántúl, the Turk crossed the Danube in force only once, in 1666. The wide river was a major barrier and relatively little was to be gained by forcing a crossing; the roads to Vienna and beyond remained south of the Danube. Thus the two major fortresses on the north bank of the river, Pozsony (Bratislava) and Komárom (Komárno), were never captured by the Turks.

The location of the fighting frontier, passing directly through the center of the Dunántúl, was a catastrophe for Hungary. The original core area of the kingdom, the region that had given birth to the kingdom, was cruelly wasted. Székesfehérvár, the old capital, was almost obliterated.

One result of the Turkish ravages was a change in the make-up of the population of the present province of Burgenland. The attacks on Vienna, and the siege of Kőszeg in 1532, had depopulated broad extents of the lowlands.[9] Following the Turkish withdrawal to the Bakony area, the border nobles turned to the task of repopulating their devastated holdings. Magyars were not available for the task, and the Germans hesitated to emerge from the safety of the mountains. On the other hand, Croats were willing to leave their homeland to the south and occupy the fertile areas closer to the protective might of the Habsburgs. Thus the majority of the new settlers were Croatian. At the present time in Burgenland the Croats form clusters of villages in the Sopron and Bruck gateways and in the flat areas north and south of Kőszeg. This initial colonization took place in the first half of the sixteenth century.[10] Later, new Croatian settlement areas were carved out of the forests on the upper surfaces of the gravel terraces.

In 1683 the Turks moved en masse over the flat terrain north and east of Lake Neusiedl, and every village in the area was destroyed. However, when the lowlands were recolonized later, the threat of the enemy no longer hung over the Little Alföld. The Ottoman had been driven out of the land for good, and for the first time in almost two centuries the settlers could feel secure. Germans poured out of the crowded Alpine valleys and migrated from southwestern Germany to occupy the available land. Since that time, the region has been predominantly German speaking, with but a few Croatian islands. Thus, the part of Burgenland which most resembles the Alföld in appearance and way of life came to be almost thoroughly German.

The Turkish period witnessed also a change in the religious affiliation of many of the people of Hungary. Mohács coincided with the beginnings of the Protestant Reformation. Most of the kingdom's higher ecclesiastics had fallen at Mohács, and the lower clergy, left leaderless, vacillated between the old and the new forms of Christianity. Lutheran preachers soon made their appearance and for a time there seems to have been considerable religious confusion. For the nobility the new system of belief presented a unique opportunity; the faith was still clearly Christian, and yet seemed to sever the bond that forced submission to the emperor or king. Whether through religious conviction, or through political expediency, many of the nobles of Hungary turned Protestant.

Seen in retrospect, the concept of the state, the Holy Crown of King St. Stephen, seems to have been firmly established on Catholic belief, but this fact was not recognized at the time. Just as Catholic churches could be readily transformed into Protestant churches, so the crown could remain a religious symbol for the Protestants. What was clear, especially by the seventeenth century, was the fact that the Habsburg claimant to the crown was an avowed Catholic and a champion of the Counter Reformation. Religion and state policy were intimately tied together, and opposition to the Habsburgs, which became virtually an obsession in eastern Hungary and Transylvania, almost predetermined that the nobility of the east would be Protestant. Yet, the Magyar nobles would not become Lutheran, since that religion would have implied a tie to a German faith. Thus, in eastern Hungary the nobility became Calvinist,[11] whereas in western Hungary the nobility either remained Catholic, or if they had changed their affiliation, were convinced by Habsburg persuasion to return to Catholicism. The city dwellers, most of whom were German speaking, generally turned Lutheran. The peasants, by and large, everywhere followed the religion of their masters.

Along the western border most of the nobility was by the seventeenth century once again Catholic; however islands of Protestantism remained, principally among the upland peasants. Though the Calvinists and Lutherans were repressed, they could not be forced back into the old faith simply because they were within Hungary. The nobles of eastern Hungary considered an attack on their religion to be an attack on the nation, and often fought for their religious freedom and national identity under one banner. The rebellions of Bocskai in 1604, Bethlen in 1620, George Rákóczy in 1644, Tököly in 1678 and 1683, and Francis Rákóczy [12] in 1703–11, were all against Austrian attempts to control Hungary in religion as well as in administration. As a result of these struggles against Austrian control, the Protestants of Hungary enjoyed relative freedom of worship at a time when such freedom was not possible within Austria.

These religious struggles must, however, be placed within the context of the thinking of the time. It is unjust to project present attitudes into the past and automatically to consider the Habsburg as the villain. The Austrian emperors acted in this regard much as did the other rulers of the time. In fact, it is probable that the principal reason why Hungary did not become uniform in religion was that she was not ruled by a hand strong enough to enforce such a uniformity, either Catholic or Protestant.

In the seventeenth century national unity, and the assimilation necessary to produce this unity, were thought of in religious rather than in linguistic terms. Just as we now rarely consider uniformity of religion to be vital to the existence of a European state, so the rulers of that time did not believe linguistic uniformity to be important. A commonly held religious belief was a means of securing the loyalty of illiterate peasants. In most countries the citizens were expected to adhere to the religion of their ruler, and heresy was often considered to be treason. This was true of almost all the states of Europe at the time. For the Habsburg, therefore, the Counter Reformation was more than a return to the ancient faith; it was also a means of bringing about the unification of his lands. For the Magyar lord, in contrast, the Reformation was a means of asserting and maintaining the separateness of Hungary from Austria.

In view of this, it is interesting that both Catholicism and Protestantism contributed essentially to the Hungarian state idea. Even during the Habsburg centuries the Catholics of Hungary were strongly nationalistic, but their nationalism was based on that historic symbol, the Crown of St. Stephen. They remained generally loyal to the Habsburg but insisted that the crown of Hungary was distinct from the crown of the Holy Roman Empire or of Austria. They emphasized the historic individuality of the kingdom, whereas the Protestants fought for the contemporary individuality of the nation. In the nineteenth century the two religious traditions joined forces in the rebellion of 1848–49, and later in the reconstruction of the Hungarian state.

Pozsony (Bratislava, Pressburg)

The principal city of Hungary during the Turkish occupation was Pozsony. Following the capture of Buda and Székesfehérvár, the center of Hungarian government was transferred to this place further to the west and north of the protective Danube barrier. The royal crown and scepter were moved to Pozsony, and the city's Gothic cathedral became the new coronation church of the Hungarian kings. For two hundred and forty-three years (1541–1784) Pozsony was the capital of Hungary, and it remained the meeting place of the Hungarian parliament until the revolution of 1848. The city came to symbolize the survival of the kingdom despite the Turkish occupation, and despite Austrian attempts to absorb Hungary into a centralized Habsburg state. Until the sudden growth of Budapest at the end of the eighteenth century, Pozsony remained the largest and wealthiest city in the kingdom.

The city is situated on the northern bank of the Danube at the foot of the Little Carpathians. The location of Pozsony is much like that of Vienna; here also the Danube issues from a gorge and begins to braid into several channels. The spread of wet land below Pozsony is considerably larger than that below Vienna, and one of the islands was large enough to be the subject of a special discussion at the Paris Peace Conference in 1919. The center of the city has always been immediately below the hills, at the crossing point, where the roads along the eastern flank of the Carpathians and around the Danubian marshes come to the river. This site has long had military significance, and perched on the hill above the city is the famous castle with its four towers high in the air.

In the first centuries A.D. Pozsony seems to have been a minor commercial center; it served as the link between Carnuntum and present Slovakia. However the principal Roman posts were west of the Little Carpathians in the March valley.[18] As Brezalauspurc, Pozsony was important to the Moravian state, but the mouth of the March at Devín was still the more significant site. The March valley was the principal north-south routeway, and Brezalauspurc was separated by the mountain spur from this route.

Pozsony did not become important until the establishment of the Kingdom of Hungary. In that sense it has been a Magyar-created city. Even though German-speaking merchants and artisans developed the site, the city depended upon the settlement of the Carpathian Basin for its growth and greatness. The location of the boundary along the March had destroyed the ancient north-south road; consequently just as the Austrians built a new road further west (towards Brno), so the Hungarians constructed a counterpart to the east and focused it on Pozsony. As a result of the position of the boundary, Pozsony became, along with Vienna, a replacement for Carnuntum as a trading center of the Danube-March confluence area.[14]

During the five centuries of Hungarian power, Pozsony was one of the two or three largest cities of the kingdom. All of the trade of Upper Hungary (Slovakia) to and from Vienna was funneled through this frontier post. Because of the attenuated Carpathian ridge, traffic from Vienna moved along the Danube corridor to this point, and then from here fanned out into present Slovakia. (No Hungarian city south of the Danube had such a control of trade routes.) Upper Hungary was from the thirteenth century an important source of minerals. The mining towns of the Slovakian valleys poured a stream of precious metals into Europe. The metals that were exported passed through Pozsony on their way to Vienna. Even if the metals were not exported, the value of the minerals was reflected in the increased purchasing power of the lords and burghers of Upper Hungary; the goods that these wealthy men wished to import from Western Europe passed through Pozsony.

Pozsony controlled not only the trade of Upper Hungary with Vienna, but also the traffic that tried to by-pass Vienna. Most of the production of the vineyards of the Dunántúl was not permitted to enter Austria, so this wine was shipped through Hungary to the markets of Moravia, Poland, and Silesia. From Sopron, Rust, Eisenstadt, and even the Bakony hills, the fine wines moved northward and crossed the Danube at Pozsony.[15] In return, the manufactured products that had been imported from Cracow and Brno crossed the Danube at Pozsony to reach the rich markets south of the river. By the fourteenth century the city had become one of the major markets of East Central Europe.

With the crushing of the Hungarian armies at Mohács, Pozsony gained added significance; it became the repository of the precious crown. Thus, in a political as well as a commercial sense, it served as the link between Vienna and Hungary. Since most of Habsburg Hungary lay north of the Danube, almost all contact between Vienna and Hungary passed through Pozsony. Whatever wealth remained in

Hungary was likewise north of the Danube, and thus was controlled by Pozsony. The rebellious Transylvanian lords always marched on the new capital, and unless they gained control of the city their rebellion could not be considered a success. Here the Magyar nobles met in their parliament; here they defied Vienna, and here they set down the conditions which the Habsburg emperor had to meet if he were to be crowned king of Hungary.

Buda was recaptured from the Turks in 1686, but Pozsony remained the capital and coronation city for one more century, and the meeting place of the parliament for still another sixty years. The Austrian rulers preferred to have the Hungarian government close to Vienna. Although Pozsony was surpassed by the new cities of the Alföld in the nineteenth century, it remained a symbol of the national will to survive. Its award to the newly created Czechoslovakia in 1919 was one of the most bitter losses imposed by the post–World War I peace treaties.[16]

The most famous events of the Turkish wars were undoubtedly the advances on Vienna, for in these two assaults the Ottoman Moslem was assailing the gate to Western Europe. It is a significant sign of the politics of the time that both advances were undertaken at the request of the nobles of eastern Hungary.

In 1529 John Zápolya, the candidate of the eastern nobles, re-quested Turkish aid in his struggle with the Habsburg claimant to the throne. A huge Turkish force under Suleiman the Magnificent ad-vanced from Belgrade to Buda to secure the Hungarian capital for Zápolya, and then, almost as an afterthought, turned toward Vienna. The main army moved through the Győr gap and the Bruck and Hainburg gateways, while smaller units penetrated the Sopron Gate-way and laid siege to Wiener Neustadt. With a force of over 100,000 men, the sultan besieged Vienna, guarded by only 16,000 men. Turk-ish units scoured the countryside for scores of miles in all directions, but after a siege of only twenty-four days the Turks withdrew into Hungary. Possibly time as much as any other factor had saved Vienna. Because of the delays en route the Turks did not lay siege to the city until late September. They were then far from their base of operations, and amid strange surroundings, with the approach of winter threaten-ing their long march back into the Balkans. On October 14, the Turks retired.

In 1683 the Magyar leader, Tököly, who was vigorously opposing the efforts of the Habsburgs towards imposing centralized control from Vienna upon all their holdings, called upon the Turks for assistance. Once again an army of a quarter of a million men moved across Hungary towards Vienna. This time, however, the purpose of the advance was clear, and by mid-July the host, under the command of the Grand Vizier, Kara Mustapha, had laid siege to the city. Vienna was defended by only 10,000 troops, and was forced to care not only for its normal population but for crowds of refugees as well. The emperor had fled westward to Passau, and, because of the anti-Habsburg diplomacy of Louis XIV, could turn only to the Poles for assistance.

The response of King Sobieski to the appeal of the emperor is the last outstanding example of that chivalry which had once been the pride of Europe. The medieval concept of Christendom was being supplanted by the concept of the amoral national state, and the theory that "might makes right," which motivated so many of these states, was within a century to destroy Sobieski's feudal kingdom. Twenty-six thousand Polish troops marched to the relief of Vienna, and on the Kahlenberg overlooking the city they joined the imperial troops that the emperor had been able to muster. The magnificent charge on September 12, 1683, is certainly one of the greatest military acts of European history. The Polish-German forces were heavily outnumbered, and yet they swept all before them.[17]

This victory did more than save Vienna; it marked the end of effective Turkish power in Europe. In the next three decades a succession of imperial victories drove the Turks out of Hungary and back into the Balkans. Sobieski himself did not wait in Vienna to enjoy the plaudits of the burghers and of the emperor, but continued after the fleeing Turks and defeated them twice more that autumn. The Treaty of Passarowitz in 1718 sealed the complete liberation of the Kingdom of Hungary from the Turks. For the first time in two centuries the entire Carpathian Basin was under one political jurisdiction.

Because of its successful resistance to the Ottoman sieges, Vienna gained fame as the final defender of Western Europe. Yet, while the significance of the Viennese victories cannot be overstated, it must be realized that the Turkish threat that faced Vienna and Austria was never as serious or as sustained as the threat that faced Hungary during the fifteenth and sixteenth centuries. The feat of Hungary in withstanding the Turks for over a century was a far greater achievement than that of Vienna in withstanding two sieges.

The southern Balkans had early become the core of the Ottoman Empire. As has been pointed out, the Turks conquered the Balkans before they gained control of Asia Minor. All the pathways towards

Central Europe from this Balkan center of the Ottoman state ran through Hungary. Thus the kingdom was in the tragic position of bearing the entire frontier of Central Europe with the Turks. The mountains along the southern periphery of the Carpathian Basin were but scant protection for Hungary; these uplands lay south of the Sava frontier, and so could be held only weakly by the Hungarians. The hills of northern Serbia faced northward; they overlooked the plain and made a fine defensive position for the Turks but a very poor defensive line for the Hungarians. The valleys of the Balkans offered broad, direct paths to the southern borders of Hungary. These paths converged on Belgrade, and once the Turks had taken this key point, Hungary lay open to the north. Only the massed armed might of the kingdom could stop a Turkish advance northward from Belgrade.

The situation was very different for Vienna. The mountains behind the imperial capital formed a mighty bulwark upon and behind which defending troops could muster. Toward the east a series of natural defense lines protected Vienna and all of Austria. Furthest to the east was the line of Lake Balaton and the Bakony hills. Behind the forested hill chain was the Rába River, and then Lake Neusiedl and the Hanság marshes. Finally, behind the marshes was the Leitha Range, with the fortresses of Hainburg, Bruck, and Wiener Neustadt guarding the gateways into the Vienna Basin. Only a concerted, driving attack by the Turks could hope to reach Vienna.

These natural means of defense were highly important in the defense of Vienna; however, of even greater importance was the fundamental contrast for the Turks between the Balkans and Hungary as a base of military operations. The Balkans were an integral part of the Ottoman realm and formed an ideal base of operations for the Turkish forces. Suleiman's army which assembled at Belgrade in 1526 had only to cross the adjacent Sava River to enter Hungary. Behind Belgrade the lines of communications were well developed and secure. In contrast, Hungary never became a base of operations for further Turkish advances. The Alföld had been severely depopulated by the campaigns of 1526–41; the broad plains were desolate. A Turkish army wishing to advance beyond Hungary was forced to transport its equipment, as well as the troops themselves, from the Balkans through the breadth of the kingdom. On the open plains lines of communications were dangerously exposed, and the remnant population could offer but paltry supplies to the passing soldiers. (It is little wonder that the troops of Suleiman and Kara Mustapha scoured the landscape like locusts when they reached the lush, productive, pre-Alpine valleys.) Sheer distance, made more difficult by the four hundred miles of utter wasteland, was as responsible for maintaining the freedom of Vienna from Turkish conquest as was the armed might of Austria. Even in her hundred and sixty years of desolation, Hungary remained the principal bulwark of Europe against the Turk.

Within Hungary, the twenty years of warfare required to drive out the Turks completed the devastation that had been started two centuries previously. The southern portions of the plain were almost completely depopulated. In 1692, after Austrian troops had reconquered the Dunántúl, the area between Lake Balaton, the Danube, and the Drava (roughly the southeastern half of the Dunántúl) had a total population of only 3,221, and half of this pitiful number was in the city of Pécs.[18] The Hungarians maintained that these lands were "recovered," but the Austrians claimed that they were "conquered." Thus, while the Hungarian administration requested the return of all the lands of the old kingdom, the Viennese authorities retained direct control of the southern areas for over a century.[19] During these important decades the empty areas were extensively resettled, but generally not with Magyars. The Viennese, who had had their fill of Hungarian rebellions, understandably preferred to introduce other ethnic groups. Germans were given preference,[20] but many other linguistic groups were also invited in to occupy the land. As a result, the Banat of Temesvár became the home of an intriguing mixture of peoples. Germans, Romanians, Serbs, Slovaks, even French and Italians were settled in a scattered pattern over the flat plains. In the Banat the Germans formed a plurality, but not a majority, and gained control of the key cities. The southernmost portions of the plain were populated with Serbs who readily moved northward onto the southern fringes of the Alföld from the mountains, which remained under Turkish control. In the Dunántúl the Germans were favored as settlers, and they occupied the Bakony hills and the southeastern corner near Pécs.

The patterns of resettlement sewed the seeds of dissolution of the old kingdom. The Turkish occupation had not destroyed the kingdom because the concept of the crown and the nation had remained alive among the survivors of that critical time. But with the mass importation of new peoples, most of whom did not share this concept, the durability of the kingdom was seriously threatened. The Magyars had been in a special sense the bearers of the state idea, and it was the Magyars who had suffered the most seriously. The other linguistic groups had occupied the mountainous periphery of the basin and had escaped the Turkish wars relatively unscathed, whereas the Magyars, the plainsmen, had borne the full rigors of the occupation and warfare. Thus Hungary became a state of minorities just before language was to become a major factor in the life of European states. With the advent of the principle of linguistic nationalism early in the nineteenth century, Hungary was faced with the need to redevelop her state idea, but with too little time to effect this essential redevelopment.

Within present Burgenland, the principal social change during the Turkish decades was the rise of a new nobility. During the numerous Hungarian rebellions, the Habsburg emperor replaced several of the older, disloyal nobles with new lords whose loyalty was unquestioned. These new magnates then became enormously wealthy by acquiring vast estates in the reconquered Alföld. The fertile plain was parceled out by the Habsburg monarchs among their favorites, so that the empty lands could be put rapidly into production.

The most outstanding of these favorites was Prince Eszterházy. Considering their enormous wealth in recent centuries, it is natural to suppose that this family is very old and began as feudal estate holders during the early centuries of the kingdom. Actually, the Eszterházy family did not become wealthy or prominent until the early part of the seventeenth century. They were initially natives of Upper Hungary (Slovakia), from the vicinity of Pozsony. The family name was first taken by Miklós Alispán, a member of the lesser nobility, who acquired some land through his two marriages, and later gained royal favor by negotiating the treaties between the Habsburg and Transylvania.

Because of its continued loyalty to the Habsburg during the seventeenth century, the Eszterházy family increased its holdings enormously. With the treaty of 1626, the Hungarian nobility under Bethlen Gábor demanded that the emperor return to Hungary the border estates that the Habsburgs had gained at the Treaty of Pressburg in 1491; as a result Frederick II sold the estates, over a period of years, to his close friend and loyal supporter, Nicholas Eszterházy. Thus Nicholas gained possession of Eisenstadt and Forchtenstein in the Sopron Gateway, as well as Kobersdorf on the south flank of the Sopron Range; in 1702 a later prince gained Hornstein, adjacent to Eisenstadt. By the early part of the eighteenth century the Eszterházy prince was the largest landowner in Hungary, and the representative of the king (the palatine) in Hungary. Within western Hungary his holdings included Lockenhaus, Köszeg, and areas around Sopron, in addition to the afore-mentioned estates. So great did his holdings become that when Burgenland was ceded to Austria in 1921 Eszterházy became the largest landowner in Austria as well as within Hungary.[21]

The seventeenth and eighteenth centuries witnessed the strengthening of those tendencies generally associated with feudalism. The *robot* (forced labor on the lord's lands), the virtual slavery of the peasants, and the lack of freedom to leave the estates were in Hungary more a product of the "Age of the Enlightenment" than of the Middle Ages.[22] The forces of nationalism helped to maintain the power of the nobles. The opposition of Hungary to the centralization tendencies of the Habsburgs was until the late eighteenth century the responsibility of the nobles, and the nobles in turn depended upon the land for their power. By their control of the kingdom's revenue the nobles were able to force the hand of the emperor. Land was of vital importance, particularly in Hungary, which had no industry and little commerce. As Austria and Western Europe became more and more urbanized the market for Hungarian grain and meat expanded accordingly.[23] Large-scale agriculture was an increasingly profitable enterprise, and the landed nobility became, in consequence, fabulously wealthy.

The Eszterházy princes were for almost two centuries among the richest men of Europe.[24] During the early days of the Industrial Revolution in the West, Hungary was an important source of raw wool, and the Eszterházys led all of Hungary in the export of wool. In Eisenstadt, their principal manorial center within present Burgenland, the princes built one of the first (1673) large palaces of Hungary. Here the prince was entertained by his court orchestra, chorus, and theatre; here Joseph Haydn served as music director and composed many of his masterpieces. Later, even this palace became too simple for the luxurious tastes of the Eszterházys, and they built a new, fabulous palace, Eszterháza, at the edge of the marshes south of Lake Neusiedl. Esterháza served as a summer palace for royalty as well as nobility; its grandeur was said to be rivalled only by Versailles.

During the seventeenth and eighteenth centuries many lesser palaces were built within the western fringe of Hungary. The lords spent the winter in Vienna, but in summer they moved to these immense, baroque "summer houses" in the hills and plains of the western Dunántúl. Burgenland contains many of these mansions; they were severely damaged during the Russian occupation of 1945–55 but still remain as symbols of the ostentatious way of life of the lords of the land. Kittsee, Halbturn, Eisenstadt, Lackenbach, Deutschkreutz, Pinkafeld, Rechnitz, Rotenturm, Güssing, and St. Martin an der Raab are just the larger of these palaces; many lesser structures dot the land throughout Burgenland and in the neighboring portions of Hungary. Within these palaces the nobles enjoyed a manner of living that was rare in Western Europe by the late eighteenth century. One of the reasons why these Hungarian magnates were so fascinating to their western contemporaries may have been the fact that they seemed to be such anachronisms. Western Europe had advanced to a city culture; Hungary had regressed to an extreme form of a manorial culture.

For most of the nobles the unceasing flow of riches led to a certain debilitation and stagnation of social development. The accumulation of wealth required no initiative; the nobleman had little to do but spend his income as pretentiously as possible. He commonly left his estates (too numerous to be supervised personally in any case) in the hands of trusted, efficient land managers. The lord himself could then spend the summer months in his palace(s), and the winter months in either Vienna or Budapest. If this life proved monotonous, there was always the possibility of travel to a fashionable spa. A trip through present-day Burgenland is almost a sermon on the demoralizing effects of unearned wealth. The palaces, with a few exceptions such as Eisenstadt, are all in ruins—shattered, destroyed, burnt, sometimes (Rechnitz) even levelled. The cause was not in all cases merely the Russian occupation; often the decline of the family itself brought about such ruin. The family members have scattered, become dissolute, committed suicide, or just disappeared. Large landholdings still remain in Burgenland, but they are far fewer than they were in 1922, and few of the old noble family names survive in the area except as memories.

For almost three and a half centuries Hungary had been the frontier of Western Christendom against the Turk, and for almost two of those centuries the Turkish wars had been fought principally within her borders. Largely because of the results of this age of devastation the kingdom entered the nineteenth century out of step with the times. While the Industrial Revolution was beginning to transform Western Europe, a baroque feudalism characterized Hungary. Whereas in the West the powers of government were gradually being extended to include the majority of the population, within Hungary the magnates clung jealously to their political power on the basis of a medieval constitution. And when language and nationality were to become synonymous terms and the bases of fanatical emotions, Hungary had become a polyglot state. To many nineteenth-century observers Hungary seemed an anachronism within Europe; she seemed a medieval state within a modern, revolutionary world.

9

NATIONALISM

Throughout the centuries of Turkish occupation and Habsburg rule the state idea of the Kingdom of Hungary remained alive and vigorous. Hungarians may have divided into eastern and western factions on the question of whether or not the Habsburg was to be the king of Hungary, but the continued individuality and separateness of Hungary was never questioned. The country was *not* to become just another province of Austria; she was to remain the Kingdom of Hungary.

After 1526 the primary fear of the Hungarians (particularly of the east) was of an Austrian strangulation of the kingdom. Even during the Turkish occupation, the nobility of eastern Hungary felt that the Austrian monarch posed a greater threat to Hungary's individual existence than did the sultan.[1] Perhaps it seemed evident that the Turkish occupation, no matter how prolonged, was nothing more than an occupation, and that the essential character of the kingdom could not be changed by the imposition of a completely alien rule. The Habsburg, however, threatened to absorb Hungary within the German empire.

The nobles, who were for two centuries the guardians of the state idea, fought Vienna on every proposed administrative and social change. These changes were often intended for the greater prosperity of the inhabitants of Hungary, so that the Hungarian leaders were placed in the dilemma of having to choose between economic advancement and the complete retention of their medieval constitution.[2] Almost invariably the maintenance of the constitution was preferred to the acceptance of any imposed changes. Since the venerable statute granted the Hungarian nobility full political power and freedom from taxation, self-interest was obviously involved in the attitude of the nobles.[3] Yet, for three centuries little opposition to this ultraconservative policy developed within Hungary. Any Viennese edict that would alter the old constitution was resisted, literally to the death, because its acceptance would mean the certain loss of a part of the true sovereignty of Hungary.

By means of the many revolts of the seventeenth century, the Magyar lords succeeded in retaining their constitution and in forcing the Habsburgs to return the major western manors to Hungarian nobles. Transylvania was too far from Austria to be long held by the imperial armies, and it served as a secure base of opposition to the Habsburgs for two centuries. In the greatest of all the rebellions (1703–11), the forces of Francis Rákóczy came so close to Vienna that a ring of fortifications was constructed around the city. Before the Habsburg could be crowned king of Hungary he was made to promise to uphold the individuality and intactness of Hungary, and not until after the Rákóczy rebellion did the Habsburg succession to the throne of St. Stephen become automatic.

In contrast to the stormy seventeenth century, relations between Hungary and Austria were singularly peaceful in the mid-eighteenth century. Empress Maria Theresa well knew how to mollify the proud Hungarian nobles and how to make the most of their chivalrous feelings towards their queen.[4] The Magyar nobles erected fine homes in the center of Vienna, and came to spend much of their time in the imperial capital.

The time of amity ended suddenly in 1780 with the accession of Joseph II to the throne. Joseph was an idealistic product of the Enlightenment, and he made a concerted effort to centralize the administration of his domains. The royal crown and scepter of Hungary were moved from Pozsony to Vienna, the old Hungarian megyek were replaced by larger administrative districts, and German was declared to be the official language of the entire Habsburg Empire. Hungarian reaction to these measures was, true to the national character, spontaneous and unyielding; the chauvinism that became so characteristic of nineteenth-century Hungary can be said to have had its beginnings in the virulent resistance to the edicts of Emperor Joseph. So extreme was the Magyar resistance to his edicts that Joseph abrogated most of them upon his death bed, in 1790.

With the start of the nineteenth century, new emotions were added to the older nationalisms. The significance of language and "race," or *Volk*, was emphasized and strongly intensified the self-consciousness of ethnic groups. In Hungary at this time poets and intellectuals replaced the nobles as the bearers of the nationalistic ideal, and the newly released feelings were superimposed upon the centuries-old passion for the intactness of the lands of the Crown of King Stephen. This emotional-intellectual fermentation culminated in the revolution of 1848–49, which the Hungarians had virtually won until the intervention of the Russian Army crushed the rebellion.

Although Hungary was once again suppressed and the megyek were again replaced with administrative districts, it was only a matter of time before the Hungarians succeeded in having their demands for virtual independence met, since Hungary had in fact become too powerful to be controlled by Vienna. Following the doubtful victory in 1849, Franz Joseph attempted several solutions of the Hungarian problem. For the Hungarians, however, any measure which threatened the intactness of the kingdom or militated against her historic autonomy was unacceptable. It was not until after the Prussian defeat of the Austrian armies, in 1866, that Franz Joseph officially yielded to the Hungarians. The *Ausgleich* of 1867 confirmed the separateness of Hungary from Austria; it virtually established an independent Hungary.[5] The military and foreign affairs remained in the hands of the emperor, but in all other matters Austria and Hungary were separate. It is interesting to note that many Hungarians objected even to this remaining tie with Austria.

The decades after 1867 were difficult ones for the emperor-king. Although Hungary did not contain Vienna or the majority of the population, the kingdom was indispensable to the Habsburg Empire. She occupied the strategic central portion of the Dual Monarchy; Austrian territory formed a narrow, elongated arc around the bulk of Hungary. In addition, the newly acquired Balkan territories, Bosnia and Herzegovina, were separated from all other Austrian territory by the Fiume corridor of Hungary. If Hungary had ever chosen to secede from the Dual Monarchy, Austria would probably have collapsed, since without Hungary Vienna could scarcely hope to maintain control over Bohemia, much less over the remote Galicia, Bukovina, and Bosnia.

During the half-century following the Ausgleich, the Hungarians remained true to their old ideal. Their primary loyalty was not to the Habsburg, much less to the Dual Monarchy; it was simply to Hungary. All their thinking was focused on Hungary, and if Austria suffered as a consequence, that was unfortunate. Adult Hungarians remembered only too well the brutal repressions of the 1850's, and after 350 years of conflict with the Habsburg, the Hungarians could scarcely be expected to trust the emperor. They felt too that the Ausgleich was nothing to be grateful for, since they realized that Franz Joseph had not had much choice in 1866–67. Nevertheless, this distrust might have been softened through mutual self-interest had it not been for the repeated renegotiation of the Ausgleich. Every ten years the Austrian and Hungarian leaders had to agree upon the proportions of the mutual expense of the empire that was to be met by each of the two partner states. Thus once every decade the continued existence of the Dual Monarchy was jeopardized, as the Hungarians tried to gain new concessions. As long as Franz Joseph lived, the loyalty to the emperor-king remained a unifying force, but Franz Joseph died in 1916, on the eve of the deliberations for the new Ausgleich. The 1917 negotiations were very prolonged, and it is interesting to speculate what might have happened, with the old king gone, had not World War I been in progress at the time.

Following the Ausgleich of 1867, Austria and Hungary attempted to develop their territories as if they were independent of each other. Of course, Hungary could not avoid the commercial and industrial predominance of Austria, and particularly Vienna. Yet, as much as possible the Hungarians made Budapest the center of national life. The rail net, which was constructed in the late nineteenth century, drew all parts of the kingdom to the capital. As a result of these efforts, the government of Hungary became far more centralized than that of Austria; within Hungary Budapest gained a predominance above that of Vienna within Austria. There were in Hungary no local centers on a par with Innsbruck, Salzburg, Prague, or Cracow.

As far as the area of Burgenland was concerned, attempts were made to turn the border dwellers away from Vienna and towards Budapest. Outstanding examples of these efforts were the routes of railroad construction; except for the international connections, the Hungarian rail lines either paralleled or stopped short of the Austrian border. Thus, in southern Burgenland a line led from the rail hub of Szombathely up the Pinka valley to the last village within Hungary, Pinkafeld. The stub end of this line was only five miles from an Austrian line connecting to both Vienna and Graz, but no contact was effected. On the Austrian side of the boundary the "Aspang Line" paralleled the Lafnitz boundary but never touched Hungarian soil. Roads were similarly directed away from the border. The deterioration of Hungarian roads as one approached the Austrian boundary became legendary in Burgenland.

Obviously the border areas could not be turned completely away from Vienna. The metropolis was too large, too glamorous, too much of a job hunter's paradise, and much too close to the boundary to be ignored. The animals, grain, sugar, fruit, wine, and milk of the plains around Lake Neusiedl moved in a continuing flow towards the great urban market of Vienna. On weekends crowds of workers shuttled back and forth between their jobs in Vienna and their families in what is now northern Burgenland. Even beyond this local movement, Vienna continued to control traffic between Hungary and Western Europe. Thus, no matter how much Budapest came to dominate the internal life of the kingdom, the connections between Hungary and the rest of the world still passed principally through Vienna.

BUDAPEST

Few cities dominate their countries as completely as Budapest does Hungary. The capital is the center of all the administrative, educational, cultural, intellectual, commercial, and industrial life of Hungary. In fact, there are few non-Hungarians who know of any other Hungarian city; Budapest is uniquely "the city of the Magyars."

The setting of Budapest is, like that of Vienna and Bratislava, at the eastern end of a river gap, but unlike Vienna, Budapest straddles the broad Danube. Budapest differs from Vienna also in that the present city center is not on the site of the Roman city. Since A.D. 376 the urban core has moved five miles south and across the river. This shift in the location of the urban core has been due to the settlement of the Alföld and to the length of the gorge cut through the Bakony-Börzsöny range by the Danube. The gorge begins opposite the mouth of the Hron (Gran) River; there the Danube has cut into the flank of the Pilis Hills, the last clump of the Bakony. At this point, on the sides and top of the steep slope is Esztergom (Gran), the first capital of Hungary. Adjacent to Esztergom is a small lowland, from the southern end of which a narrow valley cuts across the curve of the river and separates the Pilis from the remainder of the Bakony (see Map 5).

Ten miles east of Esztergom the Danube passes through the narrowest portion of the gorge, where steep slopes border the river on both banks. On the heights above the southern bank is Visegrád, a fortress city which enjoyed considerable importance in the Middle Ages and gave its name to an important commercial treaty. Visegrád was in a position to control river traffic much as was its Austrian counterpart, Dürnstein, in the Wachau.

Just to the east of Visegrád the Danube begins its sweeping curve toward the south. In the middle of the curve, on the northeastern bank, is Vác (Waitzen), another of the historic towns of Hungary. At

Vác a road leaves the Danube and runs northward into the Ipel valley, and thence into the broad valleys of eastern Slovakia. Because it was the link between these valleys and the heart of the state, Vác was one of the original bishoprics of Hungary.

Fifteen miles south of Vác on the western bank is the site of Roman Aquincum. A small lowland extends for several miles back from the Danube, and at the inner end of this plain is the narrow valley which cuts across the river bend from Esztergom. Whereas on the eastern bank the uplands extend no further south than the general vicinity of Aquincum, on the western bank they again approach the river. At the base of these hills is Óbuda (Old Buda). In the middle of the Danube is the last of a number of small islands, the Margit Sziget (Margaret Island).

South of Óbuda the upland breaks into a number of separated heights. These isolated, mesa-like features were admirable for defensive purposes in medieval times, and the center of present Buda is at the foot of two of them. Directly across the river, upon the flat plain, is the center of Pest. Two miles south of the centers of Buda and Pest the Danube is split by a large island, the Csepel Sziget. At Budafok, three miles further south, lies the last hill along the western bank. Beyond Budafok the Danube meanders across the Alföld. Until the age of modern engineering there was no satisfactory crossing point of the Danube south of Budapest, at least as far as Novi Sad, near the mouth of the Tisza.

For several reasons the Romans chose the Bakony gorge for the location of one of their principal military camps and centers of administration, Aquincum. The gorge provided the only good crossing of the north-south portion of the Danube and offered protective sites there; furthermore the Danube at this point turned away from the direct routeway between Carnuntum and Dacia. The city of Aquincum protected Pannonia from the marauders of the Alföld, governed Pannonia Inferior, and became a base for the traffic moving across the plains to Dacia.

As was pointed out in the analysis of Vienna, Roman camps were placed at major routeway junctions because such locations enabled the troops to move quickly in all directions. Since the Danube was not only the imperial boundary but also an important water highway, the Romans placed Aquincum at the point where the road system met the river. Evidently, the Roman limes road used not the gorge itself but the direct valley from Esztergom across the bend. The Pilis valley road not only was a short cut (the Romans loved straight roads), but was also less subject to floods and rock slides than a road through the gorge. At the point where this short-cut road met the

Danube was a small plain which facilitated the erection of a camp
and provided land for the garden plots of the frontier garrison. A
Celtic village nearby may have supplied food and labor, and gave its
name to the camp.[6]

For over five centuries after the abandonment of Aquincum in
376, the Danube gorge lacked an urban center, although Esztergom
and Visegrád may have been fortresses of the Moravian state. Any
Moravian settlements in the area would have been no more than villages, since they were on the periphery of the "state" and faced an
empty Alföld.

Following their conquest of the Carpathian Basin, the Magyars
established their first capital at Esztergom. The first town to develop
at the southern end of the gorge was Óbuda, adjacent to Aquincum.
Although Buda was at first overshadowed by Esztergom, and perhaps
even Óbuda, Vác, and Visegrád, by the thirteenth century it was the
principal city at the gorge. Because of the development of the southern parts of the Dunántúl and of the Alföld, the focal center of urban
life had, in effect, moved southward from the older towns.

The first portion of Hungary to be developed had been the northern Dunántúl, the area including the Bakony and the Little Alföld. The
first important routeways were, consequently, along the Danube;
these roads met at Esztergom and then followed the Pilis valley to
the Danube. It is clear then that the factors that had led the Romans
to the site of Aquincum also led the Magyars to the site of Óbuda.

Settlement was soon extended into the southern parts of the Dunántúl. The roads from Pécs (and Belgrade) and Székesfehérvár (and
Croatia) approached the Danube crossing not from the northwest
but from the south. These roads remained south of the hill clumps
and reached the Danube at or near Budafok. Because of the adjacent
large marshy island, Budafok was not a good site for a crossing, and
the roads continued northward to the present site of Buda, where the
river was narrow, easy to approach, and relatively easy to cross. There
too were the mesa-like Castle Hill (Vár Hegy) and St. Gerard's Hill
(Gellért Hegy) which were ideal for defensive purposes. Since Óbuda
was less satisfactory as both a crossing site and a fortress, the roads
from the northwest as well as the southeast were extended to the foot
of the Vár Hegy.

Across the river a similar shift had taken place. Initially the favored
location had been at Vác, but as soon as the Alföld began to be settled the vast fertile plain became far more productive than the northern valleys. By the early thirteenth century Pest had evidently replaced Vác as the principal town on the eastern bank. The rapid
growth of Pest was due not only to the growth of Buda across the

river, but also to the development of three major routeways which carried the produce of the Alföld toward the Buda-Pest crossing of the Danube.

The southernmost of these three highways [7] was the link between the core of Hungary and the plains along the lower Danube. The route from the western end of the Walachian Plain led not through the terrible Kazan Gorge of the Iron Gate of the Danube but instead through the far easier Porta Orientalis, which cuts a gateway through the Transylvanian Alps just north of the Iron Gate. From this pass the route followed the Timis valley to the fortress city of Temesvár (Timişoara), and thence on to Szeged. The Tisza was crossed at Szeged, since a more northerly path would have necessitated crossing not only the Tisza but also the Maros (Mureşul) (see Map 3). East of Szeged this highway was joined by the road which followed the Maros valley out of southern Transylvania. From Szeged, at the river junction, the highway ran directly to the Bakony-Börzsöny gorge. The road approached the gorge from the south, so that the first crossing it reached was just north of Csepel Island. Since this place was opposite Buda, and was the best crossing site in any case, there was no reason for travelers or freight to move further north.

The second highway came from the east and was the principal link between northern Transylvania and the core area of Hungary. The broadest entries from Transylvania into the Alföld were north of the Bihar Massif, along the Szamos (Someşul) and Körös (Crişul) rivers which flowed westward onto the great plain. The roads following these valleys met in the eastern part of the Alföld, at Debrecen, and then turned southwestward to cross the Tisza at or near Szolnok, since broad areas of marsh flanked the Tisza further north. From Szolnok the road ran directly to the Bakony gorge and approached it from the east-southeast. Again the closest and the best crossing site was just above the end of Csepel Island, at Pest.

The third of these highways was possibly the oldest of the three; Árpád had followed this route in his advance into the Carpathian Basin. This road followed the southern flank of the southernmost range of the Carpathians. It connected the core of the nation with the critical passes leading to the Eurasian steppes and carried the traffic flowing southward out of the Slovakian valleys. The palace town of Gödöllő, the old fortress and ecclesiastical city of Eger, the present industrial city of Miskolc, the wine center of Tokay, and the battlefield of Mohi (Sajo), are all located along this route. The highway approached the Danube at the southern end of the gorge, but since it came from the north rather than the south, it could have led to Vác or Óbuda as easily as to Pest. However, because all the other route-ways focused on the Buda-Pest crossing, this road did so also.

Thus, once the Alföld and the southern part of the Dunántúl had been brought into intensive production, the key location in the vicinity of the Bakony gorge came to be at the southern end of the gorge, at the point where the river left its constricted channel and began to braid. Because of the concentration of the principal roads of Hungary upon this crossing site, Buda-Pest became the one location from which all portions of the kingdom could be readily reached and controlled. In 1361 the capital of Hungary was moved to Buda and, except for the enforced move to Pozsony during the Turkish occupation, the capital has remained there ever since.

Since the early centuries of the kingdom, Buda and Pest have served different functions. Buda has been the administrative center, Pest the commercial center. Buda is on the west bank of the Danube, and the original core of Hungary lay west of the river. For several centuries the cultural, administrative, and ecclesiastical life of the kingdom lay to the west of the Danube in the Dunántúl. At Buda were the hills which facilitated the construction of the fortress designed to control the vital crossing and to protect the Dunántúl from any new invaders from the east. The palace, the cathedral, and the great city walls were all in Buda.

Pest, on the other hand, has always been a commercial city. Two-thirds of the area of the kingdom and all of the Alföld lay east of the Danube. The market for agricultural produce was chiefly to the west, so that as soon as the Alföld had been occupied by sedentary agriculturists its produce moved westward toward the Dunántúl and Western Europe. Since there was no satisfactory crossing of the Danube south of Pest, nearly all of this traffic concentrated on that city. Cattle, horses, and pigs were driven along the great roads from the east, and where the roads met the animals were gathered together. Merchants came to Pest to buy the animals, grain, and wine that had been collected there and shipped them to the western markets. Furthermore, those merchants who wished to sell western manufactured goods to the people of the Alföld made Pest their distributing center, since from Pest roads led to all portions of the Alföld and Transylvania. Even before the Mongol invasion Pest was a thriving commercial site, and though it was destroyed by the Mongols in 1241, King Béla IV seemed so certain of its continued importance that he made it a free city in 1244.

The Turkish occupation ruined Pest more than it did Buda. Buda was the capital of Turkish Hungary, the seat of a pasha, but Pest became little more than a transriver outpost of the capital. True, most of Pest's hinterland was also under Turkish control, but the Alföld had been ravaged and depopulated; its productivity was slight, its exports negligible. Of even greater significance was the location of the fighting frontier just to the west of Buda-Pest, cutting the cities off from their contacts with Vienna and Western Europe. Pest had prospered as the commercial link between Western Europe and the Alföld, and the cessation of the east-west traffic meant the death of Pest. When it was recaptured from the Turks in 1686 it was but a heap of ruins.[8]

With the resettlement of the Alföld in the eighteenth century, Pest was reborn and was soon growing more rapidly than Buda. In the nineteenth century the centralization of Hungary brought all the railroads and highways of the kingdom to the capital. The Alföld again became the productive core of the country, one of the bread baskets of Europe, and since the market for agricultural produce was still in the west, Pest resumed its role as the link between Western Europe and the Alföld. Budapest became the greatest milling center of the world and one of the great meat-packing centers of Europe; these mills and slaughter houses were all on the Pest side of the Danube. The nature of the terrain also favored Pest, for it was situated on the plain, whereas Buda was confined close to the river by the hill slopes behind it.[9]

Although population statistics from the fifteenth century are not available, it seems that Buda was always a larger city than Pest until the end of the eighteenth century. In the census of 1799 Pest passed Buda for the first time. The two cities were united legally in 1872, by which time Pest was overwhelmingly the larger of the two. In the nineteenth century the united city grew at a rate exceeded in Europe only by Berlin; between 1799 and 1900 the population increased from 54,000 to 732,000. By the end of World War I Budapest had over one million inhabitants.

Budapest has suffered much since 1918. In 1919 it lost much of its national hinterland and was looted by the Romanian army. Nevertheless, it remained somewhat more prosperous than Vienna, since it had not been as dependent on the far reaches of the Habsburg Monarchy as Vienna had been, and since it possessed in the Magyar Alföld an area capable of maintaining a large city in times of prosperity. Unfortunately, Buda has remained the ideal fortress from which to oppose an invader from the east. In 1944 the city endured a harrowing seven weeks' siege during which the Russians in Pest tried to dislodge the Germans from the hills of Buda. In 1956 the capital endured most of the chaos and destruction attending the unsuccessful Hungarian revolt against the Soviet-dominated government.

Budapest contains few mementos of its early history. Unlike Vienna, it has few relics of the Gothic, or even of the Baroque, for the desolation wreaked by the Mongols, the Turks, the Germans, and the Russians has destroyed most of the old landmarks. However, the city occupies a site of much beauty and great significance. No matter how often or how completely Budapest is destroyed, it remains the controlling funnel between Western Europe and the eastern two-thirds of the Carpathian Basin. As long as the Alföld remains productive Budapest will be the site of an important city.[10]

Linguistic Nationalism

In the nineteenth century linguistic nationalism spread throughout Europe. Nationalism as such had existed previously,[11] but this feeling had been of a different nature; it had been based on the established historic-political units rather than on language. There had been a Hungarian, not a Magyar, a Bohemian, not a Czech nationalism. Following the French Revolution, international languages such as Latin and French were replaced by the vernacular languages. The teaching of the mother tongue was encouraged with great zeal, and the language of the "nation" was soon regarded as the sacred repository of the essence of the "nation."

Emphasis was placed not only on individual languages, but also on the linguistic groupings. Scholars of the time favored research into the beginnings of language families, and numerous mystical conclusions were drawn from these studies. Various "pan" movements resulted, the most striking of which was Pan-Slavism, which became the dream of the Slavists and the nightmare of the non-Slavs.

Though the origins of linguistic nationalism are to be found in the ideas of the eighteenth century, much of the fervor with which the new doctrine was spread was undoubtedly due to the democratization of education in the nineteenth century. No longer was instruction limited primarily to the nobles, the wealthy, and the clergy; in the nineteenth century education was extended to the majority of the population. Such schooling had to be, of necessity, in the vernacular, since Latin could scarcely be the language in which millions of sons of the peasantry could be taught. This necessity was reinforced by that Romantic idealism which was focused on the individual languages and on the community of those who shared the language. Unfortunately, learning which is limited to one language generally results in a feeling of superiority for the culture associated with that language over the cultures of which the student knows little. The student learns the glories of his own history, heritage, and culture, but little of the glories of others. All too often lack of knowledge has bred contempt and hatred. Before this time, the noble or the king had been the moving spirit of nationalism, but in the nineteenth century the school teacher became a symbol of this spirit. The most devoted and influential worker for the transfer of Burgenland to Austria was a high school teacher of German literature.

The linguistic virus soon infected the Magyars as well as their neighbors. Yet, it must be stressed that Magyarization was a relatively late phenomenon; it was precisely its tardy appearance that gave it its desperate vigor. The Hungarians used Latin long after the practice had been abandoned elsewhere. When the Magyar nobility opposed the efforts of Joseph II to make German the official language of the Habsburg domains, they were not upholding Magyar, but rather Latin as their administrative tongue. Until 1848 the Hungarian Diet used Latin as its official language, and the University of Budapest, then the only university in the country, instructed in Latin. Not until the surge of nationalism which preceded the revolution of 1848 did the Hungarians make Magyar their official administrative language.[12]

The rise of linguistic nationalism among the Magyars intensified both pride and fear, and it was the combination of these two passions that produced the much publicized Magyar chauvinism. The Magyars recognized that they differed from all their neighbors. They had always sensed this distinction, but now it was accentuated by the new emphasis on language. The Magyar tongue is unlike any other in Central Europe; it is not even a member of the Indo-European family of languages, to which all the other languages of Central Europe belong. The Magyars were different, and they wished to remain different; above all else they wished to maintain their national identity.[13]

As was true elsewhere, this sense of difference bred a feeling of superiority which was then augmented by many studies of the national history. The Magyars remembered too well that they had come as conquerors; the others, those who had been in the Carpathian Basin when Árpád arrived, were the conquered. The nobility of the nation was consequently Magyar or Magyarized. With the new emphasis on language, the Slovak, for example, was not only a peasant, he was also a non-Magyar and hence automatically placed on a much lower cultural level. However, the non-Magyar could easily join the superior culture by becoming Magyarized, and the Magyars were always pleased to welcome converts.

Two views of Carnuntum. *Above:* The Hainburg or Carnuntum gap of the Danube. The Danube flows to the left (north) of the hill in the middle of the picture—the Braunsberg (site of Celtic Carnuntum). Uplands at left are southernmost extent of the Little Carpathians, in Slovakia. Upland at right is the northern edge of the Hainburg Hills, bearing the Hainburg fortress. The city of Hainburg lies in the gap between the fortress and the Braunsberg. *Right:* The Heidentor, a Roman arch which may have marked one of the principal entrances to Carnuntum. It now stands in the fields southwest of Petronell.

Above: The Hungarian border, seen from highway between Mogersdorf and Deutsch Minihof, west of Szent Gotthárd. The boundary is at the edge of the highway, so that the fence in foreground is within Hungary; the "dirt road" beyond is the mine field. *Below:* Neusiedl am See, from the rim of the Parndorf Heath. Note the narrow strips of cultivated land. Beyond these is a mile-wide belt of reeds and then Lake Neusiedl.

Village architecture typical of Burgenland. *Above:* The principal street of Mörbisch. The houses are all whitewashed. Note the ears of corn hanging from the side of the house. *Below:* An old peasant home in Unterwart. This was a "typical" home three decades ago but is now a picturesque rarity. Most newer houses have tiled roofs, but the same shape and internal organization as the old.

Two views showing Alföld characteristics in Burgenland. *Above:* Pamhagen, on the edge of the Hanság. The open space is a village "commons"; another row of houses is behind the photographer. Note the geese. *Below:* Inside the *Hof*, or work camp, at Eberau. The equipment, animals, and hired laborers are housed in this quadrangle. Note the long-handled well and the poultry, both typical of the Alföld.

Two of the historic fortresses of Burgenland. *Above:* Schloss Schlaining, which dominates the point where the old road around the south flank of the Köszeg Range climbed from the lowland to the Bucklige Welt. Stadt Schlaining, the "city," is on top, behind the fortress. Note the two towers, typical of most Burgenland fortresses—an old, rounded one strictly for military purposes, and a newer, baroque one largely for decoration. *Below:* The medieval fortress of Güssing, sitting atop a basaltic plug which rises sharply above the water and marsh at the confluence of the Strem and the Zicken. In the Middle Ages the lords of this castle dominated most of present southern Burgenland.

The provincial capital, Eisenstadt. *Above:* The Eszterházy Schloss, largest and most famous palace of Burgenland, and the scene of the activities of Joseph Haydn. Because the Soviet occupation troops had destroyed the old governmental building, this palace was being used for the provincial government. The banner hanging in front indicates the Landtag is in session. *Right:* The entrance to the former ghetto (Unterberg), immediately adjacent to the Eszterházy palace. The ghetto was for the Jews who managed the prince's estates. It was a distinct political subdivision, and all Gentiles were excluded after sundown by a chain stretched across the archway. Since most of the Jews were killed or deported during the Nazi regime, this is now merely an area of low-grade housing and is a part of the city of Eisenstadt.

The people and their dress reflect some of the "difference" of Burgenland. *Above:* A peasant couple of Deutsch Minihof. *Below:* Near Hagensdorf, three peasant women returning from a pilgrimage to Gaas. They had already walked over ten miles, to get there and part way back, and were asking for a ride. The emphasis on black dress is typical of most peasant women in Hungary, but note that the youngest of the three (center) has bits of white showing, and also a store-bought bag in contrast to the homemade ones of the older women.

Left: A Croatian peasant woman in Trausdorf. The boots, kerchief, and apron are typical of Burgenland and unlike Austria. She was very proud of the homemade basket on her back and pleased that I wished to have it in the picture. The basket contains reeds that are much used for weaving containers of various kinds. *Below:* Croatian peasant costumes. Unfortunately these brilliant *Trachten* can be seen only at rare public festivities. This picture was taken at Frankenau, in June, 1961, at a celebration attending the unveiling of a monument to the Croatian poet, Miloradić, who was born in Frankenau.

The Magyars were also intensely conscious of the fact that they had created the Hungarian state. Before the arrival of the Magyars there had been no Hungary, in fact there had never been anything but a dangerous power vacuum in the center of the Carpathian Basin. The state was their state, the crown was their crown, and it had undoubtedly been their efforts that had maintained the concept of a separate Hungary through the troubled centuries from 1526 to 1867. Linguistic nationalism did not, therefore, replace or even supersede the old Hungarian state idea; it added new strength to the old ideal of the kingdom and crown. A new, powerful wine had been poured into the traditional skin.

Among the high nobility, the continuing semi-feudal character of the kingdom encouraged excessive pride. The great magnates of the nineteenth century often acted as though they did not consider their serfs to be human. Even those serfs and landless peasants who were Magyars suffered from the effects of this inordinate pride, but the worst effects were felt principally by the non-Magyar peasants. Thus, in Transylvania the noble families often looked upon their Vlach (Romanian) peasants as only slightly above the level of field animals. Linguistic nationalism added little impetus to this feudalistic arrogance. To the downtrodden peasants, however, the newly developed linguistic ties with people beyond the boundary gave some hope that the conditions of servitude might be abolished. Undoubtedly some of the irredentist feelings of the Romanians within Hungary were caused by the nobles' arrogance and linguistic pride.

In addition to pride, the Magyars also came to feel a profound fear; above all other factors, it was this fear that gave Magyar nationalism its fanatical quality. The Magyars sensed their difference from the Germans and the Slavs, but they recognized too that they were but a pitiful number compared to the huge linguistic groups around them. The Magyars were surrounded by Germanic, Slavic, and Latin groups, each of which was beginning to claim special rights and to predict future glories for itself. The Germans were, in fact, to become among the most fanatical of all the linguistic nationalists.

At this time, the various Slavic groups were beginning to stress their underlying kinship. The Magyars could scarcely fear a Slovakian nationalism as such, but Pan-Slavism seemed to bring the full power of the Russian Empire to the northern fringes of the Alföld. In recent years many writings have belittled the supposed strength of Pan-Slavism, but this opinion, no matter how true an appraisal, is based on the clarity gained in retrospect. At the time the Magyars, and many Europeans, were convinced of the power of Pan-Slavism, and trembled within its shadow.[14] Pan-Slavic writers aggravated

Magyar fears; they were quick to point out the strategic location of Hungary and the anomalous character of the Magyars. The northern and southern Slavs were closest to each other in western Hungary, so that the obvious bridge for a union of the two lay within Hungary. Pan-Slavists expressed little sympathy for the Magyars; they were considered by them as interlopers, steppe ravagers who had entered Europe as raiders and who had, in destroying the Moravian state, broken the pre-existing link between the northern and southern Slavs.[15] Though Pan-Slavists were not usually explicit as to what was to become of the Magyars within a Slavic superstate, it was clear to the Magyars that at the very least such a union would have meant the Slavicization of the Magyars and the destruction of the Magyar "nation."

This anxiety caused by the overwhelming power of the Slavs and the Germans was heightened by the pressure of time. The Magyars had not been able to secure an independent Hungary until 1867, and by then the other linguistic nationalisms were in full flower. Vast areas of the old kingdom had been resettled during the eighteenth century, and the Magyars had become a minority within Hungary. It has been estimated that at the time of the Turkish invasion approximately four-fifths of the population of the kingdom was Magyar speaking.[16] Yet, in 1787 only 29 per cent of the population was Magyar. By 1840 this figure had risen to 37 per cent, and in 1880, when Magyarization began in earnest, 41 per cent.[17] The mass influx of non-Magyar inhabitants, at a time when language was soon to become important, brought the nationalists of the 1840's to the point of desperation. Louis Kossuth is said to have warned, "Make haste to Magyarize the Slovaks, Romanians, Serbs and Germans or else we will perish."[18] Unless the other peoples could be Magyarized, the kingdom would collapse under the pressures of Pan-Slavism and Pan-Germanism.[19]

There are few fanaticisms stronger than that of a group which feels itself to be the guardian of a sacred trust and yet in danger of being overwhelmed by barbarians. This was roughly the position of the Magyars, as they saw it. They felt that they could not safely wait for the natural processes of assimilation to bring the new settlers into the Magyar "nation." In the anxiety to accelerate the process of assimilation, Magyar nationalism turned into an extreme form of chauvinism.

After 1867 the Magyars attempted to transform the non-Magyars of the kingdom into Magyars as quickly as possible.[20] Activities which glorified Germanic or Slavic culture were hampered and often repressed, while Magyar activities were encouraged vigorously. All non-Magyar names of cities, villages, mountains, rivers, and forests were Magyarized.

The principal effort of the Magyarizers was made in education, since the obvious way to Magyarize the Slav, Romanian, or German was to teach him the Magyar language. Schooling could not force him to use the language, but it was felt that national pride and the pressures to communicate would lead to the use of the language. Yet, it is significant that not before 1879 was there a law in Hungary requiring that Magyar was to be a subject taught in all schools. After 1883 teacher candidates for the upper schools had to pass examinations proving their ability to handle Magyar.[21] Only in 1907 was a law promulgated which stated that all teaching in primary schools was to be in Magyar.

The Apponyi School Law of 1907 has become famous as a symbol of the policy of forced assimilation. Yet, the law itself may have been as much a response to outside pressures as it was part of a concerted, planned campaign. From almost the first years after 1867, nationalistic Germans of Germany and Austria were focusing their attention on the German-speaking inhabitants of Hungary. In 1881 the Allgemeine Deutsche Schulverein of Berlin stated that its first task was to help the Germans of Hungary. Seven years later a pamphlet entitled, "Don't let them steal your German place names; preserve your mother tongue!" was circulated within Hungary. Another pamphlet of 1888 bluntly demanded the cession of western Hungary to Austria, "German West Hungary to the Rába River belongs to the German *Volk* and *Reich*." Then in June, 1906, a school teacher named Josef Patry [22] contributed a long lead article to the chauvinistically pro-German (pro-Bismarck, anti-Semitic, anti-Catholic, anti-Hungarian) Viennese newspaper, *Das Alldeutsches Tagblatt*. This article urged the transfer of all of Hungary west of the Rába River to Austria. The area concerned would have included more Magyars than Germans (this discrepancy was to be solved by a population transfer), and 100,000 Slavs who were, Patry felt, actually pro-German. Though this plan (complete with maps, tables, and a historical analysis stressing Charlemagne) appeared in a minor, extremist paper, it caused considerable comment in both Hungary and Austria, and Patry was later considered to have been one of the precursors of Burgenland. In the next year, 1907, Patry and other nationalistic Germans formed a Viennese organization named "The Society for the Maintenance of the German Nationality in Hungary." Though the initial attempts at Magyarization may have led to these Pan-German moves, the German moves in turn may well have prompted the Apponyi School Law of 1907.

Despite the rigorous manner in which it was urged, the Magyarization campaign enjoyed much success. For the people around them the Magyars have always possessed a fascination; whether one loved them or hated them it was impossible to ignore them. Their aristocratic bearing, their fierceness in defense of a cause, their emotional romanticism, have all drawn converts to them, so that next to the Magyar there has always been the *Magyaron* who fervently accepted the ways and beliefs of the lords of the kingdom. One reason for the surprising concentration of talented men and women in so small a nation may well have been the ability of the Magyars to attract and hold the best minds of the non-Magyar peoples. Thus, Louis Kossuth, the political leader of the revolution of 1848, was a Magyarized Slovak, while Petőfi, the poetic harbinger and martyr of the revolution, was born Petrović. The composer, Franz Liszt, is perhaps a yet more famous example of this tendency towards voluntary assimilation. Liszt was born in Raiding, a village within present Burgenland, which was and is completely German speaking. Of his great grandparents all but one had an obviously German name. His father spelled the name List; it was Franz himself who Magyarized the spelling. Liszt spent most of his life outside Hungary, and yet he was always considered to be, and evidently considered himself to be, a Hungarian. Similarly, the great nineteenth-century violinist and friend of Brahms, Josef Joachim, was born within present Burgenland but was always thought of as a Hungarian. The famous doctor and discoverer of puerperal fever, Ignaz Semmelweiss, was the son of a Burgenland family that had moved to Budapest; Semmelweiss did his life's work in Vienna, and yet remains known as a Hungarian. Even in 1919, when linguistic nationalism was at its zenith, nearly all the local leaders, the administrators, clergymen, attorneys and teachers of present Burgenland, though often of German-speaking ancestry, worked strenuously to keep their territory within Hungary.

The figures of the censuses of the nineteenth century, before as well as after 1867, reveal a steady rise in the percentage of the total population that declared itself to be Magyar.[23] These statistics may, of course, be challenged,[24] but they are probably accurate in showing the trend even if not the actual numbers. The rate of increase of the Magyar proportion of the total was continuous and fairly consistent.

In addition to the attraction of the ruling Magyars, the principal factor that aided the progress of Magyarization was probably not the forced learning of the language but rather the gradually increasing urbanization of the country. An isolated, self-sufficient peasantry may preserve a language or dialect for centuries, but townsmen quickly adopt the national language. City dwellers must deal with governmental officials and with merchants and artists not only at home but in other parts of the state. In Hungary the predominance of Budapest in all the social, political, and economic life of the country made it necessary for the inhabitants of all the other cities and towns to use Magyar. These towns became thoroughly Magyar during the last decades of the nineteenth century; even the towns along the Austrian border were transformed from German speaking to predominantly Magyar speaking. Thus, although one cannot now evaluate fully the power of the linguistic nationalisms of the time, it may well be true that one of the principal reasons why Hungary failed in her attempt to Magyarize the non-Magyars of the kingdom was that she did not have sufficient time to complete the task.[25]

Within western Hungary the Magyarization program attempted to encompass all forms of the local cultural life, although the principal emphasis was placed on education. Magyar theatres were established in Sopron and Pozsony (Bratislava) and were subsidized initially by the government so that they could compete with the existent German language theatres in those cities. To make certain that children would learn Magyar as soon and as thoroughly as possible, Magyar kindergartens were established. Various Magyar cultural societies made their appearance. By 1835 Eisenstadt and Sopron had Hungarian literary clubs.

The initial purpose of these efforts by the government and by nationalistic citizens was to make Magyar the language of intellectual and cultural intercourse. These efforts succeeded completely, and by the start of the twentieth century the educated people in western Hungary used and preferred the Magyar language. The use of Magyar became a sign of intellect and cultured bearing, a status symbol, an entry into the groups and the circles that "mattered." As statistics show, these social pressures were extremely effective in the cities. Even a dwarf city such as Eisenstadt was affected. In 1874 a German plaque was dedicated, honoring the great anatomist, Josef Hyrtl; in 1898 a plaque honoring Haydn was in Magyar. The city's newspaper was founded as the *Eisenstädter Zeitung* in 1882, but changed to the *Kismartoner Zeitung* in 1884. Nevertheless, this paper continued to publish in German as did the principal Sopron newspaper. In 1896, in the surge of patriotism that accompanied the millennial celebration of the Magyar entry into the Carpathian Basin, many of the local streets and squares of Eisenstadt were renamed after Hungarian heroes.[26]

As much as was possible, the Hungarians surrounded the peasants with Magyar names and titles. Not only were place names Magyarized or returned to their old Magyar forms (Kismarton and Sopron seem to be older names than Eisenstadt and Ödenburg), but also all employees of the government were urged to Magyarize their names. Herr Karl Semmelweis of the Landesbibliothek reports that his father, a school teacher, was able to resist these urgings because of the fame of his relative, Dr. Ignaz Semmelweiss, in Budapest and Vienna. However, personal pressure of this sort was probably not as strong as the German nationalists have claimed, since the number of pro-Hungarians with German names in 1919 suggests that most did not Magyarize their names. Those who did probably did so voluntarily. Nevertheless, Magyar first names became very common, among the peasants as well as among the intellectuals.

German nationalists have often accused the nobility of the border area of having been active agents of the Magyarization program. Certainly the nobles were all strong nationalists. In the decades before the first world war many of their manorial work centers were populated with Magyars from inner Hungary. The importation of these Magyars may have been an attempt to further Magyarization, or it may merely have been an attempt by the nobles to obtain cheaper labor, workers who would not be as tempted to leave the puszta as would the inhabitants of a nearby village.

In the villages of present Burgenland none of these measures had much effect. The typical village had no contact with the kindergartens, the literary clubs, or the theatres. Within the villages the peasants lived a life centered on the village; outside the village they were either periodic visitors to the markets, or "commuting" workers on the manors or in the factories of the nearby cities. In the villages three individuals, the notary, the pastor, and the teacher, became the agents of the Magyarization program.

The notary (*jegyző* in Magyar, *Notar* in German) was usually a Magyar, not native to the area. His duties were to help the peasants in legal matters of all kinds, to keep the village records, and to collect the land taxes. Since few of the peasants had had more than a few years of schooling, they were often incapable of deciphering governmental forms, laws, and regulations. Therefore the notary became the legal counsellor and the official scribe of the village. Such a position seemed predestined to serve the forces of Magyarization, and evidently the governmental authorities, who appointed the notaries, saw to it that Magyars were placed in every post. In any case it was almost essential that the notary be a Magyar, since the laws, regulations, and forms with which he had to deal were all in the Magyar language.

In practice, the notary generally had a negative rather than a positive effect on the progress of Magyarization. He had almost no friendly contact with the peasants. He was an agent of the government and hence automatically subject to peasant suspicions; worse yet, he was the hated tax collector. The notary was an educated man, who spoke nothing but Magyar, whereas the uneducated peasants spoke a dialect of German or Croatian. He was frequently a member of the Magyar gentry, so that the peasant often encountered not only the scorn of the Magyar for the non-Magyar, but also the scorn of the educated person of "good" family background for the ignorant peasant. He demanded shows of respect from the peasants and in return often treated them with extreme discourtesy. Thus, the notary became the local symbol of the repressive aspects of the program of Magyarization; in many villages he was thoroughly hated. In 1921–23 many of those notaries who had not left the area were dismissed, and the powers of the notary were severely diminished. For many peasants it seems that the transfer to Austria was desirable simply because it rid them of the arrogant, hated Magyar notary.

The key figures in the village were, consequently, the pastor and the teacher. Since the schools were under the direction and control of the churches, these two men usually worked closely together. Ultimately it was these two men (or several if the village was very large) who regulated the degree of force with which the Magyarization program was actually applied. Technically the teacher had to follow governmental directives, but, as many peasants still recall, the government was far away, and the degree of success of the Magyarization program depended on the efforts of the pastor and the teacher.

The Catholic priest was usually of the same linguistic background as were his parishioners, although in most cases he had been Magyarized in his education. The bishops of Győr and Szombathely were reportedly strongly nationalistic, but it was obviously church policy to place in a village a priest who knew the language of the villagers. In villages of mixed languages, Magyar could be favored, of course, if a Magyar priest was available for the assignment. Although the bishops and priests were ardent Hungarian patriots, their fundamental concern was always that the peasants under their religious charge be able to understand the sermons, their catechisms, hymns, and services, and be able to confess their sins. As a result of this policy the Church became, despite its nationalism, the guardian of the German and Croatian peasant cultures.

The Lutheran pastors were more divided in their nationalistic loyalties than were the Catholic priests. In 1848 the Lutheran teachers' training school in Oberschützen became a center of pro-Hungarian agitation, and its director, Gottlieb Wimmer, translated into German Kossuth's call to rebellion. However, in the half century after 1867 the loyalties of the Lutheran pastors appear to have been drawn as much towards Germany as towards Hungary. Virtually all of the Lutherans of present Burgenland were German speaking, so that the Church did not have to accommodate itself to Croatian or Magyar; furthermore, Germany had an obvious appeal for a Lutheran. Thus the school in Oberschützen continued to stress German long after other teachers' training schools had become committed to Magyar only, and it continued to maintain ties with Vienna, and with the Lutheran educational centers of northern Germany. In the critical years 1918–21 several Lutheran pastors worked for the union with Austria, whereas all the Catholic priests strove to keep their villages within Hungary.

Since the principal efforts towards Magyarization were in the field of education, the teacher more than anyone else was responsible for the speed with which the program advanced. Like the pastor, the teacher was usually of local origin. A German village generally had a teacher of German origin, a Croatian village, a Croatian teacher. These teachers had all been through teachers' training schools in Hungary and were imbued with the spirit of Hungarian nationalism. Nevertheless, in the same way as the pastor, the teacher had to face the fact that the people in his village spoke a certain language. As a result, the language of the village remained the language of instruction until the promulgation of the Apponyi School Law of 1907. Even then not all instruction was in Magyar, although that language predominated. Everywhere instruction in religion continued to be given in the local language; the amount of Magyar used in the teaching of the other subjects varied with the teacher. In some villages it appears that everything else was in Magyar; in others evidently both Magyar and German readers were used, so that instruction was actually bilingual.

The school inspector of Moson megye is reported to have said in 1908, "Scarcely one year has passed since the promulgation of the new law and already Magyar has become the teaching language in all our primary schools." [27] This boast suggests that almost a year was required to make the Magyar language predominant in all the schools of that comitat. However Moson megye cannot be accepted as typical; it is completely flat and unwooded and contains large but few villages. In such an area the imposition of the language would have been relatively simple, whereas in the numerous tiny, remote villages of present southern Burgenland such uniformity must have been much more difficult to achieve.

The efficiency of village education at that time should not be overrated. It is clear that many of the peasants considered that the time spent by their children in school was much less worthwhile than the time they spent on the land. Whenever such parents felt that they needed the help of their children, they tended to keep them home from school. In those villages which were too small to support their own schools the children received very little education, since on sunny days they were often needed on the land and on wet days the journey to the school in the next village seemed too difficult. Teachers also varied greatly in their dedication to their profession. Teachers were not required to send detailed reports to the county school authorities, and the school inspector rarely visited all the schools under his direction. In practice the local teacher was often largely autonomous. He was usually given a home and a piece of land in addition to his salary, since in areas of subsistence farming it was necessary for him to raise part of his own food needs. In Burgenland one can still hear stories of teachers who assigned their students to tasks on their holdings instead of teaching them the expected course work.

The Hungarian authorities utilized both threats and awards to increase the efficiency of their teachers. A teacher could be dismissed if his students did not demonstrate a basic knowledge of Magyar by the end of their primary schooling. This appears to have been little more than a threat, since there is no report of such a dismissal ever having been carried out within present Burgenland. In any case, the teachers did support the program, even though they may have found the new policy more difficult than the previous method of teaching in the vernacular. Far more successful than the threats as incentives were the awards given to those teachers whose students demonstrated an exceptional command of Magyar in their graduation examinations. The award was not only a proclaimed recognition of superior teaching ability but also a sum of money worth roughly one sixth of the teacher's annual salary. Few teachers of any country, at any time, have been able to resist the appeal of such an award.

Whereas the success of the Magyarization program in the lower schools can be questioned, there can be no question of the success in the upper schools. The Hungarian government seems to have realized that the most that it could hope for from the peasants, at least of the first generation after 1907, was simply that they gain a rudimentary knowledge of the Magyar language.[28] At that time there was little prospect that the average peasant would enter into the national intellectual life; rather he would stay in his village, tend his land, and converse in his dialect with his compatriots.

The upper schools were another matter. Contrary to general Western opinion there does not seem to have been any ethnic criterion for being able to advance to the upper schools. The Magyar language was necessary, of course, but the brighter boys would have achieved a sufficient command of that by the end of their lower school years. Here the determining factor seems to have been, as in all countries at this time, the social class to which the boy belonged. The son of the peasant had little chance of advancing, since his parents often lacked the funds, frequently lacked sympathy for higher education, and always wanted the help of their son on the land. As a consequence it was usually the sons of the educated class, the government officials and the professional men, who attended school beyond the first six years. Since the educated class was almost always either Magyar or strongly Magyarized, the percentage of "Magyars" attending the upper schools was far in excess of their proportion of the total population.

Higher education was kept within Hungary, which, after 1867, was a separate country and had a different educational system from Austria's. Thus the student from the German or Croatian Burgenland village advanced to Győr, Sopron, or Szombathely, and, if he continued on to the university, to Budapest. Students very rarely crossed the boundary into Austria. Within the Hungarian upper schools the young men invariably were caught up in the fervor of Hungarian nationalism. They were led to admire Kossuth and Petőfi as their heroes, and to acquire an extreme distrust of Austria. "Never trust the Austrians" seems to have been one of the slogans of these patriotic student groups. They believed sincerely that the troubles of Hungary were the result of Austrian actions in the past and present, and that Austrian bankers and manufacturers were still attempting to keep Hungary underdeveloped. As one German-born person who went through this experience said, if anyone had asked him what "nationality" he was, he would have answered unhesitatingly "Magyar." Consequently the number of avowed non-Magyars attending upper schools, colleges, or universities in Hungary appeared to diminish even further.[29]

As a result of this educational experience, almost all of the Burgenlanders who were educated beyond primary school, regardless of their ethnic origin, became fervent *Magyaronen* (Magyarized non-Magyars). Although they often returned to Burgenland as teachers, priests, lawyers, and government officials, they conversed among themselves in Magyar, were closely attuned to Hungarian (Magyar) intellectual life, and were ardent believers in the sacred integrity of the Kingdom of Hungary. As Miltschinsky mentions (p. 32), in the large village of Deutschkreutz, the priest, Stephen Kaufmann, the doctor, Julius Hesz, and the teachers, Josef Hafner, Theiner, and Riedl, all fought the transfer to Austria, and together with the notary, Udvárdy, and the postmaster, Mesterházy, founded the "Magyar Országos Vedö Egyesület" (Society for the Defense of Hungary) in Deutschkreutz. Of all the educated men then in Burgenland, only three, Wollinger, Walheim, and Wolf, worked actively for the transfer to Austria; Wollinger was educated in Germany, Walheim and Wolf in Vienna.

The position of the Magyaronen in Burgenland became difficult after 1921. As one confided, they not only feared the actions of the Austrians, but many also felt that "they would not be able to breathe in Austria"; they felt that for them life in Austria would be intellectually and emotionally impossible. Thus many fled when the Austrians entered the area, but most of them returned to their homes when the feared repressions did not materialize. Although they have enjoyed a little political and cultural prominence in Burgenland since 1921, their life has not been without some persecution. "Magyaronen" is still a slur, an insulting word, and there is a widespread belief in Burgenland that the Magyaronen were traitors; one encounters the word *Verräter* often.

The Magyarization program was most effective in the cities, for it was there that the educated persons gathered. The cities were also centers of government and communications, the focal points uniting the surrounding areas with the remainder of the state, and with Budapest. Within a few decades all the cities on the German-Magyar linguistic frontier changed from German to Magyar (see Table 1).

TABLE 1

City	1880		1900		1920	
	German	Magyar	German	Magyar	German	Magyar
Moson	3,583	933	2,984	2,077	2,557	3,649
Magyaróvár	2,125	998	1,727	1,805	2,111	4,837
Sopron	17,115	4,877	17,924	13,540	16,911	17,166
Köszeg	5,290	1,458	4,146	3,575	3,314	4,978
Szt. Gotthárd	643	639	577	1,400	375	2,198

Bratislava (Pozsony, Pressburg) was an especially interesting case (see Table 2), since this city was first German, then partially Magyarized, then transferred to Czechoslovakia and made the capital of Slovakia.

Within the villages of present Burgenland three factors appear to have contributed to the Magyarization of the community: the presence of government offices, of manorial centers, and of a large popu-

TABLE 2

Year	Population	% German	% Magyar	% Slovak
1852	36,742	84	6	10
1880	48,006	66	16	11
1890	52,411	60	20	16
1900	65,867	52	31	15
1910	78,223	42	41	15
1921	93,189	29	21	46
1930	123,844	28	16	51

lation. Those settlements that served as county seats became increasingly Magyar, not only because of governmental policy, but also because the bureaucracy consisted entirely of the educated, and hence of Magyars and Magyaronen. The manor was a strong influence towards Magyarization, because not only the noble household itself was Magyar, but also the men who worked the estate for the nobleman, the managers, accountants, scribes, bankers, buyers, and sellers, were all of the educated class. Sheer size of the community was of importance, because the larger the village the more teachers, clergymen, lawyers, doctors, and other educated persons lived there. These Magyarized inhabitants invariably formed an intellectual and cultural nucleus whose influence on the community increased more rapidly than did their own numbers.

These factors can be noted in operation during the decade 1900–1910 in present Burgenland. During this decade Magyarization was pushed in earnest, and the chaos and ferment of the war had not yet confused the process. In the north, Moson megye, the villages were all large and manorial centers abounded; almost every one of these villages showed a substantial increase in the number of Magyars during that decade. In Kittsee, with 3,000 inhabitants and the Batthyány palace, the Magyar total increased from 493 to 756 (19 to 24 per cent of the total population). Further south the number of Magyars in the large manorial center of Rechnitz increased from 399 to 807 (11 to 25 per cent). Those settlements in which all three factors were combined were uniquely vulnerable to being Magyarized. In that one decade the Magyars in Eisenstadt increased from 842 to 1,255 (16 to 26 per cent), and in Güssing from 641 to 984 (32 to 45 per cent).

In the smaller, often remote, villages these three factors had little effect. Very few of the citizens had progressed beyond primary school, and except for the hated notary, there had been no immigration of educated persons. In these villages the process of assimilation of the village minority into the majority, primarily through inter-marriage, continued. In the few years after 1907 no generation had yet learned sufficient Magyar in the schools for that language to threaten the predominance of the local dialect. Even access to a Magyar or Magyarized center did not hasten Magyarization in the smaller villages, since the sparse vocabulary of necessity which the peasants learned could not yet bring them to the point of altering their linguistic identification. Thus in Hasendorf, Krottendorf, Tobaj, and Sulz, all of which are within three miles of Güssing, the number of Magyars declined between 1900 and 1910.

Therefore, the success of the Magyarization program can be said to have been almost complete among those persons who advanced beyond primary school, but among the peasants, slight if any. Yet, even though the peasants were not noticeably Magyarized in the few years between 1907 and 1914, their sense of separation from Austria appears to have been strong. The "Thousand-Years Boundary" continued to exert its psychological separating force despite linguistic ties across the frontier. In present middle Burgenland, for example, the peasants on either side of the line had little to do with each other, and used uncomplimentary names when referring to each other; the west Hungarians called the Austrians *Pregner*, while the Austrians in return used the name *Krowotten* (Croats).

It seems clear that at least until late 1918 few of the peasants had any conception of being "repressed" in the nationalistic sense. They found the arrogance of many of the Magyars insufferable, but they accepted the fact that they lived within Hungary, within St. Stephen's kingdom. Actually, the peasants were very little concerned about the policy of Magyarization. The government was far away; in their work on their land the peasants were almost untouched by the na-tionalistic passions then raging among the intellectuals of Europe.[30]

The Croats of present Burgenland deserve special attention, since they occupied a neutral position in the struggle between the Magyars and Germans for the possession of Burgenland. In contrast to the other two ethnic groups, the Croats had no contact with the main group of their linguistic compatriots. Croatia was distant, and ties with the ancestral homeland were broken soon after the time of the migration into the Austro-Hungarian border area. Reportedly the Croats of Croatia did not even know of the existence of these Croats until 1879, when a Croatian scholar on his way to Vienna heard Croatian spoken in a village through which he was passing. The Croats of Burgenland remembered that they had come from Croatia but had forgotten from which areas of the homeland, and their memories were set down in the form of legends and ballads rather than in established records. Not until the investigations of the twentieth century has it become clear from which parts of Croatia the inhabitants of the various villages came.[31] Not until the cultural awakening of this century were there ties of any kind between the Croats along the Austro-Hungarian frontier, and Croatia itself. For these Croatian peasants there does not seem to have existed either the desire for or the possibility of such contacts. All their political, economic, religious, and educational ties were focused east-west on the adjacent Hungarian and Austrian cities, and ultimately on Budapest or Vienna.

The settlement of the Croats in the border area was largely the result of the Turkish wars. Most of the settlement occurred in the first half of the sixteenth century, although some of the forested terraces of the south were opened to settlement as late as the mid-seventeenth century. The Croats immigrated to re-establish or found villages, and to supplement the population of those villages which still contained some German or Magyar inhabitants.

As a result of this immigration numerous islands of Croats sprang up throughout the flatter parts of western Hungary, the Vienna Basin and the Marchfeld. Many villages in the Vienna Basin are known to have been Croatian in the seventeenth century, and a solid cluster of Croatian villages, larger in area and population than any cluster in present Burgenland, occupied the southern portion of the Marchfeld. Within present Burgenland 90 of the present 320 townships had a Croatian element at the time, although it is probable that in at least half of these the population was mixed.

The present system of detailed censuses was unknown until the nineteenth century; consequently, most of the studies of the number of members of each ethnic group in a village were based on deductions gleaned largely from family names and from church records, and partially from other documents, names of pastors, drawings and descriptions of costumes and customs, and from old tombstones. Such deductions gave at best a spotty record, but it seems certain that a gradual assimilation of the Croats into the surrounding German majority occurred in the mixed villages on both sides of the boundary. Intermarriage, as well as the use of German in the neighboring villages and market towns, worked toward such a gradual assimilation. By 1900 there were within present Burgenland fifty-six villages with a Croatian majority. In those areas where Croatian villages formed clusters, the language had maintained itself strongly and probably absorbed German and Magyar elements.

By 1900 a sharp contrast was noticeable on the linguistic maps. The Croatian clusters and individual villages still existed in western Hungary but had disappeared in Austria. According to Hûrský, around the year 1600 there were some 20 villages in present northern Burgenland and 24 in the Vienna Basin, all with a substantial Croatian population.[32] In 1900, of these villages, 18 in northern Burgenland were still largely Croatian; none remained in the Vienna Basin. The huge cluster in the southern Marchfeld had disappeared as well. By 1900 there was not one Croatian village left within Lower Austria, while, on the other hand, within Hungary the original pattern had maintained itself through the three centuries.

This contrast between Austria and Hungary in the continuance of the Croatian language and culture cannot be attributed to a greater isolation of the Hungarian villages. Northern Burgenland is almost as flat and open as is the Vienna Basin, and it was through this area that the principal highways between Vienna and Hungary ran. From the earliest days of their residence within western Hungary, the Croats there had almost as easy and as frequent contact with Vienna as had the Austrian Croats just across the boundary. Many of the Hungarian Croats became *Wanderarbeiter*, working in Vienna and returning at regular intervals to their home villages. Even today the Viennese sometimes use the term *Krowotten* in reference to all Burgenlanders.

The critical difference between Hungary and Austria was in education. The Croatian villages within Hungary had Croatian teachers; those within Austria had German teachers. In fact, it can be said that, contrary to general opinion, Hungary was more tolerant of her minorities than was Austria, and that the reason for the presence of a Croatian minority within Burgenland today, just as for the presence of a Protestant minority, is simply that this area was within Hungary.

The introduction of widespread education in both countries took place in the reigns of Maria Theresa and Joseph II, although a few schools had existed in the larger villages of both Austria and Hungary before this time. But there was a fundamental difference between the schools established in Austria and those in Hungary; in Austria the schools were almost entirely under state control, while in Hungary they were nearly all under the direction of the churches. The state schools, particularly during the reign of Joseph II, worked towards the molding of a culturally uniform population, and education was in German. Within Hungary, on the other hand, the churches based their educational procedures on the local situations. Since the Croats were all Catholic, it was the attitude of the Catholic Church that was all-important. The Catholic Church was both conservative and practical; it treasured the indigenous cultures, and it tried to bring its teachings to the people in terms of their language and customs.[33] Until the late nineteenth century the Hungarian state exercised only a very loose supervision of the church schools and made no attempt to interfere with their use of the vernacular.

As far as can now be ascertained, the Croats within Austria in no way resisted their Germanization. Rather they reportedly favored the establishment of German-language schools, since they felt that a knowledge of German would be essential if their children were to advance economically or politically within Austria. The close contacts with Vienna had given them all a speaking knowledge of dialect German; now they felt that they would be able to master the reading and writing of "real" German. It seems also that the Croats came to experience a mass "inferiority complex"; they felt that their language and customs branded them as ignorant peasants, as "hicks." The Germans in Central Europe have often claimed the superiority of the German language and culture over those of the Slavs and Magyars. This attitude was soon absorbed by the younger people, and as soon as a generation knowing German had grown up, Croatian was relegated to the position of those embarrassing customs that had to be kept up for the sake of the parents and grandparents. Although around 1800 the southern Marchfeld was still solidly Croatian, by mid-century it had become Germanized, and by 1870 the peasants were ashamed to be seen in their *Trachten* (the lovely peasant costumes). Approximately a half century had been sufficient to Germanize a solid cluster of over a dozen Croatian villages, and very few Austrians or Hungarians now realize that there were once Croatian villages in Lower Austria.

In 1961 in Burgenland, some persons who remembered the years before 1918 commented that had Hungary had another fifty years without the Great War, she would have succeeded in Magyarizing most of her non-Magyars. Looked at in restrospect, Hungary, in contrast to Austria, may have suffered from too much tolerance, and perhaps what was wrong with her policy of forced assimilation was that it came too late.

All the Croats who were in school at the time remember the changes around the year 1907. Whereas before, teaching had been principally in Croatian, now it became chiefly in Magyar. Religion continued to be taught in Croatian, however. There appears to have been no marked reaction among the Croats; they simply accepted the change and, if anything, welcomed the new policy.

At the beginning of the twentieth century migrant labor was common among the Croats of present Burgenland. To supplement the family income the younger men and women moved seasonally to the Hungarian or Austrian cities and manors. Consequently, the Croatian parents felt that it was essential that their children learn Magyar and German. Croatian they would learn at home in any case, and more than a colloquial village tongue, Croatian could not be; it had no economic, political, or intellectual possibilities. As a result, a remarkable system of short-term apprenticeship developed. The child was placed as a servant in a Magyar village, and then in a German village. Each of these terms lasted about two years on the average. In this manner the child learned the language, and earned at least his or her room and board. The introduction of Magyar teaching into the schools meant that the two years in a Magyar village could be eliminated, and the family could procure the use of the young person's work on the land or earnings in the city two years earlier than previously. Thus, just as the Croats welcomed German teaching in Austria, so many Hungarian Croats welcomed Magyar teaching in Hungary. Again it appears that the mistake of the Magyars in this regard may have been their tardiness rather than their rigor.

Thus, a generation of Croats learned Magyar in the schools, but, as with the Germans, unless the student continued his education past the primary school, he continued to use the village dialect, and he continued to identify himself as a Croat. There was no movement, no stirring, no voice raised in protest against the educational system. The Church, which was the ultimate guardian of the language, was strongly pro-Hungarian. Not until the early part of 1919, when the Germans had already been promised their autonomy, did the Croats begin to press for their cultural autonomy on the basis of the principle of self-determination. In retrospect, it seems clear that the educated Croats had become Magyaronen just as much as the educated Germans had, and that in 1919–23 they distrusted the Austrians far more than they did the Hungarians.

BURGENLAND

THE TRANSFER OF
BURGENLAND TO AUSTRIA

At the end of that cataclysmic European tragedy, World War I, the Habsburg Empire disintegrated. Where formerly there had been a union under one monarch, now there were a number of fragments which were regrouped by the victorious Western Powers.

In the Paris peace deliberations which formalized all these changes, Hungary was perhaps treated the harshest of all the losing states. It is true that Austria lost an empire, but the ancestral Austria remained relatively intact, and Germany surrendered only a small proportion of her area, population, and resources. In contrast to these, Hungary was utterly shattered. Five different states obtained territory at the expense of Hungary, and one of these alone, Romania, received a territory larger than the portion left to Hungary. It would seem that Hungary was simply dissected for the benefit of her neighbors.[1]

There appear to have been several reasons for this intentional destruction of a historic European state.[2] First of all, it was common knowledge throughout Europe that the Magyars had attempted to suppress the linguistic strivings of the non-Magyars within the kingdom. The work of Seton-Watson and others had publicized widely the methods used by Magyar officials against the Slovaks. To this damning evidence was added the propaganda of the Czech and Serbian groups in the Western capitals during the war. Both the Czechs

and Serbs felt that they had brethren within Hungary, and they publicized this kinship well.

Once Croatia and Bohemia had been separated from the Dual
Monarchy, the direction of Czech and Serbian expansion led chiefly
into Hungary proper. If Bohemia was to increase her area and population she could do so only by annexing Slovakian Upper Hungary.
The non-Magyar "Succession States" all shared the desire to obtain
territorial contact with each other, and such contact could be acquired
only through Hungary, which occupied the center of the Danubian
lands. Czech leaders in Paris used their linguistic and strategic arguments skillfully and thus had a promise of Slovakia (and eventually
Ruthenia, extending to the new Romanian border) even before the
start of the peace deliberations.

Pro-Slavic sympathy was well developed in the West, in any case.
France had been bled white by the slaughter of World War I. In this
frightful war, Russia had for three years helped contain the armies
of Germany, and though Russia had become Bolshevik, the Slavs to
the east of Germany still enlisted the sympathy of France. French
cultural ties with Eastern Europe had been strong before World War
I, and the French looked upon the numerically smaller Slavic and
Romanian peoples as their protégés. After the war these lesser Slav
peoples could act as the friends of France to protect her against the
continuing German menace. The new nations to the east were expected to form a wall against the Germans, and it was to the interest of
the Western Powers, notably France, to make these states as strong
as possible. Since one way to strengthen them was to give them larger
and larger bits of Hungary, such pieces were liberally awarded.

Then too, the Magyars undeniably suffered from their singular
heritage. It was precisely their much treasured individuality and
uniqueness that helped turn the Western Powers against them. They
were not like the rest of the Europeans and their language was incom-
prehensible to others. The Magyars boasted of the days when they
had been the scourge of Europe. To have been horsemen of the steppe
was to the Magyars a source of pride, but to Western Europeans it
was a mark of brutal inhumanity. The Germans had been labelled
"Huns," since that name implied the extreme degree of barbarity;
yet, the Magyars actually claimed kinship with the Huns. The Slavs
had emphasized this, and had suggested that the rigor of the Magyarization program was due to the Asiatic characteristics of these plunderers, who did not belong to the European family of nations. On
reading the literature of 1919 on this subject, one cannot fail to be
struck by the attitude taken by some Western observers toward the
severe losses imposed on Hungary; the cutting away of three-quarters

of her territory was looked upon as a simple act of justice, as a compensation to the other nations for enduring her unspeakable domination for so many centuries.[3]

The aristocratic bearing of the Magyars only aggravated this attitude. At a time when the word "democracy" had become almost a fetish, the Magyars claimed to be a nation of aristocrats. All descendents of the original Magyars considered themselves to be of noble blood, and the great landowners lived as potentates. The Magyars made little pretense of being "democratic," whereas all the other national groups now espoused the cause. Again, it was considered by some only a matter of justice to make Hungary pay for the centuries of feudal repression of the non-Magyar peoples.

This development of animosity towards the Magyars was brought to a climax when the proximity of communism sent a shiver of dread through the Western governments. During the complete chaos at the end of the war, a Communist government under Béla Kun assumed power in Hungary. Suddenly, the Red terror had been extended into Central Europe; the Bolsheviks were only thirty miles from Vienna. The Communist government of Hungary lasted for only four months, March–August, 1919, but it was during these months that the terms of peace were set at Paris.[4]

Finally, the influence of maps must be mentioned. Towards the north, east, and south, the Magyars lived intermixed with the other linguistic groups of Hungary. However there was a basic distinction: the Magyars were principally city dwellers, the others peasants or herders.[5] The maps of linguistic distributions stressed not the numbers of people but areal distributions of people. On such maps cities vanished, and one hundred shepherds on a broad, barren upland could make a greater visual impression than 100,000 people in a city below. The peacemakers worked with statistics, true, but the boundaries were delimited on the basis of these maps, so that many Magyar cities were separated from Hungary because the surrounding hilly countryside was principally Romanian or Slovakian. Within Transylvania, for example, the lowland center and the cities were principally Magyar or German, whereas the far broader upland surfaces of the Carpathians and the Bihar were populated by Romanians. Thus, though the proportion of Magyars to Romanians was approximately two to three, the language maps of Transylvania implied that a small island of Magyars was surrounded by a vast sea of Romanians.

The severe peace terms bred a Magyar fanaticism which made the previous program of Magyarization seem mild in comparison. Not only had the intactness of the old kingdom been shattered, but Hungary had had to surrender her former capital, Pozsony, and the cradle of her rebirth, Transylvania, as well as her port, most of her forests and minerals, and the headwaters of her rivers. It is understandable why, at least until the end of World War II, the desire for a revision of the Treaty of Trianon dominated the foreign and domestic policies of Hungary.

During the collapse of the Habsburg Empire three nationalistic forces contended for the territory that is now Burgenland. Each of these groups stressed a different argument: the Magyars, tradition; the Germans, language; and the Slavs, strategic considerations. For the Hungarians this western borderland was a part of the kingdom of St. Stephen and, as such, to be defended against outside occupation. The Hungarians were especially bitter at the Austrian attempts to acquire this territory; they felt that it was dishonorable of Austria, for whom Hungary had fought for four years, to take land from her former ally.

German (Austrian) claims on this strip of land were based on linguistic nationalism. The inhabitants spoke German, therefore their home should be within a German state. Economic arguments (the need to feed Vienna) and historic precedents (this had been part of the Reich of Charlemagne) were used to buttress the linguistic cause.

The Slavic (mainly Czech) claims on the area were based, ideologically, on the Pan-Slavic dream of a territorial union of all the Slavs. The principal argument was, however, stated in more practical terms. A land connection between Slovakia and Croatia would not only allow for economic and military coöperation between the Czechs and the South Slavs, but also insure the strategic separation of Austria and Hungary. This territorial passageway was formulated as a "corridor" between the new Czech-Slovak and Serb-Croat-Slovene states.

The corridor idea was not fashioned in 1918. As early as 1848 the Slav Congress, meeting in Prague, had adopted the plan of Jan Kollár calling for the creation of a corridor, through western Hungary, to join the north and south Slavs. The existence of the Croatian enclaves in the area seemed to make the proposal reasonable. As Czech groups began to concern themselves with the coming Bohemian state, the corridor idea became increasingly popular. In 1900 the future Czech finance minister, Raschin, stressed the need of the future Czech state for an outlet to the Adriatic; in 1910 the mayor of Zagreb made an attempt to win the Croats of the western Dunántúl to the ideal of a Croatian state. In 1914 the Czech, Karl Kramař, presented to the Russian ambassador in Paris, Izvolskij, a planned "Constitution of the

Slavic Empire," which dreamt of a greater Slavic realm including Russia, Poland, Czecho-Slovakia, Bulgaria, and Jugoslavia (with the Tsar as ultimate ruler) and a corridor in western Hungary to join the northern and southern Slavs. During World War I, Czechs and South Slavs, in various Western capitals, worked on planned divisions of the Habsburg Monarchy, with the corridor usually figuring in these plans.

The leader of the Czechs, Thomas Masaryk, realized that the stated linguistic (the Croatian enclaves), historical (a medieval corridor had been destroyed by the Germans and Magyars), and economic (ties with the Adriatic) arguments were rather weak. In his Memoir II, to the British foreign minister (concerning the boundaries of the future Czech-Slovak state) in April, 1915, Masaryk tried to meet the expected objections by maintaining that since the principle of self-determination could not be followed completely, it must, in this case, give way to a higher political interest, namely that of isolating the Germans and Magyars to prevent their alliance against the Slavs. The actual plan was worked out in correspondence between Masaryk and the Croat, Lorković. Of the total population of approximately 850,000 in the area concerned, only 55,000 were Slavs (all Croats). This plan was laid before the Russian ambassador and French Foreign Minister Briand in 1916; to insure French support, the corridor was depicted as forming part of a "Slavic wall" reaching from the Baltic to the Adriatic, to prevent German expansion.

The pro-Austrian forces were centered outside of western Hungary, and most of the initial, and outspoken, leaders had had little, if any, contact with the area whose annexation they were demanding. As mentioned previously, the first pro-German voices were heard in Berlin. The Viennese movement for the transfer of present Burgenland to Austria may be considered to have its beginnings with the Patry article of 1906, although similar statements, and poems, had appeared in print in Vienna in the previous year. In 1907, under the leadership of men such as Patry, the "Society for the Maintenance of the German Nationality in Hungary" [6] was organized in Vienna. The expressed aim of this group was to acquire German West Hungary (the westernmost portions of the Dunántúl) for Austria. These men formed a cadre of the forces agitating for the transfer of the area to Austria, yet as late as October, 1918, only one of the members could call himself a "West Hungarian."

Tactically, the society pursued two goals. The first of these, and evidently the most important, was to kindle enthusiasm for the cause among the German-speaking people of Austria. The second aim was to gain support for the move among those actually concerned, the

Germans of West Hungary (as the area was then called).[7] These aims were advanced through newspaper articles, the dispatching of committees to call upon governmental officials, and the distribution of pamphlets among the peasantry of West Hungary. Until the collapse of the monarchy in October, 1918, the response to these efforts varied from lukewarm support to outright opposition.

A marked intensification in the society's propagandizing after October, 1918, was attributable primarily to the efforts of one man, Alfred Walheim, a Gymnasium professor of German literature in Vienna.[8] Between October, 1918, and the time of the Sopron Plebiscite, December, 1921, Walheim published at least 241 articles in twelve different publications, spoke at numerous mass meetings, and repeatedly acted as the spokesman of delegations approaching the leaders of the Austrian government.

It was through the efforts of this group that the issue was made familiar to the Viennese leaders and public. In the chaotic months following the collapse of the empire, this society gathered support for its activities not on ideological grounds but by stressing the envisioned increase in food supplies to the hungry metropolis. At the key moment the society was able to send one of its members, Dr. Beer (who knew French, German, and Magyar), as a special expert on West Hungary, with the Austrian delegation to the Paris peace conference.

Within West Hungary, pro-German agitation began in 1907, the year of the Apponyi School Law. Under the leadership of, among others, Karl Wollinger,[9] the miller in Heiligenkreuz im Lafnitztal, the Ungarländische Deutsche Volkspartei (Hungarian German People's party) was founded in Budapest to further the interests of the German-speaking people in Hungary. This man, passionately attached to the Pan-German ideal, exerted a considerable influence on the population in his local area. Under his leadership Heiligenkreuz printed tax books in German at its own expense, and in several villages German was reintroduced as the official language on the basis of the Nationalities Act of 1868. German candidates were put up for election in the local county in 1910 but without success.

In the extreme south of present Burgenland, Wollinger united a number of villages which became known as "the forty *Gemeinden* of Szent Gotthárd." In Eltendorf, on December 4, 1918, after speeches by Wollinger and pro-Hungarian officials, a meeting came to the following decision: "The Germans, gathered . . . in Eltendorf, demand for the Germans in West Hungary the rights of self-determination and ask the Austrian government to intercede, with all its means, at the peace negotiations in Paris, to have German West Hungary separated from Hungary and joined to German Austria." [10] On December 15, the representatives of the "forty Gemeinden" met in Heiligenkreuz to hear Wollinger, after which they announced their desire for union with Austria.

These "forty Gemeinden" [11] were all located in the lower Lafnitz and Rába valleys, which carried the only important through routes south of Sopron. The Lafnitz was the path of the principal highway from Graz into Hungary, the Rába the route of the railroad. Access to Graz was relatively simple, and the important Styrian market towns of Fürstenfeld, Fehring, and Feldbach, located close to the boundary, attracted much of the local trade of the border area. It is interesting that the connections by road to the local market centers, rather than the connections by railroad to the much larger, but much farther, Graz, evidently had the greater influence on local sentiments. Whereas most of the townships along the railroad were not represented in the list of the "forty Gemeinden," every township south of the Rába (road connections to Feldbach) and along the Lafnitz highway (connections with Fürstenfeld), as far as a village seven miles east of the present border, was represented in the "forty Gemeinden." Perhaps when the peasant boarded a train he felt that he was going to a far-off place with which his village had no organic connection, whereas when he walked or rode his oxcart to a nearby town he was visiting neighbors and kinsmen.

Elsewhere, however, Wollinger and his followers had scant success with either the authorities or the peasantry. By and large the inhabitants of present Burgenland accepted the fact that they were in Hungary; they believed that regardless of how the government acted, their land was a part of the unchangeable Kingdom of Hungary. In northern Burgenland connections with Lower Austria, and particularly with Vienna, were as close as those of the Lafnitz valley with Fürstenfeld, but the north possessed market centers of its own and, in Sopron, a major urban center. The north contained the major proportion of the intelligentsia, with a generally higher level of education than was true further south. With the exception of Wollinger, all the leaders of the German language group were in the north, and these had been educated in Hungary. They were imbued with a concept of the historic integrity of Hungary.

On January 27, 1919, the Hungarian government granted the Germans of West Hungary full autonomy. A new province, Westungarn, was to contain all the German-speaking areas of West Hungary, including numerous enclaves both of Magyars and of Croats.[12]

It is difficult to estimate how the situation would have developed had the Károlyi government been able to retain power. On March 21, 1919, Károlyi was forced to resign; he was succeeded by the Communist government of Béla Kun. Autonomy had already been granted the Germans and might have satisfied them had not the Red Republic been proclaimed. Undoubtedly, nothing united local opinion more than the advent of the Communist regime. Since a high proportion of the intellectuals were clergymen, Kun managed to unite, for the first time, the peasants of the south and many of the leaders of the north. Wollinger was arrested as a "counterrevolutionary."

The chronology of the Red regime was of great importance; it coincided with the time of the peace deliberations in Paris. There is no doubt that it proved to be the best possible propaganda for the transfer. Viennese newspapers were full of tales of terror and the flight of refugees. Béla Kun envisioned the loss of West Hungary in Marxist terms; he felt that he would be losing territory to capitalism as much as to Austria. In May, 1919, Kun stated that West Hungary would agree to join Austria only if that country also established the dictatorship of the proletariat. In July, 1919, when the report that the Entente had promised West Hungary to Austria was first heard, Kun remarked that he would be quite willing to have the question settled by a plebiscite, but one in which only the workers would be permitted to vote.

Rarely has a government advanced towards an addition of territory in as stumbling and irresolute a fashion as did Austria between 1918 and 1921. Despite the highly vocal efforts of the Society for the Maintenance of the German Nationality in Hungary, official Vienna did virtually nothing to obtain West Hungary, until the important plea of Chancellor Renner at the peace conference. Within the context of the events and the emotions of the time, however, this lack of action was understandable.

Austria was besieged by problems of such magnitude that the acquisition of West Hungary seemed trifling in comparison. These problems included the questions of South Tyrol, southern Carinthia, southern Styria, the 3,000,000 Germans in Bohemia-Moravia, the separatist desires of Vorarlberg, and the advisability of *Anschluss* with Germany, in addition to the critical problems of finance, transportation, commerce, and basic productivity that beset the mountainous stump of a great empire.

There was also much Austrian sympathy for Hungary—she had

remained loyal through all the bitter years of the war, and she was now being torn apart by the same groups that were rending Austria. The common fear of the creation of a Slavic corridor actually brought the Hungarians and Austrians together into a common effort to prevent this from occurring. The principal party of Austria in 1919, the Socialist party, hesitated to attempt to acquire territory at the expense of its Socialist (Károlyi) or Communist (Kun) comrades in Hungary. On the other hand, monarchism had not died suddenly in 1918 (nor has it died yet), and its adherents sympathized with the Hungarian desires to maintain the intactness of their land. The Pan-German *Deutschösterreichische Tages-Zeitung* often charged that the "Karlists" were striving for the continued areal integrity of Hungary in order to help the Habsburg Karl regain the throne of Hungary (as he actually attempted to do in his flight into Hungary in October, 1921). This legitimist thinking influenced the second major party of Austria, the Christlichsoziale Partei. When the Hungarian Red Republic was succeeded by the Horthy reaction, on August 1, 1919, the Christian Socialists felt, as the Socialists had previously, that they could not take territory from their comrades in Hungary. There was also a fear prevalent that Hungary might invoke some sort of economic sanctions, perhaps going to the extreme of stopping food supplies to a starving Austria.

The active protagonists of an annexation of West Hungary never numbered more than an insignificant minority. "The official opinion of Austria, from 1918 to 1920, in its overwhelming majority, had relatively little interest in the acquisition of Burgenland." [13]

Despite the agitation in Vienna and within Burgenland, the decisions settling the future of the area were all made in Paris. At the peace conference the Slavic claims on West Hungary were clearly given priority, and Austrian and Hungarian claims to the area were not examined until after the corridor had been studied and rejected.

On February 6, 1919, Czech Prime Minister Kramař and Foreign Minister Beneš asked the Entente Powers in Paris for a territorial connection between the new Czech-Slovak and Serb-Croat-Slovene states. "In this manner the Germans will finally be cut off from the East, and the Czechoslovak state will have gained a greater stability." [14] Beneš further maintained that it was necessary for the establishment of stability in Central Europe that Bohemia have territorial ties with both Jugoslavia and Romania. "Friendly relations with Hungary will follow as a matter of economic necessity." [15]

The Czechs won considerable support for the corridor from the Allies, particularly the French, who found the idea of a "Slavic wall," barring all German advances to the east, very appealing. France also looked upon the Succession States as her protégés, and felt that any strengthening of the future Little Entente would improve her power position in Europe. The British and Americans do not seem to have been strongly for or against the plan, though they might have acquiesced with the French support of the idea.[16] British delegate Harold Nicolson accepted the corridor as "just." [17]

The plan was killed by the Italian delegation, which expressed itself as so strongly opposed to such a corridor that the proposal had to be rejected. Since the basic assumption behind the corridor plan was the military and economic coöperation of the Czechs with the South Slavs, Italy could have looked forward to a vastly strengthened, unfriendly (because of the enmities concerning Trieste, Fiume, and Dalmatia) state on her flank. Were this plan ever to achieve its full ideologically envisioned dimensions, Jugoslavia could face Italy with the massed power of over 200,000,000 Slavs behind her.

Italy also hoped to be able to assume the role of the leading power in the Danubian areas. Since the Succession States had already been tied to France (or a Slavic union), only in Austria and Hungary could Italy find possibilities for an extension of her power and influence. Of these two, Hungary was certainly the more promising; Italy could not allow Hungary to be isolated from her and the West.

It is doubtful, however, that the corridor would have created a core of power capable of withstanding German and Russian expansion. The Slavs have never been able to work together (any more than all the "Germanic" or all the "Latin" peoples have been able to), and the largest of the Slav states was to prove a great menace to the independence of the Succession States. Both Jugoslavia and Czechoslovakia were disunited within their own borders, and these two states had different outlooks and foreign interests. Czech commerce preferred to move toward the North Sea rather than the Adriatic, and it is highly doubtful that a corridor would have altered this. The two states probably would have agreed only to oppose Hungary, and perhaps Austria (as they did), neither of which was to constitute the most serious threat to their power positions and independence.[18]

The Hungarians naturally considered the corridor to be an intolerable proposition. Hungary would have been entirely surrounded by her enemies, the three states forming the Little Entente. The corridor would have virtually destroyed the independence of remnant Hungary and perhaps even of Austria, and if it had remained in existence until 1956, it would have prevented the escape of most of the refugees fleeing Communist Hungary.

After the defeat of the corridor proposal, the matter of who should have control of West Hungary was considered to be of secondary importance. The Entente Powers established a commission to study the question but decided that as long as the Austrian and Hungarian delegations did not raise the issue, the Allies would do nothing. The Western leaders felt that since Austria had recognized the boundary in 1867, it should remain as it was.[19]

On June 16, 1919, the Austrian delegation made its first definitive move towards obtaining West Hungary. Chancellor Renner [20] transmitted the following note to the Entente Powers.

"It is correct that the Leitha has been for long the boundary between Austria and Hungary; yet, through the creation of the monarchy, this river became only an administrative boundary. . . . One must reckon on the fact that this boundary is not further than the range of heavy artillery . . . from Vienna, of only a rifle from Wiener Neustadt, and a distance of a day's march from Graz. . . . The Sopron vicinity has long been the vegetable garden of Vienna; the supply of milk and fresh meat to Vienna is met largely by Sopron, Vasvár, and Moson comitats; the city of Graz, finally, which lies at the foot of the Alps, draws its food supplies, in which it and its mountainous hinterland are deficient, largely from West Hungary. . . . One should only imagine that the boundary of France ran from Chantilly past Meaux to Melun, and that of England lay at Canterbury and ask yourselves if Paris or London could feel itself in full peace in such circumstances.

"Geography, history, and economic life indicate the way one must follow to overcome these difficulties. The outliers of the East Alps extend, they dominate, as far as that area of West Hungary in which, since the Middle Ages, predominantly Germans have lived, and since that time have stood unbrokenly in direct trade relationships with Vienna, Graz, and Wiener Neustadt. Budapest, which, on the contrary, lies far removed from this area, and, even more, speaks another language, has no need for its production since the neighboring Hungarian Basin supplies better and more richly what it needs for its food supplies. German Austria has the right, on geographic, national and economic grounds, to claim this area; yet it does not strive for an arbitrary annexation, rather it leaves this question exclusively, as in all other territorial questions, to the free decision of the nations. On these grounds we ask that the inhabitants of these areas be given the right to decide themselves, through a free plebiscite, whether or not they wish to be united to German Austria." [21]

On June 25, the Austrian delegation handed the Powers another note, asking specifically for the contiguous areas of Moson, Sopron, and Vasvár megyek that were compactly settled by German-speaking people. The request did not include the German areas near Bratislava for fear of antagonizing the favored Czechs, who had occupied that city on January 1, 1919. As a result of these formal requests, the Council of Foreign Ministers decided to study the question.

The Entente made its decision on July 11, 1919. Britain, France, the United States, and Japan voted for the transfer of German West Hungary to Austria; Italy voted against it. On July 20, 1919, the second part of the Conditions of Peace was transmitted to the Austrian delegation. The terms included the transfer of West Hungary, and delineated in its general lines the future boundary. There was to be no plebiscite because, with the Communist rule in Hungary, and the coincident chaos of the fighting between the Hungarians and the Czechs, Romanians, and Serbs, it would have been virtually impossible to carry out such a plebiscite. The delegates also felt that a plebiscite was "needless in view of the clearly defined ethnic frontier." [22]

The award was made official in Article 27, Point 5, of the Treaty of St. Germain, and in Article 27 of the Treaty of Trianon.[23] The transferred territory was not to include all the German-settled areas; the triangle of fertile, productive land east of Lake Neusiedl was to be split between Hungary and Austria. In reply to an Austrian protest, the Allies declared that the boundary would have to remain west of the Bratislava-Csorna railroad so that not all the lines for Bratislava to the south would be in Austrian hands; thus that city would be assured of access to the Adriatic through both countries. The Czechs expected that they would scarcely be the enemies of Austria and Hungary at the same time.

Throughout all the deliberations and the agitation which swirled above and around them, the attitude of the peasants of West Hungary remained obscure. No serious attempts were made to ascertain their feelings and desires. Most observers simply assumed that, because of language, the Burgenland peasants would prefer to join Austria. Though it is hazardous after forty years to make judgments on such matters, it does seem that by mid-1919 the majority of the inhabitants of German West Hungary did prefer to join Austria. There appear to have been several reasons for this transfer of loyalty from Hungary to Austria.

One of the most important factors making it possible for the peasants to accept the change was that the transfer was to be to the state to which they had, in a sense, belonged for centuries. Despite all the rebellions and strife, Hungary and Austria had been united under the Habsburgs. The move to Austria was, therefore, not a sharp break; in fact, many of the inhabitants did not consider it so much a move away from Hungary as back to Austria. This sentiment was expressed in the slogan of the time, *Zurück zu Österreich* ("Back to Austria").

The union with Austria existed also in the realm of economics. Whereas, for example, the Czechs and the Slovaks, the Croats and the Serbs, had had few economic ties with each other, the Germans of West Hungary had long focused their economic life on Vienna. The imperial capital had been the principal market for the agricultural produce, and a major employment center for the surplus labor of West Hungary. Many, if not most, of the families of West Hungary had some relative(s) living in Vienna. In this respect too, the union with Austria was looked upon more as a reunion than a transfer.

The war had also helped to intensify the familial feeling of the Burgenlanders for the German Austrians.[24] During their four years of armed service the men of German West Hungary had discovered that, since they could speak the same language, they shared more in common with the German Austrians than with the Magyars of Hungary. The Magyarization of the schools had not been in effect long enough to bring about any change in the native language of the peasants; it had merely prevented them from learning any language well. They had been taught a language which was not used, and given no instruction in the one actually spoken. The soldiers developed a kinship based on language and came to resent the form of schooling they had known.

All these factors made a move to Austria agreeable to the inhabitants of German West Hungary; however, it is doubtful that they would have sought or even approved of the move had they lacked a new idea which seemed to make the transfer both possible and just. Certainly, early in 1918 the vast majority of the peasants (and even more of the intellectuals) still clung to the old idea of the necessary integrity of the lands of the Crown of King St. Stephen. No matter how the Magyar may have looked down upon the *Svab*, the Kingdom of Hungary was an accepted fact. The hopes of the peasantry were directed towards an improvement of its lot within Hungary, and most of the initial plans of 1918–19 worked towards liberty, autonomy, and justice within Hungary.

Though a new political concept was in the air, it was first clearly articulated by President Woodrow Wilson. The impact, in Central Europe, of his "right of self-determination" cannot be overestimated. Technically, "self-determination" does not necessarily mean that national units are to be based on the areal extensions of language, but the principle was quickly placed within the mold of linguistic nationalism. As a consequence, linguistic nationalism was, for the first time, proclaimed as a *right*. Suddenly the non-Magyar peasant felt that he was no longer necessarily held by the idea of an established Hungary; instead he was free to have his lands join a state of his language. The new idea was not automatically adopted by the peasants, the vast majority of whom seem to have accepted without question the fact that their lands belonged in Hungary. However, the Germans of West Hungary quickly noted how the victorious Czechs, Serbs, and Romanians were making the new principle supersede the old state idea. As one old peasant stated in the spring of 1957, "Wilson said that Burgenland could come to Austria." Wilson probably said nothing of the kind, but his idea was interpreted to mean this. German nationalists blame Wilson for not bringing to Austria all the Germans of western Hungary, whereas the Magyars and Magyaronen blame him for the destruction of the old political system.[25]

In the spring of 1919 all these factors coalesced into a genuine desire to join Austria. The theme *Zurück zu Österreich* formed the basis of this desire; the Communist rule in Hungary raised this desire to the point of desperation; and the principle of self-determination made the transfer seem justified. Nine centuries earlier the enduring idea of a Roman limes along the Danube had been destroyed by the symbol of the Crown of King Stephen; now the venerable idea of the lands of the Crown was replaced, at least partially, by the new idea of linguistic self-determination.

THE SOPRON (ÖDENBURG) PLEBISCITE

The territory that had been awarded to Austria included only one urban center. Eisenstadt and Rust were, technically, "cities," but neither of these, nor any other settlement in Burgenland, had 5,000 inhabitants. Sopron (Ödenburg) was the indisputable center of the transferred area. Upon the site of the Hallstatt and Roman Scarbantia had risen a new city commanding the narrow passageway between an Alpine spur and the wet lands of Lake Neusiedl and the Hanság swamp. Sopron had been, since the first centuries of Hungary, one of the key border cities of the kingdom and had developed intimate economic relations with Vienna and Wiener Neustadt. The cattle and hogs of Sopron and Vasvár megyek were brought into the market of Sopron and from this significant point of concentration were moved directly to Vienna. Since the transferred area had been separated from its other urban centers, Sopron also became the central point for all the activities aimed at organizing the new Austrian territory.

However, just because Sopron was the most vital point of German West Hungary, the Hungarians made special efforts to retain it. The chaotic conditions within Hungary aided them in these attempts, since these disturbances delayed the completion of the peace treaty for several years. The Treaty of St. Germain (Austria and the Allies) was completed on September 10, 1919, but it did not go into effect until after the completion of the Treaty of Trianon (Hungary and the Allies) on July 26, 1921. This time lapse allowed the Hungarian government almost two extra years in which to attempt to rally the Burgenlanders back to the consciousness of the sacred integrity of the "lands of King St. Stephen." Since the Red Republic had been over-thrown on August 1, 1919, these attempts met with much success.

August 20, 1921, was the date set for the transfer of Burgenland to Austria. The occupation of the territory by members of the Austrian gendarmerie was prevented, however, by bands of Hungarian "volunteers." After a brief period of small-scale warfare, the Austrian police retired completely from the area. The Hungarian government refused to accept any responsibility for the bands but utilized the situation to press for compromise settlements which would have granted Hungary substantial territorial retentions. A state of semi-anarchy existed for over a month within the disputed area.

The question of the origin and character of these "volunteer bands" has been the source of much hatred of the Hungarians by the German nationalists of Austria. The Austrians claim that the bands consisted not of Burgenlanders but of Hungarians from inner Hungary, who were brought into the area to reconquer Burgenland. These writers always place quotation marks around "volunteer bands" and often refer to them simply as "bands" or even "bandits." The atrocities committed by these fighters have been described in many Burgenland articles and speeches. On the other hand, the Hungarians look upon these men as patriotic heroes willing to die for the preservation of a part of the fatherland. The term "uprising" (*felkelés*) is always used to describe the events, and the participants are referred to as members of an uprising army (*felkelőhadsereg*).

It is clear that these bands were not formed within present Burgenland; rather, they were largely organized in the Hungarian cities along the frontier, Sopron, Magyaróvár, Kőszeg, and Szombathely. Since history records few if any organized peasant uprisings for political motives, it seems obvious that the formation of the pro-Hungarian forces must of necessity have been in the cities, none of which is now in Burgenland but all of which acted as centers for the area. Local members of the nobility and army were the organizers and leaders of the "uprising." It is clear from the Hungarian accounts that the success of d'Annunzio in Fiume had made a great impression on the Hungarians and served as their example. The students in the colleges in Sopron, Magyaróvár, and Szombathely formed a high proportion of the fighters; the ages of those killed attest to the probable student status of many of them. In addition, contingents of troops, largely from Kecskemét (far outside the area), took part in the actions. It was these bands of armed students and troops who attacked and drove back the advancing Austrian gendarmerie (entirely composed of non-Burgenlanders), and who then tried to gather recruits from among the peasants of Burgenland. An eyewitness described an incident in his home village in this way. A few of the fighters entered the village, summoned all the villagers with a drum roll, and first asked and then demanded that volunteers join them. In that particular village none joined, but this witness made clear that in other villages there were recruits. Certainly in the later stages of the action local Burgenlanders participated; at least two of the Hungarian dead were from within present Burgenland.[26]

To the Hungarian "volunteers" this was war, and many of the tales of beatings and expropriations must be understood in that light. In return the Hungarians have claimed that the Austrian gendarmes took hostages. Residents who were known to have been actively working for the transfer to Austria were severely beaten, although not executed. (Miltschinsky, on p. 32, describes the treatment of the druggist in Deutschkreutz at the hands of a band.) The bands also, of necessity, lived "off the land" and demanded their sustenance from the villagers. There is no doubt that the invasion of the bands and the resultant combat and occupation caused great hardships in some parts of Burgenland. One can still hear many stories of the time, but these tales, though often voiced in tones of horror, do not include references to murder, military-tribunal executions, rape, or outright looting. In comparison to most military actions, this appears to have been fairly mild.

The Allies saw the specter of an attempted return of the Habsburgs in the Hungarian actions and threatened Hungary with indefinite reprisals. The Czechs backed the Austrians throughout and threatened to march into Hungary. After a conference between Beneš and Austrian Chancellor Schober on September 23, Czechoslovakia and Jugoslavia expressed their willingness to mediate the dispute. Italy thereupon entered the dispute, and called the representatives of Austria and Hungary to a conference in Venice.

The result of this Italian mediation was the Protocol of Venice of October 13, 1921. This agreement was clearly a victory for Hungary. Austria agreed that she would refrain from any mass firing of officials

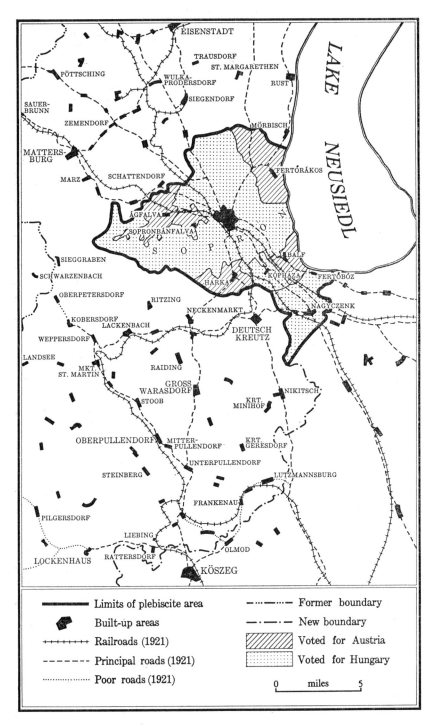

MAP 6. THE SOPRON PLEBISCITE AREA

in the acquired territory (the Pan-Germanists wished, of course, a wholesale replacement of the Hungarian officials by Germans), and would grant a general amnesty to all in Burgenland (thus preventing the prosecution of those who had committed acts of thievery and terrorism during the recent months of anarchy).[27] In reply to furious denunciations of the agreement, Chancellor Schober stated that he felt unable to refuse the offer of Italy, since such a refusal would have signified a rebuff to the entire Entente.

Most important, the Protocol of Venice called for a plebiscite in Sopron and eight surrounding villages, to determine to which country they wished to adhere. In delimiting the area of the plebiscite the Hungarians gained acceptance of the principle that no township (Gemeinde) was to be divided. This decision was of considerable significance, since the free city of Sopron included within its city limits large portions of the Sopron Range, with the coal mines of the Brennberg, and extended to within three miles of the former Austro-Hungarian border. As Map 6 indicates, the city limits of Sopron are so intricate that they virtually surround the villages of Ágfalva, Sopronbánfalva, and Fertőrákos; these were, therefore, included in the plebiscite area as forming an intimate economic union with the city. The villages of Harka, Kópháza, Balf, Fertőbóz, and Nagyczenk lay between Sopron and Hungary and were, of necessity, included also.

Everyone seems to have expected Austria to lose.[28] The ardent proponents of the transfer referred continually to the plebiscite as a "comedy" or a "swindle." They were even warned by members of the Austrian government to expect to lose since Austria could not be allowed to win.[29] General C. H. Ferrario, who was the official supervisor of the plebiscite, supposedly remarked later that the plebiscite had only had the aim of setting up the legal apparatus for an undoubted loss for Austria.

Walheim and his compatriots did not cease trying to influence a vote for Austria, but their opinions were still held by only a minority of the Viennese public. Walheim led numerous meetings and penned many articles under the title "Without Ödenburg No Burgenland." [30] He was incensed at the lack of concern or sympathy of the Viennese with the issue. "Should we lose Ödenburg because the *Wiener* feels trouble in his sleep about a bit of Burgenland?" [31]

Hungarian officials were allowed to remain in authority in the plebiscite area; they were even allowed to set up the lists of eligible voters. This was all done under the loose supervision of the Allied commission. The Austrian delegate entered complaint after complaint asking for delays. The Allied authorities allowed a delay of only three days, setting December 14 as the voting date. Chancellor Schober thereupon withdrew the Austrian delegate, telegraphing to the Allied commission in Sopron, "We do not take part in the plebiscite. Our plebiscite commissioner is being recalled immediately." [32]

The vote was a victory for Hungary, as is shown in Table 3.

TABLE 3

Township	Language	Ballots Cast	Percentages	
			Austria	Hungary
Ágfalva	German	848	83	17
Balf	German	595	60	40
Fertőbóz	German	342	22	78
Fertőrákos	German	1,370	61	39
Harka	German	581	90	10
Kópháza	Croatian	813	31	69
Nagyczenk	Magyar	1,039	0	100
Sopronbánfalva	German	1,177	81	19
			55%	45%
			(3,607)	(3,007)
Sopron		17,388	27%	73%
			(4,620)	(12,327)
Total Result		24,063 *	35%	65%
			(8,227)	(15,334)

* 502 votes were listed as void.

Most Austrians, and virtually all Burgenlanders, have maintained ever since that this plebiscite was a "swindle." [33] This assertion is based on the following, oft-quoted statements: (1) some 2,800 Germans were prevented from voting by terrorism; (2) some 2,000 citizens of Sopron were not entered on the voting lists because they had fled the city during the time of the "volunteer bands"; (3) the voting lists were completely falsified, and there was not sufficient time for the Austrian commission to check the lists; (4) students and soldiers in civilian dress were imported from Hungary to cast ballots; (5) some Hungarians voted several times; (6) Magyar Nagyczenk was included in the plebiscite area through the manipulation of the Hungarians. On the basis of these arguments Miltschinsky claims that in a fair election at least 70 per cent and probably 80 per cent of the votes would have been for Austria.[34]

Since all subsequent Austrian writings on the plebiscite have been based on these arguments as first stated by Miltschinsky, it is pertinent to this study to investigate his charges. A prime consideration in evaluating Miltschinsky's charges is the fact that his book is dated as having been written in January, 1922, within one month of the plebiscite. It seems probable that the figures given were unchecked and may have been the product of rumors, reports, and exaggerated charges. (Since he states that 100,000 Hungarian "volunteers" were guarding the boundary, his figures must be accepted with reservations.) Because the Austrian commissioner had been withdrawn prior to the plebiscite, there is no official Austrian report of the actual voting process. The number of those who are said to have fled Sopron, 2,000, is certainly suspect. Even the Viennese Pan-German newspaper, which was deeply involved in the events in Burgenland, made no mention of any such number of refugees.[35] Also, as Walheim mentioned, refugees did return to Sopron.

The origin of the figure, 2,800, given for the Germans who were prevented from voting, is interesting. Miltschinsky notes that there was a difference of 2,815 between the number eligible to vote and the number of ballots cast, and concludes that these voters must have been kept from the polls by terror. Therefore, he reasons further, this number consisted "virtually entirely of pro-Austrian votes."[36] To assume that everyone who did not vote would have voted for your side may be comforting, but it hardly seems tenable. Wambaugh discounts the effects of "terror" on the voting, and the closest approximation to an unbiased eyewitness account that we possess states that the Germans were not hindered from going to the polls.[37]

Miltschinsky further lists the number of names which the Austrian commission added and deleted from the voting lists during the checking process. The total of the figures given comes to 1,934 names added and 670 subtracted. This evidence is far more impressive than the previous charges but actually proves little. Because of the lack of time only four of the eight districts in Sopron, and one of the eight villages, were checked. Four of the districts checked were in Sopron, and yet it was Sopron which swamped the pro-Austrian results of the villages. Among the villages only Fertőrákos (Kroisbach) was checked; yet, despite the 522 names added by the Austrians in this village, Fertőrákos produced only a 61 per cent for Austria, whereas three of the "unchecked" villages produced totals of 90, 83, and 81 per cent, respectively. The charge that some Hungarians voted more than once is substantiated by some Burgenlanders stating that they spoke to persons who claimed to have done this or who knew someone else that did so. How many there were is impossible to tell.

Finally, it must be noted that Nagyczenk was included in the area awarded to Austria by the Treaty of St. Germain and hence was of necessity within the plebiscite area. Furthermore, the Austrian gendarmerie had planned in August to set up one of its posts in Nagyczenk, and therefore must have assumed that this Magyar village was to be included in Burgenland; the Hungarians can scarcely be blamed for the village's inclusion in the plebiscite area.

In her excellent, detailed discussion of the Sopron plebiscite, Miss Sarah Wambaugh repeats the above charges, and the Hungarian countercharges, and concludes that "as safeguards for a free plebiscite were lacking, the vote is not convincing one way or the other." [38] However, the attitudes and opinions expressed at the time of the plebiscite suggest that, despite a number of inaccuracies and probable falsifications, the result was probably correct; a majority of the inhabitants of the plebiscite area probably wished to remain in Hungary.

This conclusion is based on the following considerations:

1. Sopron had been strongly Magyarized. By 1920 the Magyars outnumbered the Germans, and the educated members of both groups were completely Hungarian in national consciousness. The vast majority of the intellectuals of present northern and middle Burgenland lived in Sopron and almost all were strongly pro-Hungarian. At the time of the creation of the autonomous Deutsch-Westungarn, the city council of Sopron voted to exclude itself from the new area on the grounds that Sopron was a Magyar city.[39] Walheim himself asked, "And which Ödenburg should be polled? The present one which the Magyars have made into a noticeably Magyar city, or the future one which we will have again made into a German city?" [40]

The city of Sopron had been the center of the movement for autonomy within Hungary rather than transfer to Austria. When the results of a local house-to-house poll were sent from the "forty Gemeinden of Szent Gotthárd" to the Paris peace conference, the leader of the Sopron faction made the trip to Paris to protest, in the name of 289 Gemeinden, against the transfer to Austria. In 1919, in accounting for the reluctance of Sopron to join Lower Austria, Walheim said, "The Magyaronen of Sopron . . . hope that with a separate province with its own parliament, and building its own government, [they can make] Sopron a center of Magyarism, to influence the population and prepare for a return to 'the Magyar Fatherland.' " [41]

2. Sopron was also a Hungarian political center, and much of the population was dependent for its livelihood on the governmental services in the city. Even though Sopron had already been established by the Austrians as the legal capital of the new Burgenland, the politicians and civil servants of Sopron could not be expected to trade the existent political importance of the city for a dubious status within a shadowy province. All the civil servants and lawyers must have hesitated to commit themselves to an entirely new legal system in a different language. Nor could they feel certain that they would be able to keep their positions within Austria. Of all the members of the

transferred population, they would undoubtedly have felt themselves to be the most vulnerable to replacement. And in case this was not clear to them, the Pan-German newspaper in Vienna made it starkly clear by openly discussing a replacement for the mayor of Sopron, Dr. Thurner, who "has become unacceptable because of his pro-Hungarian sentiments." [42]

3. The Hungarians made a profound impression with their argument that whereas Hungary had overcome communism and was ruled by a "Christian" government, the "Red" Socialists were either in power or very close to it in Austria.[43] The force of this appeal was strengthened by the recent experience of the population under the dictatorship of Béla Kun. On June 7, 1919, a brief peasants' rebellion against the Red regime broke out in seven villages just to the east of Sopron. This revolt was immediately crushed, and the villages were forced to pay heavy penalties in money and goods. Three of these villages were within the plebiscite area, and it may well account for the fact that German Fertőbóz gave only 22 per cent of its vote to Austria.[44]

It is to this fear of communism-socialism that Dr. Haller, whose wife was from Sopron, and who was in the city immediately after the vote, attributed the pro-Hungarian result. "The principal motive for their decision was a soberly realistic consideration. The conservative burghers of the city had no sympathy for the Austrian Marxism which at that time stood in the foreground [in Austria]." [45]

4. Among the peasants there was a general disillusionment with Austria. She had not defended them from a Jugoslav occupation in the south, a Czech bombardment and occupation in the north, or from the Hungarian bands. A Viennese newspaper quoted several as saying, "If we had known that Austria is so weak, then we would have considered carefully before we chose Austria." [46] The ineffectual actions of Austria made the peasants willing to believe the Hungarian assertion that Vienna wanted Burgenland only as a food-producing colony.

5. Apparently a clear identification of the terms "German" and "Austrian" was lacking. The German-speaking inhabitants thought of themselves as "Swabians" and believed that their ancestors had come from various parts of Germany. A German-Hungarian could feel kinship to the Germans, but not specifically to the Austrians. During the long strivings for autonomy the Sopron Germans had worked along with the other Germans within Hungary, and their political party had been organized on that basis. Austria, in turn, had left them to the hands of the Magyars in 1867 and was scarcely a fatherland. Within the new "rump Hungary," the Germans formed the only appreciable linguistic minority, and it is evident that many

Germans of present Burgenland felt that by going to Austria they would be deserting and seriously weakening the cause of the remaining Germans in Hungary. Undoubtedly, too, the German-Hungarians had inherited the feelings of all Hungarians that Austria had repressed and held back Hungary. Therefore, those Germans who felt national-istically German looked rather to the greater Germany than to Austria.[47]

6. The general fear of a move from a known into an unknown situation may have affected the vote.[48]

7. The Hungarians had made a strong appeal to the noblest patri-otic sentiments of the people. To vote for Austria became tantamount to voting against truth, faithfulness, loyalty, honor, and the homeland. Some of the banners hung from the windows of Sopron after the results became known stated, "Gott sei es gedankt—Treu geblie-ben." [49] In the victory demonstration the mayor, Dr. Thurner, made the statement that seventy million Germans would be proud of the Germans in Sopron; they would say, "These were true Germans and not villains, Germans who would not betray their country!" [50]

The above considerations cannot *prove* the validity of the an-nounced results. At this late date one can deal only in probabilities. Yet, even if one ignores all the charges and countercharges, it appears that an Austrian victory was, at best, unlikely. Fundamentally, the Austrians believe that Austria should have won because the Germans formed 55 per cent of the total population, and they assume that a German must have voted for Austria simply because he spoke German. For the reasons given above this appears an unwarranted assumption, and once we accept the probability that at least one quarter of the German-speaking people of Sopron voted for Hungary, the results seem certain; for, considering the passions of the time, it can be as-sumed that virtually all of the Magyars voted for Hungary.

The Allied commission accepted the vote as reasonably correct and, on January 1, 1922, awarded the Sopron area to Hungary.

The Hungarians regarded the victory as signifying more than the retention of a border city. They (and perhaps the Italians) seem to have hoped that a Burgenland without Sopron would be such a mon-strosity that it would fall to Hungary of its own weight; it would be forced to unite itself to its lost capital city. Walheim viewed the matter equally pessimistically, stating that with the renunciation of Sopron "nothing else would be achieved but the certain loss of the remainder of Burgenland." [51] The Hungarians were willing to accept this much also for its symbolic value; the Treaty of Trianon had been breached.

The prime agents in the entire matter of the plebiscite were the Italians. There can be little doubt that if the Allies had wished to enforce the full provisions of the treaties of St. Germain and Trianon, Hungary, despite any volunteer bands, would have had to accede. The French, British, and Americans were not especially interested in what took place between Austria and Hungary and were certainly in no mood to dispatch troops to quell the bands. The Entente Powers had been far more concerned about the possible return to power of the Habsburgs than about Sopron; they now praised Hungary for having refused to accept Karl when he made his dramatic flight into Hungary in October, 1921. The overcoming of the Communist threat was also considered in Hungary's favor. The settlement of the Sopron dispute was left entirely in the hands of the only interested member of the Entente, Italy.

In 1921 Italy found herself with a growing Slav power on her east. She had already hindered the union of the north and the south Slavs through her veto of the corridor proposal. Now she saw in a stronger Hungary her only possible ally in the event of a struggle with the new Jugoslavia. One Italian officer in Hungary declared in an interview that the Italians favored Hungary over Austria because only Hungary had the strength to prevent the erection of the corridor. Italy felt too that a Burgenland with Sopron, in the hands of an Austria so weakened that she was bound to become an economic satellite of Czechoslovakia, would become a pseudo corridor for the Czechs.

In this chaotic, protracted manner Burgenland, without Sopron, was transferred to Austria. Although the "right of self-determination" permeated all the political thinking and agitation of the time, the key decisions concerning the future of this borderland were made outside the area, by the members of the Entente. The victorious Allies alone had the power to transfer territories and, as usual, they made these transfers largely on the basis of their own foreign policies. Yet, of all the contested areas of 1919, Burgenland alone lay between two of the vanquished states, so that despite the three-cornered scramble for the area, the "right of self-determination" was largely satisfied.[52]

THE EASTERN BOUNDARY

If one drives along the eastern boundary of Burgenland (as is possible in several places), one is struck by the continued appearance of a "dirt road" in Hungary, immediately adjacent to the boundary. In and out of all the involved convolutions of this border the "dirt road" runs. This, one comes to realize, is the mine field. Along this strip are strands of barbed wire, and just behind, at frequent intervals, especially where the boundary cuts through forest, stand the wooden watchtowers. The mined strip does not appear to be a wide barrier, but for the Hungarian it is a complete barrier. The cemeteries in the Burgenland border villages contain the graves of those who died in the attempt to cross this strip.

And yet this boundary has known the largest mass migration of the past decade. Within three months in the winter of 1956–57 almost 200,000 Hungarians crossed into Austria. This was possible only because for a few months the border was not sealed. Following the Summit Conference in Geneva, an air of peace pervaded Central Europe. West and East might once more come to live together peaceably and to trade with each other. Austrians began taking trips to fabled Budapest, and delegates from almost all the countries of Eastern Europe attended the 100th anniversary celebration of the Geographische Gesellschaft in Wien. As its contribution to the new era of good feeling the Hungarian government removed the mines and the barbed wire from the frontier. Only the guards remained to watch the boundary. In the autumn of 1956 the "dirt road" was clearly visible but the mines were no longer there, and the occasional piles of rolled-up wire attested to the unsealed character of the border.

Then came the revolution, its repression, and the resultant chaos. During most of November, 1956, the border was completely open and the refugees streamed across. Later, as the Hungarian government regained control of the frontier areas, the guards returned. Then the refugees crossed at night, waiting in the forests and the marshes for darkness. To mark the boundary the Austrian government set up poles about five feet high along the entire length of the frontier; on each pole was a small red and white tuft of cloth, the Austrian flag. Burgenland peasants near the border went out after dusk, from the village centers to the fields to guide the refugees into villages for warm food and dry clothing. From these villages the refugees were usually moved to the local county seat and from there to the large *Lager* in Eisenstadt, or to the many camps in adjacent Lower Austria and Vienna.

Now the boundary is again sealed. The "dirt road" again contains its mines, and the barbed wire has been strung. Sentries stand in the wooden towers. There is almost no human movement noticeable near the border.

The peasants of Burgenland often act as if the boundary were just another feature of the terrain; they farm to within a few feet of the mines and seem scarcely to concern themselves about the fact. Yet the boundary remains strongly in the consciousness of the province and its people. They know that they are at the end of a world. As one person put it, "Here is Europe, there is Asia."

The eastern boundary of Burgenland is one of the strangest boundaries in existence. It manages to cut trade areas, lines of transportation, systems of communications, and to ignore strategic considerations with a consistency that is astounding. From north to south the air-line distance is approximately 100 miles, the length of the boundary 225 miles. Its many indentations, coupled with the topography of the province, effectively cut Burgenland into at least six separated regions.

The boundary rarely utilizes topographic features. The largest and most effective north-south barrier, Lake Neusiedl, forms the boundary for only four miles, and then *in reverse* (Hungary to the west, Austria to the east). The sharp scarp edge west of the lower Pinka valley or the less impressive forest belt east of the valley are not utilized; instead the line zigzags back and forth across the valley between them. Only in the Sopron Range does the boundary coincide with a drainage divide, for five miles. The closest approach to a concurrence of the boundary with a physical feature occurs, oddly enough, in the flattest portion of the border zone. The line has been demarcated in the middle of the Hanság marsh, a few feet north of the Einser Kanal; this, plus a tributary drainage ditch running north-south, carries the boundary for fourteen miles. This can scarcely be considered to be a major barrier, since it was in this corner that the majority of the Hungarian refugees crossed into Austria.

Broad settlement patterns do not coincide with the line. Basins and valleys are cut; in fact, the line was drawn through the areas of densest population. With a few exceptions the boundary was laid through arable areas in preference to forested areas. Nor did linguistic patterns coincide with the position of the line fixed in 1922. In the northeast the German area extended to Moson. Much of the Sopron salient was German speaking and several German villages remained east of the boundary in the south. The Croatian areas were also split by the line, particularly in the south.

A boundary commission, consisting of one Frenchman (chairman), one Englishman, and one Japanese, devoted most of 1922 to its task of determining the precise location of the new international boundary. They were accompanied by an Austrian and a Hungarian delegate. This group of five moved from village to village in the doubtful areas (but by no means everywhere), with a list of thirteen questions regarding local government, food and wood supplies, trade connections, markets, and religions, which they attempted to ask the citizenry of the concerned townships. Unfortunately, these questions were probably rarely answered honestly or completely. As soon as it was heard that the commission was coming, the villagers massed for a great demonstration, kissing the Hungarian flag or shouting *Hoch Österreich!*

The Viennese newspaper of the Great German party frequently accused the commission of making decisions that were unduly favorable to Hungary. It was alleged that the members of the commission were remaining overnight in the palaces of the nobility and having their just intentions led astray by the hospitality of the nobles.[1] At the present time one often hears in Burgenland that certain bits of territory remained in Hungary because the commission allowed itself to be swayed by the charm of the nobility. This assertion is not only repeated by peasants and schoolmasters (the latter are usually very nationalistic), but also is printed in scholarly publications.[2] Upon examination of the actual placement of the boundary it becomes clear, however, that the boundary commission performed its work as justly as was possible under the circumstances. It is true that the final line ran occasionally to the west of the vaguely delimited line of the peace treaties, but this was not the fault of the commission, as will be shown later.

The commissioners were also accused of establishing an unduly complicated boundary. As will be described, the commission had little choice in the actual placement of the line, and some of the most awkward configurations resulted from subsequent exchanges of territory between Austria and Hungary.

Even before the commission began its thankless task, two portions of the boundary had been determined. These were the sides of the Sopron salient, set by the results of the plebiscite, and the boundary between Kittsee and Petržalka in the extreme north. Petržalka (Engerau, Ligetfalu) was also German speaking but had been awarded to Czechoslovakia as a bridgehead south of the Danube and a potential suburb for Bratislava.

The boundary commission evidently felt itself committed to four principles. In order of importance these were: [3]

1. The railroad from Bratislava to Csorna must remain entirely within Hungary.

2. The self-determination of national adherence by the local population must be allowed as fully as possible.

3. Townships (Gemeinden) are not to be divided (cut internally). The boundary will, therefore, run along the township limits. If possible, counties (*Bezirke*) are to be treated as units.

4. Local trade areas and communications routes are to be kept intact as much as possible.

In practice, point 4 could rarely be followed. Problems arose, also in the northeast, on the question of residence versus ownership. Though much of the area was in the hands of pro-Hungarian noblemen, the wishes of the resident population were given preference. Special cases were the huge manorial work camps, the *puszta*'s or *Hof*'s which were scattered over the Little Alföld. These were populated by contract workers who formed their own communities, almost completely removed from the village centers. The inhabitants of these manorial centers were usually Magyar and pro-Hungary. If township limits only were to be followed these Magyar clusters would pass to Austria. In two cases, on the immediate border, these clusters were separated from their townships and allowed to remain in Hungary.

THE COURSE OF THE BOUNDARY

Neusiedl County [4]

Once it had been decided that the Bratislava-Csorna railroad must remain in Hungary and that township boundaries should not be cut, the present boundary was approximated. The townships on this flat plain are of such enormous size that the border remains well back

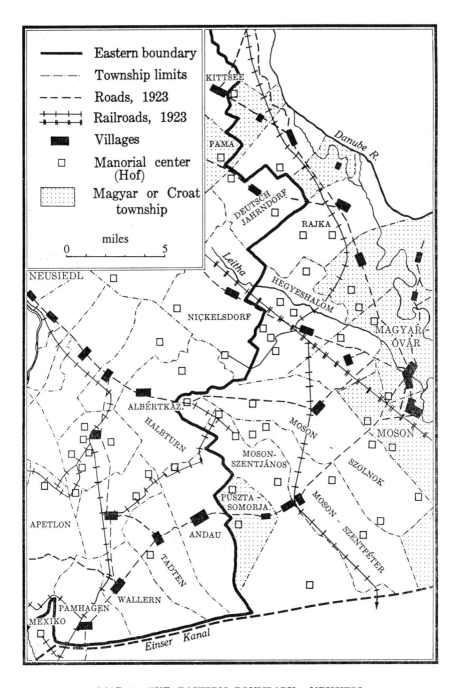

Legend

——————	Eastern boundary
—·—·—	Township limits
—————	Roads, 1923
┼┼┼┼┼	Railroads, 1923
■	Villages
□	Manorial center (Hof)
▦	Magyar or Croat township

miles
0 ————— 5

KITTSEE

PAMA

Danube R.

DEUTSCH
JAHRNDORF

RAJKA

NEUSIEDL

Leitha

HEGYESHALOM

NICKELSDORF

MAGYAR-
ÓVÁR

ALBÉRTKÁZ

HALBTURN

MOSON

MOSON

MOSON-
SZENTJÁNOS

SZOLNOK

PUSZTA-
SOMORJA

APETLON

ANDAU

TADTEN

MOSON-SZENTPÉTER

WALLERN

PAMHAGEN

MEXIKO

Einser Kanal

MAP 7. THE EASTERN BOUNDARY—NEUSIEDL

from the railroad (see Map 7). Only three exceptions are to be noted. Pusztasomorja is a township west of the railroad, and yet it remained in Hungary; its population was predominantly Magyar. Two manorial centers were cut out of their townships and also allowed to remain in Hungary. These were Albértkázmérpuszta and Mexikopuszta.[5] The former was the largest of all the manorial centers in the province, with a population of 444, most of whom were Magyar. The latter was also Magyar and was integrated economically with the huge manorial-industrial center of Eszterháza.

The southern border of Neusiedl County (along the Einser Kanal) runs through the middle of a large area of marsh, the Hanság, which has been a hindrance to movement through all recorded history. This eleven-mile stretch is the only portion of the new boundary which coincided with a pre-existing provincial boundary. This provincial boundary between Moson and Sopron megyek had evidently been in the swamp zone since the earliest organization of the Kingdom of Hungary.

Despite the flatness of the Little Alföld, this northern portion is the most satisfactory part of the entire length of the eastern frontier of Burgenland. The north-south line is located almost midway between the Hungarian center of Moson-Magyaróvár, and the county seat, Neusiedl, and almost halves the trading hinterland. It is true that Neusiedl is not as large or as important as Moson-Magyaróvár, but the principal movement in this area is towards Vienna, so that it is the Hungarian rather than the Austrian portion that has suffered from the placement of the boundary.

The Sopron Salient

Around the Sopron salient the boundary had previously been determined by the delimitation of the plebiscite area; much of the boundary coincides with the city limits of Sopron (see Map 6). For much of this distance the line runs through forest and is occasionally emphasized by the contrast between forest in one country and cleared land in the other. For approximately two miles the line crosses a cleared, open lowland along a minor stream, the Tauchenbach.

Along the southern edge of the salient the boundary runs for five miles along the crest of the Sopron Range. Even this portion of the delineation has caused inconveniences, since a locally important coal mine, the Brennbergbánya, had been developed at the crest. As the shafts ran under the boundary, an international agreement was necessitated, granting all the coal mined to Hungary.

The separation of Sopron from Burgenland was to plague the new province for decades and even to threaten its existence. Sopron was a major route node; here the boundary cut three railroads, three high-ways, and four lesser roads. The city had served as the primary market-ing and distributing center for all the nearby villages; several Burgen-land villages had road connections only with Sopron.

The railroads still exist and operate, but only to connect middle Burgenland (Oberpullendorf County) with the rest of Austria. Sop-ron thus oddly continues, despite the stringencies of the "Iron Cur-tain," to serve as an important transportation node for Burgenland. Two of the highways still exist, though their use has diminished greatly; no through, in-transit traffic into middle Burgenland is per-mitted via the highways. The lesser roads have atrophied; beyond the last village before the border they virtually cease to exist as roads.

Sopron itself has been severely handicapped by the location of the new boundary. Since the animal market was the principal economic resource of Sopron, Table 4 illustrates the effect of the boundary on the economic life of the city.[6]

TABLE 4

Year	Cattle	Swine	Total
1901	40,178	59,382	99,560
1913 (last prewar year)	36,663	134,151	170,814
1918 (last war year)	15,403	65,706	81,109
1921 (before the plebiscite)	29,663	72,456	102,119
1922 (after the plebiscite)	16,007	36,073	52,080
1925	9,388	24,236	33,624
1929	6,078	28,958	35,036

The Hungarians attempted to compensate the city for the loss of most of its hinterland by transferring a technical college from Selmetzbánya (Banská Štiavnica), which was lost to Czechoslovakia. But this was more than offset by the loss of Sopron's political signifi-cance; the remnants of Sopron and Moson megyek were joined to Győr megye. Recently, however, an increase in the population of the city has been brought about by the establishment of several new in-dustries.

The city now draws its supplies from the few surrounding villages within Hungary and from the Little Alföld to the east, but its com-mercial significance has been largely destroyed by the boundary. Not only was its immediate hinterland cut away, but Sopron was also separated from its own primary market, Vienna. The sealing of the border during the last decade has accentuated the awkward location of Sopron. The Burgenlanders who knew the city before 1922 and have seen it recently lament over its past beauty and prosperity.

Many of the fine old buildings of the inner city still show the marks of World War II, but a concerted effort is now being made to repair them. Hungarians are very proud of Sopron and refer to it as one of the most historic and beautiful cities in Hungary. However, potential tourism is severely curtailed by the Hungarian policy of preventing any approach to the border. Anyone coming to Sopron is stopped and checked at Nagyczenk, approximately eight miles east of the city; only those persons who live in the border zone or have obtained official permission to do so are allowed into the area. In fact, it is now probably easier for a Burgenlander than for the average Hungarian to visit Sopron.

Middle Burgenland (Oberpullendorf County)

South of Sopron the boundary forms a semicircle around the lowland of Oberpullendorf, with the northern and southern ends of the curve virtually severing this lowland from both north and south Burgenland, and Austria as well. Every important route ran north-south in 1922, and every one of these was cut by the boundary at both ends. The railroad and the roads focused on Sopron in the north and Köszeg in the south, and both of these cities remained in Hungary. Perhaps the most important historic route in Central Europe, the Amber Road, running from Sopron through Grosswarasdorf to Szombathely, was cut and not only has atrophied at both border crossings but has also ceased to be an important routeway within the county. Another road connected Sopron with Hungarian centers to the southeast, such as Sárvár, via the large manorial village of Deutschkreutz; this road also was cut twice, and remains now simply a local connection between Deutschkreutz and Nikitsch (see Map 6).[7]

No other portion of the entire boundary cut political and commercial areas as completely as this. The northern third of present-day Oberpullendorf County had been in Sopron County and the southern quarter in Köszeg County. The whole lowland had been commercially tributary to Sophron and Köszeg. With their loss went not only the markets and facilities themselves, but also the only connections to other centers. This situation was partially remedied by an agreement between Austria and Hungary, in 1922, which allowed unhampered passenger travel via Sopron to north Burgenland and Vienna. Freight was also allowed to pass through Sopron duty-free, in Austrian cars, but the Hungarian authorities circumvented this by raising their freight rates on these shipments. Throughout the interwar period there was acute economic dissatisfaction in this county, with frequent demands for a new railroad across the Sieggraben Saddle.

Deutschkreutz has been peculiarly affected by the demarcation of the boundary. At first it gained by taking over a portion of the animal trade formerly monopolized by Sopron. Its population of 3,929 (within present township limits) was in 1923 second only to Eisenstadt within the province, and its market was probably the most important in Middle Burgenland. Along the railroad, Deutschkreutz was the closest station in the county to the Viennese market and was advantageously located to draw on the most productive portions of the Oberpullendorf lowland. In 1934 Deutschkreutz had 4,220 inhabitants and with 433 Jews was second only to Mattersburg as a Jewish center. The Jews were the merchants, so that their number was an excellent indication of the commercial importance of a village.

Since 1938, however, Deutschkreutz has suffered a serious commercial decline. The recent development of trucking as the principal method of transporting animals to the Viennese market has almost eliminated the local animal markets. With respect to highways, Deutschkreutz is not the closest to, but the furthest from, Vienna (see Map 9). Coupled with this radical reorientation in trade routes was the extermination of the Jewish merchants by the Nazis; in 1951 there were *no* Jews in the township. At the present time there is almost no sign of commercial activity in the village; even the palace seems decayed. With a population of 3,852 (fourth largest in the province) in 1951, its appearance now is merely that of an unusually large agricultural village, with the familiar Burgenland phenomenon of numerous weekly commuters to the industrial centers in the Vienna Basin.

South of Deutschkreutz the boundary includes four stretches that were decided upon in a series of territorial exchanges between Austria and Hungary, after the boundary commission had completed its work. Th villages of Nikitsch and Lutzmannsburg received 848 acres (490 *joch*) of woodland and 43 acres (25 *joch*) of vineyard respectively in exchange for lands returned to Hungarian Szent Gotthárd further south. Nikitsch had been left with too little woodland to satisfy the needs of the township inhabitants, whereas the 43 acres of vineyard had formerly belonged to the inhabitants of Lutzmannsburg.

The major exchange in this area consisted of the Croatian village, Olmod (to Hungary), for the German villages, Rattersdorf and Liebing (to Austria). The boundary commission had awarded Olmod to Austria in order to include all of Oberpullendorf County within Austria, and Rattersdorf and Liebing to Hungary because of their proximity to and intimate connections with Köszeg. Olmod, however, petitioned to be returned to Hungary and the exchange was arranged. Rattersdorf was not returned intact to Austria. The forested upland, immediately south of the village center, was owned by Prince Eszterházy, who wished as much of his acreage as possible to remain in Hungary; south and west of the village the boundary now coincides with the edge of the forest. Though the return of Olmod to Hungary did move the line back and forth across the Rabnitz valley lowland, the exchange was fortunate for Austria. Had Rattersdorf and Liebing remained in Hungary, the only road, until 1957, connecting middle and south Burgenland, and the Zöbern valley with its county seat, would have been cut. In 1922 this road was in deplorable condition, but at least the road bed was there, and could eventually (1929) be reconstructed.

West of Köszeg the boundary does not follow the crest of the Köszeg Range, but includes a large portion of the northeastern slopes within Hungary. This forested area, largely owned by Eszterházy, was awarded to Köszeg in order to assist the city economically. This award involved 4,844 acres (2,800 *joch*) of forest land, 2,778 acres (1,600 *joch*) of which belonged to Eszterházy.

From the Köszeg Range to the Strem

Between the 2,900 foot Geschriebenstein atop the Köszeg Range and the 1,345 foot Eisenberg, the boundary crosses another flat, cleared lowland, cutting through an area of dense rural population. The railroad from Szombathely to Pinkafeld and the roads from Szombathely and Köszeg to the upper Pinka valley were cut by the line.

Similar to Deutschkreutz is Rechnitz, which, with 3,772 people in 1923, was the second largest township in southern Burgenland, and the fourth in the province. It too has had the boundary drawn along its eastern limits, and bears a relationship to Köszeg like that of Deutschkreutz to Sopron. Rechnitz, however, has suffered more than its northern counterpart, since it was never able to replace Köszeg as a market center for shipments to the Austrian market. From the very first, Rechnitz found itself at the extreme end of all important trade routes.

Because of its position in the middle of the gap between the two uplands, Rechnitz possessed, until the delineation of the boundary, a promising trade site (see Map 8). Running along the southern flank of the Köszeg Range was a medieval road, characterized by the castles of Rechnitz, Stadt Schlaining, and Bernstein. At Rechnitz a road towards Grosspetersdorf and the upper Pinka valley branched off this "noble" road. Another road connected the large village with Szombathely. The roads across the border have atrophied, as would be expected, but so has the direct connection between Rechnitz and

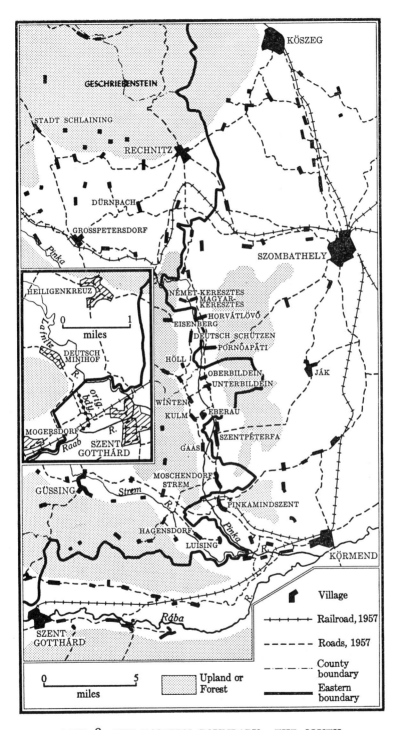

KÖSZEG

GESCHRIEBENSTEIN

STADT SCHLAINING

RECHNITZ

DÜRNBACH

GROSSPETERSDORF

Pinka

SZOMBATHELY

HEILIGENKREUZ

La fnitz R.

0   1
miles

DEUTSCH
MINIHOF

orig. bdy.

R.

MOGERSDORF

Raab

SZENT
GOTTHÁRD

NÉMET-KERESZTES
MAGYAR-
KERESZTES
HORVÁTLÖVŐ
EISENBERG
DEUTSCH SCHÜTZEN
PORNÓAPÁTI
JÁK

HÖLL

OBERBILDEIN
UNTERBILDEIN

WINTEN
KULM   EBERAU
SZENTPÉTERFA
GÁAS

MOSCHENDORF
STREM
PINKAMINDSZENT

GÜSSING   *Strem*

R.

HAGENSDORF
LUISING

Pinka

R.

KÖRMEND

R.

SZENT
GOTTHÁRD

Rába

R.

	Village
┼┼┼┼┼	Railroad, 1957
- - - - -	Roads, 1957
- · - · -	County boundary
▬▬▬	Eastern boundary

0   5
miles

Upland or
Forest

MAP 8. THE EASTERN BOUNDARY—THE SOUTH

Grosspetersdorf. Grosspetersdorf has become the most important node of transport routes in eastern Oberwart County. In 1918 there were almost 300 Jews in Rechnitz; by 1934 this number had decreased to 170, and in 1951 there were 3.

Rechnitz was also a manufacturing center, specializing in the production of special boots called *czismen*. For this business the location of the border was a disaster; these boots could be sold only in Hungary or in Burgenland. The market in Hungary was eliminated by the boundary, and most of the Burgenland market was in the north. Unfortunately, Rechnitz is situated directly in front of the middle, widest, and highest part of the Köszeg Range. In the 1920's and 1930's the peasant craftsmen attempted all manner of methods to surmount the mountain mass behind the village. (The present road was not completed until 1947.) Many tracks were utilized, but the best route, and the one most used, was through Köszeg, Hungary. However, there were the expected difficulties with the Hungarian authorities, who insisted on charging duty on all goods entering Hungary, even though it might be claimed that they were in transit to north Burgenland markets.

Rechnitz has been slowly stifled. The new road, built at great difficulty, came too late to help the *czismen* makers; very few boots are now being made. Many of the bootmakers have gone into the production of wine for the local market. The population of 3,387 is still large but it remains at this level because of the maintenance of local residence by large numbers of wandering laborers who come home every second weekend (from Vienna), every fourth weekend (from Graz), or at the end of the agricultural season.

Of all the portions of the boundary, that in the lower Pinka valley seems the most chaotic, the most senselessly drawn. It was here that the ideal of self-determination was given its fullest areal expression. The boundary commission had almost no choice but to establish the present line, yet some of the worst features resulted from a subsequent exchange of territory between the two governments. This appears to be proof of the inadvisability of making the principle of self-determination the sole controlling criterion in the delineation of the minute details of an international boundary. In the space of thirteen miles the Pinka stream was cut seven times (see Map 8). After the line was finally established only the southernmost village in the valley had road connections with its own country.

As soon as the boundary commission entered the area, various delegations came to meet it. In every village there were demonstrations for one country or the other. Slowly the commission moved through the valley, trying to ascertain the feelings of the populace in each village. It was not an easy task.

Német-keresztes and Magyar-keresztes were both German speaking. Much of the land in Német-keresztes, including an area of vineyards on the Eisenberg, belonged to a Bavarian prince, who, for political reasons, wished to have his holdings remain in Hungary. He evidently won over the villagers, who demonstrated for Hungary to the commission. Most of the land in Magyar-keresztes belonged to the Hungarian monastery of Ják. The Catholic clergy was pro-Hungarian in any case, and this village also opted for Hungary, despite language.

Eisenberg and Deutsch Schützen were German speaking and chose Austria, whereas Horvátlövő was Croatian and chose Hungary. Pornóapáti was German, but under the direction of the pastor, who organized a demonstration, declared itself for Hungary. Oberbildein, Unterbildein, Eberau, Gaas, and Moschendorf were all German and demonstrated for Austria. Pinkamindszent was Magyar and chose Hungary.

As originally drawn, the boundary would have been considerably shorter and simpler than it now is; Szentpéterfa was included in Austria while Luising was in Hungary, thus eliminating two of the present salients. The people of Luising, in notes to the commission, asked for union with Austria; they were German and had always gone to adjacent Hagensdorf to school and church. At the same time the Croatian village of Szentpéterfa asked to be reunited with Hungary. The two governments arranged the exchange.

Prior to 1922, all the political and economic contacts of the valley had been northeast, with Szombathely, and southeast, with Körmend. Only one road had existed in the valley and this ran north-south, parallel to the river; it was now cut several times by the boundary, so that all north-south movement ceased. A new north-south system had to be constructed on the Austrian side of the line. On the Hungarian side, however, the nature of the line precluded any possibility of a north-south connection; the northern villages were focused entirely on Szombathely, the southern on Körmend. Szentpéterfa was isolated by the boundary on three sides and the forest on the fourth. This situation probably accounts for the initial award of this Croatian township to Austria; it is now connected with the remainder of Hungary by a road cut through the forest. Therefore, for Hungary the lower Pinka ceased to be a continuous lowland capable of any kind of small-scale regional organization, but became, instead, three small lowland areas, completely separate from each other and connected only with the larger centers to the east.

The boundary did not become a major divide at first. The roads on the Austrian side of the boundary were not constructed until the 1930's. With the lack of roads westward and of important commercial centers to the west, the population of the Austrian villages continued to move towards Szombathely and Körmend. Familial ties kept the villages together despite the boundary, since there had been frequent intermarriage, prior to 1922, between the inhabitants of adjacent villages. Cross-boundary landholding was also common. International agreements attempted to remedy some of the difficulties produced by the disruption of holding patterns; for example, the vintners on the Eisenberg could bring their wine home into Austria.

Since 1945 the boundary between the two countries has been sealed with mines and barbed wire. The Austrian portions of the low-land have had to reorient themselves; they now focus on Grosspeters-dorf in the north, and Güssing in the south. There is no movement of any kind across the boundary at the present time. Buses between Güssing and Grosspetersdorf service most of the Austrian villages in the valley. Only the southernmost salient, Hagensdorf and Luising, is not served by public transportation; the inhabitants of these vil-lages are required to walk several miles to the Moschendorf-Strem road.

Though the boundary delimitation would seem to stifle the villagers in the valley, in actual fact they do not seem to feel that it does. They have become so accustomed to the line that, except for the fact that it represents separation from loved ones, they rarely concern themselves with it. These villages depend solely on agriculture, with animals sold as a cash crop to the Vienna market. Although the boundary limits some townships on three sides, with such a basic type of economy and the possibility of truck shipment of the animals to market, the effects of the boundary are scarcely felt by most of the inhabitants. Some of the peasants in the southernmost and most iso-lated salient, when questioned concerning the difficulties caused by the border, answered that there had been no difficulties recently be-cause the Hungarians had ceased threatening. Their replies indicated the complete absence of any idea of economic difficulties. Except for the desire to see relatives, the only complaint was that the boundary necessitated a circuitous route to reach the shrine at Gaas on certain feast days.[8]

The Extreme South

Between Luising and Heiligenkreuz, the boundary pursues a general east-west direction, approximately halfway between the Rába and Strem valleys. The line does not coincide with the drainage divide; instead it follows a saw-toothed path, crossing tributaries of the Rába at right angles and running along the divides between the tributaries. Though the entire area is populated with tiny villages, the boundary does not cut any routes and acts as a convenient divide between

Güssing and Szent Gotthárd. As such, it is one of the least bothersome portions of the boundary.

In contrast, the crossing of the Lafnitz-Rába valley is one of the most inconvenient borders imaginable. The valleys of the Lafnitz and the Rába join at the governmental and commercial center of Szent Gotthárd, yet because of the decisions of the local villages, the German villages were separated from their only local center, Magyar Szent Gotthárd,[9] and the two valleys were almost completely severed from each other.

Still, the separation of the two valleys was not complete at first. The boundary commission drew the line approximately one half mile to the east of its present position, so that the road from Deutsch Minihof to Mogersdorf remained within Austria (see inset of Map 8). This road had not been the principal connection between the two valleys; that had consisted of the roads leading from both valleys directly into Szent Gotthárd. Yet, even this last connection was to be cut, not by the commission, but by one of the post-demarcation territorial transfers between Austria and Hungary. In exchange for the woodland granted to Nikitsch and the vineyards to Lutzmannsburg, Hungary received 208 acres (120 *joch*) of rich land immediately west of Szent Gotthárd. More important than the transfer of the arable land was its position; this exchange moved the boundary westward to the base of the interfluvial ridge and cut the only remaining road in Burgenland between the two valleys.

A great outcry arose in the vicinity. Delegations approached the provincial government to demand a rectification of this transfer. The authorities replied that since the move had been accepted by both governments, it was "unfortunately a fact," but that Hungary had committed herself to build immediately, at her own expense, a new road to enable trade between the Lafnitz and Rába valleys. It was "expected" that the construction "would begin immediately." Construction did not begin immediately; two years later Representative Karl Wollinger was to demand in the federal parliament that Hungary build this road. By 1926 the road was completed, but the Hungarians had constructed it precisely on the boundary.

The road system, as established after several years of effort, had both the only connection between the two valleys and the only connection to the remainder of the province, running immediately on the boundary. This situation existed until 1960; all movement between Deutsch Minihof and Mogersdorf, and between Heiligenkreuz and Güssing, passed within ten yards of the mines and the barbed wire.

For about two miles west of Mogersdorf, the Rába River forms the boundary, but even this is not as clear and definite as it might be.

The line follows an old channel of the present stream for over half this distance. From the Rába southwestward the line runs through forested uplands, and causes no difficulties.

The short boundary between Jugoslavia and Burgenland cuts through another zone of forest. The location of the line does not coincide with the Rába-Mur drainage divide, but includes some of the headwaters of the Lendva, a tributary of the Mur, within Burgenland. The linguistic divide between the Germans and the Slovenes runs four miles south of the drainage divide, probably because the line of highest points occurs there, rather than at the watershed.

After the denial of the proposed corridor, the process of determining the eastern boundary of Burgenland consisted of two stages: the Austrian acquisition of important portions of West Hungary, and a Hungarian counterattack that nibbled away at the awarded area. As originally demarcated in the Treaty of St. Germain, the borders of Austria would have extended to the limits of the penetration of the Alpine ridges into the Hungarian Plain. In the end, the Hungarians had moved the line back onto the edges of these ridges.

In the final delineations Hungary attained footholds on almost every strong military position: [10] the Einser Kanal, the Sopron Range, the Köszeg Range, the Eisenberg, and the Rába River. The boundary cut the transport lines between the north and the south of Burgenland and, in several places, brought the line up to a position immediately adjacent to an important road. None of these strategic positions was ever used militarily, but Hungarian revisionist warnings kept the new province in a continual state of anxiety, at least until 1938. At present these positions bear armed troops in watchtowers, and anxiety still underlies the feelings of the inhabitants of Burgenland.

A boundary so contrary to communications and trade was probably certain to breed border troubles. The difficulties encountered by peasants were partially met by a 1926 agreement between Hungary and Austria. A zone fifteen kilometers wide was to be duty-free for the transport of goods intended by the local peasants for their own use: meat up to three kilograms, milled grain and legumes up to three kilograms, milk up to two liters, and all the materials to be used in their work. Doctors and veterinarians could practice on both sides of the border. The agreement also included special provisions to regulate the working of properties that had been cut by the boundary.

During the depression of the early 1930's, smuggling became a large-scale operation along the boundary. In one week in January, 1934, officials estimated that over 350 wagonloads of Hungarian wheat had been smuggled across. Herds of animals were driven across the border. There were exchanges of fire, resembling armed skirmishes, between the frontier guards and bands of smugglers.

Robert Sieger has commented that the "natural trade areas" (*natürliche Verkehrsgebiete*) form the best basis for the development of political units.[11] In order to delineate an effective boundary the representatives of the Entente Powers should have taken cognizance of the existence of functioning unit areas and treated these areas, as far as possible, as units. Had the trade areas been kept in mind, Burgenland could still have been awarded to Austria on the grounds of linguistic self-determination, but Sopron should have been included also. From this point of view the plebiscite was an unwise move. In order to maintain, as much as possible under the circumstances, the close union of the agricultural areas with their market centers, Kőszeg and Szent Gotthárd also probably should have been transferred to Austria,[12] and the lower Pinka valley retained intact by Hungary.

Once the plebiscite had been held, Sopron had to be awarded to Hungary. Even after this unfortunate result, adjustments of the boundary could have been made so as to maintain, as far as possible, intimate local connections. Deutschkreutz, Nikitsch, and Krt. Minihof (Map 6), Rechnitz, Schachendorf, and the entire lower Pinka valley (Map 8) could have remained in Hungary,[13] whereas Szent Gotthárd and the ten villages to its south and southwest could have been transferred to Austria.

Unfortunately, such adjustments of the boundary to the local "natural trade areas" were not possible because the general path of the line had been decided in Paris on purely linguistic grounds, and the boundary commission had authority to fix the boundary between townships on the basis of local preference. In a few cases where the commission awarded villages, against their desires, to one country or the other, Austria and Hungary reversed the decisions in subsequent exchanges of territory.

The only manner in which the adjustments could have been made would have been for the Entente to invest some agency with the necessary authority. This did not occur because of the predominance of the principle of linguistic self-determination over all other criteria for boundary making, and because the Entente Powers were not much interested in what was decided along the Austro-Hungarian frontier.[14]

This boundary is now of special interest in that it is probably the only boundary in Europe which, through much of its length, was drawn to give precise areal expression to the principle of self-determination. The boundary in Schleswig was based on the same principle but in that case the area concerned was divided into three zones, and the final boundary was drawn along the line between two of these zones. In Upper Silesia the results of the plebiscite vote, when plotted on a map, produced so chaotic a pattern that the final line, although following township boundaries, was an attempt to satisfy the desires of the greatest number of the inhabitants of the entire area. Significantly, the Schleswig boundary has proven to be the most satisfactory of the three.

In both Upper Silesia and Burgenland a boundary was superimposed upon a maturely developed cultural landscape, on the basis of a principle which had almost no significance in the commercial life of the area. Because an industrial complex was split by the new line, the Upper Silesian boundary proved to be a greater handicap to the local economic life than did that of Burgenland, but the Silesian boundary lasted only seventeen years, whereas the Burgenland boundary has remained in effect for forty years and appears to be permanent. Within the past decade the people of Burgenland have been forced to sever all commercial and personal ties with the adjacent areas of Hungary.

The work of the boundary commission along the frontier illustrates the difficulty of attempting to poll people, in such a time of upheaval, concerning their national preference. Those who were conscious of being German chose Austria, because their children had been forced to learn Magyar and little German in school. Those who did not share this deep consciousness of being German followed the "lords" of the village, the landholders, the teachers, and the priests. Many of the peasants seemed confused when asked to decide on a nationality. They were assailed by arguments whose validity they could not evaluate. In 1922, the peasant of Hungary still focused his loyalty on his family, his land, and his village. Nationality was often an abstraction, associated only with taxation and conscription. In this situation Hungary had a tremendous advantage; she represented the known, Austria the unknown. The peasant who was not aware of being German hesitated to leave the country he and his forebears had known and belonged to. The Croats of the south almost always chose to remain in Hungary. All tradition was on the side of Hungary, tradition and the village leaders.

The boundary has, by now, become firmly fixed in the consciousness of the local population. It still does not seem "right," yet it seems permanent. The decisions made in a time of flux have solidified into perhaps the strongest portion of the "Iron Curtain." [15] Even if Hungary were freed from Communist rule it is doubtful that the line would change. Forty years of education and nationalistic preachings have turned this boundary into a sharp divide between German and Magyar.

12

THE CREATION
OF A PROVINCE

Following the Protocol of Venice, Burgenland, minus the area of the Sopron plebiscite, was joined to Austria. The details of the boundary had yet to be worked out, but the area was occupied by the Austrian gendarmerie and integrated completely into the political and economic systems of "German Austria."

Though the national status of the territory was thus at length decided, the status of Burgenland within Austria remained obscure. What was to be done with the newly acquired land? Was it to become a new, separate province in its own right, or was it to be divided and joined to adjacent Lower Austria and Styria? Unfortunately, historic precedents could not be relied upon; there had never been a Burgenland before, nor even a distinct territorial unit approximating its size and extent. In Roman times there had been a Pannonia, but this had been much larger and had included all the surrounding cities, even Vienna. The Hungarian territorial concept of the Dunántúl had never been given a concrete geo-political organization, and was also much larger than the acquired territory. The political units which existed at the time of the transfer, the Hungarian megyek, were vastly different. It had obviously never previously occurred to men to attempt to organize this ribbon of land where the hills met the plains.

The lack of a historic basis for a Burgenland was a severe handicap within Austria. In a centralized state such as France or Hungary, an arbitrarily demarcated political unit could be expected to survive even though its existence might prove highly inefficient. Within Austria, however, the provinces were highly individualized and separate. This was especially true in 1921, when the Austrian state idea seemed to have dissolved and been replaced by self-centered provinces striving towards complete autonomy. The Austria of that time was little more than a loose federation of autonomous provinces, and loyalty to the province was generally higher than loyalty to the new Austria. In becoming a province Burgenland would have to lead a semi-independent existence in competition with the firmly entrenched traditional provinces for the trickle of federal funds. Only a vital state idea could maintain a handicapped province, and Burgenland alone among the Austrian provinces lacked that historic continuity which is the base of an effective state idea.

Until the time of its transfer to Austria, Burgenland had consisted of the western portions of three Hungarian megyek. Each of these comitats had been focused on its own central town and, beyond, on Budapest and Vienna. With the exception of those meetings working for autonomy within Hungary in the year 1918–19, north, middle, and south Burgenland had never worked together politically. Differences in dialect and in tradition (the southerners termed themselves *Heinzen*, the northerners *Heidebauern*) separated the various portions.

Just as the lack of a common tradition seemed to militate against a separate Burgenland, so did the topography of the territory. The physiographic barriers of Lake Neusiedl, the Sopron Range, the Köszeg Range, and the uplands along the Lafnitz fragmented the area into several distinct portions and turned these portions in different directions. As a consequence, there was an almost complete lack of economic contact between northern, middle, and southern Burgenland. All the major routeways ran across the territory; none ran along the north-south axis of the territory.

If a province is to be effectively organized and governed it must possess at least a modicum of communications between the various parts. The peasant of the outlying district must be able to contact the capital. Yet, within Burgenland the lone railroad between the Sopron and Köszeg ranges ran into Hungary at both ends, while two of the rail lines of the south led only into Hungary. The difficulties of transportation were augmented by the four years of war and the three years of indecision; in 1921 the Burgenland railroads were in almost total disrepair. Only a few through highways were passable for motor

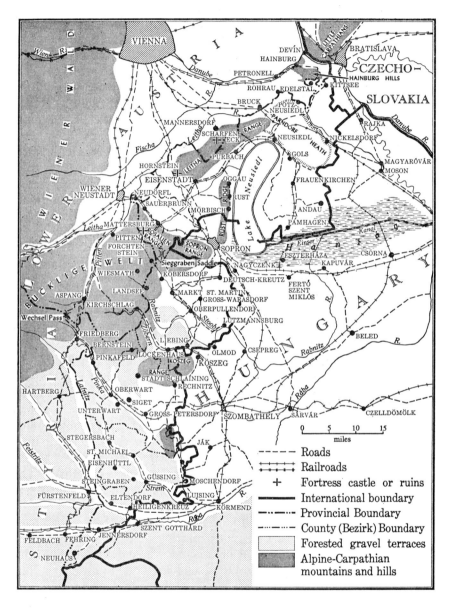

MAP 9. BURGENLAND

209

traffic, and these ran across the territory. Without leaving Burgenland there was no connection between north and south. In 1921, and for several years thereafter, the lack of passable roads divided Burgenland into six distinct areas. In addition to the major breaks there were numerous examples of local isolation. Few villages could boast of all-weather connections with the next village in any direction.

But, the problem went deeper than the lack of adequate communications; Burgenland lacked the urban centers which inevitably become the centers of communications and within which political life is concentrated. With the loss of Sopron, Burgenland lost its only large city, its capital. The largest "city" remaining in the area contained less than 5,000 inhabitants. Burgenland's closest approximation to a core area, the Sopron Gateway (Eisenstadt Basin), lacked a core center; all the routeways focused on Sopron or on Wiener Neustadt, both of which were outside the province. With the loss of Sopron the choice of a capital became an issue of unusual gravity, since there was no obvious second choice. Because Moson and Szombathely had also remained in Hungary, Burgenland was cut off from the facilities and records necessary to effective government.

Not only were these facilities lacking, but so also were the local sources of wealth capable of creating them. Containing no urban centers, Burgenland was devoid of structures that could house the meetings of the governmental agencies, or of living quarters for the bureaucracy. There were no large halls (except in some palaces), no apartments, no hotels (except in two minor spas); only 129 hospital beds, only 1 Gymnasium and 5 *Bürgerschule* (junior high schools) remained for 286,000 people. The cities of western Hungary had had 47 upper schools, 14 in Sopron alone. Schools, apartments, office buildings, plus cultural centers, would have to be constructed if Burgenland was to become a province. Yet, there was virtually no industry or commerce to support the necessitated expenditures. The west Hungarian cities that had possessed the required facilities had also possessed the taxable sources of wealth.

Finally, Burgenland lacked the local leadership which could have attempted this gigantic task of reorganization. It was an area of peasants, most of whom had at most completed primary school. The educated class lived in the cities, and these had remained in Hungary. The local political figures who had acted as the governing force were Magyar or Magyarized, and many had left the area as soon as it was transferred to Austria. The dearth of educated men meant not only a lack of leadership but also a lack of potential civil servants.

These negative factors inevitably made a profound impression on all disinterested, objective observers. Many analysts of the time drew the conclusion that the only rational solution to the problem of Burgenland was to divide it between Lower Austria and Styria. "The north tends towards Vienna; the south towards Graz," was a much quoted refrain between 1918 and 1945. Certain it was that few political units had as many and as impressive reasons for *not* being established as had Burgenland. And yet, the province was established.

Whenever a Burgenlander was asked why, in view of the many reasons for not doing so, Burgenland was established as an autonomous province, he replied that it was because of the differences between Burgenland and its people, and "Old Austria." [1] The word "different" was always used. "We are a different people with a different history and a different way of life." It was this sense of difference from the remainder of Austria which, more than any other factor, produced a feeling of unity among the inhabitants of Burgenland, and, in so doing, gave birth to the state idea of the province. Though the north, middle, and south had had, prior to 1918, little contact with each other, they had nevertheless shared a common history in that they had all been portions of Hungary. They had undergone a common historical development that was distinct from that known in Old Austria, a development that had produced cultural and economic manifestations distinct from those visible in Old Austria.

Symbolizing this separation was the western boundary of Burgenland. For much of its length this line had remained fixed since the time of King Stephen; nowhere had it been altered in over two centuries. The peasants who lived near this boundary continued to feel that beyond that line was another country.

West Hungary knew a way of life that was by 1900 almost unknown in Austria or Western Europe. The dividing line between the remnants of feudalism and the Western, complex, urban-commercial economy followed the Austro-Hungarian boundary. Western Europe had a city culture, West Hungary a baronial culture. Burgenland's greatest center of the arts, Eisenstadt, was more a palace than a city. The only prominent structures were the medieval castles and the baroque palaces. With the transfer of Burgenland to Austria most of the large holders became foreigners; they retained their Hungarian citizenship and usually lived in Hungary. Paul Eszterházy lived in Budapest and rarely visited Burgenland. In 1928, 26 per cent of the total area of Burgenland was held by foreigners, mostly Hungarians.[2]

Not only the large palaces, but also the manorial work centers, the *Hof*'s, *Meier*'s, *puszta*'s, and *major*'s, developed their own pattern of living, removed from the township centers. They resembled smaller villages, with their lines of homes around a central courtyard, and often with schools and chapels. Though the workers were contracted year by year, in practice they usually remained on the *Hof* for many years, and many of their children graduated from the local school into the service of the landholder.

As part of Hungary, Burgenland had utilized a legal code different from that of Austria. This variance was exemplified in different laws, the most famous, and disputed, of which was to be the marriage law. Hungarian law recognized both civil marriage and divorce; Austrian law recognized neither.

Hungary and Austria had also had differing religious histories. As a result of the relative tolerance of Hungary, Burgenland has now a higher proportion of Protestants, 14 per cent, than any other province of Austria. (The national average is 6 per cent.) The two counties (Oberwart 32 per cent, and Jennersdorf 21 per cent) and the ten townships with the highest proportion of Protestants in Austria are in Burgenland. West Hungary also became a place of refuge for Jews, who found not only a relative security but also ready employment in the service of the great land barons. The decrees of banishment of 1491 and 1671 had such little effect on the lords of West Hungary that Jews frequently established legal residences in present-day Burgenland and carried on trade in Vienna.[3]

Though no religion was granted a position of special favor within Hungary, the faiths all enjoyed a position of greater power and influence in the important field of education than they did in Austria. In Austria almost all education was secularized; in Hungary it was almost entirely in the hands of the various religious communities. The teachers were usually laymen, but they were under the supervision of the Catholic, Lutheran, Calvinist, or Jewish clergy, who both owned and operated the schools. The contrast between the confessional and the state-operated schools was to become one of the greatest political issues in Burgenland.[4]

Burgenland was also a province of linguistic minorities. While the adjacent provinces of Lower Austria and Styria were almost 100 per cent German speaking, in 1923, after the exodus of many of the Magyar officials, Burgenland was only 79 per cent German speaking. The Germans had been partially Magyarized, so that the influence of the Magyars and the Magyar-sympathizers who remained was far out of proportion to their numbers. The members of the minority groups did not look favorably towards union with the completely German adjacent provinces, and, above all, not with Styria, which had the reputation of being militantly pro-German. In addition, Burgenland possessed that special minority, the gypsies, who constituted a problem completely outside the experience of Old Austria.

Another linguistic difference is always mentioned locally as significant; Burgenlanders speak a dialect which differs from that spoken in either Lower Austria or Styria. This difference is evident in the extreme flattening of some vowels, the diphthonging of others, and in the use of other expressions. In northern Burgenland this contrast in dialects can be noted on the map as the difference between the "p"s in Burgenland and the "b"s in Lower Austria; only the Leitha River separates the villages of Deutsch Brodersdorf, and Leithaprodersdorf.[5]

Finally, Burgenland differed in appearance from the rest of Austria. This is the "difference" which is probably the most important for the non-Burgenlander; it has resulted in a sharing of the concept of "difference" by the people of Old Austria as well as the people of Burgenland. To an Austrian everything about Burgenland has a Hungarian look. A Viennese picture of the province focuses on its flatness, its steppe lake, its flocks of geese, its low-spreading villages composed of similar long houses each with its narrow end towards the road, its puszta-type long-handled wells, its oxcarts. To the Viennese, Burgenland represents a portion of the broad, semi-barbaric yet fascinating expanses of Hungary.[6]

When the transfer of Burgenland to Austria was first announced in mid-1919, the Austrian government could easily have made plans to integrate the acquired territory into the two adjacent provinces, Lower Austria and Styria. However, the Viennese government, faced with the wreckage of an empire torn apart by "self-determination," seemed to be in mortal fear of the word "annexation." Within Burgenland the Magyars were asserting that the Austrians wished to annex Burgenland in order to requisition the food supplies of the peasants. It was stated that the Socialist government of Austria would annex the new territory as a granary for the hungry masses of Vienna. Therefore, the Viennese leaders attempted to avoid any semblance of an annexation in their treatment of the area. Dr. Renner said, "The liberation of Burgenland is in our eyes no annexation, either in aims or methods."[7] The inhabitants of Burgenland were to be allowed to decide for themselves in what manner their territory was to unite with Austria.

In the initial, provisional Austrian constitution (*Verfassungsgesetz vom 1 Oktober 1920*), Burgenland was not listed with the provinces of the new Federal Republic of German Austria. An article stated,

"Burgenland will be taken into the Federation as an autonomous and equal province, as soon as it has so expressed its will." [8] Since it could not as yet express its will, it was listed separately by the constitution, and placed in the ambiguous position of being national territory (*Bundesgebiet*), but not a province (*Bundesland*).

This special status was promptly criticized by the Walheim group in Vienna; they called for the deletion of the special clause so as to bring Burgenland firmly into the constitution. In reply, future Chancellor Dr. Ignaz Seipel explained that this special status represented the attempt to allow the people of Burgenland complete freedom of choice; they were to decide their own political status.

Meanwhile it seems to have been generally assumed that Burgenland would be set up as a separate province. In January, 1920, Chancellor Renner promised a delegation of the Vienna Burgenland leaders, "You will govern your land and your people yourselves. I hope that Ödenburg [Sopron] will be the capital of the province. . . . The *Burgenvolk* [will] constitute a province and will, as a province with its own constitution and self-government, work together with the other provinces to build the Federal Republic of Austria." [9]

On January 25, 1921, the "Burgenland Law" was passed by the federal parliament: "Federal law concerning the establishment of Burgenland as an autonomous and equal province in the Federation, and concerning its provisional arrangement." [10] Burgenland was now a separate and equal province.

It must be emphasized at this point that all the preceding developments occurred *before the Sopron Plebiscite*, and while the city of Sopron (Ödenburg) seemed to be securely a part of the new province. When Burgenland was initially established, eleven months before the plebiscite, it still had its capital city and node of transportation, as well as all the wealth, facilities, and educated personnel that were part of the city of Sopron.

After the loss of Sopron, the advisability of setting up this strip of territory as a new province was seriously questioned. However, by then the matter had been virtually decided, and the Austrian government wished to avoid any possible charges that it was not allowing the Burgenlanders complete freedom to choose their own political status. On January 20, 1922, Chancellor Schober assured a delegation from Mattersburg County that there would be no division of Burgenland. The Burgenland parliament, when elected, could decide as to the future status of the area. [11]

The long-delayed election was held on June 18, 1922, supposedly to elect the Landtag that would decide the status of Burgenland. However, this election was in no sense a referendum on this key issue; the vital question was never debated and rarely alluded to. The campaign was waged by parties whose leaders, issues, and even, in many instances, candidates were imported from Old Austria; it seemed as if the only vital issue was to see which of the parties could gain a majority in the first Landtag, and an increase in its membership in the federal parliament. A provincial parliament was elected and began to govern. It was scarcely to be expected that the newly elected delegates would vote themselves out of their positions by deciding to destroy Burgenland as a province. There was not then, nor has there been since, a debate or a motion, much less a vote, in the Landtag on this issue.

Once the province was operating as such it could not be abolished by any power except itself. Article 3 of the Constitution of October 1, 1920, stated, "An alteration in the federal territory that is, at the same time, an alteration in the territory of a province, can be effected only by agreement between the federal government and the province concerned." [12]

The decision to establish Burgenland as a separate province was made, in a most indecisive manner, in Vienna; and then it was a Burgenland with Sopron, a Burgenland which never existed. The decision, never clearly stated, agreed with the opinion of Viennese leaders that the new territory had had an economic and political history differing from that of Old Austria. Though it never came to a vote, the majority of Burgenlanders probably agreed with the decision. They had by this time been bound together by their history, recent hardships, fear of the Magyars, and their name. Though their union was scarcely strong, they undoubtedly preferred to "try it alone."

"WER WEISS EINE HAUPTSTADT?" [13]

If any city can be said to have been "predestined" to become the capital of a political area, Sopron (Ödenburg), within the limits of the original Burgenland, was that city. With a population of 34,000, it was over seven times as large as the second largest "city," the only center of transportation routes, the site of the governmental buildings, hospitals, upper schools, offices, apartments, hotels, etc., and the home of the only locally available educated group who could be expected to take on the tasks of running a government. There was no other candidate for the role. Article 1 of the "Burgenland Law" stated, "The capital of Burgenland is the city of Ödenburg." [14]

The loss of Sopron was a disaster for Burgenland, one that seemed to produce a psychological fixation in the minds of Burgenland politicians. Even today, as soon as one discusses the capital of the province, in any connection, with a Burgenlander, he is told, "Of course, Öden-burg should have been our capital." The city is often referred to as the "natural capital" of Burgenland. Perhaps one reason why every Burgenlander is convinced that the plebiscite was a fraud is that he cannot, otherwise, resign himself to so grievous a loss.

During the more than three years that the capital question was argued in the Landtag and discussed in the press, almost every speech and article began with the remark that Ödenburg was, and would al-ways remain, the natural and true capital of Burgenland. Probably the principal reason why the problem was allowed to remain unsolved for so long, without ever coming to a vote, was that many, perhaps most, of the delegates to the Landtag nurtured the hope that within a short time Burgenland would surely regain Sopron. There were even suggestions in the press that Hungary should return Sopron to assure herself of the friendship of Austria, since all her other neighbors were aligned against her. Provincial Vice Premier Leser summed up the prevailing attitude: "For Burgenland there is no capital question, only a question as to the seat of the provincial government, since the nat-ural capital of our province is, and remains, Ödenburg." [15] As late as two and a half years after the loss of the city, Alfred Walheim, him-self born in Sopron, felt it necessary to warn his fellow delegates, "We cannot dream of obtaining Ödenburg—it lies in the realm of fables. Hungary will never willingly give up Ödenburg. We have to help ourselves without Ödenburg." [16] When the vote was finally taken in April, 1925, it was expressedly for the "provisional capital" of Bur-genland. Even on that day the only city whose mention was awarded noisy acclaim was Ödenburg.

In August, 1921, as the Austrian gendarmerie prepared to occupy the newly acquired territory, the provisional government of Burgen-land, in Vienna, headed by Dr. Davy, prepared to begin its opera-tions in Sopron. Dr. Davy was in Sopron before the official occupa-tion, when the fighting erupted between the "volunteer bands" and the advancing gendarmerie. The provisional government withdrew from the Sopron area, along the railroad, to Mattersburg, which was the first large township west of the contested city. For a short time therefore, Mattersburg served as the capital of Burgenland. As the gendarmerie evacuated all of Burgenland, the government retired to Vienna.

When, under the terms of the Protocol of Venice, Austrian gen-darmerie occupied all of Burgenland except the plebiscite area, the provisional government returned along the same railroad line as be-fore. It did not return to Mattersburg, however, since that large vil-lage lacked the buildings that could be used to serve as offices or as dwellings for the bureaucracy. Instead it established itself in the spa of Sauerbrunn, halfway between Mattersburg and Wiener Neustadt.

Sauerbrunn had more hotels than any other community in Burgenland. These quarters provided the needed facilities for government offices and for some of the necessary housing, but, unfortunately, there was not a room in the spa large enough to serve as the meeting hall for the Landtag. The only building in the vicinity and yet in Burgenland that could satisfy this requirement was the military academy in Eisenstadt. "And now there developed a most singular relationship. When the Landtag meets, the trucks of the provincial government rush, with documents, typewriters, officials and delegates, overland to Eisenstadt, where the otherwise dead-still rooms of the buildings awake to active life for a few hours. But yet on the same evening—the sessions of the Burgenland Landtag are often very short —everything is dead again." [17] Sauerbrunn and Eisenstadt are over twenty kilometers apart, and the roads were in very poor condition in the 1920's. Yet this bizarre situation was allowed to exist for over three years before a decision on one capital was reached in the Landtag, and actually for over eight years, until the completion in 1930 of the new governmental building in Eisenstadt.

In the consideration of the individual townships as possible sites of the Burgenland provincial government, several factors were held to be of critical importance. The candidate village not only had to have good connections to Vienna and with most of the province, but also had to offer facilities, and the materials and labor to construct new facilities for the government and the civil servants. Thus, only a township that formally submitted its candidacy could be considered. The shortage of funds was so serious in Burgenland that unless a township agreed to help share the cost of construction, it could not be considered. On the basis of the transportation network, however, middle Burgenland would have been impossible, since its only link with the rest of Burgenland (or Austria) ran through Hungary. The most promising areas were, therefore, the southern portion of north Burgenland or the northern portion of south Burgenland. By coincidence, these were also the most highly developed portions of both the north and the south, the Eisenstadt Basin (Sopron Gateway) and the upper Pinka valley. All four of the announced candidates were from these two areas, three from the north and one from the south. The south was at a disadvantage because of its distance from Vienna.

The northernmost of the four candidates was Eisenstadt city, which, within present city limits, had a population of 4,767, the largest in the province. The claim of Eisenstadt was based chiefly on its proud title of "Free City." Only Rust was also a "city," but it was both small and poorly located. (All unbiased discussion of the capital question began with the consideration that there were only two "cities" in the province.) During the chaotic days of September, 1921, the Hungarian government reportedly proposed the return of Sopron to Hungary, with the suggestion that Eisenstadt become the capital instead. Added to the glamour of Eisenstadt's title was the glory of its past. This was the city of the fabulous court of Prince Eszterházy, the city of Josef Haydn and other locally famous cultural figures. Eisenstadt was able to offer to the provincial government land donated by Eszterházy, the military academy which was already being used by the government, financial contributions from its citizens, free use of the city brickworks, and a free supply of sand and vehicles.

The opponents of Eisenstadt always stressed its awkward transportational situation. It was not on one of the railroads between Vienna and Sopron, but on a branch of the less important of the two lines. According to its detractors, people riding to Eisenstadt from Vienna or the south would have to change trains twice. It was stressed that because of its position off the main trade routes, Eisenstadt had only small possibilities for commercial growth and would always remain a minor center.

Eisenstadt gained its support from the two northern counties of the province, which were quick to point out that they paid half of the taxes of the province. Neusiedl County had railroad connections with the "Free City" but none with the other candidate villages.

Fifteen miles south of Eisenstadt, at the base of the Sopron Range, was Mattersburg; this village had a population of 3,706, third largest in the province (but fifth largest if Eisenstadt and Deutschkreutz are totaled within their present limits). It was located on the principal railroad between Wiener Neustadt and Sopron.

The claim of Mattersburg was based primarily on its commercial promise. It had taken over some of the functions of Sopron and had become the largest animal market in Burgenland. Because of its position on the railroad it claimed to be the candidate for the south. However, it is clear that when the proponents of Mattersburg said "the south" they meant middle Burgenland, via the railroad through Sopron. Mattersburg's contacts with the south, as well as those of Eisenstadt, were of necessity through Wiener Neustadt. One of the most interesting arguments advanced in favor of Mattersburg was that its selection would hasten the return of Sopron: "The more Mattersburg grows, the more Ödenburg sinks and the more Ödenburg's citizens will cry out for a union with Burgenland." [18]

Though Mattersburg promised land, lumber, gravel, sand, supplies, and financial contributions, it was handicapped by its lack of existing facilities. This proved such a barrier to its selection that in the final consideration Mattersburg united its cause to that of adjacent Sauerbrunn.

In 1923 Sauerbrunn had a population of only 1,357. It was a completely atypical township, in that its village life was centered on the mineral spring within it; it had no agricultural base. (Only 7 per cent of its population is dependent on agriculture for a livelihood.) In contrast to the usual peasant homes, its houses were hotels and inns. It was on the Wiener Neustadt-Sopron branch of the *Südbahn*, halfway between Mattersburg and Wiener Neustadt. The provincial government had settled itself in this spa late in 1921 because it contained the buildings that could be utilized for the offices of the government.

The inhabitants of Sauerbrunn, most of whom had previously been supported in one capacity or another by the spring, were not anxious to have their township chosen to be the capital. The host of bureaucrats was acting as a plague on their business. The hotel owners petitioned the government several times to leave the spa, or at least to select the capital, so that they could try to regain their former trade before the time lapse killed it completely.

Who then supported Sauerbrunn, and why? The bureaucracy itself supported Sauerbrunn. Since Burgenland had had no available educated class, whereas Austria, after the loss of her empire, had a surplus of former and potential civil servants, the bureaucracy was an imported force. It had had no previous ties with Burgenland and was motivated more by its own necessities than by any loyalty to Burgenland. Many of the officials were from Vienna and they preferred to remain as close as possible to their home area. The Sauerbrunn Beamtenschaft (a union of civil servants) declared itself unanimously against Eisenstadt, saying that it was a "place of horrors." [19]

Housing was a matter of prime importance to the imported officials. Sauerbrunn had better housing facilities than any of the other candidates, but even these were pitifully inadequate. "We know of cases where for weeks judges have had to sleep on straw heaps in their courtrooms, because not even the smallest room was available." [20] Under such circumstances, the families of the bureaucrats were forced to remain in Vienna, so that many of the civil servants kept two households, commuting to Vienna on weekends. Yet the situation was far better than it would have been in Eisenstadt, because only a few miles west of Sauerbrunn, along the railroad, was the important city of Wiener Neustadt. Very few of the officials actually lived in Sauerbrunn, but many did live in Wiener Neustadt. This would have been difficult from Eisenstadt.

Sauerbrunn also afforded, along its railroad, a quick and easy route of evacuation. Most Burgenlanders were convinced that Hungary would be certain to occupy Burgenland at the first opportunity. The bureaucracy was scarcely immune from this fear; it remembered well the "volunteer bands," and with its weak ties to the new province preferred to be in a place from which quick withdrawal by rail or by foot would be possible. Compared with Sauerbrunn immediately on the former frontier, Eisenstadt, with the ridge at its back, was most insecurely located.

The only candidate from the south was Pinkafeld, and it was the last to announce itself. In 1923 Pinkafeld had a population of 2,573 and was the major manufacturing center. It was located at the west end of the Pinka valley railroad. During the time of the deliberations over the capital, it had only bus connections with the Austrian rail system at Friedberg, but the important rail link was well under construction when the selection of the provincial capital took place. Pinkafeld proposed to purchase the large local palace of the Batthyány family for the use of the Landtag, and offered financial assistance, land, lumber, sand, vehicles, and 1,000,000 bricks.

Pinkafeld was suggested as the candidate of the south, though officials in the north accused the Peasants' party, which was concentrated in the south, of bringing forward this candidate merely for political purposes. The north, which held the power in the government, never took the candidacy of Pinkafeld seriously.[21]

Though the choice of the capital was, under the constitution, to be Burgenland's own, because of the difficulty the province had in arriving at a decision, the federal government was increasingly involved. Federal agreement with the selection was essential in any case, for without federal funds no government building could be built.

Since Burgenland official opinion did not resign itself to the loss of Sopron for some time, there were early suggestions that a temporary seat of government be chosen outside the province. The Pan-German newspaper in its lead article once urged the selection of Wiener Neustadt (Lower Austria), since Eisenstadt was, in its view, the candidate of "Eszterházy, the Magyar-sympathizers, and the clerics." Provincial Vice Premier Leser opposed the selection of Eisenstadt because he felt that as long as Sopron was not reunited to Burgenland, the province could be governed from Vienna, Wiener Neustadt, or Graz.

Of all the possible centers mentioned, Wiener Neustadt was the best located to act as the capital of Burgenland. This city was for half the province the most important commercial and transportational center and occupied the key position for all rail traffic from the south to either Vienna or north Burgenland.[22] Sauerbrunn was little more than an advance post for Wiener Neustadt; the officials cramped into the tiny spa would have felt not the slightest hesitation in moving the few miles westward to the city that was acting as the center in every way except in the narrowest political sense. Wiener Neustadt also had available a large building, the military academy, which could be used for the Landtag and the government offices; this fact would save the federal government the expense of constructing a new building. In June, 1923, Chancellor Seipel and federal financial officials met in Wiener Neustadt to inspect the military academy with a view to making it the home of the Burgenland government.

Burgenlanders, at least in the north, considered the Wiener Neustadt plan to be a great danger to the existence of their new province, as it undoubtedly was. The Eisenstadt newspaper in full-page, front-page editorials pleaded that the title be given to any other Burgenland community rather than have the government moved outside the province. Some Burgenlanders announced that they would accept the Wiener Neustadt proposal only if the academy, its grounds, and a connection eastward to the border were annexed to Burgenland. In view of these protests, the federal government ceased its attempts to help settle the matter for Burgenland; it was to be the province's decision.

Whereas northern Burgenland was embroiled in this controversy for over three years, southern Burgenland scarcely seemed to be concerned. Neither of the two southern newspapers showed any interest in the problem. Even the final decision was greeted with apathy. The announcement of the selection of Eisenstadt in the Oberwart paper was astounding for its lack of emphasis.[23] Under the small headline, "Burgenländische Landtag," the actions of the provincial parliament were reported in routine fashion. The last of these actions had decided the capital question. There was no headline, no subheadline, not even heavy type, and no comment elsewhere in the paper to mark this momentous decision.[24]

Nowhere else could there be found any indication of southern interest or involvement in this issue that kept the north in a furor for over three years. The south seems to have felt that this was strictly a northern affair, and watched it with the same degree of apathy with which an Andean Indian might watch the struggles among the cliques of the capital for control of the country.

If one is to credit the account of the Bürgermeister of Eisenstadt at the time, it required the intervention of the Viennese newspapers to obtain the selection of Eisenstadt. In a meeting held in Wiener Neustadt, the members of the Landtag decided in secrecy to vote for Sauerbrunn.[25] This resolution came to the attention of Eisenstadt's

Bürgermeister Koller, who, in a last minute attempt to gain public support for his city, invited representatives of the Viennese press to take a special bus tour of the three northern candidates. All the principal newspapers of Vienna agreed, and twelve reporters made the trip. The bus load of newsmen completely surprised Mattersburg and Sauerbrunn; after viewing these two townships, the reporters were driven to Eisenstadt where a tour of the city culminated in a reception in the palace of the Eszterházys. The results were most gratifying for the proponents of Eisenstadt. All the newspapers featured the tour and a comparison of the three competitors; all favored Eisenstadt. The consensus of their reports was that only Eisenstadt could pretend to the title of "city," that Mattersburg was but a large market village, and Sauerbrunn a spa. The cultural tradition of Eisenstadt was stressed.

Herr Koller maintained that these newspaper reports won the vote for Eisenstadt. It is hard to tell if this is true or not, or even if the articles exerted any influence on the delegates. However, it is significant that when the mayor found himself in a desperate position he did not try to influence a Burgenland newspaper; he did not try to organize any demonstrations or protest marches; he turned to Vienna. He reasoned that the politicians in Burgenland would find it difficult to take a stand contrary to Viennese public or official opinion. Even if Herr Koller's bus tour did not decide the election, it was indicative of the fact that almost every important decision concerning Burgenland was made not within the province, but in Vienna.

The vote was taken on April 30, 1925; Eisenstadt was selected on the second ballot.[26] However, Eisenstadt was not chosen to be the "capital" (*Hauptstadt*), but the "seat of the provincial government" (*Sitz der Landesregierung*). This was so specified in the subsequent Burgenland constitution of January 15, 1926: "The seat of the provincial government is Eisenstadt." Sopron was still the *Hauptstadt* of Burgenland.[27]

The selection of the provincial capital was made when the railroads constituted the only feasible means of transportation. Despite its location near the "waist" of Burgenland, Mattersburg did not enjoy a favorable position in this regard. Both Mattersburg and Eisenstadt had a railroad connection with Vienna, to Wiener Neustadt, and, through Sopron, to middle Burgenland. Eisenstadt was not on a through line but it soon became evident that it was no difficulty for the railroad management to run a train directly from Vienna to Eisenstadt, despite the switches en route. Rail connections to the south, while slightly better from Mattersburg, were also possible from Eisenstadt. Therefore, contrary to prevailing opinion, Mattersburg's rail position was inferior to that of Eisenstadt, since Eisenstadt had the railroad to Neusiedl which Mattersburg could not duplicate.

Mattersburg's central location was mostly potential. The fulfillment of Mattersburg's potentialities could not come until the construction of the highway across the ridge behind it, in 1929. With the completion of this road Mattersburg symbolized the connections of the north with the south. However, this stage of technological development came five years too late for Mattersburg. Had the capital been chosen on the basis of the present day transportation system, it seems probable that, despite Eisenstadt's title and history, Mattersburg would have become the capital.

Although, from the contemporary viewpoint, Mattersburg would seem to be the best located of the four candidates, in the final voting the choice was between Sauerbrunn and Eisenstadt. These two townships represented the contest between the internal and the external forces trying to control the future of Burgenland. It was not stated in those terms, of course, but the contrast was there. Eisenstadt represented a Burgenland past, a Burgenland culture, and, by virtue of the ridge behind it, was turned away from Lower Austria and towards the Hungarian Little Alföld to the east. Sauerbrunn represented virtually nothing of Burgenland, nothing of its life, its past, its culture; Sauerbrunn's strongest argument was that it was close to Wiener Neustadt and Vienna.

Had Sauerbrunn been selected, it is doubtful that Burgenland could have developed a provincial consciousness and loyalty capable of enduring the extreme trial of its seven-year dissolution. Sauerbrunn was, politically, little more than a satellite of Wiener Neustadt, and selecting Sauerbrunn as capital would have meant, in effect, the selection of Wiener Neustadt. In choosing Eisenstadt, Burgenland was electing to go its own way, and to develop itself along the lines of its own patterns and experiences.

THE VIABILITY
OF A PROVINCE

By 1922 the questions concerning the status of Burgenland had been settled, but the problems facing the area did not automatically cease to exist. The new province now had to be made to work. In the stringencies of month-to-month existence the legislators had to wrestle with the profound difficulties facing a province which would have to organize itself without facilities and without money.

For the first decade of its existence, *lebensfähig* ("viable") was the key word in the thinking and the oratory of the leaders of Burgenland. In the budget reports, in articles, in speeches, in debates the word constantly appeared. It was as if the members of the Landtag felt it necessary to convince themselves, the statesmen in Vienna, and the inhabitants of Burgenland that the new province was indeed capable of existence. Every principal issue, the budgets, the selection of a new capital, the construction of governmental facilities, had the appearance of a serious crisis.

Burgenland was trapped in a dilemma: a transportation network had to be constructed to provide the basis for commercial growth, but only an increase in commercial life could provide the funds necessary to construct the railroads and roads.[1] Unable to find a way out of this circle, the Landtag turned toward, and against, Vienna. Burgenland officials adopted the attitude that since Austria had signed the treaty with Hungary, recognizing the loss of Sopron, Vienna had the "moral duty" to supply the facilities lost with Sopron.[2]

Since the help was not forthcoming in the amounts hoped for, bitter charges were hurled at the federal government. Franz Binder, a member from Burgenland of the national parliament, condemned the other provinces for seeking their own interests first when Burgenland obviously required preferential treatment. "We cannot and will not . . . let it happen that we be treated as a stepchild. We are not a colony. We possess the full rights of a Bundesland within the Federal State of Austria, and demand nothing but our rights."[3] "Without investment by the Bund I can tell you already, there will not be a lebensfähig Burgenland. . . . We don't want to be always the stepchildren; we want to be treated as having the full rights of sons of the republic."[4] Landeshauptmann (Provincial Premier) Rauhofer accused the federal government of slighting Burgenland. One of the bitterest commentaries on the situation was an article by Walheim entitled, *Ist das Burgenland lebensfähig?* "This time in the Landtag, sharp words have again fallen against Vienna. We cannot, of course, know the heavy financial position of the federal government . . . but a little more love Burgenland had believed it could expect. Our . . . retardation has its basis not only in the financial needs of Austria. . . . There were and are circles who pin their hope of a restoration on Hungarian help and therefore . . . look for a return of Burgenland to Hungary, and, on these grounds, refuse any investment in Burgenland. . . . In the division of the tax funds we came out too low; there remain yet the hopes based on the always mythical remnant of the League of Nations credits. Let us say it strongly, that this hope is not very strong. And so we can become easily disillusioned."[5]

The fear of division was strong. Provincial Vice Premier Stesgal warned a meeting in Güssing, "Voices can already be heard in Old Austria [saying] that Burgenland is not ready to rule itself and must therefore be divided."[6] Chancellor Seipel tried to reassure Burgenland leaders by stating that there would be no division of Burgenland "even though in circles, in Burgenland and out of Burgenland . . . much is said of it. The autonomy of the province is anchored in the constitution of the Federation and can be changed only if the Landtag itself decides thus."[7] Still, the fears of attempts on the integrity of the province continued. In 1925 the Güssing newspaper directed a stern warning towards the premier of Styria, Rintelen, who was advocating the establishment of a Betriebsleitung (district office) for eastern Styria and southern Burgenland, in Hartberg, Styria: "The province does not want to know of Graz or any other Betriebsleitung

in the south. . . . It would be about time to let Herr Rintelen understand, finally, that Burgenland will not be given over to him. . . .
Hands away from Burgenland, Herr Rintelen!" [8]

During the sixteen years between its creation and its destruction,
Burgenland drifted along on a minimal level of political existence.
It could not be destroyed, and it could not raise itself. In his many
articles, Walheim tried to counter the doubts concerning the new
province. "One can ask doubters what Hungary . . . would have
done for German West Hungary. As little as for the 'most loyal city
of Sopron' ! And the friends of partition should be asked if they really
believe that we would be better off if in January, 1922, one part of
our province had gone to Lower Austria, and the other to Styria.
Certainly not! . . . Austria is the torso of a large Reich . . . we
are the torso of an ideal Burgenland of which we had dreamed but
which will never exist. We are entirely without tradition, and dis-
inherited. Despite that we will not fail." [9]

Finance

The fundamental tests of the ability of Burgenland to maintain itself
occurred in the realm of finance. Could Burgenland meet its opera-
tional expenses, and could it embark on the program of building that
was essential to its development?

Heavy criticism greeted the first announced budget. One delegate
went so far as to launch an attack on the existence of Burgenland;
he predicted that when the taxes became too heavy the housewives
of Burgenland would ponder whether it would not be expedient to
join the province to Lower Austria and Styria. Provincial Premier
Rauswitz replied to the critics, most of whom had only recently entered the province, that they should not base their judgments on past
experience.

Thereafter, there was little criticism of budgets; on the contrary,
officials seemed to outshout each other in maintaining that the budget
on hand proved that Burgenland was indeed lebensfähig. This occurred in 1922, 1923, and 1925, when Provincial Premier Rauhofer
claimed that the budget presented "irrefutable proof that Burgenland
is lebensfähig," [10] and 1926, when Walheim stated that "the proposed budget has a special significance, since it is the proof of the
lebensfähigkeit of the province." [11]

Actually, as Rauhofer stated, the province could cover its ordinary
expenses with its normal income. Burgenland could continue to exist;
in that sense it was economically viable. If the budget was limited
to the expenses of ordinary maintenance, it could be balanced, but

if it attempted to devote funds for construction work, there was a deficit.

During the interwar years Burgenland was hampered by the Austrian system of revenue collection and distribution. In this regard Burgenland suffered from too much autonomy. Each province was permitted to establish its own rates of taxation, and to collect the funds. This revenue was then divided with the federal government to meet the needs of the nation, the province, and the townships. As a result of this system, each province received a proportion of the funds it had collected; the wealthiest provinces had more money available for their own use, the poorer ones less. Burgenland, which had the greatest need of funds, received the lowest amount per capita.

Burgenland was forced, therefore, to ask for supplementary funds from the federal government, which was hard-pressed to prove itself lebensfähig. Considering the conditions at the time, the federal government assisted Burgenland as much as could reasonably be expected. It built the governmental building in Eisenstadt, apartments for officials, and necessary governmental buildings in various county seats. When the Pinkafeld-Friedberg railroad connection was being constructed, all other railroad construction in Austria was halted to concentrate the available funds. For approximately a decade (1927–38), Burgenland received one million schillings per year above its share, and, on the tenth anniversary, a gift of ten million schillings from the federal government. It was these supplementary funds that made possible the progress of road construction which, though slow, gradually knit together all the isolated sections and villages of the province.

Since the close of the second world war, finance has ceased to be a life-and-death matter for Burgenland. A new system for the collection and division of the revenues of the country has been devised, and this has brought about a great change in the province. The federal government now collects the tax revenue, and these funds are distributed among the provinces on the basis of an *Ausgleich* law which attempts to take into account the needs of each province. This method of distribution works in favor of the poorer provinces, and, above all, Burgenland.

With this steady, increased source of revenue, Burgenland has "bloomed." This is evident above all in the road system, which now rivals that of any other province. So conscientiously has Burgenland devoted itself to the construction of roads, that today the provincial boundary with Lower Austria can often be located precisely by the sudden deterioration of the road as it leaves Burgenland. New governmental buildings and schools have been built, and there is a gradual improvement in the condition of the homes of the peasants. Burgenland is still the poorest of the provinces of Austria and is notably short of facilities for the traveler, but throughout the province there is evident a new pride in the advances that have been made.

Actually, Burgenland is now being partially subsidized by Old Austria. It is being allowed to raise itself with the funds supplied by the other provinces. It could still, therefore, be asked, "Ist das Burgenland lebensfähig?" since it is questionable if the province could meet the expenses necessary to its maintenance and growth without outside help. However, such a subsidy is hardly unusual. There is scarcely a government in existence that does not keep some political units in operation by direct or indirect payments to them.

Placing the powers of collection and division of revenue in the hands of the federal government represents a marked centralization of authority within the Austrian state. Probably as a result of the Nazi rule and the war, the provinces have come to recognize the needs of the country above those of the autonomous province. Between the wars this was not true; the autonomy of the provinces was jealously guarded against possible encroachment by the government in Vienna. The ordeal of the second world war seems to have bred the sense of an individual nationality in the people of Austria, so that they think of themselves as Austrians and not only ethnically as Germans and politically as Tirolians or Styrians. In a union of largely independent provinces, all of which were workable topographic-economic units based on ten centuries of tradition, Burgenland could at best but exist; within a centralized Austrian state, Burgenland could bloom.

Landholding

The extreme disparity between the size of the holdings of the large magnate [12] and that of the individual peasant was considered to be a critical handicap to the well-being and development of Burgenland. In Burgenland the division of property by the peasants, mainly through inheritance, had reached the stage where the provincial parliament felt it necessary to pass a law stating the minimum dimensions below which a parcel of land could not be subdivided. The minimum for a vineyard was set at 4 meters (13 feet) in width and 360 square meters (one-ninth of an acre) in area. Beyond this law the Landtag would not go. In this, as in every important matter except transportation, the Landtag was split into two ineffectual halves by party warfare. From their traditionalist point of view, the members of the Christian party could never agree to the confiscatory type of land reform envisioned by the Socialists.[13] Though charges were hurled back and forth, nothing was accomplished.

In landholding, as in other matters of grave importance to the province, the problems were resolved by the gradual introduction into Burgenland of the fruits of the technological revolution of the twentieth century. It soon became obvious that the old semi-feudal order could not long exist within Western Europe. This fact was made strikingly apparent by a sharp rise in the taxes levied on the large holdings. (In Hungary the nobility had been almost immune from direct taxation.) The nobility in Burgenland began to sell and rent its arable land.

More important than the immediate increase in taxation was the introduction of good highways and bus lines into Burgenland. By the 1930's it had become feasible for local laborers in all parts of Burgenland to commute to the urban centers to the west; the poor peasant was no longer necessarily tied to his or the nobleman's land for his livelihood. The increase in transportational facilities helped to produce an agricultural revolution in Burgenland.

In the interwar period many of the large holdings were sold and, in effect, parceled out among the peasants. In Neusiedl County 2,956 hectares (7,300 acres) had ben subdivided by 1937. However, the division of the land was not always managed as wisely as it might have been; the 129 hectares (320 acres) in Podersdorf, belonging to the Heiligenkreuz monastery, were divided among 180 purchasers. The largest landowners, Eszterházy in the north and Draskovitsch in the south, did not sell any of their lands.

After 1945, the Soviet occupying forces accelerated the process of subdivision. Soviet troops were often quartered in the larger palaces and performed a magnificent feat of wrecking when they withdrew. The Soviet authorities did not indulge in wholesale expropriation, but they did look favorably upon township decisions in that direction. The most notable Soviet action was the declaration that the properties of Prince Eszterházy were *Deutsches Eigentum* (German property) and therefore subject to confiscation. This declaration was based on the fact that German troops had made use of the properties. These properties were then managed by Soviet organizations (known in Burgenland as USIA Betriebe) which parceled out the land among Communist-minded peasants.

When the Soviet forces withdrew in 1955, the peasants on the land were placed in an uncertain position. The governments of Austria and Burgenland would never recognize the expropriations but neither would they act to invalidate them. On the Eszterházy lands the situation remained unchanged because Prince Eszterházy had been in a Hungarian prison since the advent of Communist power in Hungary. During the revolution of October–November, 1956, a group of his loyal workers made a dramatic dash into Hungary and brought Prince Észterházy back into Austria. Upon achieving his freedom, Eszterházy announced that he would sell most of his arable land, principally to the people then on it. Community committees were to be established to divide the land and to take care of the financial details involved in the transactions. In Kobersdorf (middle Burgenland), the division of 222 acres (90 hectares) was the first to be agreed upon. The land was sold at prices of from 60 to 160 groschen per square meter (roughly $92 to $254 per acre). Eszterházy retained all his forest holdings, which constituted 68 per cent of his total holdings.

Despite the political overtones in the breakup of some of the arable portions of the Eszterházy estates, these moves fit into the general pattern of the division of the large landholdings. Even had Communist rule not been imposed within the Carpathian Basin, it is doubtful that Eszterházy would have retained his arable acreage for long. The old style of agriculture had depended on low taxation, an abundance of cheap labor, and a relatively high price for food. Perhaps complete mechanization would have made the operation of the large estates profitable, but certainly none of the noble landholders seems to have attempted it.[14]

Among the peasants there has also been a reversal in the trend of the size of the holdings. The flight from the land has reached such proportions that the holdings of several families are being amalgamated, through purchase or marriage. Few of the young people wish to remain on the land. In the northern townships the villagers prefer to work in the cities and come home on weekends. (A complete weekend free is a great temptation to a peasant.) Yet, the flight from the land is notable everywhere, not only in the north. The Lutheran pastor in Neuhaus am Klausenbach, in the extreme south, stated that in two years he had lost 120 of his 1,500 parishioners. In several localities there were instances of local men who wished to live on the land but could not find girls to marry them; very few young women are willing to assume the life of a peasant woman.

Within Austria, Burgenland has remained consistently the principal source of emigrants to America.[15] Besides the overseas movement there is a growing migration to Vienna. The lure of the big city cannot be overestimated; what is "modern" is sought after just as avidly by many Burgenlanders as by Americans. The Burgenlanders of Vienna have formed several singing groups and mutual-aid societies, and the greatest annual festival of Burgenland, the Martinifest, is held in Vienna, not in Burgenland.

There is scarcely a village in Burgenland that is not losing population; only the largest townships have gained in the last two decades. In the seventeen years between 1934 and 1951 the southern four counties lost 10 per cent of their population, Jennersdorf losing 14 per cent. Since the population was still rising in 1934, most of this loss can be assumed to have occurred during and after the second world war. The loss has been most severe in the areas that were formerly the most remote. In the hill country of northern Oberwart County, Schreibersdorf lost 50 per cent between 1934 and 1951, Holzschlag 43 per cent, Mönchmeierhof 42 per cent, Weinberg 38 per cent, Sulzriegel 36 per cent, and Unterschützen 26 per cent. Isolated self-sufficiency is no longer the goal of the young peasant.

Because of this continuing decrease in population, a steady amalgamation of the smaller holdings is taking place. The people who stay behind can, through purchase or marriage, acquire the property of the family that has been left without a son on the land. Signs of incipient mechanization are appearing. Even in the south, tractors are becoming obvious; the peasants are willing to sell much of the lumber of their wood lots to acquire agricultural machines. In 1957, Moschendorf, in the formerly isolated lower Pinka valley, with a population of 600, reportedly had 25 tractors.

The problem of landholdings has been solved primarily by the social aspects of the technological advances of the twentieth century. The larger and the smaller holdings are giving way to parcels of intermediate size. The poverty of the peasant has been alleviated by the improvements in transportational facilities, and the breaking down of his isolation has suddenly widened his choice of ways to earn a livelihood. Even the vaunted peasant conservatism has crumbled before the technological lure of the cities. In this sense, Burgenland was saved from its problems by being born at the correct time. Tradition created the province, but modern technology made its existence feasible despite the ineffectiveness of the provincial and national governments.

Transportation

In Burgenland the improvement of the transportational system was placed ahead of every other task of the provincial and federal governments. It was felt that this was the life-and-death question for the province. Such importance was placed on this that the construction of railroads became a panacea; if the rail lines were built, automati-

cally industry would enter the province, tourists would come throng-
ing, and every isolated village would flourish. In the critical period
between the wars, the future importance of highways could not be
appreciated. Buses and automobiles had not yet entered the province
in sufficient numbers to transform the problem. All emphasis was on
railroads. When funds were sought for a north-south connection, it
was always a rail line, crossing the mountain areas, that was envisioned.

The proposed railroad construction had two aims: to connect
all parts of Burgenland to Vienna, and to tie together the various
portions of the province. The first of these was suggested for economic as well as political reasons; the second was considered vital to
the existence of Burgenland. "As long as the south Burgenlander
needs three days to come to north Burgenland, the feeling of belonging together cannot attain a strength necessary to defy the danger
of a division [of the province]. Only when the rail line runs through
the whole Burgenland will Burgenland present a completed unity."[16]
Although over two dozen railroad construction proposals appeared in
the Burgenland press, only one was carried out.[17] The reason was
simply that there was no one to pay the costs of construction. The
provincial government could not sustain more than a minimal proportion of the costs; the determining factor came to be which projects
the federal government was willing or able to construct out of federal
funds. Private sources of revenue were never available.

In considering a specific proposal, the federal government distin-
guished between those in the national interest and those of only
local, or provincial, importance. If a line was considered to be of
interest to the province alone, the federal government would contribute one-third, the provincial government two-thirds of the cost
of construction. If a line was said to be in the interest of the entire
country, the federal government would contribute up to 90 per cent
of the costs. The federal government was itself in continual financial
difficulties throughout the interwar period. Only the Pinkafeld-Friedberg link[18] was considered to be in the national interest, and only
this ten-mile-long connection was built. In 1925 the Ministry for
Trade and Commerce stated its willingness to build the three stretches
necessary to complete a north-south railroad,[19] but that Burgenland
would have to contribute 60 per cent of the "36 milliarden Kronen."
In Burgenland this was considered to be "unjust and impossible."

Of all the proposed railroads it is clear that only the Pinkafeld-
Friedberg connection, and possibly a Güssing-Stegersbach-Oberwart
line, could have paid their way. Every other project, if completed,
would have involved not only heavy expenditures for the initial construction but also a continuing deficit thereafter. The north-south

railroad undoubtedly would have meant much to Burgenland politically, helping to unify the province, and would have been a great convenience for the relatively few people who had any reason for going to Eisenstadt, but financially it would have been a severe liability. Actually, the costs of constructing a railroad across the upland barriers of the Sopron and Köszeg ranges relegated this project to the realm of visionary dreams; even a wealthy province within a prosperous country could scarcely have afforded such an idealistic luxury as the north-south railroad. The fact is that except for those people actively involved in the provincial government, everyone and everything continues to move across rather than along the axis of the province. Burgenland continues to be a rural hinterland for the cities, above all Vienna, to the west. It is fortunate for Austria, in this respect, that her financial condition and that of Burgenland were so weak in the interwar period that these railroads could not be built; had they been constructed they would now be a continuing drain on the national treasury.

In the interwar years most of the road construction in Burgenland was limited to local connections. Villages which had had no contact with each other except via field tracks were connected with adequate roads. Otherwise, roads were thought of as being supplementary to railroads.

As local roads were improved or newly built, and it became evident that railroad construction would be halting, and perhaps nonexistent, attention came to be focused increasingly on the more important road connections between the separated portions of the still fragmented province. The vital road across the Sopron Range (the Sieggraben Saddle), connecting north and middle Burgenland, was completed in 1929, as was the important road between Liebing and Lockenhaus, which finally joined the Zöbern valley to the remainder of Oberpullendorf County. The mid-1920's marked the completion of the road, Heiligenkreuz to Mogersdorf, joining the Lafnitz and Rába valleys; the 1930's saw the construction of the roads joining the south and north ends of the isolated lower Pinka valley to the rest of Austria.

With the development of a highway system, bus lines were slowly introduced to reach the many areas far removed from the railroads. The first bus routes were those which were intended to join the upper Pinka valley to the "Aspang Line," prior to the completion of the Pinkafeld-Friedberg rail link. November, 1926, witnessed the first bus connection between Vienna and Eisenstadt. In September, 1926, the first bus run within north Burgenland (Eisenstadt-Mattersburg) was initiated, and in December, the first within south Burgenland (Güssing-Grosspetersdorf). Gradually the number of bus lines increased, but bus transportation was not to become an adequate unifying force until after the second world war.

Since the reconstitution of Burgenland in 1945, the motor bus, utilizing a rapidly expanding highway system, has become the principal means of tying the province together. With the new revenues granted to Burgenland, a fine network of roads, centered on the Eisenstädter Bundesstrasse (Eisenstadt Federal Highway), has effectively bound the fragmented province together. It is still a chore for a person from the south to come to Eisenstadt, but at least it is now possible without a long detour westward.

The Eisenstädter Bundesstrasse is the modern version of the old dream of a north-south railroad. The highway is still far from being a direct route, but it is being constantly improved. It has been designated a federal highway, and is therefore supported by federal funds. The portions of this highway that had existed before 1938, such as the section over the Sieggraben Saddle, have been improved. The connection across the Bernstein hill lands (the southernmost part of the Bucklige Welt) has been made into a fine highway. Those portions that remained immediately adjacent to the Hungarian boundary have been reconstructed at a distance from the border. Early in 1957 the Güssing-Heiligenkreuz connection was moved two miles to the west of the boundary, and a new route was constructed between Lockenhaus and Oberpullendorf to replace the older highway along the boundary. In the extreme south, a new road crosses the steep interfluvial upland between the Lafnitz and the Rába, due north from Jennersdorf, to eliminate the former total dependence of Jennersdorf on the frightening road just west of Szent Gotthárd. In order that Rechnitz and its surrounding villages could have adequate connections with the north, a road across the broadest and highest portion of the Köszeg Range was completed in 1947.

The basic pattern of bus routes now consists of four lines radiating from Vienna towards the southeast, to Neusiedl, Eisenstadt, Oberpullendorf, and Oberwart, and two lines eastward from Graz, to Oberwart and Güssing. Connecting these local centers is the north-south system centered on the capital, Eisenstadt. The five mentioned Burgenland centers act as cores for short lines which radiate in all directions from them.[20] Each of these five is a county seat. Of the remaining two county seats, one, Mattersburg, acts as the focal point for traffic crossing the Sieggraben Saddle behind it, whereas the other, Jennersdorf, serves virtually no transportational function.

In Eisenstadt, Oberpullendorf, and Güssing are the Burgenland offices and service stations for the Postautolinien, the governmental system of bus lines. Eisenstadt is, for its size, the most important bus center in Austria. On an ordinary weekday approximately 150 buses pass into, out of, or through the city. Oberpullendorf has great local significance as the node for all the routes within middle Burgenland, and as the junction point for the longer routes north, west, and south. Güssing is less important as a local center, since it has lost most of the area to the north and northeast to Oberwart and its forepost, Grosspetersdorf. Neusiedl and Oberwart are centers of private bus lines. Oberwart is the headquarters of Südburg, the largest private bus company in Burgenland, and is the only major transportation node of the south. Of the three bus centers south of Eisenstadt, only Oberwart has direct, non-change connections with Vienna. Oberwart is the only city in the province with direct connections to both Vienna and Graz.

Yet, though the bus routes have tied Burgenland together, they have not completed this task. Many townships do not have any kind of public transportation, but these are usually in the remote, forested uplands. The scheduling of the runs is often far from perfect. The local lines serve the primary purpose of affording easy connections between the outlying communities and the county seats. The convenience of connections to the longer runs out of the province, or even to Eisenstadt, is evidently considered to be secondary.

Despite the overwhelming emphasis on railroads in the early planning, Burgenland became united without them. Buses and trucks, on an expanding highway system, brought the various regions together, notwithstanding the presence of formidable topographic barriers between them. In the problems concerning transportation, as in those concerning landholding, Burgenland was assisted greatly by the unforeseen technological developments of the twentieth century.

The Lack of Cities

Many of the initial problems that beset Burgenland were attributable to the separation of this territory from the cities that had formerly acted as its political and commercial centers. The most serious initial problems stemmed from the necessity of finding ways to compensate for the loss of Sopron.

As a result of a railroad agreement between Austria and Hungary, connections between north and middle Burgenland were quickly re-established along the former routeway through Sopron. Sopron thus remained the principal link between north and middle Burgenland. Connections between the north and south were initially established through Wiener Neustadt. In relation to Burgenland this city was in a position somewhat analogous to that of Sopron. Through the interwar years Wiener Neustadt was the principal transport center for Burgenland and, as we have seen, was for a brief time considered to be the best location for the capital of the new province.

With the development of a highway system, utilized by buses and trucks, the primary line of north-south communications has been located entirely within the province, about halfway between Sopron and Wiener Neustadt. Instead of the original single node of transportation, Sopron, there are now three lesser centers of communications. Eisenstadt, northwest of Sopron, is the primary focal point for bus routes in north Burgenland, but all the routes from Eisenstadt, as well as those from Wiener Neustadt, must funnel through Mattersburg before crossing the hill barrier at Sieggraben. Oberpullendorf has become the principal transport node of middle Burgenland.

Sopron was also the principal market center of north and middle Burgenland, and again, Wiener Neustadt at first assumed this function. However, since it was necessary to have local hubs for the concentration of goods to be shipped to Vienna and Wiener Neustadt, two townships, one to the north and one to the south of the Sopron Range, became substitute market centers. Mattersburg, north of the range and along the principal railroad to Vienna, became the most important animal market center in Burgenland; Deutschkreutz, on the same railroad but beyond Sopron, became the principal market center of middle Burgenland. In both cases these were the closest large townships to Sopron on the railroad through Sopron.

Until December, 1921, Sopron was also the capital of the province. Just as the transportational and commercial functions of this city were dispersed, so were the political functions. For nine years the capital of Burgenland was, in practice, in two locations, Sauerbrunn and Eisenstadt, on two of the railroads fanning out of Sopron. In 1930 the political functions were concentrated in Eisenstadt, which was at the time considered to be only a substitute for Sopron.

Initially, therefore, the loss of Sopron was compensated for largely by the extension of the influence of Wiener Neustadt into the new province, with three Burgenland townships, Eisenstadt, Mattersburg, and Deutschkreutz, forming a semicircle of local substitutes around the lost city. Since the advent of trucking and buses, Sopron has been compensated for primarily by Vienna, with Eisenstadt functioning as the local governmental and transportational center.

Köszeg was formerly an important commercial center for the southern half of middle Burgenland. Since the movement of goods and labor in middle Burgenland is northward toward Vienna, no substitute center has developed across the boundary from Köszeg. Oberpullendorf, which has become a bus center as well as the county seat, has assumed the local commercial functions of middle Burgenland that were formerly served by Sopron in the northern half and Köszeg in the southern half. The transport connections between middle and south Burgenland that passed through Köszeg prior to 1921 have been diverted westward across the uplands. South of the Köszeg Range the previous commercial and transportational functions of Köszeg, Szombathely, and Körmend have been assumed by Grosspetersdorf and Güssing close to the border, and by the larger centers, Oberwart and Fürstenfeld (Styria) further west. The north-south routeway that had run from Sopron through Köszeg and Szombathely to Körmend has been replaced by the north-south highway from Eisenstadt through Oberpullendorf and Oberwart to Güssing.

In summary it can be said that the separation of Burgenland from the Hungarian cities has been compensated for primarily by the increasing extension of the economic influence of Vienna into Burgenland. Economically, most of the province has been annexed by the metropolis. This extension of Viennese influence existed even prior to 1921, but since most of the traffic then moved by rail, it was limited largely to those portions of north Burgenland which enjoyed rail connections with Vienna. Since 1921 this trade has expanded greatly. The movement of foodstuffs and laborers is no longer limited to rail routes; rather most of it now moves by truck or bus. All of Burgenland is now an actual or potential hinterland for Vienna. Even so remote a village as Moschendorf, in the southeastern corner of the province, ships its meat animals by truck directly to Vienna.

The attractiveness of Vienna is increased by the lack of any important commercial center within Burgenland. Eisenstadt and Oberwart are important only in relation to the other villages of the province. Three decades after the establishment of the province, the capital, Eisenstadt, had only 5,464 inhabitants. Eisenstadt is off all the important trade routes and is an important bus center only because it is the capital. Because there is no important commercial center within the province, all improvements in local transportation manage only to facilitate movement to Vienna. With continuing improvements in both the system of highways and the forms of motorized transportation the people of Burgenland tend more and more to move toward Vienna.

The Great Crisis—1938

In March, 1938, the German Army marched into Austria, annexing her to the German Reich. All newspapers were taken over immediately by the Nazi party, so that it is impossible to locate any unbiased printed appraisals of the events. The federal system of Austria, which had been subjected to one-party rule by Dollfuss and Schuschnigg, now vanished completely in the absolute dictatorship of Hitler and his party. The tense interactions between Vienna and the provinces were replaced by the simple hierarchy of rule from above. At first the Nazis allowed the existing political subdivisions to remain as they had been, with Nazi officials in complete control. A new government was established for Burgenland; this consisted of thirty members, twenty of whom were chosen to represent the counties. Nazi Burgenland was, however, of short duration. In May the new rulers of Austria promulgated a vast reorganization of the federation, destroying or altering the areas of the provinces in favor of the system of *Gaue* and *Kreise* characteristic of Germany. There were not one but two reorganizations of territory.

On May 24, 1938, it was decreed that the entire province of Burgenland plus the Bezirke of Wiener Neustadt, Neunkirchen, and Bruck an der Leitha of the former province of Lower Austria were to be added to Gau Styria. This award seems to have been intended as a reward to Styria for its support of the Nazi cause. It would have brought Styria to the Danube at Hainburg and increased its area from 6,310 to 8,880 square miles. Though communications between Graz and Hainburg might have been feasible over the Semmering Pass, this new Styria would have been somewhat of a monstrosity. Unfortunately for Gau Styria, the affected population of Lower Austria protested against being detached from its traditional province, and a new decision was promulgated. On May 31, 1938, the Nazi power announced the dissolution of Burgenland. The four northern counties were to be joined to Lower Austria (Niederdonau), and the three southern counties to Styria.[21]

At present it is impossible to ascertain how the majority of the people of Burgenland felt about the destruction of their province. No one will admit that he was in favor of anything that the Nazis did, yet, everywhere people say, "Of course, there were many circles who favored it, because it does make sense economically"; however, these "circles" are never identified. Burgenlanders add, "What could we do?" "We couldn't say anything." It appears that most of the inhabitants were against the destruction of Burgenland, but that few, if any, cared deeply. As one person said, "Very few tears were shed." There seems to have been only one case of local opposition to the attempted rearrangement; the inhabitants of Sieggraben protested successfully against being separated from Mattersburg and joined to Kreis Oberpullendorf. On a provincial or a regional scale there was no sign of any opposition to the move.

Burgenland had experienced a very difficult seventeen years of existence and in that time had not been able to surmount the enormous difficulties confronting it. The political life of the province had not yet come to rest in its citizenry; most of the party leaders had been immigrants from Old Austria, as had been almost the entire bureaucracy. There were, therefore, few articulate persons who felt any deep identification with a Burgenland.

1945

In February, 1945, the Soviet Army entered Burgenland. Within two months the Nazi rule of Austria came to an end. In many ways Austria was back to where she had been in 1918: a ruined country, shattered by a disastrous war. And once more leading the country was Chancellor Renner. For several months there was no effective self-government in the provinces. During these early months of 1945 the future status of Burgenland was uncertain. Reportedly there were movements within Lower Austria and Styria to keep their portions of Burgenland. In May, 1945, at a meeting in Eisenstadt of the mayors of Lower Austria, Provincial Vice Premier Helmer stated that he was certain that, despite attempts to reintroduce a government for Burgenland, the majority of the people of north Burgenland would not feel this to be the time to tear the ties that bound them to Lower Austria. ". . . All the less so when the only question may be whether or not five hundred more officials will find employment." [22] "In certain circles there was very great opposition to the resurrection of Burgenland. Leading positions in our state were of the opinion . . . that the Burgenland people . . . did not have the ability to govern themselves." [23]

Nonetheless, a delegation representing party leaders of the former Burgenland formally appealed to the provisional government of Austria for the re-establishment of the province, and its request was quickly granted. A special act, a second "Burgenland Law," was enacted on August 29, 1945. Article 1 stated, "Burgenland is re-established as an autonomous province of the republic," and Article 2 stated that its boundaries were to be the same as they had been previously. [24]

Though Burgenland was now once more a province, its immediate resumption of its rights, privileges, and functions was not assured. The matter was debated at the September 8 session of the provisional national government. Chancellor Renner suggested the naming of a special commissioner who, with the help of a council chosen from the three permitted political parties, was evidently to oversee the government of the province. This would have signified that Burgenland was to be handled as a "second-class province," considerably less than autonomous. Herr Figl, the leader of the Austrian People's party (Volkspartei), and who later became chancellor, fought this proposal, energetically supporting the complete self-government of Burgenland. On October 1, 1945, Burgenland again became an autonomous and equal province, and on November 10, 1945, the August 29 "Burgenland Law" was accepted by the Allied occupation authorities.

In the moves that returned self-government to Burgenland, the population of the province was very poorly represented. Except for the delegation of interested persons that went to Vienna to request the re-establishment of the province, all activity concerned the leaders of the provisional national government in Vienna. Did the majority of the population wish a resurrection of Burgenland? As far as we can now tell, it seems that they did; the inhabitants of Burgenland wished to have their province back. There remain yet the important questions: Why was Burgenland re-established? Why did its inhabitants want the province back? Why did they get it back so easily? No clamor, no demonstrations, no floods of letters to Vienna or Eisenstadt were required. There appear to have been several reasons:

1. There was a revulsion to everything Nazi. After the catastrophic war Austrians seemed seized with the desire to reverse everything the Nazis had done, just because they had done it. Unless there were compelling reasons for not doing so, everything was returned to its pre-1938 status.[25] The presence of the Allied occupation forces strongly augmented this tendency.

2. The Allied Forces, in effect, reconstituted Burgenland even before the enactment of the Burgenland Law by the Austrian government. The foreign ministers of the United Kingdom, the United States, and the Soviet Union had announced in the Moscow Proclamation of November 1, 1943, that the Nazi occupation of Austria was to be treated as null and void. The Allies entering Austria considered her to be returned to her status as of March 13, 1938. To the Austrians this implied a return to all the internal political units and boundaries of that date as well, and hence the resurrection of Burgenland.

Early in August, 1945, in the Allied agreement on the zones of occupation, the Soviet zone was specified to include all of Lower Austria, that portion of Upper Austria north of the Danube, one quarter of Vienna, and the former Burgenland. Burgenland was thus separately designated as part of a zone of occupation, distinct from Styria, which was occupied by the British. The principal reason for the demarcation of Burgenland as separate from Styria was probably based on its location; by occupying this strip, the Soviet Forces prevented any direct contact between the Western Powers and Hungary. Furthermore, the Soviet authorities may have favored a separate Burgenland as granting them an added opportunity to influence political activities.

The occupation boundary was strictly enforced, turning the Burgenland-Styria border into a milder version of the "Iron Curtain." Barbed wire was strung along the border. People could cross back and forth with a pass, but the checking was often a dangerous and uncomfortable procedure; the Soviet authorities used the border check points as convenient places for apprehending wanted persons. As a result, south Burgenland was forced to turn north. This dependence of the south on the north was of great importance, because it was in the north that political power in the province had been centered, hence it was there that the desire to have the province re-established was most strongly concentrated. The north had always feared that the south tended towards Graz; now the south was being forcibly turned away from Graz towards Eisenstadt and Vienna. The occupation boundary exerted a definite pressure towards the resurrection of a Burgenland government.

3. The war had produced a solidifying of the Burgenland provincial consciousness. Just as in the first world war, when the local men had served as soldiers of Hungary but had returned with an intensified consciousness of being German, so now the men returned with an intensified consciousness of being Burgenlanders. They had felt themselves different from the other German, or even Austrian, soldiers; when they met a serviceman from some other portion of Burgenland they would greet him as a provincial kinsman, as someone who could understand the mutual problems. Among the civilians, this consciousness of a difference was strengthened also. The people of the south, who were supposedly so similar to the Styrians, felt the difference keenly and referred to themselves as "New Styrians," in distinction from the Styrians themselves. This conscious separation was based on the many "differences" mentioned previously. Because of their heritage, even because of the economic backwardness of their area, these people felt themselves to be different from their neighbors.

4. The *Grenzland* ("borderland") consciousness rekindled the desire to try it alone. The Burgenlanders felt themselves a border folk, in a border area. They had once been the "stepchild" of the Hungarians; recently they had been the "stepchild" of the Styrians and Lower Austrians. Theirs was a borderland which was always neglected in favor of other areas or provinces, and they had grown to suspect any rule by an outsider. "For the Lower Austrian government Burgenland was only an area for the procurement of the necessities of life for the Lower Austrian market, but nobody concerned himself

whether or not the needy areas of Burgenland were supplied." [26] The prevailing opinion of the people of south Burgenland is that in Styria they paid their taxes but received little in return; in Burgenland there is less money to work with, but they know that they will get their share. As long as they remained somebody's borderland they would be neglected. They wished to rule themselves.

5. All the county seats that had lost their political functions wished to regain their positions and offices. This was true of Neusiedl, Mattersburg, Güssing, and Jennersdorf. Not only the county seats themselves desired this resumption of political power, but all the surrounding areas as well wished a return to the former system, if only for the reason of convenience. Thus a peasant in Steingraben explained that he had favored the re-establishment of Burgenland because Güssing was close at hand, whereas Fürstenfeld, the Kreis center from 1938 to 1945, was several hours away by foot or wagon. Since this factor also carried weight in every village to the east of the former county seats, it may have had some influence on almost half of the inhabitants of Burgenland.

Thus Burgenland survived the most rigorous test a political area can endure, the test of dissolution. The destruction and division of Burgenland had long been contemplated as a possible, and perhaps a preferable, solution to the organizational problems confronting it. During the Nazi regime this alternate suggestion had been given the benefit of a trial, albeit under poor circumstances. It must be noted too that the act of dissolution had occurred before the special unifying features of added finances and integrated road and bus systems had become operative. However in two decades the Burgenland state idea, based on a complex of "differences," had grown from nothing to a power capable of maintaining the concept of a province when the organization of the area had been abolished.

14

TIES ACROSS THE BORDER

Among the peasants of Burgenland the emotions of linguistic nationalism could not eradicate all traces of sympathy for Hungary. Burgenlanders were keenly aware of the fact that until 1921 theirs had been a Hungarian tradition and history; it was in fact this Hungarian tradition which had given birth to a separate Burgenland. At least until 1938 the feelings of these border folk towards their former compatriots remained a matter of serious concern to the Viennese political leaders. Even today the inhabitants of Burgenland feel a special compassionate tie with the suffering land to the east.

Yet, after World War I, fear in one form or another was the most notable reaction of Burgenlanders to Hungary. In the critical years between 1918 and 1921, most people in Burgenland believed that the Magyars would never allow this territory to be taken away from Hungary and given to Austria. The protracted negotiations, the apparent weakness and lassitude of Austria, the intense propaganda efforts of the Hungarians, and, finally, the onslaught of the "volunteer bands" seemed to corroborate this belief. The Sopron Plebiscite and the boundary delimitations then returned bits of the awarded area to Hungary. Few, if any, Burgenlanders thought that the Hungarians would cease their revisionist efforts once the final treaty had been ratified.

In the decade that followed, the Hungarians seemed to live for nothing but the return of their lost lands. *Nem, nem, soha!* ("No, no, never!") was the national rallying cry. Special demonstrations were staged adjacent to the border in the hope that the Hungarian revisionist ideals would seep into Burgenland. A Magyar newspaper, *Hétfő*, was printed in Sopron and distributed in Burgenland; the revisionist propaganda of this paper caused resentment in Burgenland and led to official objections to its publication. Two other newspapers, *Vasvármegye* (Szombathely) and *Heideboden* (Magyaróvár), were banned from distribution in Burgenland.

The continuing fear of a Hungarian return was expressed several times in the newspapers in 1926. During the bloody Socialist riots in Vienna on July 15–17, 1927, rumors circulated through Burgenland that the Hungarians would march into the province if the "Red revolution" succeeded.[1] Later that year Chancellor Seipel attempted to allay the fears of a Hungarian return by announcing that Hungary had definitely renounced all claims to Burgenland. However, the next year Prime Minister Bethlen of Hungary stated that Hungary had *not* renounced Burgenland and asked for a plebiscite in the province. This fear was ultimately lessened by the rise of Hitler and the incorporation of Austria into the mighty German Reich.

Since the second world war, Hungarian revisionism has evidently been superseded, at least temporarily, by the greater issues confronting Central Europe. The fear of a Hungarian return is still not dead, however. In 1957 and 1961, in three widely separated villages, I encountered anxiety that the Hungarians would be back someday.[2] In a powerful way that fear has been transformed and enlarged to mean the return of a huge force from the east. The predominating fear at the present time is not a return of the Hungarians themselves but of the Russians, through Hungary. During the Hungarian Revolution of October–November, 1956, this fear gripped many portions of Burgenland, reaching panic proportions in at least one village.[3]

Fear of Hungary is felt not only in terms of a threatened force from the east, but also in all traces of the Hungarian history and culture which still permeate Burgenland. One cannot read many Burgenland publications, or observe the archival research that is being pursued, without coming to the conclusion that much of this labor has one end: to prove that Burgenland was never actually a part of Hungary. When the new province was searching for a flag, the committee in charge rejected the colors of Charlemagne (red and green) as bearing too close a resemblance to the colors of Hungary (red, white, and green). Instead the colors of the *Vandals* were selected![4] (The Vandals had moved rapidly through the Carpathian Basin in A.D. 401.)

An intriguing manifestation of this fear of history is the series of six murals on the wall of the city hall in Eisenstadt. These sketches depict six important dates in the history of the "Free City": (1) the "Hallstatt" settlements in the area, approximately 1000 B.C.; (2) the Roman times; (3) the settling of the Germans in the area by Charlemagne; (4) the transfer of the city to Austria *in 1445;* (5) the raising of the settlement to the status of "free city" in 1648; and (6) the raising of the city to the status of provincial capital in 1925. This sequence is significant in that every connection with Hungary is omitted. The date chosen for the transfer to Austria is medieval. That this transfer was shortly reversed, that Eisenstadt was founded in Hungary, that most of its history was spent in Hungary, that the greatest glory of the city occurred while it was within Hungary (the times of the Eszterházy court with Josef Haydn)—none of these points is alluded to, whereas the Hallstatt and the Roman times are chosen for special attention. The Hungarian experience is evidently still too close, too much a part of the local culture and memory to be safely publicized.

Coupled with the fear of an attack from the east has been a feeling of antagonism against the Hungarians. This feeling is now held by surprisingly few people, however, and is based more on nationalistic resentment than on memories of past injuries. It is the German nationalists who feel the antagonism most deeply; they still harbor a grudge against the Hungarians for having "robbed" Burgenland of its "natural capital."

The anti-Hungarian feelings were considerably inflamed by the post–World War II expulsion of the *Volksdeutsch* from Hungary. This expulsion meant that many of the Germans who had been left behind in Hungary by the boundary delimitation of 1921–23, and who populated what has often been referred to by the German nationalists as the "Hungarian Burgenland," were dispossessed of the lands they had held for centuries. Some of the intelligentsia had hoped for an ultimate union of the "two Burgenlands," the Austrian and the Hungarian, into a truly viable Burgenland. Many of the border peasants had had close relationships with the Germans across the line in Hungary. Though by no means all the Germans were forced out, the mass expulsion destroyed many old ties, seemed to shatter forever the hopes of an ultimate reunion of adjacent areas, and intensified the nationalistic animosities that had existed since 1918.[5] In Nickelsdorf, one of the principal border crossing points, it was said that some of the villagers had refused to help the Hungarian refugees who surged across the boundary there in the winter of 1956–57 because "they had it coming to them. . . . Now it is their turn to be driven out."

Despite the fear, an emotional bond underlies much of the feeling of the Burgenlander for Hungary. The younger people do not feel this much, but it is common among the older peasants who remember Hungary. They definitely prefer to be in Austria, but they have not completely lost their feeling for the historicity of Hungary. Austria has granted them freedom and ties with the advances and prosperity of Western Europe, but these do not have the emotional power of the lure of the Alföld or the fierce grandeur of the Magyars. Especially among the older clergymen this feeling is still alive. Several people confided that it is not easy to change one's national loyalties. Sympathy for Hungary was intense in October–December, 1956. It was more than "there, but for the grace of God, go I"; it was a sympathy based on a deep affection.[6] With but few exceptions, the charity of the Burgenlanders was magnificent that winter.

The historical and geographical situation of Burgenland meant for many hopeful Austrians that the new province could serve as a "bridge" between Austria and Hungary. This was to be the "mission" of Burgenland. Given other circumstances and developments, it is possible that Burgenland could have served as some kind of "bridge" between the two countries. The events and the passions of the mid-twentieth century have made such a role difficult. Strange to say, Hungary cut herself off from Burgenland more than Burgenland cut itself off from Hungary. Burgenland would have favored the continuation of the old personal ties and the old economic ties with the border cities, but it was Hungary who forced the separation. The "Iron Curtain" was erected from the Hungarian side of the boundary, albeit under outside pressure.

Burgenland is the least German of the Austrian provinces.[7] The 1951 census indicated that 13.2 per cent of the population of Burgenland was primarily non-German speaking. This figure is clearly too low; approximately 15.5 per cent of the population of the province belongs to a linguistic minority (Magyar or Croatian).[8] Burgenland also contains a higher proportion of Protestants, 14.1 per cent, than any other province of Austria.[9] Since most of the members of the linguistic minorities are Catholic, 29 per cent of the people of Burgenland are members of a minority group.

This figure has an interest beyond sheer numbers or percentages. The present Magyar minority had been, until 1921, a part of the national ruling group, and the Croats had known only a Hungarian existence, since even Croatia was within Hungary until the shattering of the Dual Monarchy. The transfer to Austrian sovereignty was a reversal in national ties for both these groups. For the Protestants

(mostly Lutherans) the transfer to Austria also meant a major alteration in situation, a move from Hungary, with her tradition of Protestant revolutionaries, to "Catholic Austria," the home of the Habsburg
Counter Reformation.

MINORITY GROUPS

Table 5 lists the numbers and the percentages of the three principal
linguistic groups in Burgenland. The census figures are, however, misleading; the census questionnaire did not ask for *Muttersprache*
("mother tongue"), but rather for *Umgangsprache*. Supposedly the

TABLE 5

Year	Total Population	Germans	Magyars	Croats
1920	294,849	221,185 (75%)	24,867 (8.0%)	44,753 (15.0%)
1923	275,851	222,401 (81%)	14,931 (5.2%)	40,196 (14.1%)
1934	292,288	241,280 (81%)	10,430 (3.5%)	40,487 (13.5%)
1951	276,136	239,687 (87%)	5,251 (1.9%)	30,599 (11.1%)
1951 Revised *		233,441 (85%)	7,669 (2.8%)	34,427 (12.6%)

* The "Revised" figure represents the transfer of the German-Magyars from the
"German" to the "Magyar" column, and the German-Croats from the "German" to
the "Croat" column.

latter term meant the language used within the home, but many Burgenlanders interpreted it to mean the language used outside the home.
As is common in such circumstances, many members of the minority
groups have felt it expedient to declare themselves as being members
of the majority group. For example, in Siget in der Wart, which is
considered to be a Magyar village and in which the religious services
are still conducted in Magyar, the census lists 217 Germans and 45
Magyars. Fortunately, the census of 1951 gives a detailed breakdown
of the figures for Burgenland. The totals for German *Sprachzuge-
hörigkeit* are subdivided into German, German-Magyar, and German-
Croat.[10] Since it can safely be assumed that no German would move
towards a minority status, the best indication of the actual totals for
each linguistic minority is obtained by adding the German-Magyars
to the listed Magyars and the German-Croats to the listed Croats. These
in-between classifications are significant also in granting a good approximation of the proportions of each group that are on the threshold
of linguistic assimilation.

Because the prominent leaders of the movement for transfer to
Austria placed so much emphasis on German nationalism, both of
the principal linguistic minority groups demanded, in 1922, autonomy

for the province and guarantees of political freedom for themselves.[11] The fears of the minorities were recognized and eased by I Article 5 of the Burgenland Constitution: "German is the official language of Burgenland, but without harming the constitutionally established rights of the linguistic minorities."[12] The cultural and political rights of the minorities have been carefully protected except for the years of the Nazi government.

The Magyars

As depicted on Map 10, the Magyars of Burgenland are concentrated in two small areas, the centers of Oberwart and Oberpullendorf counties. These Magyars are the descendants of colonies settled by Hungarian kings on strategic sites to guard the western frontier.

As indicated in Table 5, the Magyars have declined greatly, both in numbers and in their proportion of the total population. The precipitous drop between 1920 and 1923 was due primarily to the mass emigration of Hungarian officials and intellectuals. The 1923 total of 14,931 Magyars included 4,376 "Foreigners," most of whom probably emigrated subsequently, since the 1934 census listed but 10,430 Magyars. The extreme nationalism of the Nazi years and the maturing of a generation that has no recollection of Hungarian rule have helped to lower the Magyar total to only 7,669. (If the German-Magyars are not included, the total is only 5,251.) Of the 7,669 Magyars, 31 per cent chose, for one reason or another, to declare themselves as being German first and Magyar second and can, therefore, be considered to be well on the way to becoming Germanized.[13]

Oberwart city is generally considered in Austria to be the center of the Magyars in Burgenland, and yet the 1951 census listed more Germans than Magyars. Table 6 reveals that even if the German-Magyars are added to the Magyar total, the number of Germans exceeds the number of Magyars. Thus Oberwart has become German, and the Magyars are being rapidly Germanized; 26 per cent of the Magyars

TABLE 6

Township	1951 Census		Revised Figures		German-Magyars and their proportion of the Magyar total
	Germans	Magyars	Germans	Magyars	
Oberwart	2,854	1,603	2,277	2,180	577 (26%)
Unterwart	148	789	147	790	1 (0%)
Siget in der Wart	217	45	23	239	194 (81%)
Oberpullendorf	860	504	691	674	169 (25%)
Mitterpullendorf	85	362	59	388	26 (7%)

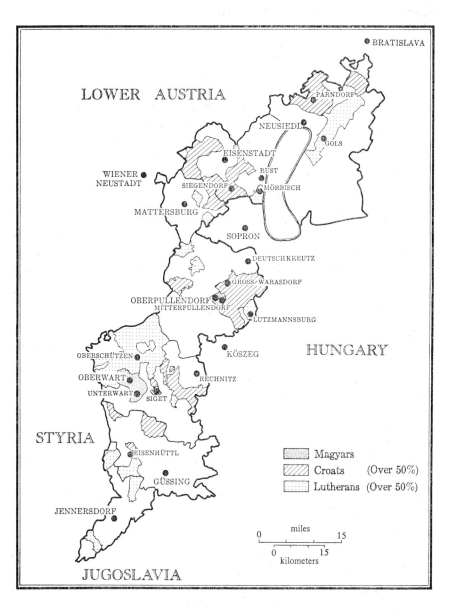

BRATISLAVA

LOWER AUSTRIA

PARNDORF

NEUSIEDL

GOLS

EISENSTADT

RUST

WIENER
NEUSTADT

SIEGENDORF

MÖRBISCH

MATTERSBURG

SOPRON

DEUTSCHKREUTZ

GROSS WARASDORF

OBERPULLENDORF
MITTERPULLENDORF

LUTZMANNSBURG

KÖSZEG

HUNGARY

OBERSCHÜTZEN

OBERWART

RECHNITZ

UNTERWART

SIGET

STYRIA

EISENHÜTTL

GÜSSING

JENNERSDORF

	Magyars
	Croats	(Over 50%)
	Lutherans	(Over 50%)

miles
0   15

0   15
kilometers

JUGOSLAVIA

MAP 10. THE MINORITIES OF BURGENLAND

listed themselves as primarily German. There is still a strong core of Magyars surrounding the only Calvinist church in Burgenland. This church, with its parish, forms a distinct community in the south-western third of the city.

Within Burgenland, Oberwart is second only to Eisenstadt in population and in economic and political importance. Because of its importance Oberwart has been subjected to intense pressure to Germanize. The development of the city as the principal governmental center of the south was accompanied by an influx of German-speaking officials. The locally born members of the bureaucracy were rapidly Germanized, since all the provincial and county governmental agencies had to conduct their operations in German. As the most important market center of southern Burgenland, Oberwart was Germanized in its commercial as well as its political life.

Linguistic pride and the religious community have worked for the continuance of the Magyar language, but the local inhabitants recognized that their children would have to speak German fluently if they were to advance in the commercial or political life of the city, province, or country. In the interwar years the activities of the civic government were conducted in Magyar, but since the war (and the Nazi occupation) these too have been Germanized.

Unterwart adjoins Oberwart on the southeast and presents the prime example of a minority-populated township that has succeeded in maintaining its original language and culture despite the continuing pressures towards linguistic assimilation. Only one German-Magyar was listed in 1951. The persistence of the Magyar language and culture has been the result of three sociogeographic factors. First, Unterwart is not a political or commercial center and does not, therefore, have to meet the other areas of Austria on their terms. Second, all the contacts of Unterwart with the outside world flow through Oberwart, which thus serves as a protective shield for the smaller Magyar community. Though the inhabitants of Unterwart can all speak German (it is a required subject in the Magyar local school), they are able to use Magyar in their commercial and political dealings with Oberwart. Third, Unterwart has become, through the efforts of some of its local leaders, the center of an active Magyar cultural group. A local schoolteacher, in close coöperation with the local (Catholic) church, has organized a group to perpetuate the Magyar costumes, songs, dances, and literature. When folk festivals are held in Vienna or elsewhere, it is usually a group from Unterwart that presents the Magyar dances.

Siget in der Wart is an excellent example of a minority-populated village that is rapidly being Germanized. Eighty-one per cent of these Magyars declared themselves to be Germans first and Magyars second.

This rapid assimilation is attributable to the location of the village and the religious adherence of the population. Siget is only three miles from Oberwart and Unterwart, but the immediately adjacent villages are non-Magyar. Probably of greatest significance has been the fact that the Magyars of Siget are Lutheran. Whereas the Calvinists of Oberwart look towards Hungary, and the Catholics of Unterwart towards the richness of their tradition, the Lutherans of Siget look towards Germany.

Oberpullendorf, the center of the second Magyar enclave, strongly resembles Oberwart. It too is a county seat, and it too has experienced the influx of German-speaking civil servants and the same pressure to Germanize for political and economic reasons as has Oberwart. Its German, Magyar, and German-Magyar proportions are almost identical with those of Oberwart. The Magyars in Oberpullendorf village are Catholics. Their church, which was built in 1935, is an interesting combination of the two linguistic influences. The church is dedicated to St. Clement Hofbauer who is a patron saint of Vienna and had no connection with Hungary or the Magyars, but three of the stained glass windows picture Hungarian saints. The window depicting King St. Stephen was donated by the then Chancellor of Austria, Dr. Kurt Schuschnigg. The congregation sings the same Haydn-type hymns that are sung by similar congregations in Vienna.

Mitterpullendorf strongly resembles Unterwart. The former adjoins Oberpullendorf, just as the latter adjoins Oberwart. Mitterpullendorf is also agricultural and Catholic. But the strong cultural life of Unterwart is not duplicated in this village, perhaps because the number of Magyars in the vicinity is much smaller than the number in the vicinity of Unterwart.

The Magyars of Burgenland never attempted to form a political party. They felt themselves to be too weak, too few in numbers. An obviously Magyar party would have had to endure the violent denunciations of the German nationalists who, in 1922, appeared to have assumed many of the positions of power and influence within Burgenland. The efforts of the Maygars and the Magyaronen were funneled into the existing Austrian party structure, which had been promptly introduced into the new territory. Since the Magyar-Magyaron intellectuals were mostly clerics and members of the middle class, the party chosen was the Christian party.[14]

The publication of a Magyar weekly newspaper was begun, but this attempt failed. A Magyar paper, *Hétfő*, was printed in Sopron and distributed in Burgenland until 1940. This strongly revisionist newspaper was a frequent target of the newspapers of the Great German party. After the second world war a Magyar Communist paper, *Magyar Ujság*, was founded in Vienna, but it ceased publication in the summer of 1956. A Catholic newspaper, *Magyar Szó,* was published in Vienna from 1954 to 1957.

In 1921, and throughout the interwar period, Vienna was beset by the constant fear of irredentist desires among the members of the Magyar minority. It was recognized that the Magyars were few, but it was feared that their influence was still great. The transfer to Austria was not, however, the shattering experience it may now seem to have been. The older Magyars knew Hungary only within the unity of the Habsburg Empire. Those who do look back with nostalgia to Hungary, look to the Hungary of Franz Joseph, not to the Hungary of Horthy, Rákosy, or Kádár. The situation since 1945 has also had a great effect on Magyar opinion. As one member of the nobility stated, "We were all against it [the move to Austria] but we are thankful now that we are not in Hungary."

An important deterrent to any development of irredentism has been the wise decision of the Austrian government to allow the minorities their primary schools, the full freedom to use their language and pursue their culture, and to avoid any policy of suppression, intimidation, or even watchful supervision. As a result the Magyars of Burgenland feel no sense of injustice. They profess to be *zufrieden* ("satisfied"). The willingness of the Austrians to trust the Magyars is exemplified by the high position enjoyed by the principal Magyar centers of Burgenland, Oberwart and Oberpullendorf. No Magyar could feel that he was being discriminated against when his particular township was retained as the local political center and made prosperous by the attendant construction of government buildings, schools, and hospitals. Though financial considerations probably motivated the Austrian decision to keep the county seats (*Bezirkshauptstädte*) where they had been, this development of political activities in the two Magyar centers was astute, since it assured the rapid assimilation of the Magyars without coercion or attendant dissatisfaction.

The younger Magyars are content with their situation within Austria to the point of considering themselves to be completely Austrian. The leader of the Magyar cultural group in Unterwart clarified this feeling by stating that he considers himself to be "a Magyar but not a Hungarian." According to him (and this was corroborated by others), there is not the slightest desire among the Magyars for a return to Hungary; even if Hungary were freed from communism there would be no favorable response to possible Hungarian demands on Burgenland. Austria has given them ties with the West and greater prosperity than has been the rule within Hungary. He then stated that the Magyars were no longer looking to this or that small state, but beyond, to a united Europe.

The Croats

One of every eight Burgenlanders is a Croat; the Croats are also maintaining their language far more effectively than the Magyars. Of the forty-three Croatian townships in Burgenland, none is of any political or commercial significance, so that the Croats have not, in their home villages, had to meet the rest of Austria on its terms. The Croatian villages also show a marked tendency toward clustering; this also has facilitated the retention of their language.

The decline in numbers and proportion of the Croats between 1923 and 1951 is not entirely attributable to the effects of Germanization. A study of the population totals indicates that over 50 per cent of the decline in numbers is the result of a decline in the total population of the Croatian townships; the Croatian villages have been losing population at a faster rate than the provincial average. This is in direct contrast to the case of the Magyars, who have suffered a precipitous decline in the same twenty-eight years, despite a rise of 11 per cent in the total population of the Magyar townships (Gemeinden).

Though the Germanization of the Croats is a relatively slow process, it has, nevertheless, been continuous since the Croats first settled these areas four centuries ago. The prevalence of persons with Croatian names who consider themselves to be German is striking. Persons with names such as Sinkovitz (pronounced Shinkovich), Dujmowitz, Kositz, Villovitz, Sinowatz, and Szmudits insist that they are *rein Deutsch.*

The Croatian villages of the northern five counties of Burgenland tend to form clusters (see Map 10); only a few are relatively isolated. These villages are also fairly large, so that even in those villages where the Croatian proportion of the total population is less than 50 per cent, the number of Croats is high. In Neusiedl County (the extreme north), the distance between the villages is so great that they tend to have little close contact with each other, so that each village forms the equivalent of a cluster. Under such conditions the rate of Germanization has tended to be low even though these villages all have close contact with Vienna, Wiener Neustadt, Bruck, and Hainburg.

Güssing County, in the south, forms an interesting contrast to these other counties; its Croatian villages are scattered rather than clustered, they are relatively small, and they are located in varying topographic situations. An analysis of the changes in this county in the past fifty years may help one to understand the forces and processes that are involved in the assimilation of a linguistic minority.

The accompanying diagram shows all the villages in the western two-thirds of Güssing County. The lines joining most of the village

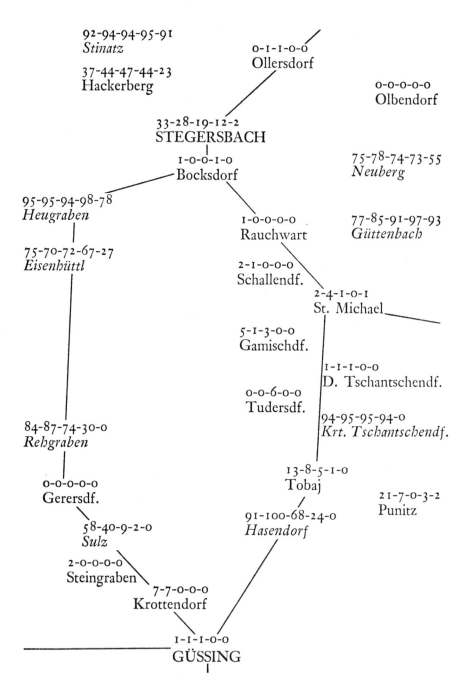

92-94-94-95-91
Stinatz

37-44-47-44-23
Hackerberg

0-1-1-0-0
Ollersdorf

0-0-0-0-0
Olbendorf

33-28-19-12-2
STEGERSBACH

1-0-0-1-0
Bocksdorf

75-78-74-73-55
Neuberg

95-95-94-98-78
Heugraben

75-70-72-67-27
Eisenhüttl

1-0-0-0-0
Rauchwart

77-85-91-97-93
Güttenbach

2-1-0-0-0
Schallendf.

2-4-1-0-1
St. Michael

5-1-3-0-0
Gamischdf.

1-1-1-0-0
D. Tschantschendf.

0-0-6-0-0
Tudersdf.

94-95-95-94-0
Krt. Tschantschendf.

84-87-74-30-0
Rehgraben

13-8-5-1-0
Tobaj

0-0-0-0-0
Gerersdf.

21-7-0-3-2
Punitz

58-40-9-2-0
Sulz

91-100-68-24-0
Hasendorf

2-0-0-0-0
Steingraben

7-7-0-0-0
Krottendorf

1-1-1-0-0
GÜSSING

Note: The five figures above each name represent the Croatian proportion of the population of the village in the censuses of 1910, 1920, 1923, 1934, 1951. The airline distance between Stegersbach and Güssing is ten miles. North is towards the upper right-hand corner of the page.

names represent the surfaced roads. Two large villages (3,000 inhabitants each), Stegersbach and Güssing, lie at opposite ends of the local road network. The right-hand vertical road, Stegersbach-St. Michael-Güssing, is the principal highway and a portion of the Eisenstädter Bundesstrasse, which joins this region to Oberwart in the next county, and ultimately to Vienna and Eisenstadt. The road on the left is also paved but is only of local importance. The six villages which are shown as being off the roads entirely are connected to the outside world by dirt roads and field tracks. The five figures by each name indicate the Croatian proportion of the total population of the village in the censuses of 1910, 1920, 1923, 1934, and 1951. The names in italics are of villages with a Croatian majority in 1910. Of the 26 villages in this diagram, 9 were Croatian in 1910; four of them over 90 per cent. The three successive villages along the left-hand (side valley) road formed the closest approximation to a cluster in the area. The other Croatian villages were either flanked by German villages or isolated in the forests.

Since the first two censuses, 1910 and 1920, were both taken by the Hungarians, and since Magyar continued to be the principal teaching language in Croatian villages until 1921 (in German villages until 1919), the first two figures may be taken to show the effects of a decade of the Magyarization program in such an isolated rural area. (Of course, the announcement in 1919 that this area was being transferred to Austria certainly diminished the effects of Magyarization.) In these first two figures a sharp contrast is notable between those villages that had a Croatian majority, and those that had a German majority in 1910. In the Croatian villages the Croatian proportion tended to maintain itself or even increase. In the German villages, on the other hand, the Croatian minority decreased. Such changes are what one could expect under such circumstances, the assimilation of the village minority into the majority.

Between 1920 and 1923 Burgenland was transferred to Austria, and the two censuses were taken by different governments. Although not shown on this diagram, the number of Magyars decreased sharply; yet, except in the county seat, Güssing, the emigration of Magyars had no noticeable effect on the German and Croatian proportions in these villages. What is striking in the comparison of these two figures is the sudden drop in the Croatian proportion of those villages close to Güssing: Hasendorf, Sulz, and Rehgraben. The other Croatian villages were not as sharply affected by the move to Austria.

As county seat, Güssing had been the focal point of the Magyarization program; now with the setting up of a German administration and the importation of German officials, it became the center of the forces pressing towards Germanization. Whereas the Magyarization program had not noticeably affected these small Croatian villages, the Germanization program evidently had an immediate impact. Since emigration from this area was extremely heavy in those three years, it is possible that the Croats chose to emigrate in especially large numbers once the area was transferred to Austria; however, emigration cannot account for the drop from 100 to 68 per cent in Hasendorf.

Perhaps the most important reason for the sudden drop in the number of avowed Croats was the psychological impact of the move to Austria. Within Hungary the Croats had been expected to learn Magyar, but they felt that they belonged in Hungary. They had been within Hungary proper for four hundred years; there was no reason to think of themselves as strangers in the area. Within Austria this was not so. In the minds of the Croats there was no doubt that they had entered a new country to which they did not "belong" in the same sense as previously. Now they were "strangers" in a "strange" country. The constant propaganda of the time that this was *Deutsches Boden* aggravated this feeling. It is understandable that those Croats who had acquired a working knowledge of German may have felt it advisable or expedient to announce themselves as "German," whereas they had not felt it necessary to announce themselves as "Magyars" previously. However, away from the immediate vicinity of the county seat this sudden tendency towards Germanization does not appear to have existed strongly.

In 1951 only four of the original nine villages were Croatian, and only two were still over 90 per cent. Three of these four were isolated in the forests; the fourth was the furthest from the county seat of the cluster in the side valley. Of the five other villages, four had become 100 per cent German, and one of them, Hasendorf, had changed from 100 per cent Croatian to 100 per cent German (without a single German-Croat) in thirty-one years.

It is obvious that location was a critical factor in the tendency of a village to be Germanized. In the forty-one years between the first and the last of these censuses, both Croatian villages along the principal highway became completely German. Both of these villages had close contact with the county seat and, via bus, with Vienna. The only village in the area with the word "Croatian" in its name, Kroatisch Tschantschendorf, is now solidly German; in just seventeen years it changed from 94 per cent Croatian to 100 per cent German. In the large village of Stegersbach the decline in percentage has been gradual and not as impressive as the drop in the smaller villages, but in numbers the Croats of Stegersbach have decreased from 982 to 36.[15]

In the side valley (left-hand side of the diagram) the assimilation process has not been as rapid as along the highway, because of the relative isolation of the valley and because three of these villages formed a Croatian cluster. The statistics indicate an obvious progression in the rate of Germanization; the closer the village was to the county seat, Güssing, the more rapidly it became Germanized.[16] Only the two furthest of these villages now contain any admitted Croats and only the furthest, Heugraben, is still officially Croatian. Stegersbach is a large village of approximately the same size as Güssing, and yet it has had no appreciable influence on the rate of assimilation. This may be because Croatian is understood by enough persons in Stegersbach to make the use of that language by visitors possible, or it may also indicate that a governmental center exerts far more pressure towards assimilation than does a marketing center in which German may be required.

Six of the villages on this diagram are located on the forested interfluvial terraces; these are: Stinatz, Hackerberg, Olbendorf, Neuberg, Güttenbach, and Punitz. Although their inhabitants frequently come out of the forests to the villages along the highway, the villages themselves have remained relatively isolated. In these communities the local majority, of whatever language, has maintained itself and even tended to assimilate the minority in its midst. Thus Stinatz and Güttenbach are still over 90 per cent Croatian. On the other hand, in Punitz the Croatian minority has gradually been assimilated into the German majority. (The "o" in 1923 suggests a possible fear of German pressure.) In Neuberg and Hackerberg the Croatian proportion has decreased, but far more slowly than in the villages along the highway.

The villages in the forests are famous in Burgenland as the homes of crowds of migrant workers. In American terms, these peasants are trying to work submarginal farms on the poor, gravelly soils of the terraces, and in locations far removed from markets. Outside sources of income are necessary, and every spring hundreds of men leave Neuberg, Güttenbach, and Stinatz to work on the large landholdings throughout, and even beyond, Austria, and in the factories of Vienna, Graz, and Wiener Neustadt. It is said locally that if one wishes to see the men of these villages, he must visit the village during winter, since in summer only the women, children, and old men are at home.

In their work throughout Austria, Germany, and Switzerland these men speak German constantly, using Croatian only among themselves, if at all. Yet, their linguistic identification has usually not been changed, despite their obvious command of German. This observation suggests that in the assimilation of a minority it is the situation in the home village that is all-important. If the village is Croatian, then the person from that village continues to consider himself Croatian, because he is a member of that village. Similarly when these people move permanently to Vienna or Graz their knowledge of German is scarcely increased, but they then consider themselves "German" because they are no longer of Stinatz or Neuberg, but rather of Vienna. The home village in turn remains Croatian (or changes very slowly) if it is in some way a self-contained unit (isolated or very large), or is surrounded by other Croatian villages.

During the critical years of the transfer to Austria (1918–22), the national desires of the Croats of Burgenland were never investigated. The pro-German propagandists alleged their support; the Magyars claimed them as non-Germans, who lacked all vital ties with "German Austria"; the Czechs looked to them to form the linguistic base of the corridor. Yet, no one bothered to ask the concerned Croatian peasants how they felt. It is now difficult to determine what the Croats wished in 1921; too much time has passed and it is still unpopular to admit that one might have been for Hungary. But the following points can be made as probably correct.

The Croats of Burgenland were not in favor of any corridor to link the northern and southern Slavs. Their interests had always been oriented east-west and never north-south. They had had no ties with the Czechs or Slovaks and were far removed from all Pan-Slavic agitation. They probably would have opposed the corridor, since its creation would have separated them from Vienna and Budapest.

They had never considered uniting with the Croats of Croatia, having had almost no contact with the main body of Croats for four centuries. (The southernmost county of Burgenland is also the only county without a Croatian township.) Prior to 1918 the main body of the Croats had also been within Hungary; therefore, there was not a Croatia outside the state to look towards until the post–World War I breakup of the greater Hungary.

Where local considerations were paramount and the peasants rarely left the area, the Croats showed a tendency to favor Hungary. This tendency was based on the traditional claims of Hungary and on the attractiveness of a known condition in contrast to a move into an unknown situation. These Croats already knew their own language and they knew some Magyar; they often did not know German. A shift to Austrian sovereignty meant a transfer to a new language and culture. However, the Croats in the northern three counties of Burgenland (the northern half of the Croats) were decidedly for Austria. These Croats lived adjacent to the railroads leading to Vienna, and they had close commercial and personal ties with the nearby metropolis. Many of them spent their weekdays in Vienna as migrant industrial workers; these had become Austrian Socialists and subscribed to the

Viennese *Arbeiterzeitung*. In contrast, the Croats of the southern counties were clearly pro-Hungarian. Vienna was distant, and all the close urban centers were Hungarian.

The Croatian intellectuals, predominantly the clergy and the teachers, were very pro-Hungarian. Where the situation allowed it, they used their influence to persuade the villagers to declare themselves for Hungary.

Finally, the Croats of Burgenland do not seem to have been especially impressed by the arguments that they were leaving Hungarian "repression" to join a "free" Austria. This idea, which became so widespread later, seems to have had little support in this area at the time. Along the eastern boundary of middle and southern Burgenland every Croatian village that was clearly given its option chose Hungary, and two villages which had originally been awarded to Austria petitioned to be returned to Hungary. Yet, over two dozen Croatian villages south of Sopron were awarded to Austria.[17]

Ever since 1918 (and perhaps previously) there has been a sharp north-south split in the political and cultural activities of the Croats of Burgenland. The divide between "north" and "south" in this case is at the "waist" of Burgenland, where the Sopron salient almost cuts the province in two. The northern Croats have for long been closely tied to the industrial and commercial life of Vienna and Wiener Neustadt; the southern Croats have not. The northerners are principally industrial workers; the southerners are principally land-based peasants. The northerners are overwhelmingly members or supporters of the Socialist party; the southerners have tended to support the Christian party (since 1945 the ÖVP). The northern Croats were assimilated into the Austrian economic and political life even before 1918, but the southern Croats did not readily accept the pre-existing Austrian political system.

Late in 1918 the Croats were attracted by the ideal of self-determination, although not to the same extent as were the Germans of the area. There were no known attempts by the Croats to obtain "the right of self-determination" from the Hungarian government. They probably felt themselves to be nothing more than a scattered minority with no outside source of support. Instead, many of the Croats, especially of the educated class, became increasingly concerned at the strong emphasis that was being placed on the "German" character of West Hungary. The local strivers for an autonomous province, as well as the Viennese propagandists, constantly referred to the area as "German"; it had a "German" history, a "German" culture, and was soon even given a "German" name, Deutsch Westungarn. In the articles, reports, editorials, and books of the time there was virtually no mention made of the Croats, nor even of the Magyars except as government officials; the non-Germans were ignored.

In response to this continual German emphasis, the Croatian leaders of Oberpullendorf County (middle Burgenland) organized a *Volksrat* ("people's council") at the end of 1918 to safeguard their own "right of self-determination." On January 20, 1919, various Croatian leaders from this area met with government officials in Sopron to ascertain what the status of the Croats was to be in the new German West Hungary; they were promised equal rights with the Germans. However, on this same date Croatian delegates from the northern villages of Steinbrunn (then Stinkenbrunn) and Trauersdorf declared that they "would have nothing to do with the *kroatische Volksrate*." [18] Nevertheless, this council acted as if it were representing all the Croats within West Hungary, and in March, 1919, sent a Dr. Pinezich with a Sopron delegation to Budapest to ask for the right of self-determination for the Croats within the new German autonomous province.

In 1920 the Croatian intellectuals of Oberpullendorf County founded the Croatian Culture Society,[19] whose avowed purpose has been to maintain the Croatian language and culture within Burgenland. Although the Treaty of St. Germain had already been signed, Burgenland was still within Hungary, so that for the first two years of its existence the Culture Society did little. Many of the local inhabitants believed at the time that the Hungarians would never surrender Burgenland to the Austrians; it was expedient to sit quietly until the status of the area had been definitely determined.[20] During these two years the autonomous German West Hungary remained in existence, but Magyar continued to be the principal language taught in the schools of the Croatian villages.

The occupation of Burgenland by the Austrian gendarmerie in November–December, 1921, increased the fears of many of the Croatian intellectuals; their villages were now within a German state, and the emphasis on German culture seemed to mount. The pressures towards Germanization were augmented by the influx of German politicians, civil servants, and teachers. The Hungarians who had left or had been dismissed were replaced by Austrian civil servants, of whom Austria had a vast surplus after 1918. (In 1922 of the six Burgenland school inspectors, only one was a Burgenlander.) According to these Croatian leaders, many of these immigrants were from the lost Austrian territories, especially the Sudeten areas. They were often strongly nationalistic, and many had chosen to leave the new Czechoslovakia rather than work with or under the Czechs.

A particularly strong force working towards the Germanization of the minorities was the Deutsche Schulverein Südmark. This organization was powerful in the neighboring province of Styria, where it had worked for the complete Germanization of that province. It sent free textbooks, pencils, paper, etc., to the schools of Burgenland, but in return urged that members of each village join their organization. Some of the Croats single out this organization as the most potent force which worked against the continuance of the Croatian culture in Burgenland in the 1920's and early 1930's; evidently much of the work of the Croatian Culture Society at that time was designed to combat the efforts of the Schulverein. After 1934 the influence of the Schulverein declined greatly. Following the assassination of Chancellor Dollfuss, the Nazis were outlawed in Austria, and many of the Schulverein members had been involved in Nazi activities.

Since the obvious way to assure the success of their aims was to gain some political power, the Croatian intellectuals of Oberpullendorf County organized the Burgenland Croatian party in 1922.[21] The platform of this party revealed the basic fears of the southern half of the Croatian minority. Included in this platform were demands for complete autonomy for the province, and the enactment of the measures, designed to perpetuate the Croatian language and culture, that had been specified in Articles 64–69 of the Treaty of St. Germain.[22] In the election of 1923 the first candidate of this party was Lorenz Karall, a young lawyer of Grosswarasdorf.

However, in northern Burgenland most of the Croats were Socialists, and the more outstanding men had gained positions of prominence in the Burgenland Socialist party. In the election of 1923 the Croatian party received only 2,454 votes, 80 per cent of which came from Oberpullendorf County. Though over half of the Croats lived in the northern three counties, only 272 votes were cast for this party in the north. The largest Croatian township, Parndorf, did not cast one vote for Karall.

The Croatian party never ran again; instead it amalgamated with the Christian party. Eager to gain the support of the non-Socialist Croats, the Christian party leaders were willing to guarantee that their future ballots would be so arranged that at least two Croatian delegates would be certain to be elected to the Landtag in every election. Reportedly Dr. Karall (who had received his LL.D. from the University of Budapest) had been against the transfer of Burgenland to Austria. If this is true it indicates that both the German and the Croatian Magyaronen entered the Christian party, and each group produced a future provincial premier.[23]

After the amalgamation of the Croatian party with the Christian party, the north-south split became obvious in the voting returns. In the elections of 1927 and 1930 (the last elections prior to 1945), the composite results of the fifteen Croatian townships of the north were, Socialist—23, Christian—6 (and one tie); and of the twenty-eight Croatian townships of the south, Socialist—10, and Christian—46.

During World War II the Croats served in the German Army, as did all the other men of Burgenland. In 1942, those men who had declared themselves to be Croats at the time of their induction were separated from their companies and sent into Jugoslavia to help fight the Partisans. Subsequently, many of these men were captured by Tito's Partisans, who were infuriated that they should call themselves Croats, and yet have fought against them; the captured men were imprisoned and threatened with execution. Thereupon twelve of the elder Croats from Burgenland traveled to Belgrade to see Marshall Tito and explain the situation to him. Perhaps to gain the good will of the Burgenland Croats, Tito released the imprisoned men. Later in London Tito suggested that the Croats of Burgenland be repatriated to Jugoslavia to take the place of the Germans who had been driven out. In the mild panic that followed the announcement of Tito's request, the committee of twelve was accused of having bartered their countrymen for the freedom of a few prisoners who would probably have been freed eventually anyhow. Fifteen years after the event one can still hear this charge in Burgenland. Merely because the twelve elder Croats had some kind of contact with the Communist government, both they and the Culture Society to which they belong have become the objects of suspicion.

The Austrian State Treaty of 1955, in Article 7, "Rights of the Slovene and Croat Minorities," carefully guaranteed the rights of the Croats within Austria. This treaty went into effect on July 27, and four months later the Culture Society published a memoir which it had presented to the Austrian government. This paper [24] made specific reference, point by point, to the pertinent clauses of the treaty, and thereupon made sweeping demands for increased Croatian educational facilities and representation in the bureaucracy. The memoir closed with the warning that it was being brought to the attention of the signatory powers of the treaty, the United States, the Soviet Union, Great Britain, and France.[25] Since the Austrian government did not accede to these proposals, the representatives of the Culture Society and of a similar group from among the Slovenes, on January 15, 1957, petitioned the Powers that the rights enunciated in the treaty be put into effect.

These actions of the Culture Society have drawn violent denunciations from the Socialist Croats of the north. At the time of the initial memoir, a gathering of the "Mayors and Assistant Mayors of the

Croatian and mixed-language townships of Burgenland" met in Siegen-dorf, an industrial, Socialist, Croatian township of the north, and passed a resolution rejecting the memoir and declaring that the Culture Society had no mandate to speak for the Croats of Burgen-land. The Socialist newspaper of Burgenland, *Burgenländische Frei-heit*, echoed the resolution of the mayors, and Croats from the north contributed articles denouncing the memoirs. The note to the Powers was interpreted as "an attack against Austria." [26]

Since the leaders of the Culture Society are adherents of the Chris-tian party, the Socialist party demanded that the Christian party (ÖVP) accept responsibility for the actions of the Culture Society. In a heated editorial the Socialist newspaper asked the leadership of the Christian party, "Do you agree with the resolution of January 15, 1957? Do you agree with the charges made against the Ministry of the Interior? Do you agree with the charges made against the Courts? Do you support this Croatian Kadar who is giving strange powers, including Russia, opportunities for intervention in Austria? We ask you Herr Landeshauptmann. . . . We ask your party!" [27]

It was unfortunate but probably inevitable that the question of minority cultural rights should have thus become entangled in politics. At the present time the Croatian intelligentsia is sharply split between the Socialist and the Christian party. All the acrimony that separates these two doctrinaire parties (the "Reds" and the "Blacks") has been poured into the local evaluations of the actions of the Croatian Culture Society.

The Culture Society is, of its very nature, conservative; it is striv-ing for the maintenance of a tradition and a culture—in effect, a peasant culture. Under such circumstances a tie with the Catholic Church seems inevitable, and in practice has existed since before the transfer to Austria. Without the active support of members of the Catholic clergy, the Culture Society would have lacked some of its most effective leaders. The tie with the Christian party, now the ÖVP (People's party), since 1922, was also virtually inevitable and has emphasized the close connections between the leaders of the society and the Church. The Christian-ÖVP party has been, and still is, the conservative Austrian party and bases its ideals on the traditional respect for private property, the land, the peasants, the Church, the home, and the family.

In contrast, the entire outlook of the Socialist party militates against any sympathy for the aims of the Croatian Culture Society. At least until World War II the Socialist party was strongly anti-Church, anti-clerical, anti-private property. It was sharply anti-traditional in that it sought to sweep away the encumbrances of the past in order to be able to advance towards its own view of the future. The Socialists thought in terms of the industrial proletariat, not the peasant, and for the urban industrial workers the continuance of peasant cultures was not only unnecessary but perhaps even a hindrance to the march of progress. Although the positions of the Socialist party have become milder since the turmoil of the 1930's, the basic point of view has not changed and remains out of sympathy with all the aims and actions of the Culture Society. In addition, since the society's leaders are obviously supporters of the ÖVP, the Culture Society is looked upon as "Black," and hence automatically in the enemy camp.

The Socialist party professes to be international in outlook, but this internationalism is based on the vision of a union of similar proletariats in all the countries of the world. The Christian party is more local in outlook, but it treasures all the cultural variations from valley to valley as well as from ethnic group to ethnic group within its country. Intentionally or not, the Socialists tend to look towards an international homogeneity, whereas the ÖVP tends to look towards a national heterogeneity. Thus, there exists the paradox that the internationally minded Socialists do not concern themselves about the preservation of minority cultures, whereas the nationally minded conservatives do. Yet, it must be stressed that in Burgenland the Socialists are not working towards the Germanization of the Croats either; the Socialists, rather, simply are not involved in linguistic issues. To the Socialist these ethnic distinctions are relatively minor and have little importance; the leaders of the Culture Society are considered to be "fanatics." [28]

Thus the influence of the Croatian Culture Society is felt very weakly in the Socialist villages of the north. The society's leaders complain that the Socialist mayors often prevent the society from holding meetings in their villages, and in at least one township the mayor is said to have attempted to do away with Croatian language teaching in the school.

Despite the memoirs, and the other complaints of the conservative Croatian leaders, it is generally believed that the vast majority of the Croats feel themselves to be loyal and satisfied citizens of Austria. Even the few dissatisfied persons clearly prefer to be in Austria; certainly a return to Hungary is presently beyond consideration. The word *zufrieden* ("satisfied") is heard as often in conversation with them as with the Magyars. Although the Croats of Oberpullendorf County may be interested in maintaining their culture, the vast majority of the Croats, in the south as well as in the north, seem far more interested in becoming adept at German than in retaining or improving their mastery of the Croatian language.[29] (It is interesting to observe that the rate of Germanization seems to be no higher among the Socialists than among the ÖVP Croats.) We see here another example of that striking paradox, the peasants who are the bearers of the culture that is so highly prized by the intelligentsia are quite willing to surrender their inherited culture if human relationships or practical considerations so suggest.[30]

In order to make a thorough knowledge of Croatian seem worthwhile, the leaders of the Croatian Culture Society have tried to increase the intellectual desirability of the language. In 1959 school Croatian was changed from the local dialect forms to "literary Croatian" (the term "Serbo-Croatian" is not used). It was hoped that in this way the language would gain in prestige and utility, and that it would allow the Burgenland Croats to draw upon, and be supported by, the literary heritage of the Croats of Croatia. (This decision was attacked as the forging of ties with Communist Jugoslavia.) However the differences between the local dialects and "literary Croatian" have caused so many objections to this new policy that it now (spring, 1961) seems probable that the teaching language will soon be returned to the local forms.

Within Burgenland a Croatian Publications Society[31] has been established. Although technically not under the control of the Culture Society, this organization is led and supported by the same men that lead and support the society. The basic support of this venture comes from the 250 people who contribute 300 schillings ($12) per year and receive the publications. Extra copies are then sold to other interested persons. Since World War II, twenty-four books have been published, including the Bible, fairy tales, two plays, three new novels, and several translations of novels, in addition to works on local history. The aim of the publications is clearly to bring Croatian books to the average peasant; hence the emphasis on novels. An annual calendar is also published.

Beyond these local efforts, the leaders of the Croatian Culture Society find themselves trapped in a dilemma similar to that of the Magyars; they cannot identify themselves with the main body of the Croats, and any semblance of a tie with Croatia is strongly attacked by its opponents. Nevertheless, the society feels that such contacts are essential if the Burgenland Croatian culture is to survive. Four village groups have performed their songs and dances in Croatia, and, in return, music groups from Croatia have performed in Burgenland villages. Each summer some thirty Burgenland Croats attend free, concentrated courses in the Croatian language, at Zagreb. A few non-Communist books have been received from Croatia, but otherwise the reception of books from Jugoslavia is severely discouraged. Even the

Croatian "classics" and folk legends may not be imported from Zagreb to be used in the Burgenland schools.

Caught in this predicament, the leaders of the Culture Society tend toward pessimism and bitterness. At least one stated that he did not look toward any country but rather toward a united Europe. Others accuse the Austrian government of not doing as much as possible to maintain the Croatian culture within Austria. One person felt that the Burgenland administration is still dominated by the Pan-Germans, who long for the day when Burgenland will be purely German.

Most of the peasantry wishes no part of Jugoslavia. It too has been alienated by the specter of communism. More important, however, have been the facts that the Croats of Burgenland and of Croatia have not, since 1530, felt any close ties with each other, and that within Austria they enjoy a higher standard of living than would be possible within Croatia. In 1947, when Tito asked that a free exchange of population be allowed, this was misinterpreted in Burgenland to mean that the Croatian peasantry would be forced to leave its lands and migrate to Croatia. Local protest demonstrations greeted the spread of this report, and some of the peasants removed their children from the Croatian schools for fear of being identified as Croatian and forced to migrate.

Under the present circumstances, the eventual assimilation of all the Croats seems inevitable. The increasing ease of access to the cities, and to higher education, works steadily towards Germanization. Even the children of some of the most ardent Croats have become Germanized through education. Some of the Croatian teachers themselves seem to lack sympathy with the preservation of the minority culture and, directly or indirectly, assist the advance of Germanization. Although the rate of assimilation remains low in those villages which form clusters or are isolated, Germanization is observable everywhere. The principal cause seems to be not the opposition of the Socialists, the Pan-Germans, or the Austrian government, but the indifference of the majority of the Croats themselves. To the peasants, Germanization is equated with economic, social, and intellectual advancement; very few of the peasants have a love of their inherited language strong enough to combat the attractiveness of such an advancement.

The Gypsies

Though the fewest of all minority groups in number, prior to 1938 the gypsies presented Burgenland with more and greater problems than any of the other groups. This was doubly unfortunate, since of all the minority problems in the province this one was the least understood by the politicians of Old Austria. The Viennese had known the gypsies only as night-club musicians and had romanticized them in their operettas, but they had never had to face the problems resulting from the rapid growth in numbers of a nomadic population within a densely populated agricultural area.

The gypsies were a unique inheritance from Hungary. They were scattered over most of Burgenland (126 of the 325 townships had permanent gypsy camps outside the village), though the greatest concentration was in the vicinity of Magyar Oberwart-Unterwart. In 1925 there were 5,480 gypsies in Burgenland (2 per cent of the total population), but 1,419 (26 per cent) were under ten years of age. By the 1934 census there were 6,507, an increase of 19 per cent in nine years.[32] It was this almost unbelievable fertility that made the gypsy problem so pressing for Burgenland.

The problem of the gypsies was enormously complicated by their unorthodox way of life. They had no fixed places of residence and no regular marriages, hence no recorded households. They did not register their births. Most maddening of all to the governmental record keepers was their tribal system; everyone in a particular tribe bore the same last name. Of the 5,480 gypsies counted in 1925, 2,305 were in the Horvath tribe alone, and many of these shared the same first name. Tracking down a person was difficult, if not impossible. As a means of establishing some sort of records, the Burgenland government began photographing and fingerprinting every gypsy over fourteen years of age.

Of the 5,480 gypsies counted in 1925, only 354 (6 per cent) claimed regular employment of any type. Of these, almost a third (105) were unlicensed musicians, 30 were licensed musicians, 62 were smiths, and the remainder were "occupied" in a variety of crafts. Most of the gypsies would not work according to usual standards. They performed odd jobs, and often indulged in acts of petty thievery.

In April, 1924, the Oberwart newspaper gave the first outcry of distress at the growing problem. In 1926 there were numerous meetings, articles in the newspapers, and petitions to Vienna. By the early 1930's the gypsy problem was termed "a life-and-death question for Burgenland peasant economy." [33] "The gypsy problem must be solved. Forty years ago there were about 800 in all Burgenland; now there are 5,000 in Oberwart County alone." [34] With increasing vehemence, Burgenland requested special assistance from the federal government.

At the invitation of Provincial Premier Walheim, and with four other members of the Landtag also present, a "Conference on the Gypsy Problem in Burgenland" was held in Oberwart on January 15, 1933. Four resolutions were adopted by the participants of this meeting. (1) There should be a special law for the gypsies, removing the citizenship of those who would not work. (2) The welfare (*Fürsorge*) of the gypsies should be the responsibility of the federal government. (3) There should be a stiffening of the punishment meted out for vagabondage and robbery. With each repeated conviction the penalty should be doubled. (4) The townships should be granted the right to state a definite period of the year in which the essentials of life would be supplied to the gypsies.

The problem was not "solved" until the entry of the Nazis. After March, 1938, the gypsies were forced to labor ten hours a day, and in the latter years of the war they were almost exterminated.

The 1951 census did not list gypsies. Since there are no other linguistic groups in Burgenland, it can be assumed that almost all of the 599 "others" (not German, Croat, or Magyar) are gypsies. If this is true, then the gypsy total is only 7 per cent of their number in 1938. Most of these "others" are located in Oberwart County, with 89 in Oberwart and Unterwart townships. The most notable gypsy camp at the present time is the cluster of huts behind Unterwart. Although small, the huts appear to be in good condition.[35] In extensive travels through Burgenland in 1956–57 and in 1961, I saw gypsy wagons on the road only three times, and then the "caravans" totalled just four wagons.

The gypsies still do odd menial jobs. On one occasion a woman of Unterwart discussed, in Magyar, a piece of sewing work with a young gypsy woman. After the gypsy had left, the Magyar woman commented, "They are to us what the black people are to you."

The Lutherans [36]

In 1951 there were 38,995 Protestants in Burgenland, approximately 37,500 of whom were Lutheran (*Augsburger Bekenntnis*). In numbers and in their proportion of the total population (14 per cent) the Protestants have remained virtually unchanged since 1923.

As Map 10 indicates, the Lutherans are distributed through all seven counties. There is a distinct correlation with terrain features. Though the Lutherans were generally protected by sympathetic Magyar noblemen, the topography also seems to have had much to do with the locales of their survival. The largest grouping is in the rough upland area of northwestern Oberwart County. This is the most isolated and extensive area of cultivated upland surface in the province. Two other notable areas of Lutherans are in the rugged interfluvial upland along the Güssing-Jennersdorf boundary and in the southernmost tip of the province. The northwestern corner of Oberpullendorf County is, similarly, an area of upland. The prosperous wine townships of Rust [37] and Mörbisch, which lie between the ridge and the lake, are the only Lutheran settlements in their county. The only notable concentration in a flat, open area occurs in the northeast. These Lutherans may have survived largely because of their late arrival. After the Turks had devastated this area in 1683, the destroyed villages were populated partially with Lutherans who migrated from southwestern Germany to the relative tolerance of Hungary.

Religious memories are long and strong in Burgenland. For the average Lutheran pastor the Toleration Act of 1781 was enacted only yesterday, and his church is still threatened by the rigors of the Austrian Counter Reformation. The ordinary Lutheran seems to feel that he is, in fact even if not legally, still persecuted. He claims that he cannot hope to obtain one of the higher governmental positions. The Burgenland Catholic is not as conscious of religious differences as is the Protestant, and he tends to feel that the Lutherans are excessively touchy, clannish, and obstructionist.

In the interwar years the Lutherans avoided supporting the Christian party, since it was, in fact, the Catholic party. Most of the Lutherans were land-based peasants and preferred not to cast their votes for the Socialist Party. Fortunately, a third party, the Peasants' party, was available. In the four interwar elections the composite results of the Lutheran townships were: Peasants—114, Socialist—52, Great German—12, Christian—7, and Heimatblock—5.[38]

In the five elections since 1945 the Lutherans have had to choose between the Socialist and the Christian (ÖVP) parties, because the Peasants' party no longer exists. The composite results from the Lutheran townships are: Socialist—136, and Christian—104. Since the Christian party obtained a majority or plurality in every one of these five elections, these results suggest that despite their peasant character the Lutherans still prefer not to vote for the Christian party.

The Lutherans of Burgenland believed in the unity of the German people. "The *Volk* is a God-given unity," one Lutheran pastor stated. It was this belief in the essential unity of the German people that motivated the Lutherans of Burgenland to favor the transfer to Austria, despite the fact that the existence of a Lutheran minority in Burgenland was due largely to the protection of Magyar noblemen and the willingness of Magyar Protestants to oppose with force the Habsburg Counter Reformation. It was paradoxical that the Catholic clergy worked actively for Hungary, whereas the Lutherans favored a union with Austria.[39] However, the aim of the Lutherans went beyond the union with Austria to the *Anschluss* with Germany.[40] The attractiveness of a greater Germany was enhanced by the historical fact that Luther had been a German and had lived, preached, and died within Germany. The Lutherans also saw, in a union with Germany, the opportunity to change from a minority to a majority status. In a greater Germany the Catholics, not they, would be the minority group. It was an unfortunate historical coincidence that the union of Austria and Germany was effected by Adolf Hitler.

Did the Lutherans recognize the evil aspects of Nazism? They now claim that they did not. Though the persecution of the Jews had been a brutal fact for several years in Germany, there was enough latent anti-Semitism throughout Central Europe to allow this early indication of the degree of Nazi brutality to be accepted without serious qualms of conscience. The peasants in the hills of Burgenland may well not have known or believed the extent of Nazi cruelty. Even if they had heard, the Lutheran peasants may have refused to admit the shortcomings of their hoped-for saviors (a common enough occurrence among minority groups). As the wife of one pastor admitted, "shockingly many of the Lutherans became Nazis."

It must be remembered too that the 1930's were years of dictatorship. In almost every state of central, eastern, and southern Europe the powers of government were concentrated in the hands of one individual or one party. These were also years of grave economic crisis, and it was common practice for a dictatorship to focus the blame for the national plight on one group, such as the Jews, the kulaks, the Communists, or the Socialists. Between 1933 and 1938 Austria was governed by a regime which was, in the eyes of the Socialists and the Lutherans, a Catholic dictatorship. Following a brief civil war, the *Heimatfront*, led by the leaders of the Christian party, outlawed all other political parties and established hand-picked governments for the country and the provinces. In 1934 Chancellor Dollfuss signed a Concordat with the Vatican. The Lutherans viewed this as a confirmation of their belief that they were looked upon as second-class citizens of Austria. They feared a return of the persecution they had endured prior to 1781. Motivated by this fear and by their Pan-German sentiments, the Lutherans of Burgenland preferred the introduction of a German dictatorship to the Austrian variety they were then experiencing.

Prior to their dissolution of Burgenland as a province in May, 1938, the Nazis established a short-lived provincial government. Despite an attempt at regional representation (three members from each county), 11 of the 30 members, including the holders of 7 of the 10 top offices in this government were from within five miles of Oberschützen, the Lutheran educational center of the province. Four of the members were from Oberschützen itself, a village of 1,179 inhabitants in 1934. Several of the Lutheran villages of Burgenland still bear the reputation of having been Nazi centers. Gols was referred to later as having been "a Nazi paradise." [41]

After February, 1945, everyone who had had connections with the Nazi party was held suspect or imprisoned. The two resurrected principal parties of Austria, the Socialist and the Christian (ÖVP), announced that they would have nothing to do with the remnants of the former Nazi party. Some of the Lutherans thus found themselves excluded from organized political life. These persons tended to adopt an attitude of "a plague on both your houses" and cast their votes for whichever third party happened to be at hand. In 1945 the only other party was, paradoxically, the Communist. In that election the wine-producing centers of Gols and Rust gave the Communist party 12 and 34 per cent of their votes respectively. [42]

In 1949 another party, the VdU (Independent party) appeared on the ballot. This party, which has been looked upon as obstructionist by the leaders of the two major parties, became the rallying ground of the former Nazis. Now known as the FPÖ, it is locally considered to be the party of the German nationalists and the protest voters. In 1949, 35 of the 320 townships of Burgenland gave 10 per cent or more of their votes to this minor party; 20 of these 35 were Lutheran. This pattern has continued to the present. In the election of 1959, the Lutheran townships accounted for 11.7 per cent of the total votes cast in Burgenland, but 26.6 per cent of the votes cast for the FPÖ. The four townships with the highest proportion of votes for this party are all Lutheran. [43]

From the foregoing analyses it can be seen that neither of the two principal linguistic minorities of Burgenland forms the united force that statistics of their numbers suggest. Both are divided among themselves, the Croats politically, the Magyars religiously. All the Croats are Catholics, but the division by adherence to political party, based largely on economic occupation (based ultimately on location in relation to Vienna), has resulted in two antagonistic factions. The Magyars are not split into antagonistic groups, but the three religious faiths have induced differing reactions to the minority situation in which the Magyar peasants find themselves. [44]

The intellectuals among both the Croats and the Magyars distrusted the Austrians in 1921 and demanded complete autonomy for the province and precise guarantees of rights. The Croats, since they had the larger numbers, attempted to form their own party. However, by 1924 both the Croatian and the Magyar intellectuals were mostly active members of the Christian party.

The assimilation of the Croats and the Magyars was encouraged by the Austrian system of proportional representation. Had the province been divided, as in the United States, into single-member electoral units, the Magyars around Oberwart might well have been able to elect a Magyar spokesman, and certainly the Croats could have elected locally representative Croatian delegates to the provincial parliament. However, the entire province is treated as one election district for federal elections, so that all the voters of the province vote on the same party lists. Under the system of proportional representation, the larger parties, with their broadly based apparatus, were able to submerge or incorporate such political localisms. Within three years, the linguistic groups and their factions had been absorbed into the two political parties.

In contrast, the Lutherans have not been as effectively assimilated into the established political life of Austria. While the Magyars and the Croats had no common, politically virile set of ideas capable of uniting them within one party, the Lutherans did possess such an ideology, which manifested itself in political life in a negative rather than a positive fashion—against the major parties rather than for any party. The Lutherans, who entered Austria the most eagerly of all the minority groups, nevertheless became the group that supported the minor and protest parties.

Despite Viennese fears, neither of the linguistic minority groups has entertained any serious irredentist aspirations; paradoxically, the Lutherans supplied the only irredentism in Burgenland. The Croats never considered a union with Croatia, the Magyars never seriously concerned themselves with an attempted return to Hungary, but the Lutherans were supporters of the *Anschluss* with Germany and seem to have welcomed the outside force when it arrived. In this, as in all other political activities, religion has been a far more potent factor than the overly publicized linguistic differences.

The Magyar and the Croatian peasants felt from their first days within Austria that their prime task was to learn German and to become acquainted with the Austrian political and economic systems. Both groups are essentially Austrianized in their national feelings. The Croats have been linguistically assimilated far more slowly than the Magyars because the Croats have the larger number, are more compactly clustered, and have remained relatively more isolated than the two Magyar centers, both of which have become important centers of local government. Yet, unless there is a radical change in the situation of the minority groups, the Croats as well as the Magyars seem certain to be assimilated within a few decades.

The pressure towards linguistic assimilation has, since 1945, been tremendously enhanced by the introduction into Burgenland of recent improvements in transportation and communications. The outside world can now enter the most remote Croatian village, and the peasant can, with ever increasing ease, move beyond the township limits to the glamorous cities and their market and employment facilities. The fabled long-livedness of the village linguistic cultures in Central Europe was a symbol of local, circumscribed peasant self-sufficiency. At the present time the peasant will no longer so limit his vision of the world; he now not only must, but is eager to, meet the outside world on its terms. As one Magyar priest commented, "Under 400 years of supposed repression by the Magyars, the Croats kept their language and music, their dances and costumes, and now, after 30 years of Austrian 'freedom' they have lost most of it."

The Christian party intellectuals of both the Croats and the Magyars have found themselves trapped between the inexorable advance of the forces of linguistic Germanization and the destruction by communism, nationalism, and economics, of their ties with Hungary and Croatia. In this dilemma some of the intellectuals of both groups have projected their hopes for linguistic and cultural survival on a united Europe, a Europe which would be above nationalisms, and in which one language and culture would be, in fact as well as in theory, as good as another.

Location and religion have clearly been the most important factors affecting the rate of both the political and the linguistic assimilation of the minorities of Burgenland. Among the Croats, all of whom are Catholics, only the size, the relative clustering, and the isolation of the villages have an important influence on the rate of linguistic assimilation. In contrast, the Magyars are divided into three faiths, and this division is accompanied by marked variations in the rate of linguistic assimilation. Agricultural, Lutheran Siget is being Germanized at a far more rapid rate than Oberwart or Oberpullendorf, both of which are forced, by their economic and political importance, to act as German-speaking centers. At the same time, the Lutherans as a group have shown the greatest reluctance to assimilate into the political life of Austria.

The strongest efforts to halt the process of Germanization of the Croats and the Magyars are, in both cases, being made in Catholic villages by Catholic leaders. The Catholic Church's emphasis on historicity, legitimacy, and tradition would seem to be the ideological foundation of these efforts, as well as the explanation of the paradox that the Catholic clergy worked against the transfer to "Catholic Austria." Similarly, the ideal of a united Europe voiced by some Catholic Croatian and Magyar leaders may be a reflection of the constant Catholic memory, and dream, of a spiritually united Europe.

The case of Burgenland suggests that too much emphasis may have been placed on linguistic variations in East Central Europe. At least in Burgenland, religious differences have been far more important and promise to be far more long-lasting than the highly publicized linguistic variations.

THE BURGENLAND IDEA

The sense of a provincial identity has been of fundamental importance to the continued existence of Burgenland. Without this idea of a separate Burgenland, the province could scarcely have been created and probably would not have been re-created in 1945. It can almost be said, in fact, that in view of the tremendous difficulties which faced this area in 1921, the "state idea" by itself fashioned a political unit where no such unit should have been. And yet this idea, capable of such an astounding binding power, had to be in itself created from nothing after the end of World War I.

The basis of this feeling of belonging together in a specific Burgenland lay undoubtedly in the sense of "difference" which has been described previously. The inhabitants of this area felt themselves to be different from their neighbors in Old Austria. They had all been within Hungary and had experienced an economic, political, and social history different from that known in Old Austria. Their houses, fields, clothing, all had Hungarian roots. In these ways they were like each other, whether from the north or the south; in these ways they differed noticeably from their new compatriots to the west.

Yet, when these people were first approached by the German propagandists of Vienna, even when their fate was being decided in Paris, they lacked a common name. Nothing can express a union of peoples more clearly and effectively than a name shared in common by them, but this area had never had a distinctive name. In all the initial discussions concerning the future of the area, the cumbersome "German West Hungary" (Deutsch Westungarn) was used for want of a more concise title. When this area had the name "German West Hungary" it was no more than that, and its individual inhabitants felt no tie with the attenuated strip that happened to be occupied by German-speaking people. There was also a different group identification in the north from that of the south. The leaders of the movement for the transfer of West Hungary were much concerned over the lack of a name for the entire territory. Since it was not to be a part of Hungary any longer, "German West Hungary" was certainly not applicable, and the name "Hungary" was taboo among the Vienna propagandists. It seemed to imply a continued recognition of the concept of the "lands of the Crown of King St. Stephen." Since there had never been a political unit even approximating the area, no historical name could be resurrected for the purpose.

The first attempt was "Heinzenland." The Heinzen were the people of south Burgenland. They derived this name from "Schwarzen Heinz," a legendary count of Güssing, who ruled over his domain as a virtually independent monarch (1254–74). The people in the surrounding area became known as Heinz's men, or simply, "Heinzen." The inhabitants of the north, however, refused to accept the name; they were not Heinzen, and they considered the name to have uncomplimentary connotations.

The first mention of the name "Burgenland" occurred on December 24, 1918, in the Viennese newspaper *Ostdeutsche Rundschau.* Professor Alfred Walheim published a poem, which began:

> Heinzenland
> Burgenland
> Kehrst du wiederum zu uns zurück? [1]

The name as it was first used here was not derived from the castles in the area, but from the common ending of the four provinces (megyek) from which the territory was to be taken: Pressburg (Bratislava), Wieselburg (Moson), Ödenburg (Sopron), and Eisenburg (Vasvár). Because of this poem, Walheim was often given credit for coining the name. However, it is clear that he did not appreciate the possibilities of the word, but looked upon it as merely a good rhyme. Even after the name had begun to spread and be accepted everywhere, Walheim continued to propagandize for his choice, Heinzenland.

Meanwhile the name was being independently developed in the north. Late in 1918 Karl Amon of Neusiedl selected the name "Vier-

Burgen-Land" for the autonomous German area for which he was working energetically. It is thought that this name may have been in imitation of Siebenbürgen (Transylvania), since many of the most prominent German leaders within Hungary came from that region. The new name was widely accepted in the north, and in February, 1919, in Moson, a conference ended with the call, "Hoch unser deutsches autonomes Vierburgenland!" [2] In June, 1919, a new magazine, *Vierburgenland*, began publication in Sopron, although the official name of the area remained Deutsch Westungarn.

The decision, in this as in most other matters, was made by a leader of the federal government. In a telegram from Paris in August, 1919, Chancellor Renner stated that the name of the province was to be "Dreiburgenland" (three-burgs-province/land), since the area had itself chosen "Vierburgenland" when the acquisition of the German areas of Pressburg (Bratislava) comitat still seemed possible. In this decision Chancellor Renner expressed his preference for a name that had been developed within the area rather than one coined outside by the Viennese romantic nationalists. The final development seems to have occurred shortly after Dr. Renner's return to Vienna. On September 6, 1919, a delegation led by Herr Meidlinger of Frauenkirchen suggested that Chancellor Renner refer to the area as "Dreiburgenland," or perhaps more simply as "Burgenland." Subsequently the numerical prefix was dropped and the name remained in its present form. Thus, although he initiated neither action, it was Renner who made the decisive moves that brought Burgenland to Austria and gave it its name.

The new name spread with remarkable rapidity. It had a fine antique flavor and was suggestive of the many castles within the territory.[3] The Oberwart newspaper, which was at this time still working energetically against the transfer to Austria, used "Burgenland" by October 5, 1919. By the end of 1919 the name was accepted everywhere, and the inhabitants had come to refer to themselves as "Burgenländer." The provisional government for the territory accepted the name officially on January 8, 1920.[4]

It is true that the name came after the other unifying factors, the "differences" previously noted, and it was dependent upon these factors for its acceptance. Nevertheless, beyond doubt the name, more than any common history or common customs, served to unite the people of German West Hungary. In finding a name, Burgenland put into a concise, effective form its state idea. Then, just as the sense of uniqueness was crystallized by the name, a few years later this sense was localized in the selection of a capital, Eisenstadt, which represented the foremost cultural achievements of Burgenland.

Throughout Burgenland the feeling of provincial identification among the inhabitants appears now to be very strong. Yet, this Burgenland idea differs in content from that of the other provinces of Austria in that it seems to be not a consciousness of pride or glory but one of suffering and persecution. Burgenlanders are convinced that the inhabitants of no other province of Austria have suffered as they have. "Wie viel haben die Menschen hier schon mitgemacht!" ("How much the people here have endured!") The inhabitants remember all the sufferings of the past from the ravages of the Turks to the advance of the Russian troops.

These feelings of suffering and persecution are expressed frequently in the terms *Grenzland* ("borderland") and *Stiefkind* ("stepchild"). Burgenlanders maintain that their area has always been a borderland, always facing the enemy whether from the east or the west, always neglected by the national government because of its location. They believe that the Hungarians intentionally kept it economically retarded and treated it severely, and that the Austrians have allowed it to remain undeveloped, simply because it is a border area. They feel that Burgenland has always been the stepchild, the neglected, uncared-for part of the country. The years of dissolution, 1938–45, augmented this feeling; the Burgenlanders assert that Styria and Lower Austria were interested only in obtaining the material resources of the partitioned province, and that once again Burgenland was the stepchild, the borderland.

At the present time the sense of a permanent Burgenland individuality seems indestructible. Three decades of provincial existence and of education in the provincial schools have strengthened the provincial consciousness so that the continued existence of Burgenland is rarely if ever questioned. The recent development of a fine highway system and the construction of public buildings have initiated the beginnings of a sense of pride in the accomplishments of Burgenland. But though the province has "bloomed" through the use of the federal funds available to it, the people of Burgenland are still conscious that their province is the borderland. It is the easternmost frontier of German-speaking people, and the furthest extension of Western society in Central Europe. Beyond this frontier area is the Communist empire. The events of the winter of 1956–57 emphasized again in grim fashion the borderland character of this narrow strip of territory.

The case of Burgenland suggests that, granted a basic minimum of resources and of trained personnel, almost any area can be effectively organized politically if its inhabitants have the will to do so. Recent developments in means of communication have greatly diminished the separating influence of physical barriers. Topographic details, in themselves, can no longer separate political units from each other. Even before the development of air and automotive transportation, the Carpathian Basin was divided into five portions, four of which were, and still are, joined to areas beyond the mountain rim.

It appears that in the twentieth century two factors are of prime importance in the formation of an effective political unit. These are financial assistance and the will to succeed.[5] Despite great handicaps Burgenland has been able to organize its territory effectively because the will to do so was there, and, though haltingly, so was the financial assistance. Even though it is but a province, Burgenland is, in this sense, similar to some of the areas that are now groping towards statehood. In these new states, just as in Burgenland, the present and future development of an effectively functioning political unit appears to be dependent on the internal development of a state idea and the addition of funds from outside the state. Since such funds are usually available (at least to the same degree that they were in Burgenland), in the final analysis it is the *Staatsidee*, the state (or provincial) idea, the will of the inhabitants to live together despite handicaps and crises, that is the most important factor in the birth and the development of these political units.

This idea, though usually anchored in a common history, need not be an ideal of national glory. To have viable states over the world we need not necessarily look forward to the formation of a multiplicity of proud histories which, compressed into a small area, has been both the glory and the curse of Europe. Burgenland has shown that this concept can be rooted in feelings of common sufferings as well as in feelings of common glory and military grandeur. The idea must, however, be rooted in a feeling of distinctiveness. In some manner, even if only in belonging together, the inhabitants of an area must feel themselves distinct from their neighbors. Ultimately, memories of glory and national power are but superficial expressions of this essential feeling of difference. In Burgenland this sense of distinctiveness produced in a few years a provincial concept capable of resurrecting the province, despite all its internal difficulties, after seven years of dissolution.

Though prediction is foolhardy, it seems reasonable to assume that sometime in the future Russian control of East Central Europe will weaken or cease altogether. Certainly most of the East European nations are enduring the present occupation in the expectation that this will occur. For the Hungarians the present time is a second Turkish occupation which, no matter how prolonged, is certain to end.

In that hoped-for time, when the nations of East Central Europe will again attain some measure of true self-determination, they will have to face the uncomfortable fact that complete independence is no longer possible for them. Within a world of large power units and of great economic confederations, the small Danubian states could exist only precariously. To insure their self-defense and their economic well-being, the Danubian nations would almost be forced to seek some measure of unification.[6] Yet, it is certain that such a union would have to be the result of voluntary agreement; an enforced unification could not succeed. Such a union or confederation would have to be a freely entered association of the many geo-political units which characterize the "Shatter Belt." Within the broader area of this study, such units as Hungary, Austria, Bohemia-Moravia, Croatia, Serbia, Walachia-Moldavia, and perhaps Slovenia, Slovakia, and Transylvania, would have to be treated as separate entities. Most of these geo-historical units have had vital individual existences through the centuries, and all attempts to enforce unification upon them have brought merely dissatisfaction and disunity.[7]

The presence of Vienna would be highly desirable within such a federation. It would be possible for present Czechoslovakia, Hungary, Romania, and even Jugoslavia to unite without Vienna, but for all these lands (excepting only Bohemia proper), traffic to and from Western Europe would almost of necessity have to move through Vienna. It seems safe to assume that once these states are freed, they will again, as they always have in the past, turn to the west. (It is difficult to see how the present attempts of the Soviet Union to divert this movement to the east could continue for long once the Iron Curtain has disappeared.) If so, then these states will look to the west primarily through the doors of Vienna. Thus, although Austria would not be essential to the federation, it would be desirable to include her, since within or without the federation, Vienna would handle much of the traffic with the west.

Fortunately, Austria is probably no longer feared by the other Succession States. She has clearly separated herself from the Pan-German forces which, before 1945, seemed to make Austria a springboard for German advances towards the east. The Austrians have been willing to forget the fact that they once ruled an empire and have freed themselves from the desire to regain what they once controlled in East Central Europe. They have also separated themselves politically from the Habsburg heritage, and whereas theorists may feel that a Habsburg return would bring stability to Central Europe, for the other Danubian states a Habsburg in Vienna would merely resurrect the threat of Viennese domination of the other nations. During the decade and a half since 1945 Austria has become a state of avowed neutrality, the meeting ground for East and West. She manifests no desires for revision, no desires for revenge. Vienna has become once more the city of promise to the members of the Danubian nations. It is no coincidence that the majority of the people who have fled Hungary, Jugoslavia, and Czechoslovakia have moved toward Vienna.

Whatever bitterness continued as a result of the breakup of the Habsburg Empire had been removed largely by the events of 1956–57. During that terrible winter tiny Austria, facing the immense Soviet threat, welcomed without exceptions all persons who crossed her borders. She did not ask questions about diseases or past political attachments. While some other states picked and chose among the refugees, Austria accepted them all (and hence was left with many of those whom others considered to be undesirable). In recent history there have been few comparable acts of genuine charity. Affection and a feeling of comradeship are replacing the bitterness and fear which the name Austria formerly engendered in the nations of the East.

It may well be true that the fragmentation of the old Habsburg Empire was essential for the future stability of East Central Europe, since this fragmentation separated again the permanent geo-political units which had formed the empire. In the future these units could become component parts of a federation voluntarily achieved. Since the Habsburgs were not able to effect this voluntary unification, it may have been necessary for the integrants to fall apart so that a new, mutually acceptable union could result.[8]

Whereas the presence of Vienna would be highly desirable within an East Central European federation, the presence of Hungary would be absolutely essential. It is impossible, geographically, to construct a Danubian federation without Hungary. She occupies the center of the Carpathian Basin, the center of the Danubian lands. Contact between the Czechs or Viennese and the southern Slavs or Romanians is almost impossible except through Hungary.

Yet, Hungary would be the most difficult country to bring into such a new union. Although nationalistic emotions are now clouded by Communist dogma, it is probable that the Hungarians still feel acutely the heavy losses inflicted upon their nation by the Treaty of

Trianon. All the neighbors of Hungary gained at her expense, and many Magyars live as minorities beyond her borders. Consequently, discussions that have been attempted among the expatriate groups have always ended in serious disagreement on the question of the territorial terms of the unification. Since the other Succession States all gained enormously at the expense of Hungary, these states would undoubtedly work for a unification on the basis of the existing boundaries. On the other hand, the Hungarians wish rectifications that would satisfy more fully their historic, ethnic, and economic claims. It would require a tremendous act of renunciation for the Hungarians to accept the boundaries as they now are. Yet it is clear that Hungary cannot hope to regain her lost territories by herself. Not only are all her neighbors except Austria larger than she is, but they would probably meet any Hungarian aggressive intentions with joint action.

Of course, it would be preferable if the neighboring states voluntarily returned to Hungary those bits of territory populated by Magyars and close to the boundary. (Even then the Hungarians would have to accept a tremendous reduction in the area of 1918.) Such generosity might help to start the confederation in an aura of peace and good will. Yet it is highly improbable that even minor rectifications would be made. No state has ever willingly given up territory, no matter how just the claims of the other nation have been, and it is too much to expect that East European chauvinism will have died just because of a Communist occupation.

Therefore, unless chauvinism has died and the other nations are led by remarkable statesmen (and we have no right to expect either of these), a federation of the Danubian lands would be possible only if the Hungarians were willing to renounce their claims to the lost lands of the Crown of King St. Stephen. This self-denial would be extraordinarily difficult, since in all of Europe there has not been a state idea as long-lived, as unchanging, and as ardently defended as the concept of the lands of King Stephen. Yet only through renunciation can Hungary hope to regain her contact with the lost lands. The Carpathian Basin remains a remarkably distinct topographic unit, and as long as large-scale movement of goods is tied to the surface of the earth, most of the trade of Transylvania, Slovakia, and even the lands beyond, will move through Hungary and her great nodal city, Budapest.

The Hungarians must, in essence, look beyond their cherished state ideal and see the topographic features upon which the concept of the kingdom was based. The Carpathians formed the boundary before the Crown placed the seal of Christendom upon them. In a union of the Danubian lands all the portions of the Carpathian Basin would again move towards the center. Transylvania cannot be reconquered by arms, but with the removal or reduction of international boundaries, this lost bastion would almost inevitably turn again towards the Alföld, towards Budapest.

Because of its successful amalgamation of elements from both east and west, Burgenland may serve as an inspiration to the nations of East Central Europe. Burgenland has been a small borderland within that broad border zone, "The Shatter Belt." It has shared with its neighbors the menace of invasions from east and west. Like its neighbors it has experienced a Communist occupation, and though the occupation forces left in 1955, Burgenland abuts directly upon the Communist empire. The province carries the entire boundary between Hungary and Austria; no village of Burgenland is more than twenty miles from the perilous border.

Furthermore, Burgenland has demonstrated the way to blend the ideas of East and West. For nine centuries this territory shared the way of life of Hungary, and accepted the concept which fashioned and maintained a kingdom within the Carpathian Basin. And yet, although rooted in Hungary, Burgenland has made the transition to a more Western way of life with remarkable ease. Fortunately, in leaving Hungary it was not forced to surrender completely its share in the uniqueness of the Hungarian past. For Burgenland, the old state idea, although destroyed in a national sense, has been transformed into a provincial concept which, despite the transfer to Austria, has its roots in the tradition of the lands of King Stephen.

Burgenland has shown too a way in which the Eastern, semi-feudal way of life can be changed into a Western manner of living. Beyond the Iron Curtain the noble holdings have been abolished, but state farms or enforced large coöperative farms have, in a sense, maintained the system of large units worked by hirelings. In Burgenland, on the other hand, the large estate is giving way, without coercion or bureaucratic interference, to the medium-sized holdings which can support an independent, prosperous peasantry.

On a small scale, the Burgenland experience shows also the manner in which a difficult area can be organized. Whatever the problems facing a future East Central European federation might be, they could scarcely be much greater than those surmounted by Burgenland in 1922 and 1945. An almost unmanageable piece of terrain was organized —and then later reorganized; and of even greater significance is the fact that a new idea, which had the power to bind these diverse parts together, was developed and widely accepted. It is true that the various portions of Burgenland had had the mutual experience of a Hungarian past; if and when a future federation is formed, the component portions will have had the mutual experience of an imposed Communist past. As Burgenland has proven, shared suffering can bind a people together; the Danubian states will have participated in this common, painful experience unfelt by the Western states. On such a base, a sense of belonging together, and a desire to work together could develop, and the Danubian states of the Shatter Belt could form a belt of stability and prosperity between the power worlds of Western and Eastern Europe.

REFERENCE

MATTER

NOTES

CHAPTER 1

1. In this study "Carpathian Basin" will be used instead of the more common "Pannonian Basin" or "Hungarian Basin" to avoid confusion with "Pannonia" and "Hungary," both of which will frequently be used in their political sense and neither of which coincides with the full extent of the basin.

2. "Shatter Belt" is a term often used to designate the tier of states from the Baltic to Turkey and between the Germans and Russians. These countries have often been shattered or annexed by their powerful neighbors.

CHAPTER 2

1. For a detailed study of the topography of this area see Norbert Krebs, *Die Ostalpen und das Heutige Österreich* (2 vols.; Stuttgart, 1928).

2. In this study the much abused term "geo-political" is intended only as a convenient adjective expressing the combination of geographical and political factors. No reference to the doctrine of *Geopolitik* is intended, and to avoid the possibility of such an inference the term will always be hyphenated and will never be used as a noun.

3. For a detailed study of the dimensions, limits, and subdivisions of the Vienna-Marchfeld Basin see Hans Slanar, "Grenzen und Formenschatz des Wiener Beckens," in F. Heiderich, *Zur Geographie des Wiener Beckens* (Vienna, 1923), pp. 1–14. Other sections of this book deal with the climate, industry, settlement, etc., of the Vienna Basin.

4. The surface of the lake is fifty-five feet below the surface of the Danube at Bratislava.

5. Often this is referred to simply as the Alföld. In this study also, whenever "Alföld" is used without "Little" or "Great" the reference will be to the Great Alföld. In Magyar, *nagy* means large, big, great.

6. Although geographers have customarily assumed that the Alföld is a natural steppe land, a recent paper by Professor Norman J. G. Pounds has sharply challenged this belief. On the basis of the descriptions of early travelers, and of the conclusions reached by Károly Kann in his, *A Magyar Alföld* (Budapest, 1927), Professor Pounds has suggested that the Hungarian plain was formerly far more forested than in recent centuries, and that the widespread steppe conditions are largely a result of excessive deforestation, the devastation of the Turkish wars, the long emphasis on grazing in the area, and the extensive drainage of the eighteenth and nineteenth centuries. This paper was presented in April, 1960, at the Dallas meetings of the Association of American Geographers, and will be published shortly in *Essays on Eastern Europe*, one volume of the Slavic and East European Series, of Indiana University, Bloomington, Indiana. As Professor Pounds makes clear, the evidence prior to the nineteenth century is extremely scanty, and it does appear that most of the travel accounts dealt with the areas west of the Danube, where one would expect forests to have been fairly widespread, rather than with the Alföld proper, east of the Danube. Perhaps future research will help clarify the extent of the medieval and premedieval grasslands in the Carpathian Basin as a whole.

In this book I assume that steppe areas large enough to support the headquarters of the Huns, the Avars, and the Kavars of the Magyars existed east of the Danube. West of the Danube it seems certain that the Parndorf Heath is a natural steppe. On this surface the ground water is everywhere at least 63 feet, and for over half the area over 200 feet below the surface. (See A. F. Tauber, "Hydrogeologie und Hydrochemie der Parndorfer Heideplatte," *Burgenländische Heimatblätter* [Eisenstadt], Jg. 21 [1959], 7–23, with two cross-sectional diagrams and a map.) Other portions of present northern Burgenland may also have been steppe since the time of Burebista (the first century B.C.), when this area was first referred to as the *Deserta Boiiorum*. (*Deserta* does not mean "desert," of course. But the fact that the area could be depopulated and that it should remain unpopulated suggests open spaces.) This was the area left to the Avars, a steppe rider group, an area which came to be known as the *Deserta Avarorum*. The ease and thoroughness with which the Mongols (1241) devastated this area suggests again the probability of open spaces. Certainly the name *Heidebauern* ("heath peasants") has been applied to the inhabitants of this area for centuries, and descriptions from around 1800 suggest the present landscape. In 1821 much of the soil of Moson *megye* was described as unusually fruitful and black, qualities which suggest a soil developed under a grass cover. János Csaplovics, *Topographisch-statistisches Archiv des Königreichs Ungern* (Vienna, 1821), p. 188.

7. These two terms indicate both the noble origin of these camps and their

function in reclaiming a wilderness. *Hof* is a German word of many applications but here means a yard or courtyard; *puszta* is a Magyar word meaning wilderness.

8. The legend tells of a mother who called down the wrath of heaven to avenge the murder of her daughter by the jealous wife of the Lord of Forchtenstein. Overnight the water filled the present lake bed and floated the body to the eastern shore. At the spot where the body came to rest, the lord built the shrine of Frauenkirchen. The five flooded villages were named: Hauftal, Schwarzlacken, Königstal, See, and St. Jakob. The inhabitants fled to the northern hills where they founded Neusiedl am See. Josef Rittsteuer, *Neusiedl am See* (Neusiedl, 1949), pp. 33–34.

9. In 1957 all of Burgenland had 205,800 overnight visitors; this was 0.59 per cent of the Austrian total of 34,800,000. Of this small number 87 per cent were from the remainder of Austria, and only 26,900 from beyond Austria.

CHAPTER 3

1. The location of the roads, as described in the text and depicted on Map 1, has been gathered from many sources. Among the more significant have been J. M. de Navarro, "Prehistoric Routes Between Northern Europe and Italy. Defined by the Amber Trade," *Geographical Journal* (London), Vol. 66 (Dec., 1925), 481–503; E. von Cholnoky, "Die geographische Lage von Wien," *Mitteilungen der Geographischen Gesellschaft in Wien* (Vienna), Band 72, Heft 7–12 (1929), 380–94; V. Pârvan, *Dacia: An Outline of the Early Civilization of the Carpatho-Danubian Countries* (Cambridge, 1928); T. Mommsen, *The Provinces of the Roman Empire from Caesar to Diocletian* (London, 1909); A. A. Barb, "Unter römischer Herrschaft," in *Burgenland, Landeskunde* (Vienna, 1951), pp. 206–23; W. Kubitschek, "Ältere Berichte über den römischen Limes in Pannonien," *Akademie der Wissenschaft in Wien. Sitzungsberichte 209* (Vienna and Leipzig), Band I (1929), 1–336; and various atlases and maps.

2. Several other "Amber Roads" existed also, e.g. between the Baltic and the Black seas.

3. The Romans later had several military outposts along the eastern bank of the March. Presumably these were along the highway.

4. On top of the Braunsberg has been noted a wall one mile long and encompassing an area of about thirty-three acres. In some places this wall is still over six feet high. It is thought that it probably encircled a pre-Roman fortress city. Ernst Nischer-Falkenhof, "Die vorgeschichtlichen Siedlungen auf dem Braunsberg bei Hainburg a. d. Donau," *Unsere Heimat* (Vienna), Band VIII (1935), 290–94.

5. Theodore Mommsen, *The Provinces of the Roman Empire*, Vol. I, 42.

6. This is the reason given by Mommsen, *ibid.*, p. 198. According to Kenner, Emperor Vespasian wished to place the entire stretch of the Danubian limes,

from the Wienerwald to Aquincum, under one, unified, military command. "Die Römerorte in Nieder-Oesterreich," *Jahrbuch für Landeskunde von Nieder-Oesterreich* (Vienna), Jg. II (1869), 130.

7. The cities on or south of the Drava have been omitted because they do not fall within the area of this study. Among these were Sirmium (Mitrovica), Mursa (Osijek), Poetovio (Ptuj), and Siscia (Sisak).

8. For discussion, maps, and pictures of Carnuntum see Erich Swoboda, *Carnuntum, Seine Geschichte und Seine Denkmäler* (Römische Forschungen in Niederösterreich, Band I) (Vienna, 1953), 259 pp.

9. Arrabona was important because it was located where the limes road crossed the Rába and followed a tongue of dry land between the marshes of the Hanság and the Danube.

10. In 375 Savaria was the winter headquarters of the army of Valentinian; it was the capital of Pannonia Prima at the time.

CHAPTER 4

1. Ernst K. Winter attributes this shift to the greater adeptness of Byzantine diplomats in dealing with the barbarians. "The Byzantine Millennium of Vienna," *Medievalia et Humanistica*, Vol. X (1956), 5.

2. Because of the indirectness of the route and the difficulty of passing through the Iron Gate of the Danube, that river was used only as far as the mouth of the Morava (Belgrade). The principal route from Constantinople to the Middle Danube passed along the Maritza and Morava valleys instead.

3. The Huns required linen clothing, skins, grain, and arms. "Even the Mongols of the 12th century . . . had to import their weapons, chiefly from China and Khorasan." In exchange they gave horses, meat, furs, and slaves. E. A. Thompson, *A History of Attila and the Huns* (Oxford, 1948), pp. 171–74.

4. For a discussion of this question see *ibid.*, pp. 106–11, 221–22.

5. The Szeklers of eastern Transylvania claim to be the descendants of the Huns. There appears to be little other evidence either for or against this tradition.

6. The site of Favianus has been, and still is, much disputed. Tradition placed Severin's monastery in the vicinity of Vienna and during the Middle Ages the Vienna area was frequently equated with the site of Favianus. In the late nineteenth century, on the basis of a new interpretation of the chronicle of Severin's life, Dr. Friedrich Kenner and others placed Favianus at Mautern, across the Danube from Krems. The recent discovery of the possible tomb of St. Severin underneath the parish church in Heiligenstadt strongly supports the older tradition. Certainly the name Heiligenstadt (formerly Heiligen-statt) suggests some kind of medieval veneration. I do not feel competent to judge all the evidence in this case, especially as the argumentation includes so much vituperation. However, to a geographer the locational arguments of the Heiligenstadt supporters seem the more plausible. As will be explained in the

discussion of Vienna (Chapter 6), the site of Heiligenstadt may have been of considerable importance during the Dark Ages, and undoubtedly a more significant location than that of Mautern. Then too there is a legend that Severin passed through present Sopron on his way north from Constantinople; this use of the ancient highway (rather than the Danube itself) would probably have brought him to the river in the Vienna area. Whether Severin came by the river or the road, a site at or near Vienna would have served as his contact point between Noricum to the west and the centers of state and church to the southeast. Still, whether Heiligenstadt or Mautern was Favianus, it is clear that the former, and probably the latter, were the sites of settlements at the time.

The full text, in Latin and German, of the critical "Vita Sancti Severini" by Eugippius, and the description of the discovery of the tomb, may be found in Klemens Kramert and Ernst Karl Winter, *St. Severin, Der Heilige zwischen Ost und West* (Klosterneuburg, 1958). Other recent translations of and commentaries on the "Vita Sancti Severini" include Rudolf Noll, *Eugippius. Das Leben des Hl. Severin* (Linz, 1947), and Nikolaus Hovorka, *Erinnerungen an den heil. Severin* (Vienna-Berlin, 1925). The Mautern arguments were summarized most conclusively in Friedrich Kenner, "Favianus, Wien und Mautern," *Blätter des Vereines für Landeskunde von Niederösterreich* (Vienna), Band XVI (1882), 3–53. The most concise recent summary of the opponents of the Heiligenstadt thesis occurs in a long footnote, in a review by Karl Lechner of Rudolf Noll, "Frühes Christentum in Österreich von den Anfangen bis um 600 n. Chr.," in *Unsere Heimat* (Vienna), Jg. 27 (1956), 34–38. These arguments are countered by Ernst Karl Winter in *Wo Lag Favianus? Fünfzig Gründe für und wider Heiligenstadt* (Vienna, 1957). The legend of Severin passing through Scarbantia (Sopron) is mentioned in Károly Mollay, *Scarbantia, Ödenburg, Sopron. Siedlungsgeschichte und Ortsnamenkunde* (Budapest, 1944), p. 11.

7. In their movement southward the Lombards forced the remnants of the Marcomani and Quadi to leave Bohemia and Moravia and (*ca.* 489) to migrate westward along the Danube. This mixture of remnant peoples became known to their contemporaries as the men from the old home of the Celtic Boii, or the Bojuvari; this was altered through the course of centuries into the Bayern, or Bavarians.

8. This idea is explained more fully in Francis Dvornik, *The Slavs, Their Early History and Civilization* (Boston, 1956), and the consequences of the interruption in sea connections in most of the works of Henri Pirenne.

9. Karl Oettinger has postulated that a large fortress was constructed during the first half of the seventh century in the northeastern corner of remnant Vindobona. On this basis he concludes that Vienna was the capital of Samo's state. *Das Werden Wiens* (Vienna, 1945), pp. 58–79. Some other scholars have disagreed vehemently.

10. On the basis of the proportions of cavalry and infantry in the Croatian armies of the time, Stephen Kr. Sakač has estimated that the Croats consisted of approximately 60 per cent Slavs and 40 per cent Iranians, though both were heavily combined with the descendants of the Romanized Illyrians. This ratio very likely greatly overestimates the Iranian proportion of the total popu-

lation. Probably we can accept the assumption that all the cavalry was Iranian and all the infantry Slavic, but undoubtedly a higher proportion of the Iranians than of the Slavs was in the fighting force. A 90 Slav to 10 Iranian proportion would appear to be closer to the truth. Sakač, "The Iranian Origins of the Croats According to C. Porphyrogenitus," in A. Bonifačić and C. Mihanovich, *The Croatian Nation, in Its Struggle for Freedom and Independence* (Chicago, 1955), p. 45. Since Porphyrogenitus appears to be the only concrete source mentioning an Iranian origin for the Croatian rulers, this interpretation has been challenged by other scholars, and other possible origins of the Croats have been postulated.

11. Francis Dvornik feels that the Croats moved along the northern flank of the Carpathians to the Black Sea and then by ship to Dalmatia. This seems highly unlikely. To move a whole people, or even only their fighting forces, by this far longer route would have been not only a tremendous logistical problem but also senseless, since the direct Amber Road was well known. Dvornik, *The Slavs*, p. 63.

12. Erdmann D. Beynon mentions two groups in southwestern Hungary, in the forested hills just north of the Drava, which are probably of Avar origin. "Isolated Racial Groups of Hungary," *Geographical Review* (New York), Vol. XVII (Oct., 1927), 592, 596–97.

13. Reportedly St. Cyril mentioned in 860 that Christianity was being preached in the language of the Avars. Mollay, *Scarbantia, Ödenburg, Sopron,* p. 93.

14. J. B. Bury, *A History of the Eastern Roman Empire. From the Fall of Irene to the Accession of Basil I (A.D. 802–867)* (London, 1912), p. 392.

15. Dvornik feels that the Moravian capital may have been at present Staré Městvo, which is across the March River from Uherské Hradiště, *The Slavs*, p. 103. Because of the size of the ruins on the hill overlooking Devín, Friedrich Baumhackl feels that Devín (Theben) must have been the site of the capital. "Die Burgruine Theben an der Marchmündung," *Unsere Heimat* (Vienna), Band XII (1939), 87–91.

16. H. G. Wanklyn, *The Eastern Marchlands of Europe* (London, 1941), p. 199, and Emil Portisch, *Geschichte der Stadt Bratislava-Pressburg* (Bratislava, 1933), Vol. I, 19, show the boundary as being on the Rába, whereas Dvornik, *The Slavs*, p. 96, shows all of present Burgenland and northern Lower Austria as also within Great Moravia. Oettinger states that Vienna was under the control of Sviatopluk from 884 to 892, *Das Werden Wiens*, pp. 106–7.

17. The plan and pictures of this church foundation are in Aladár Radnóti, "Une église du haut moyen âge à Zalavár," *Étude Slaves et Roumaines* (Budapest), Vol. I (1948), 21–30.

CHAPTER 5

1. "Magyar" is the name this nation applies to itself. To the Latins and Slavs they were known by the more comprehensive name of the Ugrian race to

which they belonged. This led to Ugri, then Hungari or Hungarian. The Greeks on the other hand called them Τουρκοι (Turks), since they included Turkic warriors. J. B. Bury, *A History of the Eastern Roman Empire* (London, 1912), p. 492. In this book I make a distinction between "Magyar" and "Hungarian"; "Magyar" denotes the ethnic group and its language, "Hungarian" the state and all its inhabitants, non-Magyars included.

2. C. A. Macartney, *The Magyars in the IX Century* (Cambridge, 1930).

3. *Ibid.*, pp. 76–77.

4. Macartney gives the legendary route as beginning with Munkács (Mukachevo) and then Ungvár (Uzhgorod), followed by the conquest of Salanus, the ruler of the land between the Danube and Tisza; Menumorot, of the land between the Maros and Szamos; Glad, of the Banat; the "Romans" in Pannonia; the Duke of the Bohemians and Slavs in western Slovakia; a Bulgarian relative of Salanus near Belgrade; and Gelou, a Vlach Duke in Transylvania. "The First Historians of Hungary," *The Hungarian Quarterly* (Budapest), Vol. IV (Winter, 1938), 638–39. J. Berry, "Transylvania," *Geographical Journal* (London), Vol. 53 (March, 1919), 129–46, mentions and shows on a map the supposed Vlach-Bulgar "duchies" which occupied the eastern Alföld and Transylvania at this time.

5. Because this battle has been named the Battle of Pressburg, historians have generally placed the site of the engagement north of the Danube near Pressburg (Bratislava). However, the fortress of Pressburg can be clearly seen from Kittsee and its vicinity, so that the fact that the fortress was visible from the battlefield does not necessitate the battle's occurring north of the river.

6. It must be borne in mind that the frequent wars between the Franks and Moravians had largely ravaged Pannonia even before 900. On the other hand, Macartney feels that a considerable non-Magyar population, composed of slaves gained in wars and forays and of the peoples who preceded the Magyars, dwelt among the Magyars. Estimates of the density of the non-Magyar population remaining in the basin at this time depend on the author's point of view. Some scholars feel that there was an unbroken continuity of settlement and that the arrival of the Magyars meant principally a change in rulers; others feel that the Magyars established a new settlement pattern in an empty basin. German nationalists stress the former, Magyar nationalists the latter viewpoint. Unfortunately, few discussions of this question appear to be truly objective.

7. Emil Franzel, *Der Donauraum im Zeitalter des Nationalitätenprinzips* (Bern, 1958), p. 17.

8. F. Dvornik, *The Slavs, Their Early History and Civilization* (Boston, 1956), pp. 104, 171.

9. Perhaps because each comitat was governed by a "count" and because England is divided into counties, British authors have translated *megyek* as "counties." For Americans this is misleading; "province" comes closer to the meaning. The subdivision of the *megye*, known in Magyar as a *járás*, and in German as a *Bezirk*, approximates the American county.

10. By "state idea" here is meant the reason for the existence of a political unit. "Each state must seek to present to its people a specific purpose, or pur-

poses distinct from the purposes formulated in other states, in terms of which all classes of people in all the diverse areas of the region will identify themselves with the state that includes them within its organized area. This concept of a complex of specific purposes of each state has been called the 'state idea' [*Staatsidee*] by various writers following Ratzel, or by others the *raison d'etre*, or justification of the state." Richard Hartshorne, "Political Geography," in Preston James and Clarence Jones, *American Geography. Inventory and Prospect* (Syracuse, 1954), p. 195. In its strongest and most satisfactory form, the state idea would consist of a belief freely held by the inhabitants of a political unit that they belong to that political unit and to no other, whether real or imaginary.

11. Robert Sieger, "Die Grenzen Niederösterreich," *Jahrbuch für Landeskunde von Niederösterreich* (Vienna), Band I (1902), 212–13.

12. The Lendva, which the boundary crosses just before reaching the Kutschenitza, is a larger and longer river than the Kutschenitza. However, it did not serve the interests of the boundary makers, since it turns towards the east whereas the Kutschenitza flows directly south.

13. The rivulet used south of the Rába is nothing more than a gully. Two other, larger streams were available, but each of these was accompanied by flat land suitable for cultivation, and each now contains a village.

14. Sinnersdorf is probably the only Styrian village for which the Magyars have a name distinctly their own. This name is Határfalva (boundary village).

CHAPTER 6

1. According to Kurt Hetzer, the principal advance was not along the Danube but along the road south of and parallel to the river; this road ran through or by present St. Pölten, Böheimkirchen, and Lengbach and entered the Vienna Basin not along the Danube but along the Wien River. "Taktische Betrachtungen zur babenbergischen Eroberung Niederösterreichs," *Unsere Heimat* (Vienna), Jg. 23 (1952), 2–11. This route helps explain why St. Pölten was captured before Melk, and perhaps Vienna before Krems. The significance of this road will be emphasized in the discussion of Vienna which follows in this chapter.

2. This was not the first fortress erected on the Leopoldsberg. At least as early as 400 B.C. the Celts had constructed a small fortress city atop this mountain.

3. The date of the Babenberger move into Vienna has been long disputed, but it now seems that it was either in 1136, the last year of (St.) Leopold III, or in 1137, the first year of Leopold IV. The reason for the long delay in this move has also been the subject of much controversy.

4. The Danube was not regulated and clearly channelized until 1869–82.

5. The path of the Roman road westward was through the following present towns: Vienna, Purkersdorf, Neulengbach, St. Pölten, Grafendorf, St. Leonhard am Forst, and Wieselburg am Erlauf. Hermann Vetters, Friedrich König,

and Heinrich Pabisch, *Landeskunde von Niederösterreich* (Vienna, 1908), p. 111. Friedrich Kenner indicated this road on his map, "Übersichtskarte der römischen Orte und Strassen." However, like all the other historians his emphasis has been drawn to the Danube boundary of the Empire, and to the limes road, which must have run along the river bank. (Much of the route of the limes road is still only postulated.) The Wiental road is listed as one of the "other reserve and trade roads." Yet, it seems clear that because of its directness and safety the Wiental road may well have been the busier artery and, except for the watching of the immediate boundary, the more important road. The map accompanies Kenner's article, "Die Römerorte in Nieder-Oesterreich," *Jahrbuch für Landeskunde von Nieder-Oesterreich* (Vienna), Jg. II (1869), 119–214.

6. The lines Ulm-Augsburg-Munich-Salzburg-Linz, Vienna-Bruck-Győr-Budapest, Budapest-Szeged (or Subotica)-Belgrade-Aegean, Budapest-Timişoara-Bucharest, and Bucharest-Constanta are all more important than routes along the Danube. For a development of this point see Robert Sieger, "Donauweg und Rheinstrasse," in F. Heiderich, *Zur Geographie des Wiener Beckens* (Vienna, 1923), pp. 186–97.

7. Within the Roman camp the road to the west formed the Via Praetoria, one of the two principal streets of Vindobona. It entered the camp via the present Tuchlauben and coincided with the present Marc Aurel Strasse, at the western end of the Hohen Markt. The second principal street, the Via Principalis, ran at right angles to this street; its course coincided with the long axis of the Hohen Markt and the Wipplinger Strasse.

8. See note 6, Chapter 4.

9. Scholars of the history of Vienna are split into two antagonistic camps on the question of the continuity of Vienna. One faction feels that Vienna is an unbroken descendant of Roman Vindobona; the other feels that Vienna was established as a new city shortly after 1000. These two viewpoints color all the analyses of the history of this site during the Dark Ages. Thus Oettinger, *Das Werden Wiens* (Vienna, 1945), maintains that Vienna survived all the barbarian invasions, was the capital of Samo's state, was the largest center on the middle Danube in the Carolingian century, survived the Magyar storm, and was a prosperous commercial center before the entry of the Babenbergers *ca.* 1136. On the other hand, in his review of Oettinger's book, Lechner, *Unsere Heimat* (Vienna), Jg. 23 (1952), 45–67, attacks all these positions as being based on nothing more than fantasy.

10. The Semmering route to Venice is actually a union of three passes. Between Styria and Carinthia the road passes through the broad Neumarkt Saddle, and between Carinthia and Italy, the Tarviso Pass (Safnitzer Sattel bei Tarvis). Though these two passes had been known and used before the Roman conquest of the Alps, it was the discovery of the Semmering that joined all three into one highway.

11. It is intriguing to note how the new system of routeways and administrative organization caused the focal center of Moravia to be moved westward. During the days of the Moravian Empire the March valley had carried the principal north-south road, and a town on the March, near the present Uherské Hradiště, had been the capital of the state. Following the destruction of the

Moravian state the political center was shifted to Prague in Bohemia, and the international boundary was established along the lower March and the Carpathians. The March was no longer a routeway, and a provincial center on the river would have been adjacent to a dangerous border. A center on the March would also have been too far from Prague to act as the link between Prague and Moravia. At Brno, however, the roads from Prague left behind the belts of forest (that still separate Bohemia and Moravia) and entered the fertile lowlands of Moravia; Brno was therefore the link between the productive portions of Moravia and Prague, the capital of the kingdom. Brno was also on the new north-south road through Vienna, and, in fact, acted as a distributing and collecting point for the trade between Vienna and northern Europe.

12. By East Central Europe is meant all those states and peoples between Germany and Russia; it is roughly coincident with the "Shatter Belt." This subdivision of Europe follows that of Oskar Halecki, *The Limits and Divisions of European History* (New York, 1950).

13. Many authors have stressed the crossroads position of Vienna, and yet the greatness of Vienna was due not so much to the crossing of two principal highways in her general vicinity as it was to the fact that Vienna *controlled* the traffic along these highways. Vienna could not be by-passed. This city became therefore the obvious place for the interchange of goods and for the regulation and the financing of commerce. For a list of goods carried on the Semmering road in 1545 see Johann Sölch, *Das Semmeringgebiet* (Vienna, 1948), p. 22.

14. For descriptions of Vienna late in the fifteenth century see Bruno Brehm, *Wien. Die Grenzstadt im deutschen Osten* (Jena, 1937), pp. 28–30. According to the report of Aeneas Silvius Piccolomini (later Pope Pius II), Vienna had "50,000 communicants" around 1450; this has led to the estimate of 60,000 for the population of the city at that time. According to another Italian, Antonio Bonfini, the University of Vienna had 7,000 students at this time. In 1800 Vienna had 231,000 inhabitants, in 1916 (maximum) 2,239,000, and in 1951, 1,866,000.

CHAPTER 7

1. According to H. G. Wanklyn the commercial stagnation following 1500 helps to explain the strengthening of feudal tendencies in Eastern Europe. *The Eastern Marchlands of Europe* (London, 1941), p. 16.

2. Heidelberg was established in 1385, Cologne in 1388. These were the first universities along the Rhine. Buda was established in 1389.

3. The title of king was applied only to Wladislas, in 1086; Bohemia did not become officially a kingdom until 1156.

4. A few small groups of the Tatars remained behind and settled in the Carpathian Basin. The Csököly group near Kaposvár in the southern Dunántúl, and the Kalotaszeg group located just west of the present Cluj, Transylvania, are thought to be descendants of Tatar groups. E. D. Beynon, "Isolated Racial Groups of Hungary," *Geographical Review* (New York), Vol. XVII (Oct., 1927), 595, 602.

5. According to A. W. Leeper, approximately 40,000 Cumans entered Hungary at this time. *A History of Medieval Austria* (Oxford, 1941).

6. The action of the Styrian lords was probably not a result of any marked preference for the Bohemian instead of the Hungarian ruler. Whereas Styria lies open to Hungary and Székesfehérvár, it is beyond the central Alps from Prague. In addition, the Styrians may have wished to maintain their ties to Lower Austria and Vienna, which were under Ottokar, and may possibly have hoped in this way to regain the Pitten Mark, which had just been transferred from Styria to Lower Austria by the Peace of Buda.

7. According to the *Cambridge Medieval History* (London, 1936), Vol. VI, 469, 56,000 Hungarian troops took part in the Battle of Dürnkrut, and thus probably gained Austria for the Habsburg.

8. Ruins found on the Alföld indicate that before the Turkish invasion the plain was divided regularly among many cell-like communes. The present administrative area of the city of Debrecen (957 square kilometers) includes the territory of 11 to 30 abandoned communes. E. D. Beynon, "Migrations of Hungarian Peasants," *Geographical Review* (New York), Vol. XXVII (April, 1937), 219. The comparison of the number and density of settlements in southern portions of the Alföld in the fifteenth and in the late eighteenth centuries is strikingly shown on the map, "Carte Ethnographique de la Hongrie Méridionale," opposite p. 176 in G. Szekfű, *État et Nation* (Paris, 1945). According to this map, at least three times as many settlements existed in the present Bačka and Banat in the fifteenth as in the eighteenth century.

9. Wiener Neustadt profited greatly from the trade with Hungary; in the mid-fifteenth century it had an estimated population of 18,000. By the end of the sixteenth century this figure had decreased to 3,000. Fritz Bodo, "Wiener Neustadt. Eine historisch-geographische Skizze," *Unsere Heimat* (Vienna), Band IX (1936), 171.

10. The event which seems to have stimulated the signing of the Compact of Visegrád was the incorporation into Austria of Carinthia and Carniola in 1335. With these acquisitions the rulers of Vienna held a belt of territory extending to the northern shore of the Adriatic. Direct access to Italy from the Carpathian Basin was possible by land only through Austrian territory.

11. Largely for nationalistic purposes many attempts have been made by German scholars to equate present settlements in western Hungary and Burgenland with Carolingian settlements. On the basis of a Carolingian record the Burgenland "city" of Pinkafeld (which is located on the Styrian border) has claimed Frankish origin, and in 1960 celebrated the 1100th anniversary of its founding. A more significant identification has been that of the Carolingian "Odenburch" with Ödenburg (Sopron) because of the similarity of the names. Largely on the basis of this identification, German nationalists have constructed an elaborate edifice of German settlement throughout Pannonia. The continuation of the name since 860 has been taken to prove that the Germans had settled this city prior to the arrival of the Magyars, and that the city had remained German through the Magyar storm. However, Odenburch or Ödenburg mean only "devastated castle" and such features have always been common in this region. In a thorough piece of scholarship Károly Mollay has shown that this identification is impos-

sible and that the Carolingian Odenburch was probably within present eastern Styria. The first known mention of the name Ödenburg for the present Sopron occurred in 1283; the first mention of a form of Sopron in 1096. Within Burgenland and Vienna the study of the origins of these place names seems obviously motivated by the desire to prove that Burgenland (West Hungary) was always German (or Germanized-Slav) and that the Magyars exerted nothing more than a political control over the area. This fits in well with the frequent reference to the transfer of Burgenland to Austria as a "return to Austria" after the centuries of foreign (Magyar) domination. Thus, Zimmerman simply waves away Mollay's work and repeats the identification of Odenburch with Ödenburg; Kranzmayer does so also. Since in most cases the ethnic origin of a place name can only be postulated, and frequently two or more names for the one place exist, nationalistic coloration of such research seems inevitable, and truly objective studies are non-existent. Károly Mollay, *Scarbantia, Ödenburg, Sopron. Siedlungsgeschichte und Ortsnamenkunde* (Budapest, 1944), pp. 38–105; also in *Ödenburg. Helynévfejtés és Településtörténet* (Budapest, 1942). Austrian works include Fritz Zimmermann, *Die vormadjarische Besiedlung des burgenländischen Raumes* (Eisenstadt, 1954); and Eberhard Kranzmayer and Karl Bürger, *Burgenländisches Siedlungsnamenbuch* (Eisenstadt, 1957). Although clearly pro-German, the best village by village analysis of the Burgenland place names is that by Bürger in pp. 37–165 of the last mentioned work.

12. Károly Heimler, *Magyar Tájak, Magyar Városok*, Vol. I, "Sopron" (Budapest, 1932), p. 121. *Lövő* means "archer." Other *gyepü* defense settlements occurred at the present villages of Kittsee, Gols, Mörbisch, Schützen, Siegless, Hodis, and Kohfidisch. Hubert Lendl, "Die Sozialökonomische Struktur der Burgenländischen Landwirtschaft" (Unpublished Doctoral dissertation, Hochschule der Bodenkultur, Vienna, 1937), pp. 54–55.

13. This in fact occurred in Bulgaria. There the original language of the steppe Bulgars was supplanted by Slavic.

14. Matthias obtained control of Moravia and Silesia at this time. The situation in Bohemia itself was confused with the election, by a portion of the Bohemian nobility, of Vladislav, King of Poland. In 1478 Vladislav and Matthias agreed that Bohemia proper was to be ruled by Vladislav during his life and after his death was to be rejoined to Moravia and Silesia under the rule of Matthias. However Matthias died first (1490). Nevertheless the union of the Bohemian and Hungarian lands continued, first under Vladislav, and then under his descendants, until the death of Louis at Mohács in 1526. Therefore, in 1526, when the Habsburg laid claim to the crowns of Bohemia and Hungary, he was laying claim to what had been, at least dynastically, one political grouping for over half a century.

CHAPTER 8

1. Herbert A. Gibbons, *The Foundation of the Ottoman Empire* (Oxford, 1916), p. 181.

2. Aziz Suryal Atiya, *The Crusade of Nicopolis* (London, 1934), p. 75.

3. The progress of the Turks had been greatly facilitated by the plagues, including the Black Death (1347–51), which ravaged Europe in the fourteenth century. According to Gibbons, the dates of nine plagues between 1348 and 1431 coincide with the aggressive periods of the Ottomans. *Ottoman Empire*, p. 96.

4. Oskar Halecki, *The Limits and Divisions of European History* (New York, 1950), p. 78.

5. King Sobieski of Poland and Eugene of Savoy won many victories against the Turks, but these came when the Turks were declining as a military power, whereas the successes of Hunyádi came during the time of Ottoman greatness.

6. After the death of King Ladislaus at Varna in 1444, Hungary experienced another lengthy interregnum period. Although there were several aspirants for the crown, Hunyádi János seems to have been the actual ruler of the kingdom, though not the king. He, and his second son, Matthias, were the candidates of the eastern nobles; the western nobles favored the Habsburg claimant.

7. Hungary had been greatly weakened not only by the disputes for the crown but also by peasant disputes with their feudal lords. What is remarkable, however, is not the weakness of the kingdom in 1526 but rather the length of time for which it successfully resisted the Turks. By 1520 the Ottoman Empire was both in area and in population several times the size of Hungary. Suleiman had all or most of present day Turkey, Bulgaria, Greece, Albania, Jugoslavia, Romania, Syria, Lebanon, Israel, Jordan, and Egypt, and parts of Iraq, Saudi Arabia, and the U.S.S.R. behind him.

8. Székesfehérvár was captured by imperial troops in 1601, but was soon retaken by the Turks.

9. It has been estimated that the Turkish invasions of Lower Austria and adjacent areas of western Hungary cost 500,000 lives. Vetters, König, and Pabisch, *Landeskunde von Niederösterreich* (Vienna, 1908), p. 79.

10. For the terms of the contract of May, 1558, between the Batthyány lord and twenty Croatian family patriarchs concerning the settlement of St. Nicholas, Güssing, see Thomas M. Barker, "The Croatian Minority of Burgenland," *Journal of Central European Affairs*, Vol. XIX (April, 1959), 38–39.

11. Hungary and Transylvania remain the only strongholds of Calvinism east of Switzerland.

12. Francis Rákóczy was a Catholic but most of his followers were Calvinist.

13. Roman strong points north of the Danube were at present Devínska Nova Ves (Theben-Neudorf), Mast, and Stupava (Stampfen). Emil Portisch, *Geschichte der Stadt Bratislava-Pressburg* (Bratislava, 1933), Vol. I, 13.

14. The names of the city have been the cause of much discussion. "Bratislava" is probably derived from the Slavic form of Brezalauspurc (or Braslaverspurch). The German name also seems to be derived from the same source: Braslaverspurch → Preslawaspurch (1052) → Brezesburg → Pressburg. The Magyar name is, however, a mystery. *Ibid.*, pp. 30–31. Some Hungarians feel that "Pozsony" was initially the name of the megye and was later applied to the city.

15. The crossing of the Danube was a significant function of the city from the first days of the Hungarian kingdom. As early as 1001 a royal ruling specified

that the revenue gained from the ferry was to be divided: one third to the Pannonhalma monastery, one third to the "count" of Pozsony comitat (megye), and one third to the king. *Ibid.*, p. 24.

16. The functions of this city were radically altered in 1919, since the new boundaries severed it from Budapest, Vienna, and the Dunántúl. The city's primary hinterland, now named Slovakia, was united to Bohemia-Moravia, and Bratislava, because of its relatively southern location, was not the obvious link between Slovakia and Bohemia. The long valleys of northern Slovakia were connected directly to Prague by new rail links in the vicinity of the Jablunka Pass. In return, however, Bratislava has gained two new urban functions which have maintained it as a large city. It became the capital of Slovakia and hence a political center second in importance only to Prague, and it became the only Danubian port for the new Czechoslovakia.

17. The significance of terrain features on military operations was clearly shown in the entire campaign of 1683. The Turkish horde advanced through the eastern Dunántúl and was soon faced with the problem of crossing the Rába River with the fortress city of Győr (Raab) controlling the one important bridge. Following a crossing of the river by a Tatar unit, the imperial forces quickly retreated from the Rába but left a force behind to defend Győr. The Turks decided not to lay siege to Győr, but instead pressed on after the main body of the imperial troops. The first Turkish troops arrived before Vienna on July 13, and on the next day the siege began. The Turks completed the surrounding of the city by occupying the island between the city walls and the main channel of the Danube. Throughout the siege the Turks remained south of the Danube, the main body of the imperial army was north of the Danube (not in the city), and the river remained fairly open to the Austrians. Even after the first enemy units had appeared before Vienna, the Duke of Croy was able to travel by the river and along its north bank from Vienna to Győr to assume command of the key fortress city. The Poles moved southward from Poland and were able to reach the north bank of the Danube opposite Vienna without serious opposition. In this vicinity they joined the imperial forces under the Duke of Lorraine. Since an attempt to force a crossing at Vienna seemed impossible, the combined relief force marched *westward forty miles* to the next available crossing point, Krems, at the western end of the Tullner Feld. The army then retraced its steps along the southern flank of the Tullner Feld and occupied the heights of the Wienerwald by September 6. The battle was fought on the lower slopes of the Wienerwald on the morning of September 12. Perhaps because of their location so far from home, perhaps because of the fame of Sobieski as a fighter of the Turks, perhaps because of the strength of the Christian charge down the slopes, the Turks broke and fled in panic. In their flight eastward the Turks were forced to recross the Rába; since Győr was still controlled by imperial forces, Sobieski and the Poles were able to catch the trapped army and defeat it again before it had fled beyond the Rába.

18. Henry Marczali, *Hungary in the Eighteenth Century* (Cambridge, 1910), p. 199.

19. Until 1780 the Banat was under the Imperial Chamber and War Council, and not under the Hungarian government. From 1690 to 1779 the Serbs of south-

ern Hungary were under their own patriarch, who was directly controlled by the emperor; Hungarian authorities had no control over them. All the mines of Hungary were under imperial control. "The lands won from the Turks appeared to Hungarians as recovered territory—to the Viennese as conquered soil." Marczali, *Hungary*, pp. 318–19. See also C. A. Macartney, *Hungary* (London, 1934), pp. 82–89.

20. German colonists were looked upon by Vienna as "the apostles of civilization, nationality and religion." Imperial agents promised land, tools, cattle, and exemption from taxation to all Germans willing to migrate to Hungary. Marczali, *Hungary*, pp. 205–7. Over eight hundred new German settlements were established in Hungary during the years 1711–80.

21. Just prior to World War I the holdings of Prince Eszterházy totalled 570,000 acres. Oskar Jaszi, *The Dissolution of the Habsburg Empire* (Chicago, 1929), p. 223.

22. Since all the descendents of the original Magyars were considered to be noblemen, medieval Hungary had had relatively many small-holding nobles. The increase in the great power of the nobles dates from roughly the death of King Matthias "the Just," in 1490. In the sixteenth century Hungary suffered from the same kind of peasant disorders as disturbed other parts of Europe at the time; nevertheless immense landholdings did not become the rule in Hungary until after 1600.

23. The agricultural nature of Hungary at this time is revealed by the export-import statistics for the decade 1777–86 (shown in florins).

Exports		*Imports*	
Cattle	2,546,395	Linen Cloth	1,042,046
Wool	1,842,795	Woolen & Linen Goods	849,824
Copper	1,162,402	Pieces of Cloth	789,113
Wheat	865,294	Silk & Silk Goods	664,160
Wine	820,594	Cotton & Cotton Goods	518,194
Tobacco	774,854	Sugar	302,179
Rye	618,827	Harnesses etc.	261,116
Sheep	412,896	Coffee	233,794
Barley	370,650	Wood Products	229,361
Swine	363,383	Hardware & Jewelry	203,325
Oats	358,841	Thread, Yarn & Rope	183,120
Hides	257,023	Clothing	143,254
Nuts	127,585	Furs	127,129
Honey	114,817	Salt	125,595
Wax	105,215	Iron	121,919

Martin Schwartner, *Statistik des Koenigreichs Ungern* (Pest, 1798), p. 216.

24. In the late eighteenth century the annual income of Prince Eszterházy was said to exceed 700,000 florins. At this time a bushel of wheat cost less than half a florin. Marczali, *Hungary*, pp. 112–13. Yet, even this great income did not prevent the princes from later going heavily into debt because of lavish spending. Macartney, *Hungary*, p. 167.

CHAPTER 9

1. The most striking example of this attitude was the action of John Zápolya in placing Hungary under the protection of the Turks. Zápolya, Tököly, and others called upon the Turks for assistance in their fights against the Habsburgs. "The Protestants considered that this [Catholic] alliance [with the Habsburgs] imperilled their political and religious liberty [and] looked rather to the Turks for support." Henry Marczali, *Hungary in the Eighteenth Century* (Cambridge, 1910), p. 248.

2. Several Austrian rulers, notably Maria Theresa and Joseph II, had attempted to introduce economic, administrative, and educational reforms, but all these attempts were resisted. ". . . the Magyars had to choose between two alternatives—either to accept an organization conforming not to national but to foreign ideas and interests, or to maintain the older institutions already recognized as inadequate to satisfy the new needs but at all events thoroughly national in character." *Ibid.*, p. 307.

3. The privileges enjoyed under the old constitution are well summarized in Jerome Blum, *Noble Landowners and Agriculture in Austria 1815–1848. A Study in the Origins of the Peasant Emancipation of 1848* (Baltimore, 1948), pp. 34–36.

4. Hungarian opposition to the Habsburgs did not cease under Maria Theresa. She ruled almost entirely by royal edict, and much of the resettlement of Hungary occurred during her reign. Yet the forty years of her reign were years of relative peace and good feeling. This was a time of great Marian devotion, and pilgrimage shrines were conspicuous throughout much of Austria and Hungary (Burgenland contains several noteworthy baroque shrines to the Virgin Mary). It was considered to be a meaningful coincidence that the Empire was temporally as well as spiritually under a Queen Mary.

5. The terms of the *Ausgleich* of 1867, as well as the Hungarian declaration of independence of 1849, may be found in Jelavich and Jelavich, *The Habsburg Monarchy. Towards a Multinational Empire or National States* (New York, 1959).

6. The actual crossing point of the Danube was not at Aquincum but rather five miles south at the present centers of Buda and Pest. The ruins of the wall of Contra-Aquincum have been found under the oldest church of Pest, the Belvárosi Templom. Therefore both Vindobona and Aquincum were located at a highway-river junction four to five miles from a good river crossing. In medieval Vienna the highway center remained more important than the crossing, and hence the city developed on the precise site of Roman Vindobona, whereas in medieval Buda the crossing became far more important than the initial road center, and consequently the city developed not at the Aquincum camp site but at the crossing.

7. I cannot assert as absolutely true that these roads existed, as described, before the Turkish occupation. However, such places as Szeged, Temesvár,

Debrecen, and Eger were already important cities in the early centuries of Hungary, and it is known that important roads existed east as well as west of the Danube. Since the Alföld offers no barriers (except a few marshes) to the positioning of roads, it seems safe to assume that the highways of medieval times, just as the highways of today, followed the shortest possible paths between key points. If other roads existed between these highways, their existence would add to rather than detract from the arguments for the growth of Pest and Buda.

8. The constant warfare had wreaked havoc on both centers, but Pest on the plain was more susceptible to destruction than was Buda on the hills. Austrian troops laid siege to Buda and Pest in 1598, 1602, 1684, and 1686. Vilmos Kovácsházy, *Magyar Tájak, Magyar Városok*, Vol. II, "Budapest" (Budapest, 1934), pp. 19–24.

9. Until the mid-nineteenth century the advantages of expansion on the flat plain were partially negated by the recurring danger of floods. Whereas Buda was generally above the danger of flooding, Pest was often inundated. A disastrous flood occurred as late as 1838.

10. Presently the Communist rule, accentuated by the imposition of the Iron Curtain, has again separated Budapest from Western Europe. The role of the city has been somewhat reversed now, but it is still the vital crossing point. Budapest is now the link between the Dunántúl and the Soviet Union, and also between Czechoslovakia and either Jugoslavia or Romania. It seems reasonable to assume, moreover, that eventually the Iron Curtain will cease to be a barrier between east-west movement, and that when this happens most of the agricultural produce of the Alföld will again move westward.

11. Unfortunately, the word "nation" has come to have several overlapping meanings. In this work, "nation" is taken to mean a group of people who, sharing a common tradition, common customs, and common political and legal development, feel themselves to belong together. This does not necessarily mean that all the members of the nation will speak the same language, although they generally will. Since "nation" is, however, often taken to mean the totality of persons sharing a language, in other words the members of an ethnic group, a certain ambiguity seems unavoidable. Whenever in this work "nation" is used in its linguistic sense, it will be placed in quotation marks. From the first definition given above it follows that "nationalism" could have flourished, and did flourish, before the eighteenth century. Therefore, to prevent ambiguity concerning the use of the word "nationalism," this term will be used in its broadest sense, and "linguistic nationalism" will be used to refer to the special type of nationalism based on language.

12. In retrospect it seems that Latin might have been an admirable solution to the problems posed by the many languages of the kingdom. However, it was too much to expect of any ethnic group of the nineteenth century to forego its own sacred tongue in favor of the "dead" language associated with the Church. Unfortunately, Latin was also considered to be the language of the feudal system, so that the move away from Latin was seen as a move towards the contemporary age and away from an anachronistic survival of feudalism.

13. "A nation placed as the Magyars have been . . . has indeed no alternative

between extinction and an almost ferocious attachment to its own ways and manners. . . . Once across the mountain he [the nomad] must make good his ground or perish. . . . The nation which remains purely Asiatic perishes for lack of fresh blood; that which turns its face towards the West risks finding its individuality submerged." C. A. Macartney, *Hungary* (London, 1934), pp. 14, 28, 30.

14. One can imagine the effect on the Magyars of the following quotations from the Slovak Kollár's, "The Daughter of Slava": "Scattered Slavs, let us be a united whole and no longer mere fragments." He would mold all the Slavs into a mighty statue, and "All Europe would kneel before this idol, whose head would tower above the clouds and whose feet would shake the earth." Quoted in R. W. Seton-Watson, *Racial Problems in Hungary* (London, 1908), p. 53.

15. "Of all the non-Slavic peoples of Eastern Europe, it was the Magyars that Hilferding and Danilevskii least admired. There was practically nothing about the Magyars that merited grace, in the light of Panslavist doctrine. Not only were the Magyars non-Slavs; they were not even Indo-European. These Panslavists frankly regarded them as Asiatic interlopers whose usurpation of the Pannonian Plain had resulted in the separation of the Slavic peoples from each other. This was the historic crime for which the progeny of the Árpáds now had to pay the price. Moreover Hungary had been the bastion of Romanism [Catholicism] and feudalism for a millennium. Its culture and its orientation were Western. . . . Thus Hungary was nothing less than an enemy in the camp. . . . Hilferding [wrote], 'Woe to the Magyars, should they wish to interfere. The march of history has crushed better peoples.'" Michael B. Petrovich, *The Emergence of Russian Panslavism 1856–1870* (New York, 1956), pp. 275–76.

16. This figure must omit Croatia-Slavonia which was completely Croatian at the time. The estimate comes from Hungarian sources, and is mentioned by Macartney, *Hungary*, p. 68.

17. The figures are based on Oskar Jaszi, *The Dissolution of the Habsburg Empire* (Chicago, 1929), p. 305, and probably include Croatia-Slavonia. However, the figure for 1787 seems too low. The census of that date did not count the members of each ethnic group; instead it gave merely the total population of each settlement and indicated what language predominated in that settlement. In all of Hungary there were then 48 Royal Free Cities and 11,408 market towns and villages. Of these 11,408 market towns and villages, 3,668 (32 per cent) were listed as Magyar, 5,789 (51 per cent) as Slav, 921 (8 per cent) as German, and 1,024 (9 per cent) as Romanian. Unfortunately, many of the villages were actually of mixed "nationality," but there is no way of deducing accurately how many members of each ethnic group were in each village. However, two other factors can be evaluated. Roughly 5 per cent of the total population was in the Royal Free Cities; most of these urbanites were German. Also, the market towns and villages were certainly not of uniform size. Many of the Magyar market towns of the Alföld (e.g. Miskolc, Kecskemét, Hódmezővásárhely) were larger than most of the cities, so that a commentator of the time felt that there may have been as many Magyars as Slavs. On the basis of these considerations, a more plausible estimate for 1787 would appear to be: Magyar 39 per cent, Slav 41

per cent, German 12 per cent, and Romanian 8 per cent. Macartney gives figures of 45 per cent Magyar in 1720 and 39 per cent in 1778, *Hungary*, p. 86. In any case, the figures indicate a serious decline in the relative strength of the Magyars until about 1790, and a steady increase thereafter.

18. Friedrich Szmudits, "Geschichte der Angliederung des Burgenlandes an Österreich" (Unpublished dissertation, University of Vienna, 1937), p. 31. The statement appears in a slightly different form in Seton-Watson, *Racial Problems*, p. 220.

19. Not all Magyars shared this belief. The great Széchenyi stated in his 1843 address to the Hungarian Academy that the Slav movement was a reaction to Magyar vehemence. The only hope of victory for the Magyars lay in moral superiority, in the development of a vigorous national culture. The Magyars should not let their patriotic ardor tempt them to overstep the law. Other notable national leaders, among them Deák and Eötvös, urged a humane, just treatment of the non-Magyars.

20. Perhaps forced assimilation is an inevitable corollary of linguistic nationalism. The first modern nationalists of Europe, the French, as early as 1794 began a campaign to force the Bretons, Alsatians, Flemings, etc., of France to speak French.

21. As soon as Burgenland was transferred to Austria the teachers were compelled to take an examination proving their ability to handle German.

22. Patry has himself explained the origin of his feelings. He had been born in Vienna of parents from Iglau (Jihlava) in Bohemia. "With my mother's milk I sucked in the noble hatred of the cunning Czechs. . . . Out of the Czech-German situation sprang my efforts to bring help to the Germans of Hungary." From Josef Patry, "Allerlei aus der Zeit vor zum Anschluss." Festnummer, *Drei Jahre bei Deutschösterreich, Der Freie Burgenländer* (Eisenstadt), November 16, 1924.

23. The Magyar proportion of the total population increased between 2 and 3 per cent per decade, with a gradual acceleration in the rate of increase:

Year	*Magyars*	*Increase*
1880	46.7%	
1890	48.6%	1.9%
1900	51.4%	2.8%
1910	54.5%	3.1%

As several authors have pointed out, emigration was stronger among the non-Magyars than among the Magyars. Emigration may explain the sudden increase in the rate around 1890, since emigration to America did not become notable until around that time, but it can scarcely account for the total increase in the Magyar proportion of the total population.

24. Seton-Watson, by using the number of communes rather than the number of people, came to the conclusion that the policy of Magyarization was a failure. *Racial Problems*, p. 396.

25. Linguistic nationalism is usually considered to have been the principal cause of the collapse of the Austrian Empire in 1918. Yet, it seems significant

that the strongest separatist feelings had developed and been expressed in those areas and by those peoples who possessed the memory of a separate political existence, that is, by those who already possessed a state idea.

In viewing the Austrian problem, if we focus our attention not on the linguistic groups but instead on the historic geo-political entities which comprised the empire, then the history of the Habsburg Empire may be considered to have been a continuation of the centuries-old struggles between Hungary, Austria, and Bohemia. For five centuries prior to 1526 these three states had contended for supremacy in the Danubian lands, and although Hungary was usually the strongest, the three states remained separate and distinct. Therefore, in the long view of history, the conquests of Austria after 1526 may well be looked upon as only a temporary expansion made possible by the crushing of Hungary by a greater, outside force. When Hungary finally regained her strength (toward the end of the eighteenth century), she again became difficult, almost impossible, for Austria to control. Despite all the emphasis on languages, the principal problem Vienna had to face through much of the nineteenth century was that of maintaining some kind of adequate control of Hungary. Vienna may have been the communications center of the Danubian lands, but Alpine Austria formed but a poor base for national power. Had the Habsburgs been able to fashion a sense of unity, a state idea, acceptable to the Hungarians (and the others within the empire), then probably the empire could have become a truly united, integrated state. However, this did not occur. Instead, the Habsburgs seem to have chosen the wrong means to effect this essential unity; they tried to *impose* their control on Hungary, Bohemia, and the other portions of the empire, from a base insufficient for the task.

26. These Hungarian names have disappeared from the streets of Eisenstadt. The majority of street names now refer to prominent men in the early days of Burgenland, and to cultural heroes of the past.

27. Heinrich Kunnert, "Vor Zehn Jahren," *Burgenland Vierteljahrshefte für Landeskunde, Heimatschutz und Denkmalpflege* (Eisenstadt), Band II, Heft 2 (1929), 128.

28. At least within Sopron megye a local exchange student program brought promising boys from German-speaking villages to Magyar villages for a year to become more proficient in Magyar, and vice versa from Magyar villages to German villages.

29. Some scholars have used the fact that prior to World War I, 89 per cent of the students in the two Hungarian universities were Magyar, as proof of ethnic discrimination against the non-Magyars within Hungary. However, considering the social origin of the students and the passionate patriotism which accompanied higher education, such figures could be expected even without discrimination. Nor does the emigration proportion of two non-Magyars for every Magyar leaving Hungary in the decade 1900–1909 prove discrimination or repression. A simple geographical analysis shows that the Magyar areas were far more capable of absorbing increases in population than the non-Magyar areas. The Magyars were in the "booming" central parts of the country, the cities and the fertile, but yet relatively empty, Alföld; the non-Magyars were in the peripheral hill lands. As a general rule peasants emigrate not so much because of repression as because of the better economic opportunities present

elsewhere. The peak of emigration from Burgenland occurred immediately *after* the area had been transferred to Austria, in 1922–23.

30. There is a significant contrast between the attitude towards the Hungarian years held by those persons who were educated while the area was still within Hungary, and the attitude held by those educated since that time. To be sure, some of those who finished their schooling before 1921 insist there was a Magyar repression. However, many of the members of that generation do not speak of repression, but rather refer with nostalgia to the days before 1918. In contrast, the Burgenlanders who have gone through school since 1921 all believe and maintain fervently that their people suffered from a chauvinistic Magyar repression. Burgenland education seems to stress, explicitly or implicitly, that the Germans were *unterdruckt* in Hungary, that the Sopron plebiscite was *falsch*, and that the placement of the boundary was a result of Hungarian manipulations. It seems to have become a part of the official point of view to stress the "horrors" of the semi-legendary Hungarian past, much as it has been part of the Soviet point of view to stress the "horrors" of the semi-legendary Tsarist past.

31. The most complete works on the history of the Croats of Burgenland are by Direktor Ivan Dobrović (the founder and first president of the Kroatische Kulturverein.) These two works are: *Kratka povijest naših stari njihova borba s Turki i selenje u novu domovinu* (A Short History of Our Forefathers, Their Battles With the Turks and Their Migration into Their New Homeland) (Eisenstadt, 1952), 62 pp.; and *Naši Hrvati u. dobi reformacije i prva stoljeta u novoj domovini* (Our Croats at the Time of the Reformation and Their First Centuries in the New Homeland) (Vienna [Beč], 1955), 100 pp. These two works may be obtained by ordering from Direktor Alfons Kornfeind, Trauersdorf, Burgenland. Direktor Dobrović is currently working on an enlarged German version of the material in both of the above works; this will be the closest approach to a complete history of the Croats in Burgenland and the surrounding areas that has yet appeared. The title is not yet definite but will resemble, "Die Geschichte der Kroaten des Burgenlandes und der Nachbarländer"; it is expected to be published in 1962.

32. Josef Hůrský, *Vylidňovaňí a asimilace slovanských obcí v Gradišti* (The Depopulation and Assimilation of Slavic Townships in Burgenland) (Prague, 1952). This large work is entirely in Czech but the maps and some of the tables can be deciphered by one not knowing the Czech language.

33. This tendency to maintain the peasant cultures was not unique to the Catholic Church. There are many such ethnic-religious ties in Central and Eastern Europe. Within Hungary the Orthodox Church performed the same function for the Serbs, and the Lutheran Church for the Germans of Transylvania and of the "Zips."

CHAPTER 10

1. A good description of how this process worked in the field was given by the (British) president of the commission establishing the boundary between

Hungary and Jugoslavia. The most striking example was that of the Mursziget, or Prekmurje, the northernmost salient of Jugoslav territory, where Austria, Hungary, and Jugoslavia meet. In this area the local demonstrations were all pro-Hungary, the economy and the communications were completely tied to Hungary, while the broad Mur valley separated the area from Jugoslavia. Nevertheless, the area was awarded, on linguistic grounds, to Jugoslavia. D. Cree, R. E., "Jugoslav-Hungarian Boundary Commission," *Geographical Journal* (London), Vol. 65 (Feb., 1925), 89–110.

2. Of course, the Hungarians were on the losing side in the war, but most of the other peoples of the monarchy had fought just as loyally as had the Magyars. However, since the Magyars had been co-rulers of the Dual Monarchy, a distinction was made in the West between the Magyars and the other non-German "nationalities" of the monarchy.

3. "My feelings toward Hungary were less detached. I confess that I regarded, and still regard, that Turanian tribe with acute distaste. Like their cousins, the Turks, they had destroyed much and created nothing. Pest was a false city devoid of any autochthonous reality. For centuries the Magyars had oppressed their subject nationalities. The hour of liberation was at hand." Harold Nicolson, *Peacemaking, 1919* (London, 1933), p. 27.

4. "No event affected the frontiers of Hungary more decisively than the Socialist [sic] revolution which broke out in Budapest in April [sic] 1919 and enthroned Béla Kun as dictator." Harold Temperley, "How the Hungarian Frontiers Were Drawn," *Foreign Affairs*, Vol. 6 (April, 1928), 434.

5. This distribution was not, in itself, a sign of preferential treatment given the Magyars, but rather a part of the general east-west pattern of Europe. The German-Polish frontier area contained German cities in a Polish countryside, the Polish-Ukrainian frontier had Polish cities in a Ukrainian countryside.

6. "Verein zur Erhaltung des Deutschtums in Ungarn." This name was changed in 1918 to "Versammlung der Wiener Deutscher aus Westungarn und der Freunde des westungarisches Deutschtums." (Gathering of the Viennese Germans from West Hungary and the Friends of the West Hungarian Germans.)

7. "West Hungary" was the name applied to this area in 1918 and early 1919. "Burgenland" did not become the accepted name until late in 1919. The derivation of the latter name is described in Chapter 15.

8. Alfred Walheim was born in Sopron in 1874, but left to study in Vienna. He became an "Austrian citizen" in 1899. He stated as his motto: "German West Hungary to German Austria and with German Austria to Great Germany!" Though all his work concerned West Hungary he envisioned its aim as extending further: "East and West Prussia, the Heinzenland [Burgenland], Carinthia, Upper Silesia; the great gathering has begun. Great Germany is on the march; nothing in the world can stop her." From *Wiener Deutsche Tageszeitung* (Vienna), September 5, 1922; *Ostdeutsche Rundschau* (Vienna), July 8, 1919, October 3, 1919, and April 30, 1920.

9. Karl Wollinger was the son of a Rhineland German who had been settled in Heiligenkreuz by a nationalistic German society with the specific purpose of maintaining and strengthening the German language and culture in the

area. This society had purchased a holding of 99 acres and a mill for the elder Wollinger so that he and his son were among the wealthiest men in the vicinity. Karl Wollinger spent all his lower school years in Germany and then attended the University of Graz. He was evidently an early friend of the Nazi leaders. Although local stories vary, it is certain that Goering visited him at least once and probably twice: once in 1930 (?) and once in 1942.

10. Friedrich Szmudits, "Geschichte der Angliederung des Burgenlandes an Österreich" (Unpublished dissertation, University of Vienna, 1937), p. 98.

11. For a listing of the forty Gemeinden, refer to my *The Political Geography of Burgenland*, National Academy of Sciences—National Research Council Publication 587 (Washington, 1958), p. 55; or doctoral dissertation, same title (University of Wisconsin, 1958), p 79.

12. The act establishing the autonomous province may be found as "Das Volksgesetz VI/1919 über die deutsche Autonomie," in the *Amtsblatt für das Gouvernement Deutsch-Westungarn* 1/1 (Ödenburg, March 1, 1919). The villages and cities included are named in the *Amtsblatt für den Gau Deutsch-Westungarn* 1/6 (Ödenburg, May 8, 1919).

13. Josef Tschida, "Die Stellungnahme der Wiener Presse zum Anschluss und zur Einrichtung des Burgenlandes" (Unpublished Doctoral dissertation, University of Vienna, 1947), p. 298.

14. Günther Berka, *Die tschechische Irredenta in Deutschösterreich* (Graz, 1928), p. 5.

15. K. Friedrich Nowak, *Chaos* (Munich, 1923), p. 240.

16. According to F. J. Vondracek, only France favored the creation of the corridor. The United States objected for ethnographic reasons and Britain because the corridor would be indefensible in time of war. *The Foreign Policy of Czechoslovakia 1918–1935* (New York, 1937), p. 31.

17. Nicolson, *Peacemaking*, p. 240.

18. The corridor dream did not die immediately. In January, 1922, at a meeting in Vienna of the Czechs of Vienna, Lower Austria, and Upper Austria, a former minister of the Czech republic, Zahradnik, said, "The Slavic Corridor from Prague to Trieste must be created." Many of the Slav officials expected Austria to fall apart. Thus a Slovenian, Dr. Janko Brejc, could, with evident sincerity, publish two proposed partitions of Austria. In the first, Burgenland would have been split at its "waist" between Czechoslovakia and Jugoslavia; in the second, it would have been joined to Vienna, Lower Austria, and most of Styria in a rump buffer state, "The Free City of Vienna." Berka, *Tschech. Irredenta*, pp. 6–8, maps pp. 31–32. The post–World War II Czech request for a widening of its bridgehead south of the Danube was interpreted in Austria as a new attempt to form the corridor. *Burgenländisches Volksblatt* (Eisenstadt), August 17, 1946.

19. The Paris discussion concerning Burgenland may be found in greatest detail in David Miller, *My Diary at the Conference of Paris. With Documents* (New York, 1924), Vol. XVI, 227–29, 273; Vol. XIX, 510–13. A good summary of the sequence of events and discussions leading up to the award of the area to Austria is Elizabeth De Weiss, "Dispute for the Burgenland, 1919," *Journal of Central European Affairs*, Vol. III (July, 1943), 147–66.

20. Chancellor Renner (the head of the Austrian delegation) had had contact, through the relatives of his wife, with West Hungary. Heinrich Benedikt, *Geschichte der Republik Österreich* (Munich, 1954), p. 84.

21. For the complete text, in translation, see Burghardt, *Burgenland*, book, pp. 63–64; dissertation, pp. 90–91. The original German text may be found in, Beilage 28, *Bericht über die Tätigkeit der deutschösterreichischen Friedens-delegation in St. Germain en Laye* (Vienna, 1919), pp. 130–31.

22. David Miller, *My Diary*, Vol. XIX, 511.

23. Although the avowed reasons for the award were the German character of the area and the need to grant Vienna a larger food-producing hinterland, various authors have suggested other reasons also. Several observers have felt that Burgenland was intended to serve as a pseudo-corridor for the Czechs. In an article in the Czech paper *Videňsky Dennik*, April 24, 1920, Dr. Karel Zieny stated his hope of winning the Burgenland Croats to the corridor idea; they could establish it themselves from within Austria. Quoted in *Ostdeutsche Rundschau* (Vienna), May 7, 1920. According to Benedikt, *Rep. Öst.*, p. 94, and Walheim, *Wiener Deutsche Tageszeitung*, January 3, 1921, Beneš favored the award of Burgenland to Austria to place a thorn of enmity between Austria and Hungary.

24. The non-Germans are obviously ignored here.

25. The impact of "Wilson's program" favoring "the right of self-determination" can be seen in the many petitions composed in Burgenland villages in 1918–19. Folder number 36 in "Karton 26" of the *Anschluss Archiv* in the Landesarchiv, Eisenstadt, contains many of these petitions. Six protest against the Jugoslavian occupation and all six include, in their short text, the magic words *"auf Wilsons Programm"* and *"Selbstbestimmungsrecht."* There are also fifty-two petitions from villages in the Szt. Gotthárd area, for transfer to Austria; all of these were based on the ideal of the *Selbstbestimmungsrecht*, and several mentioned Wilson specifically. Later the Croats asked for their *Selbstbestimmungsrecht* within the autonomous German province, and after the announcement in 1919 that Burgenland had been awarded to Austria, the representatives of many German villages met to request that their villages remain within Hungary on the basis of *"Wilsons Programm"* of the *Selbstbestimmungsrecht*. The latter word seemed to gain magic qualities; even today it is never paraphrased, there is no synonym or substitute phrase. Always one reads and hears *Selbstbestimmungsrecht*.

26. The number of men included in the bands is not clear. Miltschinsky states that around the time of the plebiscite 100,000 Hungarians were on the Austrian border. This figure seems absurdly high. Missuray-Krúg mentions 200 men in the vicinity of Pinkafeld in August, and the Pan-German Viennese newspaper stated that the Ostermann forces which occupied Sopron consisted of 800 men. Missuray-Krúg boasts that in the battle at Pinkafeld 22 Hungarians beat back 200 Austrians, while at Ágfalva 100 Hungarians drove off 500 Austrians. These figures for the Hungarians are probably too low. What seems clear is that the military operations were on a small scale, and that the Hungarians had come to fight, whereas the Austrian gendarmerie had not. Missuray-Krúg feels that during the fighting the Hungarians numbered fewer than 3,000, and later, at their

maximum strength, approximately 5,000 men. These figures sound plausible. Officially, 1,475 Austrian gendarmes had been assigned to the initial task of the peaceful occupation of Burgenland. The addition of reinforcements and the numbers engaged on Styrian and Lower Austrian territory probably brought the Austrian forces to approximately the same strength as the Hungarians. Killed in the fighting were 29 Hungarians and 30 Austrians.

The best source now available appears to be that of the pro-Hungarian, Lajos Missuray-Krúg, *A Nyugatmagyarországi Felkelés* (The West Hungarian Uprising) (Sopron, 1938). The personal experiences of a nobleman organizer and participant are given by Count Tamás Erdödy, *Habsburgs Weg von Wilhelm zu Briand. Die Memoiren des Grafen Tamás von Erdödy*, eds. Paul Szemere and Erich Czech (Zürich-Leipzig-Vienna, 1931). A Hungarian account dealing principally with the activities of the Kecskemét soldiers is Jenö Héjjas, *A Nyugatmagyarországi Felkelés* (Kecskemét, 1929). Every Austrian publication which deals with the transfer of Burgenland to Austria mentions this border warfare, but a thorough study is lacking. The Miltschinsky work seems to be the best, but is an avowed propaganda piece and deals principally with the subsequent plebiscite. Viktor Miltschinsky, *Das Verbrechen von Ödenburg* (Vienna, 1922). A brief Austrian description from the viewpoint of the gendarmes is *Die Gendarmerie. 10 Jahre österreichische Gendarmerie in Burgenland* (Vienna, 1931). Another Austrian description is that of Alfred Rausnitz, "Die Gendarmerie im Burgenlande," in Franz Neubauer, *Die Gendarmerie im Österreich 1849–1924* (Vienna, 1925), pp. 231–63. Fortunately a fairly thorough and objective report will be available in the *Burgenländische Heimatblätter* (Eisenstadt) sometime in 1962. In its present Magyar manuscript title this is, László Fogarassy, "A Bandaharcok Burgenlandban, 28. August—4. November 1921."

27. The text of the Protocol and the mechanics of the plebiscite may be found in Sarah Wambaugh, *Plebiscites Since the World War* (Washington, 1933).

28. For example: Italy, France, and Hungary, quoted in *Deutschösterreichische Tages-Zeitung* (Vienna), on October 16, 20, and 22, 1921, respectively.

29. "A high Austrian official [said] to me, 'Austria dares not win in the Sopron Plebiscite. Naturally it would be bad if only 10 per cent of the votes were for Austria and 90 per cent for Hungary because then Hungary would immediately come forward with the assertion that the vote in the remainder of Burgenland would be against the *Anschluss*. But it would be equally bad if 60 per cent voted for Austria and only 40 per cent for Hungary because a victory for Austria would be contrary to the spirit of the Venetian compromise. We must, therefore, so regulate the agitation that Austria will be not too far in the minority but must also endeavor to hinder the attainment of a majority. On my word we must prepare for an honorable defeat!' " *Deutschösterreichische Tages-Zeitung*, October 25, 1921.

Current research supports this view. According to Walter Dujmowitz, Chancellor Schober concluded at Venice that he could retain most of Burgenland only by agreeing to the cession of Sopron. Austria was incapable of driving the Hungarian bands out of Burgenland and could turn to no one for active military support. However, the Hungarians announced their willingness to surrender the remainder of Burgenland if Sopron were returned to Hungary. Since Schober had no alternative other than losing the entire territory, he acquiesced. Therefore the subsequent plebiscite may have been little more than a face-saving method of accomplishing the return of Sopron to Hungary, and the furor over the justness of the vote of little more than speculative importance. It is to be hoped that Mr. Dujmowitz will treat this matter in detail in his forthcoming doctoral dissertation, "Die Angliederung des Burgenlandes an Österreich" (University of Vienna, 1963?).

30. For example, *Wiener Mittag*, September 5, 26, 28, October 3, 1921; *Deutschösterreichische Tages-Zeitung*, September 22, 29, 1921; *Reichspost* (Vienna), September 26, 1921.

31. *Deutschösterreichische Tages-Zeitung*, September 22, 1921.

32. *Tagespost* (Graz), December 14, 1921.

33. The Socialist leader, Dr. Karl Renner, later termed the plebiscite a "*Komodie*" in "Wie es zur Befreiung des Burgenlandes kam," *Die Gendarmerie*, p. 10.

34. Viktor Miltschinsky, *Verbrechen*, p. 106. Other pro-Austrian literature includes: J. K. Homma, "Burgenlands Vereinigung mit Österreich," *Österreich in Geschichte und Literatur* (Vienna), Jg. 4, Sonderheft (1960), 18–27; Rudolf Kiszling, "Das Problem Ödenburg," *ibid.*, pp. 28–31; Heinrich Kunnert, "Vor Zehn Jahren," *Burgenland Vierteljahrshefte für Landeskunde, Heimatschutz und Denkmalpflege* (Eisenstadt), Band II (1929); Kunnert, "Im ungarischen Nationalstaat," in *Burgenland Landeskunde* (Vienna, 1951), pp. 329–46; Friedrich Szmudits, "Angliederung." As sources for their articles Homma and Kiszling mention the works of Kunnert, Szmudits, and Miltschinsky. Szmudits has listed Kunnert and Miltschinsky as sources. In a telephone conversation, Dr. Kunnert mentioned Wambaugh and Miltschinsky as his sources for the figures. An investigation of the Wambaugh study indicates that she received her pro-Austrian figures and charges from Miltschinsky. Therefore all the pro-Austrian charges rest eventually on the Miltschinsky work.

The best Hungarian report is probably that of Lajos Missuray-Krúg, "Sopron nagy napjai" (Sopron's Day of Greatness), *A Sopron vármegye népszavazas emlékalbuma* (Sopron, 1932), pp. 45–72. Another Hungarian source is Ernö Traeger, "A Sopron népszavazás" (The Sopron Plebiscite), in Gustáv Thirring, *Sopron: Civitas Fidelissima* (Sopron, 1925); this has appeared in translation as *Die Volksabstimmung in Sopron* (Sopron, 1928); unfortunately this is little more than a sentimental paean in homage to the loyalty of the city. The report of the Swedish professor, Björn Collinder, "A leghívebb város" (The Most Loyal City), *Scarbantia. Helytörténeti Adatok Sopron és Sopron Vármegye Multjából* 3. Szám (Sopron, 1938), 11 pp., is very brief and admittedly based on the work of Missuray-Krúg.

The best and the only unbiased, complete report remains that of Sarah Wambaugh, *Plebiscites*. The closest approach to an unbiased eyewitness report that I have found is that of Dr. P. Haller, *Der Ungarndeutsche* (Munich), September 20, 1959, p. 5. Many of the reports of the ill-fated Burgenland government in Sopron, the complaints of the Pan-German Oedenburger Heimatdienst society, and charges of corruption by individuals in Sopron may be found strewn through the mass of materials concerning the first years of Burgenland in the "Kartonen" of the *Anschluss Archiv*, stored in the Landesarchiv, Eisenstadt. As far as I can tell, no thorough study of the materials in these cartons has yet been made; a friend interested in the plebiscite feels that a complete assembling and interpretation of the materials would require two years. There are forty-four such cartons, and I admit that I have looked through only a few. Yet it seems clear that since the complaints included may be the results of the rumors of the time and may overlap, they probably would be impossible to evaluate adequately and hence would add little tangible to the Miltschinsky charges. All the official voting records remain in Sopron, Hungary, and by now it would be virtually impossible to judge the listings of the eligible voters. Any attempt to do so would require not only an intimate knowledge of the city, but also several years of work, assuming, of course, that the scholar had complete and continual access to all the records, and could afford to remain in Sopron for the required length of time.

35. The most that I could find was the statement that "numerous Burgenlanders, including also many refugees from Burgenland, appeared in parliament [to speak to party leaders]." *Deutschösterreichische Tages-Zeitung*, September 25, 1921. I found none of the reports of arriving refugees and their tales of terror, none of the requests for beds, clothing, and financial contributions which normally accompany the sudden arrival of several thousand fleeing persons.

36. Miltschinsky, *Verbrechen*, p. 106.

37. "I have found no concrete facts as evidence that the Germans in Ödenburg . . . were in any way hindered from voting in the plebiscite. . . . Acts of force certainly occurred in several of the villages in Burgenland which would shortly be joined to Austria, but within Ödenburg itself, definitely not." Haller, *Ungarndeutsche*, p. 5. Eye witnesses I was able to interview in Sopron maintain that the "terror" is an invention of the embittered German nationalists.

38. Wambaugh, *Plebiscites*, Vol. I, 297.

39. See *Grenzpost* (Sopron), March 19, 20, 22 & 23, 1919. Also, Szmudits, "Angliederung," p. 114, quoting from *Die Oedenburger Zeitung*, March 21, 1919.

40. *Deutschösterreichische Tages-Zeitung*, October 8, 1921.

41. *Ibid.*, October 3, 1919.

42. *Ibid.*, August 28, 1921.

43. "One must understand the feelings in Heinzenland [Burgenland]. . . . That is primarily the fear of a return of the 'Red' danger. The remembrance of the horrors of the Red period sticks to their very bones. For months now the Hungarian propaganda has described the terrors of Red Austria in the most somber colors. . . . The burgher trembles before the returning refugee, before the Austrian soldier, before the workers. . . . The frightened ones do not consider that of the officials which Austria has sent into Burgenland there has not been one Communist or Bolshevik; to him everything Austrian is already tinted with Red." Walheim, *ibid.*, August 27, 1921.

44. Miltschinsky attributes this low Austrian vote to the extreme "terror" in the village. *Verbrechen*, p. 106. The other two villages within the plebiscite

area were Nagyczenk and Balf. *Christliches Oedenburger Tagblatt,* August 29, 1919.

45. Haller, *Ungarndeutsche,* p. 5.

46. *Deutschösterreichische Tages-Zeitung,* November 9, 1921.

47. Walheim warned that the Burgenlanders considered the Austrians to be *Fremden* ("strangers"). *Ibid.,* August 27, 1921. Haller states, "Also: I have a high regard for Austria, but one dare not forget that according to the impression prevailing then the concepts 'German' and 'Austrian' did not have the same meaning. At that time we German-Hungarians, whose forefathers had immigrated from all parts of Germany and not only from Austria, could hardly consider ourselves to be Austrian. The pro-Austrian viewpoint suffered its fall through the stepmotherly way Austria had handled the *Ausgleich.*" *Ungarndeutsche,* p. 5. Of course many of the German nationalists voted for Austria because they looked upon union with Austria as the first step in their union with all the German peoples. The Lutherans evidently acted in this way; the religious influence on the vote and the movement to Austria is discussed in Chapter 14.

48. "The Magyar was lord, the admired, loved, feared, and hated lord. People were accustomed to his dominance; in good and evil one had become satisfied with him. Now comes, as many believe, a leap into the unknown. One should exchange the old lord for a new one of whom no one knows how he will conduct himself." Walheim, *Deutschösterreichische Tages-Zeitung,* August 28, 1921.

49. ("God be thanked—remained true/loyal"), Missuray-Krúg, "Sopron nagy napjai," p. 64.

50. Traeger, *Die Volksabstimmung in Sopron,* p. 31.

51. *Deutschösterreichische Tages-Zeitung,* October 8, 1921.

52. During the struggle for control of this area, Burgenland was twice proclaimed an independent country. In December, 1918, when there seemed little hope that Austria would ask for the area, much less obtain it, a group of the Viennese Pan-German propagandists smuggled arms into West Hungary and proclaimed a Heinzenland republic at Mattersdorf. However, no spontaneous uprising followed this proclamation, and it is doubtful if any Burgenlanders except those in Mattersburg and Vienna knew anything of this incident. In October, 1921, after the Hungarian "volunteer bands" had occupied Burgenland, a new Hungarian republic, the Lajta Banat, was proclaimed in Oberwart (Felsőőr), the Magyar center of Burgenland. How much support this "republic" won from groups other than the Magyars is questionable. Since the Protocol of Venice followed within ten days, nothing more was heard of this new "state" either. Both proclamations were obviously attempts to use the principle of self-determination as a means of preventing the other side from keeping the territory. Surprisingly, none of the Austrian works dealing with the transfer to Austria does more than mention the Mattersburg incident (and the way it is mentioned always leads one to suppose that local peasants had proclaimed the republic). The only Austrian work that gives any details is an article not yet published, Fred Sinowatz, "Zur Geschichte des Landesnamens." This manuscript is expected to appear shortly in the *Burgenländische Heimatblätter* (Eisen-

stadt). The proclamation of the Lajta Banat may be found in Missuray-Krúg, *A Nyugatmagyarországi Felkelés,* pp. 183–92; Erdödy, *Memoiren,* pp. 264–74; and the *Oberwarther Sonntags-Zeitung* (Oberwart), October 9, 1921.

CHAPTER 11

1. It must be remembered that since the few urban centers near the border area were all in Hungary, the only other facilities available for the commission would have been in the large palaces. Even today Burgenland has very poor accommodations for the traveler.

2. In 1960 the retiring director of the Burgenländisches Landesarchiv und -bibliothek, Hofrat Homma, made this assertion in a scholarly publication. He attributed the Hungarian retention of Albértkázmérpuszta, Mexikopuszta, Pinkamindszentpuszta, Pornóapáti, Magyar and Német Keresztes, Szentpéterfa, several Croatian villages near Rechnitz, four German villages northeast of Szent Gotthárd, and the east end of the Köszeg Range all to the influence of the Magyar magnates on the commission. J. K. Homma, "Burgenlands Vereinigung mit Österreich," *Österreich in Geschichte und Literatur,* Sonderheft (Vienna, 1960), p. 26.

3. Article 29 of the Treaty of St. Germain specified the role of the boundary commission as follows: "They shall have the power not only of fixing those portions which are defined as 'a line to be fixed on the ground', but also where a request to that effect is made by one of the States concerned, and the Commission is satisfied that it is desirable to do so, of revising portions defined by administrative boundaries; . . . . They shall endeavor . . . to follow as nearly as possible the descriptions given in the Treaties taking into account as far as possible administrative boundaries and local economic interests." Allied and Associated Powers, *Conditions of Peace with Austria. Treaty of Peace Between the Principal Allied and Associated Powers and Austria* (Washington, 1919), p. 25.

4. The German *Bezirk,* or the Hungarian *járás* is translated as "county" throughout this study, since it approximates in size and function the United States and Canadian county.

5. Article 27, Point 5 of the Treaty of St. Germain specified that the boundary was to be fixed west of Pustasomorja "and east of Andau, Nikelsdorf, D. Jahrndorf and Kittsee"; and that Mexikopuszta "as well as the entire Einser canal" were to remain in Hungary. *Conditions of Peace with Austria,* p. 25.

6. *Der Freie Burgenländer* (Eisenstadt), January 19, 1930.

7. At least three medieval roads crossed the former border into "Old Austria," at Schwarzenbach, at Landsee, and in the Zöbern valley, but in 1922 these were unusable for trucking or for public transportation. The most important of these, the Zöbern valley route, between Köszeg and Kirchschlag, Lower Austria, was not suitable for public and commercial use until August, 1929.

8. In March, 1957, the *Lehrer* in Moschendorf described to me the events of the previous autumn, when the border was suddenly thrown open. At that time

the entire population of Pinkamindszent (technically a "Magyar" village), even the gendarmerie, came with flags to Moschendorf (a "German" village). Many people then saw their parents, children, and cousins for the first time in a decade. The next day they all returned in a great religious procession to the church. The people of Moschendorf treated all of Pinkamindszent to meals, drinks, and dancing in the *Gasthaus*. Hours of conversation bridged the silences of a decade. As we were discussing these events the wife of the *Lehrer* sadly shook her head and said, "Und es war alles umsonst." ("And it was all in vain.") Though the border was freely open for only about a week, those meetings reaffirmed the close contacts of the peasants living along both sides of the boundary. It will require at least several decades more of complete separation before the local peasants cease to be pained by the barbaric wall located in their midst.

9. The treaty terms practically determined this location of the boundary. Article 27, Point 5 stated, ". . . a line to be fixed on the ground passing . . . west of the Radkersburg-Szentgotthard road and east of the villages of Nagyfalva [Mogersdorf], Nemetlak [Deutsch Minihof], and Rabakeresztur [Heiligenkreuz]." *Conditions of Peace with Austria*, p. 24.

10. These positions were "strong" in terms of the methods of warfare in use at that time, but they still bear a strong psychological impact.

11. Robert Sieger, "Natürliche Räume und Lebensräume," *Petermanns Geographische Mitteilungen* (Gotha), Band LXIX, Heft 11/12 (1923), 254. *Verkehr* denotes all kinds of movement, not only "trade," but "trade areas" seems to be the most concise way of translating *Verkehrsgebiete*.

12. The placing of the boundary to the southeast of Köszeg and to the east of Szent Gotthárd would have separated these centers from portions of their hinterlands, but these two centers are faced, in any case, with the growing importance of Szombathely and Körmend. The transfer of Köszeg, and the five villages between that city and Rechnitz, would have made feasible the completion of a north-south railroad joining five of the seven counties of Burgenland. Had these changes occurred, Köszeg would undoubtedly have gained economically by becoming the dominating link between all of middle (and northern beyond) Burgenland, and all of southern Burgenland. Similarly Szent Gotthárd would have been the link between the southern tip and the remainder of the province.

13. Nikitsch, Krt. Minihof, and Schachendorf are Croatian. South of Sopron every Croatian village that was given a free choice chose Hungary.

14. In his introduction to the 1943 edition of *Peacemaking, 1919*, Harold Nicolson lists a number of recommendations to future peacemakers, on the basis of the experiences of 1919. The seventh of these is, "No single theory of settlement must be allowed to take precedence over other theories. . . . The Conference of Powers was unduly obsessed by the conception of nationality contained in the formula of 'Self Determination.'" P. xvi.

15. Incidents continue to occur along this boundary. In the two years 1957–58 one Burgenland newspaper announced the following incidents: February 2, 1957, a border violation; February 23, 1957, five Austrians abducted across the border; May 11, 1957, a Hungarian girl was killed trying to cross the boundary; June 1, 1957, two incidents in which a married couple and a fleeing soldier were wounded; August 9, 1958, a Hungarian crossed successfully by pole-vaulting

across the mine field. (The newspaper stated that six successful escapes occurred that July.) August 16, 1958, an Austrian trying to photograph the boundary was shot at; August 23 and 30, 1958, contained information concerning diplomatic protests relating to the border incidents. In November, 1959, a Burgenlander who, while drunk, came onto the boundary by mistake, was shot by the Hungarian guards. In December, 1960, Hungarian guards crossed sixty yards into Austrian territory to drag back a refugee who had been wounded crossing the mine field. For a description in English of the boundary and some of its effects on the local people, see Austrian Information Service, *Austrian Information* (New York, August 23, 1958), p. 7.

CHAPTER 12

1. "Old Austria" was a term frequently used to refer to all of Austria except Burgenland.

2. In 1930 the largest landholders in Burgenland were:

Paul Eszterházy	58,432 hectares
Erzh. Friedrich Habsburg-Lotharingen	8,364
Paul Draskovitsch	4,593
Sopron City	3,475
Heiligenkreuz Monastery	3,244
Count Harrach	2,835
Gabriel Batthyány	2,018
Countess Jenny Pállfy-Erdödy	2,002
Bishopric of Győr	1,886
Baron Thyssen-Bornemisza	1,508
Theodor Batthyány	1,300
Siegmund Batthyány	1,295
Alexander Erdödy	1,098
Jakob Zichy-Mesko	1,082

Jahrbuch und Adressbuch der Land- und Forstwirtschaft. Ergänzungsband 1930/1931 (Vienna, 1930).

3. After 1671 the Jewish communities in Eisenstadt, Mattersburg, Deutschkreutz, Lackenbach, Kobersdorf, Frauenkirchen, and Kittsee were under the direct protection of Prince Eszterházy, who exercised his noble prerogative to protect them from various taxes and payments (e.g. *Schutzgeldes* and *Haussteuer*). The Jewish communities of southern Burgenland, Güssing, Stadt Schlaining, and Rechnitz, developed after the expulsion of the Jews from adjacent Styria in 1496. Ghettos of astonishing size developed in small villages. In 1818, Mattersburg, Deutschkreutz, and Rechnitz, each of which had a population of approximately 4,000, contained 1,400, 895, and 738 Jews respectively. Kittsee, with a population of less than 3,000, had a ghetto of 789 Jews. In Eisenstadt, the Jewish ghetto was a separately incorporated township, Unterberg,

from which all gentiles were excluded after sundown; this continued until the entry of the Nazis in 1938.

4. In the support of the clerics, priests, and pastors, West Hungary presented an anachronism that was to plague Burgenland. In Old Austria the clergy was supported by funds from the state, based partly on a complicated compensation for past confiscations; in Hungary the parishes were under the protection and support of the local nobility. Of the 157 Catholic parishes in Burgenland in 1938, 70 were supported by Prince Eszterházy. Of greater impact yet was the continuance of the medieval barter payment, the *Giebigkeiten,* of the villages to their clergy. This endured until 1929, when a payment of 4,250,000 schillings finally cancelled these old agreements. For a listing of the *Giebigkeiten* see Burghardt, *The Political Geography of Burgenland,* National Academy of Sciences—National Research Council Publication 587 (Washington, 1958), p. 134; or, doctoral dissertation, same title (University of Wisconsin, 1958), p. 195.

5. Within the last 150 years Baumhacken has become Pamhagen, and Baumern, Pama.

6. On a field trip of professional geographers into the area around Lake Neusiedl, most of the guides referred to this territory as really a part of Hungary. Among Viennese, Burgenland is referred to less flatteringly, as "Austria's Balkans," or is described as primitive, simple, dusty, and run-down, with terrible roads.

7. *Deutschösterreichische Tages-Zeitung* (Vienna), August 21, 1921.

8. Ludwig Adamovich and Georg Froehlich, *"Die österreichischen Verfassungsgesetze des Bundes und der Länder* (Vienna, 1925), p. 58.

9. *Neue Wiener Tagblatt* (Vienna), January 29, 1920.

10. "Bundesverfassungsgesetz . . . über die Stellung des Burgenlandes als selbständiges und gleichberechtiges Land im Bund und über seine vorläufige Einrichtung," Adamovich and Froehlich, *Verfassungsgesetze,* p. 396.

11. Mattersburg County was at this time the governmental center of Burgenland, so that this delegation probably represented more a vested interest than an expression of the desires of the majority of the population.

12. Ernst C. Hellbling, *Österreichische Verfassungs- und Verwaltungsgeschichte* (Vienna, 1956), pp. 433–34.

13. "Who knows of a capital?" (Who knows where we can find a capital?). This was the title of an article by Walheim, *Österreichische Volkszeitung* (Vienna), February 24, 1924.

14. Adamovich and Froehlich, *Verfassungsgesetze,* p. 396.

15. *Der Freie Burgenländer* (Sauerbrunn), March 2, 1924.

16. *Österreichische Volkszeitung,* June 1, 1924.

17. *Ibid.,* February 24, 1924.

18. *Ibid.*

19. *Ibid.*

20. *Der Freie Burgenländer,* January 28, 1923.

21. The ommission of Oberwart from the list of candidates is interesting. Oberwart was the most important center of the south and was second only to Eisenstadt in population. The Peasants' party delegate from Oberwart ad-

mitted that he favored Oberwart but had nominated Pinkafeld instead; he said only that for reasons which he would not mention Oberwart had not offered itself as a candidate. No other reasons were ever given. However it is significant that chauvinistic pro-German statements were common at the time, and Pinkafeld was advanced as a completely German center, with a glorious German history. Hungarian connections were treated as odious, and Oberwart was the largest Magyar township in Austria and had been the locale for the proclamation of the Lajta Banat "republic" in 1921. As one Burgenlander said, the capital city of Burgenland could hardly be placed in a Magyar community.

22. The importance of Wiener Neustadt to Burgenland may be deduced from the maps of traffic density in Fritz Bodo, "Wiener Neustadt als Verkehr- und Industriemittelpunkt des südöstlichen Niederösterreichs," *Unsere Heimat* (Vienna), Band II (1929), 22, 34, 35. The extent of the Wiener Neustadt market area in Burgenland in 1934 is depicted on maps 45, 46, Bodo, *Burgenland Atlas* (Vienna, 1940), p. 22.

23. During the first two years of the dispute concerning the selection of the capital, the Oberwart paper mentioned the question just once, and then in only a general way. This silence was broken on December 16, 1923, when the entire first page was devoted to the just-announced candidacy of Pinkafeld. Three times more that winter the newspaper advocated the selection of Pinkafeld, and then, again, silence. During the twelve months preceding the decision, the *Oberwarther Sonntags-Zeitung* never mentioned the matter.

24. The other newspaper of the south, the *Güssinger Zeitung*, showed even less interest, since it never advocated the candidacy of Pinkafeld (which was distant). During those three and a half years, this paper mentioned the capital question exactly twice, and then briefly, without supporting any of the contending townships. The decision was announced under a small headline, "The new seat of the provisional government of Burgenland." The article mentioned briefly and casually that Eisenstadt had been selected; most of the article lamented the loss of Sopron (May 10, 1925).

25. Actually, if the vote had been carried through as planned, the result would have meant a continuation of the bizarre status quo; Eisenstadt was to continue as the seat of the Landtag meetings, but the actual provincial government was to remain in Sauerbrunn. Evidently the expectation was that a new meeting hall for the Landtag would be built in Sauerbrunn or Mattersburg.

26. A two-thirds majority of the 29 members present was necessary for election. Rather than have each delegate choose one candidate, the contending townships were voted on one at a time. The first ballot was indecisive. Pinkafeld had 7 for, 19 against, and 3 abstentions; Eisenstadt had 18 for and 11 against; Sauerbrunn, 12 for, 12 against, and 5 abstentions. After a recess Eisenstadt was elected with a vote of 20 for and 9 against. *Stenographisches Protokoll. 28. Sitzung der II Wahlperiode des Burgenländischen Landtages. Donnerstag den 30. April 1925* (Sauerbrunn, 1925), pp. 371–81.

27. Eisenstadt is now always referred to as the *Landeshauptstadt* ("capital") rather than the *Sitz der Landesregierung*. The dream of obtaining Sopron has vanished. However, several officials in Eisenstadt expressed the opinion (in 1957) that if Sopron were reunited to Burgenland the provincial capital would

be moved there forthwith despite the recent construction of facilities in Eisenstadt.

CHAPTER 13

1. Austrian writers have accused Hungary of having deliberately suppressed industrial and commercial development in the border area; however, the lack of development since 1921 suggests that the causes may lie elsewhere than in governmental policy. Hungarians did develop the economy of the larger towns in western Hungary, but these favored spots remained in Hungary.

2. Provincial Vice Premier Leser: "The federal government is at fault in losing Ödenburg [Sopron], therefore it must pay the consequences and contribute the necessary means." *Der Freie Burgenländer* (Sauerbrunn), July 8, 1923. Provincial Premier Rauhofer: "Burgenland with its industrious population is undoubtedly *lebensfähig* but still cannot raise the sum needed to construct the facilities necessary to its existence. The credit must come from the federal government." *Burgenländische Heimat* (Sauerbrunn), November 9, 1924.

3. *Oberwarther Sonntags-Zeitung*, March 29, 1925.

4. *Burgenländische Heimat*, June 1, 1924.

5. *Österreichische Volkszeitung* (Vienna), June 1, 1924.

6. *Güssinger Zeitung,* February 3, 1924.

7. *Der Freie Burgenländer*, February 10, 1924.

8. *Güssinger Zeitung*, October 4, 1925.

9. *Österreichische Volkszeitung*, June 1, 1924.

10. *Burgenländische Heimat*, March 22, 1925.

11. For the budget of 1929 see Burghardt, *The Political Geography of Burgenland*, National Academy of Sciences—National Research Council Publication 587 (Washington, 1958), p. 334; or, doctoral dissertation, same title (University of Wisconsin, 1958), p. 512.

12. As late as 1930, 22 large owners possessed a quarter of the land in the province. Prince Paul Eszterházy, though all his holdings were in the northern four of the seven counties, was, with 144,385 acres (58,432 hectares), by far the largest landowner in Austria, with 15 per cent of the total area of Burgenland. Though much of this holding was forested, it included some of the finest agricultural land in the province. Forty-three per cent of the area of fertile, treeless Neusiedl County was contained in the 52 holdings (0.87 per cent of the county total number) of 100 hectares (247 acres) or larger.

13. In November, 1929, the federal government purchased 554 *joch* of land from Eszterházy to be divided among small landholders. This left Eszterházy with 84,211 *joch*.

14. It is probable that this type of large-scale commercial agriculture is no longer considered to be a profitable venture. Considering the necessary investment, the production of food does not offer a financial return comparable to

that of industry. Especially in Central Europe, food prices are very low in relation to the prices of manufactured products.

15. In the two years 1922–23 (immediately prior to the United States restrictions on immigration), 17,641 persons migrated from Austria to the U.S.A.; of these, 12,019 were from Burgenland, which had less than 5 per cent of the national population. This emigration included 4.2 per cent of the total population of the province (286,000) and was especially notable in Güssing County. In those two years, of the total inhabitants of the village, 16 per cent left Tudersdorf, 9 per cent left Gaas, 8 per cent left Strem, Tobaj, and Reinersdorf, 7 per cent left Moschendorf.

The movement continues, although at a lower rate. Emigration of Burgenlanders is now facilitated by the fact that so many moved overseas before and after World War I. Many of these couples returned to Burgenland as soon as they had saved a few thousand dollars, or at the time of the great depression. Very commonly in such families one or more of the children had been born in the United States. After World War II these children, now of legal age, claimed American citizenship by birth and were able to enter the U.S.A. Being industrious they quickly established themselves and then brought over the rest of the family. Almost every Burgenland family has a relative somewhere in America. If the opportunity to move to America exists, very few of the young Burgenlanders hesitate to act upon it. Frequently one hears stories of parents deserted by their last son, on land they cannot work without him, because he (or very often his wife) insists on moving to America.

16. Provincial Premier Rauhofer, *Burgenländische Heimat*, November 9, 1924.

17. For a map and a detailed discussion of all the railroad proposals see Burghardt, *Burgenland*, book, pp. 152–58; dissertation, pp. 223–31.

18. This link connected the end of the Pinka valley line, which the Hungarians had built from Szombathely to Pinkafeld, to the "Aspang Line," which ran from Vienna to Graz over the Wechsel Pass. This connection was completed with great fanfare on November 15, 1926.

19. The three links were: Wulkaprodersdorf to Markt St. Martin (over the Sieggraben Saddle of the Sopron Range), Liebing to Oberwart (across the Bernstein hills west of the Köszeg Range), and Grosspetersdorf through Güssing to Mogersdorf (across two of the broadest and most densely forested of the terraces).

20. For a map of the bus lines see Burghardt, *Burgenland*, book, p. 164; dissertation, p. 240.

21. For a map and discussion of the division see *ibid.*, book, pp. 173–75; dissertation, pp. 255–57. The Graz *Tagespost* had labeled the first decision as "the only correct one, the best one that one could ever encounter" (May 26, 1938); the newspaper maintained a complete silence on the second decision.

22. *Neues Österreich* (Vienna), May 29, 1945.

23. *Freies Burgenland* (Eisenstadt), September 27, 1946.

24. "143 Verfassungsgesetz vom 29. August 1945 über die Wiedererrichtung des selbständiges Landes Burgenland (Burgenlandgesetz)," *Staatsgesetzblatt für die Republik Österreich, Jahrgang 1945* (Vienna, 1945), p. 191.

25. The Nazi-introduced laws allowing civil marriage and divorce, driving on the right side of the road, and the secularization of the Burgenland schools, have remained in force.

26. *Freies Burgenland,* September 27, 1946.

CHAPTER 14

1. These riots were an outgrowth of events which had occurred within Burgenland. On January 30, 1927, the *Frontkämpfvereinigung,* which was virtually an armed force of the Christian party, held a meeting in Schattendorf, a village about halfway between Mattersburg and Sopron. The *Schutzbund,* the armed force of the Socialist party, evidently decided to break up the meeting. The members of the *Schutzbund* marched into Schattendorf, and while some marched to the railroad station to intercept a small group of *Front* members who were arriving from Vienna, the remainder demonstrated outside the inn in which the *Front* was holding its meeting. In the uproar at the inn, shots were fired and two people, an elderly railroad worker and a seven-year-old boy, were killed. The sons of the innkeeper were charged with the shooting. Since Burgenland did not have its own high court, the trial was held in Vienna. On July 14, 1927, the jury freed the defendants on all counts. On the next day the Socialists of Vienna staged a demonstration which rapidly became a riot. In the ensuing three days of street fighting and general strike, eighty-nine people were killed, the Palace of Justice was burnt down, and fear of a Marxist revolution gripped all of Austria. The Marxists in Bruck an der Mur, Styria, actually proclaimed the "Dictatorship of the Proletariat" and ruled the city for two days. Burgenland remained quiet throughout the disturbances, but the three freed defendants fled across the adjacent boundary into Hungary. From this time on, armed forces of most of the political parties proliferated throughout Austria. Information from all newspapers, but primarily from the *Arbeiterzeitung* (Vienna) and *Der Freie Burgenländer* (Eisenstadt).

2. Evidently there is still a fairly widespread fear that eventually the Hungarians will try to regain the area. One person mentioned a story, which he insisted had been proven to be correct, that in 1938, when Hitler occupied Austria, Admiral Horthy, then Regent of Hungary, asked Hitler for the return of Burgenland. This person maintains that this request was one of the factors which motivated the incorporation of Burgenland into the neighboring provinces; in that way the old boundary disappeared. Oddly enough, the Communists are considered by some to be less of a danger than the expatriates, since the former think in international terms and do not regard the location of boundaries as all-important; nor do they sympathize with the feudal Hungarian past and its symbols. The expatriates are thought to be the most extreme of chauvinists, who would assuredly press demands for the lost territories if they ever gained power. (It seems most unlikely that they could ever gain power.) One person went so far as to mention the possible ways that a Hungarian advance into Burgenland could take place. In case of a European war the Russians could

move westward through Hungary and might well give Burgenland back to their ally; or, if the Soviet empire collapsed suddenly and chaos developed in Central Europe, the Western Powers might give Burgenland to Hungary as a reward for her gallant opposition to the Communists. In any case, he, and evidently others, fear that when the pressure of Soviet might is relaxed from the area, the Hungarians will again look towards their lost lands. One woman in a northern village stated that she would have preferred her village to remain with Lower Austria, because then the Hungarians could not come back. What is intriguing to the outsider is the belief that the Hungarians will never forget the kingdom of St. Stephen, and that the Austrians will not be able to prevent the Hungarians from regaining the area.

On the other hand, the Hungarians I have spoken to have expressed no interest whatsoever in the reacquisition of Burgenland. In comparison with the other lost territories, Burgenland is insignificant in area, population, or wealth; it also contains no sites of Hungarian historic importance. What Hungarian revisionist feelings still exist seem to be focused principally on Transylvania.

3. Significantly, a story was circulated in Burgenland that the Russians were all set to march into Austria on November 6, 1956 (the date of the American elections and two days after the attack on Budapest), but that on the previous evening President Eisenhower had called in the Russian ambassador and warned him that the planes were ready to deliver the atom bomb if Russia attacked Austria.

4. The details for this flag were selected from the medieval banners of Güssing and Forchtenstein because "their ancestors came from the west," and "both had feuds with the Hungarian crown." Walheim, "Wie das Burgenland zu seinem Wappen gekommen ist," *Österreichische Volkszeitung* (Vienna), February 10, 1924.

5. The expelled Germans reportedly had all been members of the Volksbund der Deutschen in Ungarn, a nationalistic German organization introduced from Germany. Those Germans who had not joined this organization could remain, and there are still many people in Sopron who can speak German. However, within Hungary I heard the assertion that the wealth of the German-Hungarian at times affected his position; those that were wealthy or had fine homes were more liable to deportation than their poorer compatriots. One village name has disappeared from the map of western Hungary; Harka (Harkau) is now known as Magyarfalva (Hungarian village). Harka had had a militantly pro-German Lutheran pastor in 1921 and was the village with the highest percentage (90 per cent) for Austria in the plebiscite.

6. The annual provincial celebration, the *Martinifest* (St. Martin's Feast), scheduled to be held on the feast day of the saint, November 11, was postponed for over a month and a half because of the events in Hungary. This postponement was decided upon before there was any hint of the crowds of refugees that were to come from Hungary.

7. Burgenland 87 per cent German, Carinthia 94, Tirol and Salzburg 98, Vienna and Vorarlberg 99, Lower Austria, Upper Austria, and Styria 100 per cent.

8. These minorities tend to be overlooked within Austria; in contrast the

Carinthian Slovenes are well publicized. The official booklet of the Federal Press Service of Austria, *Austria, Facts and Figures* (Vienna, 1958), states (p. 28) that "Carinthia is the only Austrian province with an appreciable racial minority among its population. Although about 96% of Carinthians are German speaking, 4% profess Slovene as their native language."

9. Burgenland 14 per cent Protestant, Carinthia 10, Vienna 8, Upper Austria 7, Salzburg and Styria 6, Tirol, Vorarlberg, and Lower Austria 3 per cent.

10. The other two linguistic groups are similarly subdivided, but it is the German-Magyar and the German-Croat figures that are significant, since they must indicate the members of the minority groups who have come to feel themselves, or felt it advisable to declare themselves, as being German first and members of the minority group second.

11. In April, 1922, Karl Wollinger had told a political meeting in Jennersdorf, "We will have our province German. He who is not with us we tell: Get out of here, out of this German land!" Alfred Walheim, in a visit to Eisenstadt, complained that he could still hear people "babbling Magyar." *Deutschöster-reichische Tages-Zeitung* (Vienna), April 7, 1922, and *Burgenländisches Volksblatt* (Eisenstadt), September 23, 1923.

12. Articles 66–69 of the Treaty of St. Germain had guaranteed the rights of the minorities of Austria. Allied and Associated Powers, *Conditions of Peace with Austria. Treaty of Peace Between the Principal Allied and Associated Powers and Austria* (Washington, 1919), pp. 40–42.

13. The number of Magyar language schools declined from nine schools with 2,306 students in 1921, to three schools with 723 students in 1951. Hans Nowak, "Das Erziehungswesen," in *Burgenland, Landeskunde* (Vienna, 1951), p. 540. At present there are still three Magyar schools.

14. A group of the former delegates to the Hungarian parliament met, in 1921, to demand complete autonomy for Burgenland and to protest against the influx of gendarmes, bureaucrats, and political leaders from Old Austria. This local cadre was able to gain partial control of the Christian party within Burgenland.

15. For details of the Germanization of the Croats of Stegersbach see Thomas M. Barker, "The Croatian Minority of Burgenland," *Journal of Central European Affairs*, Vol. XIX (April, 1959), 32–56.

16. In Eisenhüttl, when the present schoolmaster (who is fluent in German, Croatian, and Magyar) arrived in the 1920's, only three families in the village could speak German and most of the children knew no German. The parents were, however, not interested in, or did not consider it necessary, having their children learn Croatian in school. The peasants knew Croatian and some Magyar but would henceforth need a workable knowledge of German if they were to move outside the township confines. Therefore, the emphasis in local education was placed by the peasants themselves on learning German.

Probably Eisenhüttl could, nevertheless, have remained primarily Croatian if it could have joined with Heugraben to form one Croatian parish. However, for geographic reasons the parish boundaries were so delimited that these two Croatian villages were connected as "missions" (*Filiale*) to different German-speaking parishes. In Eisenhüttl the hymns sung at Mass remained Croatian until 1955, though the sermons had long since been held in German; now all parts of the service (except the Latin) are in German. In 1951 Eisenhüttl was listed as containing 178 Germans and 67 Croats, with 29 German-Croats in the German total. Within three decades the village had changed from Croatian to German.

The Croatian Culture Society has attempted to halt the process of assimilation before it becomes irreversible. After the close of World War II, a letter was sent to the schoolmaster in Eisenhüttl advising him to begin giving one hour's instruction in Croatian per week. The schoolmaster interpreted this move to represent the first step in an attempt to change the village back to Croatian. He brought the matter before the Bürgermeister (mayor) and the Gemeinderat (village council); they voted against the introduction of the Croatian language into the school curriculum. The secretary of the Croatian Culture Society thereupon made a special trip to Eisenhüttl to speak before the Gemeinderat, but that body still refused. In attitude as well as in language Eisenhüttl was rapidly becoming German, and that through its own choice.

17. It is evident that the location of the boundary was determined purely on the basis of the position of the German and Magyar villages. The Croatian villages were generally ignored. In Oberpullendorf County the desire to transfer the county intact, and the location of the German townships of Lutzmannsburg and Deutschkreutz, evidently determined the placement of the boundary. Had the Boundary Commission chosen to ignore the 1,500 Germans of Lutzmannsburg and a smaller adjacent village, a full quarter of present-day Oberpullendorf County, including the Magyar county seat, could have been kept in Hungary as non-German (see Map 10). In northeastern Oberwart County the site of the large German township, Rechnitz, was the decisive factor. Had the 3,700 Germans of Rechnitz and a smaller adjacent village been ignored, most of northeastern Oberwart County could have been retained by Hungary as non-German. A slightly further extension would have included the large Magyar cluster around Oberwart within this non-German area. It can be seen, therefore, that south of Sopron, contrary to prevailing opinion in Austria, the position of the boundary probably favored Austria more than it did Hungary.

18. *Grenzpost* (Ödenburg [Sopron]), January 24, 1919.

19. Kroatische Kulturverein or Hrvatsko Kulturno Društvo u Gradišću.

20. This attitude did not end with the occupation of the territory by the Austrian gendarmerie. Numerous parents kept their children in schools within Hungary, or even started their children in Hungarian schools because they felt that there was a strong possibility that Burgenland would return to Hungary shortly.

21. Burgenländische Kroatische Partei or Gradjansko Hrvatska Stranka.

22. The platform of the Croatian party consisted of the following points: (1) the protection of the Croatian language in schools and in the government as promised in the peace treaty; (2) complete autonomy for Burgenland; (3) the preservation of the ethnic individuality of the Croats in Burgenland, though in the closest agreement with the German majority; (4) the furthering of the

economic welfare and the cultural advance of the Burgenland Croats; (5) the representation of the Croats in the provincial parliament, the federal parliament, and the bureaucracy. *Güssinger Zeitung,* April 30, 1922.

23. In 1929 Rev. Thullner, one of the former members of the Hungarian parliament, was selected to be the provincial premier. Dr. Karall served as provincial premier from 1945 to 1956 (the longest term in Burgenland's short history).

24. *Naš Tajednik, Neodvisni Glasnik Gradišćanskih Hrvatov, Denkschrift des Kroatischen Kulturvereines* (Vienna, 1955).

25. The Powers were, under the terms of the treaty, to supervise the execution of the terms of the treaty by Austria, for a period of eighteen months.

26. *Burgenländische Freiheit* (Eisenstadt), February 10, 1957.

27. *Ibid.*

28. An indefinite number of persons belong to the Culture Society. In the past it was generally assumed in Burgenland that the active leaders were its only members. Barker (*Journal of Central European Affairs,* Vol. XIX [April, 1959], 56) stated that the membership was said not to exceed eighty. According to the present president of the society, the constant charges that the society represented only a minimal proportion of the Croats led him to engage in a membership drive as soon as he entered office three years ago. He maintains that within a few weeks the society had signed 2,500 members, and then ceased its efforts, since it felt that it had proved that it did represent a considerable number of Croats. On the grounds that church authorities generally claim all the "Catholics" or all the "Lutherans," he feels he can claim that the society represents all the Croats.

29. According to Austrian law, if a Gemeinde is 70 per cent or more Croatian, teaching will be in Croatian. Although teaching could be entirely in Croatian, legally, the Croats wish to learn German also. If a Gemeinde is between 30 and 70 per cent Croatian, then both languages will be utilized in instruction. If under 30 per cent, then parents can still obtain some Croatian instruction, provided twenty or more parents in the village so request. In 1934, some 59 townships had Croatian instruction; by 1961 this had dropped to 44 townships. Individual language courses are given in the various Gymnasia of Burgenland, and in many of the other schools as well. Unfortunately such courses are given in the afternoon (all normal, prescribed instruction is in the morning), so that only a peasant who has a strong desire for his child to learn Croatian will allow him to take the course (children help at home or on the land in the afternoons).

30. Even in the Gymnasia little interest is shown in the language. In the Eisenstadt Gymnasium, which has an enrollment of approximately 600, only 16 young men attend the voluntary Croatian course, whereas 139 attend the voluntary shorthand courses which are also given in the afternoons.

31. This is now known as the Štamparsko Društvo; until 1960 it was called Nakladno Društvo. Its German title is Der Kroatische Verlagsverein.

32. In the village of Schreibersdorf, though slightly less than half of the population of 450 was gypsy, in eleven years there was an increase of 84 people, 74 of whom were gypsy children.

33. *Der Freie Burgenländer* (Eisenstadt), October 2, 1932.

34. *Ibid.*, January 1, 1933. (The figures are exaggerated.)

35. According to Burgenlanders these figures do not give a good indication of the actual gypsy total. Following the end of the war many are said to have returned from the work camps and concentration camps and used their indemnity payments to purchase homes in the middle of the villages, rather than on the outskirts. In return for the legal and financial assistance given by the Communist party to the gypsies, many reportedly vote Communist. Since most of the gypsies now declare themselves to be "German" in the censuses, there is no way of determining their correct total.

36. There are approximately 1,500 Calvinists in Burgenland; most of these live in Oberwart and have already been mentioned. In 1951 there were also 39 Jews, 445 no religion, and 475 "Other" and "Unknown." For a discussion of the Jews, see Burghardt, *The Political Geography of Burgenland*, National Academy of Sciences—National Research Council Publication 587 (Washington, 1958), pp. 299–300; or, doctoral dissertation, same title (University of Wisconsin, 1958), pp. 454–55.

37. Rust is 42 per cent Lutheran and hence is not indicated as Lutheran on Map 10. However, the leading vintners and merchants of the "city" are almost all Lutheran and exercise an influence beyond their "minority" status.

38. The results from two townships are missing from the 1922 election.

39. The returns of the Sopron Plebiscite reveal a possible correlation between the religious character of some of the villages and the results of the vote. No one factor alone can explain all the variations in the results of that confused election, but it does appear probable that religion had a considerable influence in those villages with a Lutheran majority.

Township	% Lutheran	% For Austria
Harka	94	90
Ágfalva	86	83
Balf	72	60
Sopronbánfalva	70	81
SOPRON	28	27
Fertőbóz	1	22
Nagyczenk	1	0
Fertőrákos	0	61
Kópháza	0	31

40. The desire for an *Anschluss* with Germany was hardly unusual in Austria at the time, but within Burgenland it was unusual.

41. One must not, obviously, infer any intrinsic relationship between Lutheranism and either Nazism or extreme German nationalism. The situation of the Lutherans in Burgenland was clearly unique and in no way comparable to the situation of the Lutherans in Germany, Scandinavia, America, or elsewhere.

42. The large Communist vote in Rust is generally attributed to the presence of many landless fieldhands. However, it is notable that the Communist vote was cut in half by the emergence of the new third party, the VdU (now FPÖ).

In the election of 1959 the total of the Communist and the FPÖ votes closely approximated the Communist total in 1945. This observation suggests that many of the burghers may have voted Communist in 1945. A Catholic priest in a nearby village stated that many of the vintners had supported the Communist party in 1945 in order to avoid being prosecuted for their Nazi activities in the preceding years.

43. The following townships gave 20 per cent or more of their total votes to the FPÖ:

Township	% Lutheran	% FPÖ
Pöttelsdorf	87	33.0
Gols	81	22.7
Kukmirn	78	22.0
Eltendorf	70	21.8
Krottendorf	31	21.6
Kalkgruben	71	21.1
Mörbisch	78	19.5

44. Although the Unterwart Catholics and the Oberwart Calvinists seem to be holding on to their Magyar heritage more effectively and enthusiastically than are the Siget Lutherans, they have little close social contact with each other. Instead, the Calvinists and Lutherans often coöperate with each other simply because both groups are Protestant, whereas neither group has much social contact with the Unterwart Magyars because the latter are Catholics.

CHAPTER 15

1. "Heinzenland/Burgenland/ Are you returning to us?" This issue of the newspaper is missing from the Nationalbibliothek in Vienna, but the poem can be found in its entirety in *Burgenland, Vierteljahrshefte für Landeskunde, Heimatschutz, und Denkmalpflege* (Eisenstadt), Band I (December, 1927), 1–2.

2. "Long life to our German autonomous Four-burgs-land!" Fred Sinowatz, "Zur Geschichte des Landesnamens," manuscript of article expected to appear shortly in the *Burgenländische Heimatblätter* (Eisenstadt).

3. Inside as well as outside of Austria there exists the misconception that the name was derived from the many castles in the area. The official booklet of the Federal Press Service of Austria, *Austria, Facts and Figures* (Vienna, 1958), which is distributed to many visitors, including Fulbright scholars, states on p. 34, "The province derives its name from the number of castles which were erected here in former times as the last bastions on the edge of the great plain against incursions from the east." In reality these castles were built as bastions against incursions from the west, not the east. Similarly, it is probably the antique ring of the name that prompted James Mitchener to refer to "the ancient province of Burgenland (Land of Castles)" in his *The Bridge at Andau* (New York, 1957), p. 238. Sarah Wambaugh realized that the name was of very recent origin but she asserted, "To endow their own [Austrian] claim with a more

poetic appeal, the name of 'Burgenland' was invented for the strip of territory."
Plebiscites Since the World War (Washington, 1933), Vol. I, 274. As far as I
can determine, this idea has no foundation in fact.

4. Hungarian nationalists were loath to accept the new name, and continued
to refer to the area as "Nyugatmagyarország" (West Hungary). One Hungarian stated that the Austrians had given the name to the area improperly
since there was on this territory not one settlement in whose name "Burg" appeared. Therefore, he went on, the Austrians were "compelled" to change the
name of Matters*dorf* to Matters*burg!* István Nagy, "Nyugatmagyarország Ausz-
triában," in Miklós Móricz *et al., Észak-Kelet-Dél-és-Nyugat* (Pécs, 1937), p. 57.
Actually, the name was changed from "-dorf" to "-burg" in accordance with the
raising of the Gemeinde to the status of *Stadt* ("city"). This action was taken
on January 15, 1926, partly in recognition of the size of the settlement, and
partly as a compensation for the lost honor of provincial capital. As far as I
can ascertain, the motive given by Mr. Nagy occurred to no one at the time,
nor has it occurred since.

5. Obviously some sort of a resource base and a sufficient number of trained
persons are essential to the stability of a state. Generally (but not always) these
two prerequisites are present. Note too, that this argument does not postulate a
democracy, but rather simply a viable state.

6. At the present time the East European "Satellites" are already joined in
an economic federation, the Comecon (The Council for Mutual Economic Assistance). Conceivably, Comecon could continue to function in the future,
when these states are free of Soviet domination, but at present it is closely tied
to the Soviet Union and excludes both Austria and Jugoslavia; yet it could
form a basis for future federation.

7. Obviously the new federation would be faced by many serious problems,
among which would be the question of languages and the problem of selecting
a site for the federal government, no matter how slight that government may be.
It is not the function of this study to go into these problems, but as a geographer
I feel that I am entitled to nominate a potential "capital," Bratislava. Bratislava
is a historic city for the Slavs, the Germans, and the Magyars, and yet is not
associated with present or past political power, as Vienna or Budapest certainly
are. It is located in the area of the Slovaks, a people who have never been a
threat to any of their neighbors. It is located too, on the Danube, at the meeting
zone of the Carpathian Basin, the Austrian valleys, and the Moravian corridor.
It is doubtful if any other candidate city could offer as many advantages as
Bratislava-Pressburg-Pozsony.

8. "However it seems quite possible that exaggerated nationalistic dreams had
first to be led *ad absurdum* before the true meaning, purpose, and in the long
run, necessity of an economic and political Danubian Cooperative had its historic chance to be rediscovered." Kurt Schuschnigg, "The National Minority
Question in Austria Before and After 1918," *Journal of Central European
Affairs*, Vol. XVII (Jan., 1959), 371. From another viewpoint, A. J. P. Taylor
concluded that the Habsburg had to be removed from the scene before a
viable unification could be achieved. *The Habsburg Monarchy 1809–1918* (London, 1948), p. 226.

BIBLIOGRAPHY

The following bibliography includes only the works that were utilized in the writing of this book. Obviously there are hundreds of other available works dealing with the Danubian lands. Because this study consists of two differing portions—a broad historical survey until 1918, and a detailed analysis of Burgenland since 1918—the bibliography has been divided into two portions also.

A. Bibliography for Parts I and II

Many of the following works will be well known to the student of East Central Europe and require no comment. The lesser known works generally deal with but one topic which is usually obvious in the title. However, since the items in the Magyar language may be unfamiliar even to the expert, the translation of the title and a brief annotation where necessary follow the Magyar titles.

Books

Alföldi, Andreas. *Der Untergang der Römerherrschaft in Pannonien.* Berlin, 1924.

Atiya, Aziz Suryal. *The Crusade of Nicopolis.* London, 1934.

Belitzky, János. *Sopron vármegye története.* (The History of Sopron Megye.) Budapest, 1938. In 1,015 pages this book gives the history of the megye from prehistory to 1490. As far as I know, no further volumes have appeared.

Biricz, Eugen. "Geschichte der Einwanderung der burgenländischen Kroaten." Unpublished Doctoral dissertation, University of Vienna, 1949.

332   *Bibliography*

Blum, Jerome. *Noble Landowners and Agriculture in Austria, 1815–1848. A Study in the Origins of the Peasant Emancipation of 1848.* Baltimore, 1948.

Bonifačić, Antun, and Mihanovich, Clement S. *The Croatian Nation in Its Struggle for Freedom and Independence.* Chicago, 1955.

Brehm, Bruno. *Wien. Die Grenzstadt im deutschen Osten.* Jena, 1937.

Burgenland, Landeskunde. Vienna, 1951.

Bury, J. B. *A History of the Eastern Roman Empire. From the Fall of Irene to the Accession of Basil I (A.D. 802–867).* London, 1912.

Cambridge Medieval Histories. Vol. VI, *The Victory of the Papacy,* Cambridge, 1929; Vol. VII, *The Decline of the Empire and Papacy,* London, 1932; Vol. VIII, *The Close of the Middle Ages,* London, 1936.

Childe, V. Gordon. *The Danube in Prehistory.* Oxford, 1929.

———. *The Dawn of European Civilization* (6th ed.). New York, 1958.

Clark, J. G. D. *Prehistoric Europe, the Economic Basis.* London, 1952.

Csaplovics, János. *Topographische-statistisches Archiv des Königreichs Ungern.* Vienna, 1821.

Demián, János A. *Statistische Darstellung des Königreichs Ungern und der dazu gehoerigen Laender.* Vienna, 1805.

Dvornik, Francis. *The Slavs, Their Early History and Civilization.* Boston, 1956.

Erdélyi, Gyula. *Veszprém Város Története, A Török Idők Alatt.* (The History of the City of Veszprém, During the Turkish Times.) Veszprém, 1913.

Franzel, Emil. *Der Donauraum im Zeitalter des Nationalitätenprinzips.* Bern, 1958.

Geschichte der Oesterreichisch-Ungarischen Monarchie. Vienna, Pest, and Leipzig, 1875? (No author given.)

Gibbons, Herbert Adams. *The Foundation of the Ottoman Empire. A History of the Osmanlis up to the Death of Bayezid I (1300–1403).* Oxford, 1916.

Halecki, Oskar. *Borderlands of Western Civilization; a History of East Central Europe.* New York, 1952.

———. *The Limits and Divisions of European History.* New York, 1950.

Hantsch, Hugo. *Die Geschichte Österreichs.* 2 vols. Graz, 1953.

———. *Die Nationalitätenfrage im Alten Österreich.* Vienna, 1953.

Hassinger, Hugo. *Boden und Lage Wiens.* Vienna, 1946.

Hayes, Carlton J. H. *The Historical Evolution of Modern Nationalism.* New York, 1931.

Heiderich, Franz. *Zur Geographie des Wiener Beckens.* (Professor Dr. Franz Heiderich zum 60. Geburtstag Gewidmet von Freunden und Schülern.) Vienna, 1923.

Heile, Gerhard. *Der Feldzug gegen die Türken und die Eroberung Stuhlweissenburgs.* Rostock, 1901.

Heymann, Frederick G. *John Žižka and the Hussite Revolution.* Princeton, 1955.

Hůrský, Josef, *Vylidňovaní a asimilace slovanských obcí v Gradišti.* (The

Depopulation and Assimilation of the Slavic Townships in Burgenland.) Prague, 1952.

Jaszi, Oskar. *The Dissolution of the Habsburg Empire.* Chicago, 1929.

Jelavich, Charles, and Jelavich, Barbara. *The Habsburg Monarchy. Toward a Multinational Empire or National States.* ("Source Problems in World Civilization Series.") New York, 1959.

Kann, Robert A. *The Habsburg Empire. A Study in Integration and Disintegration.* New York, 1957.

———. *The Multinational Empire; Nationalism and National Reform in the Habsburg Monarchy 1848–1918.* 2 vols. New York, 1950.

Kohn, Hans. *The Idea of Nationalism.* New York, 1944.

Kosáry, Domokos. *Bevezetés a Magyar Történelem Forrásaiba és Irodalmába.* (An Introduction to Hungarian Historical Sources and Writings.) 2 vols. Budapest, 1951, 1954. This is an excellent annotated bibliography of everything that is known to have been written concerning Hungary before 1825. The chapter and section headings are in Magyar but the inclusion of many German, French, and Latin titles makes it possible for the person knowing little or no Hungarian to locate himself.

Kralik, Richard. *Geschichte der Stadt Wien und ihrer Kultur.* Vienna, 1933.

Kramert, Klemens, and Winter, Ernst K. *St. Severin, Der Heilige zwischen Ost und West.* Klosterneuburg, 1958.

Kranzmayer, Eberhard, and Bürger, Karl. *Burgenländisches Siedlungsnamenbuch.* Eisenstadt, 1957.

Krebs, Norbert. *Die Ostalpen und das heutige Österreich.* 2 vols. Stuttgart, 1928.

Lamb, Harold. *Genghis Khan, the Emperor of All Men.* Garden City (New York), 1927.

Leeper, A. W. A. *A History of Medieval Austria.* Oxford, 1941.

Litschauer, Gottfried F. *Bibliographie zur Geschichte, Landes- und Volkskunde des Burgenlandes, 1800–1929.* Wels (Austria), 1938.

Macartney, C. A. *Hungary.* London, 1934.

———. *The Magyars in the IX Century.* Cambridge, 1930.

Magyar Tájak, Magyar Városok. (Hungarian Landscapes, Hungarian Cities.) I. "Sopron," Heimler, Károly, Budapest, 1932; II. "Budapest," Kovácsházy, Vilmos, Budapest, 1934; III. "Debrecen," Vásáry, István, Budapest, 1934.

Marczali, Henry. *Hungary in the Eighteenth Century.* Cambridge, 1910.

Marriott, John A. R. *The Eastern Question; an Historical Study in European Diplomacy* (3rd ed.). Oxford, 1940.

Maull, Otto. *Politische Geographie.* Berlin, 1956.

Mayer, Josef. *Geschichte von Wiener Neustadt.* Wiener Neustadt, 1924.

Merriman, Roger B. *Suleiman the Magnificent 1520–1566.* Cambridge (Mass.), 1944.

Miltchinsky, Viktor. *Das Verbrechen von Ödenburg.* Vienna, Zürich, 1922.

Mollay, Károly. *Scarbantia, Ödenburg, Sopron. Siedlungsgeschichte und Ortsnamenkunde.* Budapest, 1944. The section on Ödenburg was published in slightly shorter form two years previously as *Ödenburg. Helynévfejtés és Településtörténet,* Budapest, 1942.

Mommsen, Theodore. *The Provinces of the Roman Empire from Caesar to Diocletian.* Vol. I. London, 1909.

Móricz, Miklós, *et al. Észak-Kelet-Dél-és-Nyugat.* (North, East, South, and West.) Pécs, 1937. A discussion of the areas lost to Hungary under the terms of the Treaty of Trianon. Unfortunately, this is largely a propaganda piece, characterized by much wishful thinking.

Nagy, Lajos. *Három Magyar Város.* (Three Hungarian Cities.) Budapest, 1933. Includes a description of Győr.

Oettinger, Karl. *Das Werden Wiens. Thesen und Hypothesen zur Frühgeschichte der Stadt.* (Schriften des Kunsthistorischen Institutes der Universität Wien Nr.8.) Vienna, 1945.

Ohrenberger, Alois. "Die Jungsteinzeit des Burgenlandes." Unpublished Doctoral dissertation, University of Vienna, 1949.

Ostrogorsky, George. *History of the Byzantine State.* Oxford, 1956.

Pârvan, Vasile. *Dacia: An Outline of the Early Civilization of the Carpatho-Danubian Countries.* Cambridge, 1928.

Peter, John. *A Relation or Diary of the Siege of Vienna.* London, 1684.

Petrovich, Michael B. *The Emergence of Russian Panslavism 1856–1870.* New York, 1956.

Pirenne, Henri. *Medieval Cities.* Princeton, 1925.

Pogány, Béla. *Die Südmarken in der ungarischen Geschichte.* Budapest, 1941.

Popovici, Aurel C. *Die Vereinigten Staaten von Gross-Österreich.* Leipzig, 1906.

Portisch, Emil. *Geschichte der Stadt Bratislava-Pressburg.* 2 vols. Bratislava, 1933.

Priester, Eva. *Kurze Geschichte Österreichs (Aufstieg und Untergang des Habsburgreichs).* Vienna, 1949.

Rittsteur, Josef. *Neusiedl am See.* Neusiedl (Austria), 1949.

Rostovtzeff, M. *The Social and Economic History of the Roman Empire* (2nd ed.). 2 vols. Oxford, 1957.

Schilcher, Helmut. "Die Grenzen Niederösterreich, ihres Entwicklung und Funktion." Unpublished Doctoral dissertation, University of Vienna, 1950.

Schmidt, Heinrich, Schilling, Rogerius, and Schnitzer, Johann. *Das Deutschtum in Rumpfungarn.* Budapest, 1928.

Schwartner, Martin. *Statistik des Koenigreichs Ungern.* Pest, 1798.

Seton-Watson, R. W. *Racial Problems in Hungary.* London, 1908.

Sieger, Robert. *Die geographischen Grundlagen der Österreichisch-Ungarischen Monarchie und ihrer Aussenpolitik.* Leipzig and Berlin, 1915.

Sinowatz, Fred. *Reformation und katholische Restauration in der Grafschaft Forchtenstein und Herrschaft Eisenstadt.* Eisenstadt, 1957.

Sölch, Johann. *Das Semmeringgebiet.* Vienna, 1948.

Spore, Walter. "St. Pölten. Eine stadtgeographische Untersuchung." Unpublished Doctoral dissertation, University of Vienna, 1944.

Statisztikai Hivatal. *Magyar Statisztikai Közlemények. 1900 Évi Népszámlálása.* Budapest, 1902. (Hungarian census)

———. *1910 Évi.* Budapest, 1912.

———. *Recensement de la Population en 1920.* Budapest, 1925.

Strong, D. F. *Austria (October 1918–March 1919). Transition from Empire to Republic.* New York, 1939.

Swoboda, Erich. *Carnuntum, seine Geschichte und seine Denkmäler.* (Römische Forschungen in Niederösterreich, Band I.) Vienna, 1953.

Szekfű, Gyula. *Állam és Nemzet.* (State and Nation.) Budapest, 1942. Although the title is the same as that of the following work, the two books are not identical. This is a compilation of longer articles dealing with various aspects of the "nationalities" question, by the leading Hungarian authority on the subject.

———. *État et Nation.* Paris, 1945. Another compilation of material from the author's Magyar works; it is probably the best work discussing the "nationalities" question from a moderate Magyar viewpoint that is available in a language other than Magyar.

———. *Három Nemzedék és Ami Utána Következik.* (Three Generations and What Followed After.) Budapest, 1938. A history of Magyar nationalism in the middle and late nineteenth century.

——— (ed.). *A Magyarság és a Szlávok.* (Magyardom and the Slavs.) Budapest, 1942. Twelve articles by different authors dealing with the relationships between the Magyars and the Slavs in general, and the individual Slavic groups.

——— (ed.). *Mi a Magyar.* (What Is a Magyar?) Budapest, 1939. Thirteen articles by different authors investigating the Magyar character as seen in history, literature, music, poetry, relations with foreigners, etc.

Taylor, A. J. P. *The Habsburg Monarchy 1809–1918.* London, 1948.

Teleki, Paul. *The Evolution of Hungary and Its Place in European History.* New York, 1923.

Thompson, E. A. *A History of Attila and the Huns.* Oxford, 1948.

Tóth, Zoltán. *Magyar Történeti Bibliográfia, 1825–1867.* 3 vols. (Hungarian Historical Bibliography.) Budapest, 1950–52. The three volumes are devoted to: I—General; II—Economic; and III—Political, Legal, Educational, Scientific, Cultural, Press, and Religious works. This bibliography is not as complete as that of Kosáry, nor is it annotated; however, it is very well organized. It deals with non-Magyar as well as Magyar works, and despite its title, includes some works well past 1867.

Vetters, Hermann, König, Friederich, and Pabisch, Heinrich. *Landeskunde von Niederösterreich.* Vienna, 1908?

von Voltelini, Hans. *Die Anfänge der Stadt Wien.* Vienna and Leipzig, 1913.

Walter, Friedrich, *Wien. Die Geschichte einer deutschen Grossstadt an der Grenze.* Vienna, 1944.

336 *Bibliography*

Wanklyn, H. G. *The Eastern Marchlands of Europe.* London, 1941.
Zarek, Otto. *Die Geschichte Ungarns.* Zürich, 1938.
Zibermayr, Ignaz. *Noricum, Baiern und Österreich: Lorch als Hauptstadt und die Einführung des Christentums.* Horn (Austria), 1956.
Zimmermann, Fritz. *Die vormadjarische Besiedlung des burgenländischen Raumes.* Eisenstadt, 1954.

Articles and Pamphlets

Albrecht, Ferenc. *A Kiegyezesi korszak nemzetiségi politikájának értékítélete.* (A Jancsó Benedek Társaság Kiadványal, 4.) (An evaluation of the Hungarian nationalities policy following the Ausgleich. Publication 4 of the Jancsó Benedek Society.) Budapest, 1931.
Austrian Information Service. *Austrian Information.* (Biweekly Newsletter.) New York, 1958–60.
Balogh, Joseph. "The Political Testament of St. Stephen, King of Hungary," *The Hungarian Quarterly* (Budapest), Vol. IV (Autumn, 1938), 389–98.
Barb, A. A. "Zum Awarenzeitlichen Friedhof von Leithaprodersdorf," *Burgenländische Heimatblätter* (Eisenstadt), Jg. 20 (1958), 16–18.
———. "Unter römischer Herrschaft," in *Burgenland, Landeskunde.* Vienna, 1951. Pp. 206–23.
Baumhackl, Friedrich. "Die Burgruine Theben an der Marchmündung," *Unsere Heimat* (Vienna), Band XII (1939), 87–91.
———. "Die Kroaten im Marchfeld," *ibid.*, Band XIII (1940), 90–108.
Belloc, Hilaire. "The Geography of War," *Geographical Journal* (London), Vol. 45 (Jan., 1915), 1–13.
Bernleither, Ernst. "Das Turkenjahr 1529 und die Marchfeld-Kroaten," *Unsere Heimat* (Vienna), Jg. 20 (1949), 1–12.
Berry, James. "Transylvania and Its Relations to Ancient Dacia and Modern Rumania," *Geographical Journal* (London), Vol. 53 (March, 1919), 129–46.
Beynon, Erdmann D. "Isolated Racial Groups of Hungary," *Geographical Review* (New York), Vol. XVII (Oct., 1927), 586–604.
———. "Migrations of Hungarian Peasants," *ibid.*, Vol. XXVII (April, 1937), 214–28.
Blum, Jerome. "Transportation & Industry in Austria, 1815–1848," *The Journal of Modern History*, Vol. XV (March, 1943), 24–38.
Bodo, Fritz. "Wiener Neustadt. Eine historisch-geographische Skizze," *Unsere Heimat* (Vienna), Band IX (1936), 169–74.
Brunner, O. "Der burgenländische Raum zwischen Österreich und Ungarn, 800–1848," in *Burgenland, Landeskunde.* Vienna, 1951. Pp. 245–328.
von Cholnoky, Eugen. "Die geographische Lage von Wien," *Mitteilungen der Geographischen Gesellschaft in Wien* (Vienna), Band 72, Heft 7–12 (1929), 380–94.
Csatkai, Endre. "Idegenek a régi sopronról 1487–1841." (*Scarbantia. Helytörténeti Sopron és Sopron Vármegye Multjából*, 2 Szám.) Sopron,

1938. 42 pp. The old Sopron as seen in the reports of foreign visitors.

Cvijić, Jovan. "The Geographical Distribution of the Balkan Peoples," *Geographical Review* (New York), Vol. V (May, 1918), 345–61.

———. "The Zones of Civilization of the Balkan Peninsula," *ibid.*, Vol. V (June, 1918), 470–81.

Deák, Imre. *A Magyarországi Nemzetiségi Kérdés*. (The Hungarian Nationalities Question.) Budapest, 1940. A strongly pro-Magyar pamphlet.

Dercsényi, Dezső. "Székesfehérvár, St. Stephen's City," *The Hungarian Quarterly* (Budapest), Vol. IV (Spring, 1938), 87–96.

Faluhelyi, Ferenc. *A Kisebbségi Kérdés. Eredte és Jelentösége Általános és Magyar Szempontból.* (A Pécsi M. Kir. Erzsébet-Tudományegyetem Kisebbségi Intézetének Kiadványai III.) Pécs, 1937. (The Minorities Question. Its Origin and Significance from the General and the Hungarian Viewpoints. Publication III of the Minorities Institute of the Queen Elizabeth-of-Hungary University of Pécs.) A short pamphlet trying to summarize the minorities question.

Faust, Ovidius. "Wien und Pressburg," *Unsere Heimat* (Vienna), Band XIII (1940), 119–26.

Fuchs, Richard. "Die Kroaten-Ansiedlung von Landegg," *ibid.*, Band IX (1936), 83–90.

Gamber, Emil. "Das Amphitheater bei Deutsch-Altenburg," *ibid.*, Jg. 18 (1947), 135–37.

Gruszecki, Oskar. "Die Geschichte Eisenstadts bis 1648," in *Eisenstadt, 300 Jahre Freiheit.* Vienna, 1948. Pp. 9–12.

———. "Maximilians Feldzug nach Ungarn im Jahre 1490," *Burgenländische Heimatblätter* (Eisenstadt), Jg. 17 (1955), 162–71.

Hartshorne, Richard, "Political Geography," in Preston E. James and Clarence F. Jones, *American Geography. Inventory and Prospect.* Syracuse, 1954. Pp. 169–221.

———. "Suggestions on the Terminology of Political Boundaries," *Mitteilungen des Vereins der Geographen an der Universität Leipzig,* Heft 14/15 (1936), 180–92.

Hassinger, Hugo. "Die Grenzen unseres Heimatgaues," *Jahrbuch für Landeskunde von Niederösterreich* (Vienna), Vol. 27 (1938).

Hetzer, Kurt. "Taktische Betrachtungen zur babenbergischen Eroberung Niederösterreichs," *Unsere Heimat* (Vienna), Jg. 23 (1952), 2–11.

Heydendorff, Walther. "Die römische Flotte auf der norischen und oberpannonischen Donau," *ibid.*, Jg. 23 (1952), 149–57.

Homma, Josef K. "Zu den Grenzverhältnissen zwischen der Herrschaft Thalberg bzw. Bärnegg (Stm.) und dem Landesgericht Pinkafeld von 17. bis 19. Jahrhundert," *Burgenländische Heimatblätter* (Eisenstadt), 13/4 (1951), 272–82.

———. "Die letzten Akte des Pinkafelder Hochgerichtes," *ibid.*, 13/2 (1951), 50–76.

Horváth, Eugene. "Medieval Hungary," *South Eastern Affairs*, Vol. I (Jan., 1931), 1–30.

Hydrographischen Zentralbureau in Bundesministerium für Land- und Forstwirtschaft. "Temperaturmittel 1896–1915 und Isothermenkarten von Österreich," *Mitteilungen der Geographischen Gesellschaft in Wien* (Vienna), Band 72, Heft 7–12 (1929), 245–80.

Jánko, Johannes. "Resultate der wissenschaftlichen Erforschung des Balatonsees," *Magyar Földrajzi Társaság* (Vienna), Vol. III, part ii (1906), entire issue.

Kemény, Gábor G. *A Magyar Nemzetiségi Kérdés Története.* (The History of the Hungarian Nationalities Question.) Budapest, 1947. A short pamphlet.

Kenner, Friedrich. "Favianus, Wien und Mautern," *Blätter des Vereines für Landeskunde von Niederösterreich* (Vienna), Vol. XVI (1882), 3–53.

———. "Die Römerorte in Nieder-Oesterreich," *Jahrbuch für Landeskunde von Nieder-Oesterreich* (Vienna), Jg. 11 (1869), 119–214.

Kranzmayer, Eberhard. "Herkunft und Geschichte der Namen Wiens. Gedanken zu den namenkundlichen Exkursen Oettingers 'Das Werden Wiens,' " *Unsere Heimat* (Vienna), Jg. 23 (1952), 67–73.

Kubitschek, Wilhelm. "Ältere Berichte über den römischen Limes in Pannonien," *Akademie der Wissenschaft in Wien. Sitzungsberichte 209* (Vienna, and Leipzig), Band I (1929), 1–336.

Kunnert, Heinrich. "Im ungarischen Nationalstaat," in *Burgenland, Landeskunde.* Vienna, 1951. Pp. 347–56.

Lampel, Josef. "Die Leitha Grenze," *Blätter des Vereines für Landeskunde von Niederösterreich* (Vienna), Vol. XXXIII (1899), 113–33.

Lechner, Karl. " 'Das Werden Wiens—Das Werden Österreichs.' Ein neues Buch über die Frühgeschichte Wiens." *Unsere Heimat* (Vienna), Jg. 23 (1952), 45–67. (A review.)

———. "Die territoriale Entwicklung von Mark und Herzogtum Österreich," *ibid.,* Jg. 24 (1953), 33–55.

———. "Frühes Christentum in Österreich von den Anfängen bis um 600 n. Chr." *ibid.,* Jg. 27 (1956), 34–38. Review of book by Rudolph Noll.

Lendl, Egon. "Der Beitrag Niederösterreichs zur deutschen Südostkolonisation der Neuzeit," *ibid.,* Band XI (1938), 1–6.

Litschauer, Gottfried F. "Zur Geschichte der deutschen Besiedlung des Burgenlandes," *Burgenland Vierteljahrshefte für Landeskunde, Heimatschutz und Denkmalpflege* (Eisenstadt), Band II (1929), 185–92.

Macartney, C. A. "The First Historians of Hungary," *The Hungarian Quarterly* (Budapest), Vol. IV (Winter, 1938–39), 630–41.

Marek, Richard. "Die Entwicklung des Deutschtums im österreichischen Burgenland," *Petermanns Mitteilungen* (Gotha), Band LXXXIII, Heft 7/8 (1937), 193–97.

Marle, T. B. "In Turkish Times, an Early English Traveller in Hungary," *The Hungarian Quarterly* (Budapest), Vol. IV (Summer, 1938), 324–31.

de Martonne, Emmanuel. "The Carpathians: Physiographic Features

Controlling Human Geography," *Geographical Review* (New York), Vol. III (June, 1917), 417–37.

Marz, Edward. "Economic Conflict in the Habsburg Empire," *Journal of Central European Affairs*, Vol. XIII (July, 1953), 123–35.

Mitscha-Märheim, H. "Die germanische Völkerwanderungszeit," in *Burgenland, Landeskunde*. Vienna, 1951. Pp. 224–44.

de Navarro, J. M. "Prehistoric Routes between Northern Europe and Italy. Defined by the Amber Trade," *Geographical Journal* (London), Vol. 66 (Dec., 1925), 481–503.

Neunteufel, Josef. "Das Klima," in *Burgenland, Landeskunde*. Vienna, 1951. Pp. 137–45.

von Nischer, Ernst. "Das Vorland des norisch-pannonischen Limes," *Unsere Heimat* (Vienna), Band V (1932), 227–52.

Nischer-Falkenhof, Ernst. "Die vorgeschichtlichen Siedlungen auf dem Braunsberg bei Hainburg a.d. Donau," *ibid.*, Band VIII (1935), 290–94.

Patsch, Carl. "Beiträge zur Völkerkunde von Südosteuropa. IV. Die quadisch-jazygische Kriegsgemeinschaft im Jahre 374/375," *Akademie der Wissenschaft in Wien. Sitzungsberichte 209* (Vienna & Leipzig), Band 5 (1929), 1–36.

Pittioni, Richard. "Das Geschichte der Urzeit," in *Burgenland, Landeskunde*. Vienna, 1951. Pp. 185–205.

Pounds, Norman J. G. "Land Use on the Hungarian Plain," manuscript copy of article to appear shortly in *Geographical Essays on Eastern Europe*. Bloomington (Indiana).

Radnóti, Aladár. "Une église du haut moyen âge à Zalavár," *Étude Slaves et Roumaines* (Budapest), Vol. I (1948), 21–30.

Rapaics, Raymund. "The Wines of Hungary," *The Hungarian Quarterly* (Budapest), Vol. IV (Spring, 1938), 109–17.

Rath, John R. "The Viennese Liberals of 1848 and the Nationality Problem," *Journal of Central European Affairs*, Vol. XV (Oct., 1955), 227–39.

Roth-Fuchs, Gabriele. "Beobachtungen über Wasserschwankungen am Neusiedlersee," *Mitteilungen der Geographischen Gesellschaft in Wien* (Vienna), Band 76, Heft 7–9 (1933), 195–205.

Rumi, Károly G. "Verzeichniss einiger Gegenden im Oedenburger Comitat in Niederungern, die eine pittoreske Beschreibung und eine Abzeichnung mit der *Camera obscura* oder aus freyer Hand verdienen," *Vaterlaendische Blaetter fuer den oesterreichischen Kaiserstaat* (Vienna), Erster Band (1814), 357–59.

Sakač, Stephen Kr. "The Iranian Origin of the Croats according to C. Porphyrogenitus," in Bonifačić and Mihanovich, *The Croatian Nation in Its Struggle for Freedom and Independence*. Chicago, 1955. Pp. 30–46.

Schuschnigg, Kurt. "The National Minority Question in Austria Before and After 1918," *The Journal of Central European Affairs*, Vol. XVIII (Jan., 1959), 367–79.

Semmelweis, Karl. "Das Esterhazysche Schloss in Eisenstadt," in *Eisenstadt, 300 Jahre Freiheit*. Vienna, 1948. Pp. 28–32.

――――. "Die Geschichte der Orte Stotzing und Loretto am Leithagebirge," *Burgenländische Heimatblätter* (Eisenstadt), Band XI, Heft 2 (1949), 66–70.

――――. "Podler. Ansiedlung von Kroaten durch Adam Batthyány im Jahre 1650," *ibid.*, Heft XI (1949), 189–90.

Sidaritsch, Marian. "Die landschaftliche Gliederung des Burgenlandes," *Mitteilungen der Geographischen Gesellschaft in Wien*, Band 67, Heft 1–8 (1924), 118–39.

Sieger, Robert. "Die Grenzen Niederösterreich," *Jahrbuch für Landeskunde von Niederösterreich* (Vienna), Band 1 (1902), 169–225.

――――. " 'Natürliche' Grenzen," *Petermanns Geographischen Mitteilungen* (Gotha), Band LXXI, Heft 3/4 (1925), 57–59.

Siklóssy, Ladislas. "The Centenary of the Great Flood in Pest," *The Hungarian Quarterly* (Budapest), Vol. IV (Spring, 1938), 143–46.

Stanoyevich, Milovoy S. "Czecho-Slovakia and Its People," *Geographical Review* (New York) Vol. VIII (July, 1919), 31–36.

Steers, Mrs. J. A. (Harriet Wanklyn). "The Middle People: Resettlement in Czechoslovakia," *Geographical Journal* (London), Vol. 112 (July–Sept., 1948), 28–40.

Sylvester, Hans. "Franz Liszt und das Burgenland," *Burgenländische Heimatblätter* (Eisenstadt), Band I (May, 1936), entire issue.

Tauber, A. F. "Hydrogeologie und Hydrochemie der Parndorfer Heideplatte," *ibid.*, Jg. 21 (1959), 7–23.

Thirring, Gusztáv. *Az első soproni népszámlálás.* (The First Sopron Census.) Sopron, 1937. A brief description and summary of the results of the census of 1784 in the city of Sopron; only the number of houses, dwellings, and inhabitants are given.

――――. *Sopron népessége a 18-ik század elején.* (The Population of Sopron at the Beginning of the 18th Century.) Sopron, 1937. The results of the house count of 1720, with a comparison with previous estimates. Includes the number of houses, total population, and estimates of the religious and linguistic proportions.

――――. *Sopron vármegye községeinek népesedési fejlődése az utolsó 150 év alatt.* (The Patterns of Population Increase in the Townships of Sopron Megye during the Past 150 Years.) Sopron, 1937. Includes the number of houses, total population, and number of Jews in each township of the megye for 1785, 1828, 1880, and 1934.

Ulbrich, Karl. "Die Grenzkarte Ungarn-Niederösterreich von C. J. Walter (1754–56)," *Burgenländische Heimatblätter* (Eisenstadt), Jg. 15 (1953), 108–21.

――――. "Die Schlossriegel von Strem in Südburgenland," *ibid.*, Band XI, Heft 2 (1949), 54–60.

Vorbeck, Eduard. "Carnuntum," *Österreich in Geschichte und Literatur* (Vienna), Jg. 4, Heft 3 (1960), 138–40.

Wallis, B. C. "Central Hungary: Magyars and Germans," *Geographical Review* (New York), Vol. VI (Nov., 1918), 421–35.

———. "Distribution of Nationalities in Hungary," *Geographical Journal* (London), Vol. 47 (March, 1916), 177–88.

———. "The Peoples of Austria," *Geographical Review* (New York), Vol. VI (July, 1918), 52–65.

———. "The Peoples of Hungary: Their Work on the Land," *ibid.*, Vol. IV (Dec., 1917), 465–81.

———. "The Slavs of Northern Hungary," *ibid.*, Vol. VI (Sept., 1918), 268–81.

Wanklyn, Harriet (Mrs. J. A. Steers). "The Role of Peasant Hungary in Europe," *Geographical Journal* (London), Vol. 97 (Jan., 1941), 18–34.

Wendelberger, Gustav. "Die naturwissenschaftliche Schriftum über das Gebiet des Neusiedler Sees," *Burgenländische Heimatblätter* (Eisenstadt), Band XI (1949), 122–34.

Wiche, Konrad. "Die Oberflächenformen," in *Burgenland, Landeskunde*. Vienna, 1951. Pp. 98–136.

Winter, Ernst Karl. "The Byzantine Millennium of Vienna," *Medievalia et Humanistica*, Vol. X (1956), 1–31.

———. "La Tène in Niederösterreich hinsichtlich der Sozialorganization," *Unsere Heimat* (Vienna), Band I (1927), 102–16.

———. *Wo Lag Favianus? Fünfzig Gründe für und wider Heiligenstadt*. Vienna, 1957. Pamphlet, 32 pp.

B. Bibliography for Part III

The following categories of sources are listed in the order of their significance to the research for this study. By far the most of my material was obtained from newspapers. Even many of the listed "articles" appeared in newspapers rather than in periodicals.

Newspapers—Burgenland

On this and the following list, an asterisk has been placed before the name of those papers which were especially useful.

Burgenländische Freiheit (Socialist), Sauerbrunn-Eisenstadt, 1922–34, 1946–61.

Burgenländische Heimat (Christian), Sauerbrunn, 1924–26.

Burgenländisches Leben mit Burgenland Kurier, Vienna, 1954–60.

Burgenländisches Volksblatt (Christian-ÖVP), Sauerbrunn-Eisenstadt, 1922–24, 1926–38, 1945–61.

Der Freie Burgenländer (Great German), Sauerbrunn-Eisenstadt, 1921–34.

Freies Burgenland (Communist), Eisenstadt, 1945–61.

Grenzland Kurier (Independent), Neusiedl, 1954–57.

Güssinger Zeitung (Christian), Güssing, 1922–38.
Naš Tajednik, Neodvisni Glasnik Gradišćanskih Hrvatov, Denkschrift des Kroatischen Kulturvereines, Vienna, 1955.
Neue Eisenstädter Zeitung, Eisenstadt, 1923.
Oberwarther Sonntags-Zeitung, Oberwart, 1919–November, 1921; December, 1922–38; 1949–57.

Newspapers—Old Austria

The most valuable Viennese papers were those of the extremist Great German party. This party was intensely involved in the acquisition and establishment of Burgenland and hence gave the area full coverage, whereas the larger, more important of the Viennese newspapers referred to Burgenland only in times of crisis or sensational news.

Alldeutsches Tagblatt (Great German), Vienna, 1905–6.
Arbeiterzeitung (Socialist), Vienna, 1919–34, 1946, 1961.
Deutschösterreichische Tages-Zeitung (Great German), Vienna, 1920–22.
Neue Freie Presse, Vienna, 1919–21.
Neues Österreich, Vienna, 1945–61.
Neue Wiener Tagblatt, Vienna, 1920–21.
Ostdeutsche Rundschau (Great German), Vienna, 1919–20.
Österreichische Volkszeitung (Christian), Vienna, 1918–30.
Die Presse, Vienna, 1961.
Reichspost, Vienna, 1921.
Tagespost, Graz, 1918–38.
Wiener Deutsche Tageszeitung, Vienna, 1920–22.
Wiener Mittag, Vienna, 1921.

Newspapers—Non-Austrian

Christliches Oedenburger Tagblatt, Ödenburg (Sopron), 1919.
Grenzpost, Ödenburg (Sopron), 1919.
Hétfő (*Burgenlandi Magyar Hirlap*), Sopron, 1936–37.
Der Ungarndeutsche (*Heimatzeitung der Deutschen aus Ungarn*), Munich, 1959.
Vierburgenland (*Offizielles Organ des Kulturbundes für Deutschwestungarn*), Ödenburg (Sopron), 1919–20.
Weckruf, Ödenburg (Sopron), 1919.

Articles

Ambroschitz, Hans. "Das Burgenland," *Das Deutschtum des Südostens, 1928, 1929, 1930*. (Schriften des Deutschen Schulvereins Südmark über das Grenz- und Auslanddeutschtum.) Graz, 1929, 1930, 1931.
Barker, Thomas M. "The Croatian Minority of Burgenland," *Journal of Central European Affairs*, Vol. XIX (April, 1959), 32–56.
Bodo, Fritz. "Wiener Neustadt als Verkehr- und Industriemittelpunkt des südöstlichen Niederösterreichs," *Unsere Heimat* (Vienna), Band II (1929), 11–24, 33–44, 70–74.

Bothar, Michael F. "Magyarische Wörter im Heinzischer Sprachgebrauch," *Burgenländische Heimatblätter* (Eisenstadt), Band XI (1949), 182–85.

Collinder, Björn. "A leghívebb város" (The Most Loyal City). (*Scarbantia. Helytörténeti Sopron és Sopron Vármegye Multjából*, 3 Szám.) Sopron, 1938. 11 pp. This professes to be "an objective presentation of the events of 1921" in Sopron and Burgenland by a Swedish professor. However, the article is very short and admits to being dependent on the work of Missuray-Krúg.

Cree, D. "Yugoslav-Hungarian Boundary Commission," *Geographical Journal* (London), Vol. 65 (Feb., 1925), 89–110.

Davy, Robert. "Das Burgenlandproblem," *Neue Wiener Tagblatt* (Vienna), June 29, 1921.

De Weiss, Elizabeth. "Dispute for the Burgenland in 1919," *Journal of Central European Affairs*, Vol. III (July, 1943), 147–66.

Fogarassy László. "A Bandaharcok Burgenlandban, 28. August—4. November 1921," (The Bands' Fighting in Burgenland). This is now the most objective and complete study of the fighting. A manuscript copy, expected to be published in the *Burgenländische Heimatblätter* (Eisenstadt) sometime in 1962.

Graupner, Ludwig. "Die Amerikawanderung im Güssinger Bezirk," *Burgenländische Forschungen* (Vienna), Heft 3 (1949), 1–36.

———. "Die Güssinger Landschaft. Ein übervölkertes österreichisches Grenzland," *Geographischer Jahresbericht aus Österreich* (Geographischen Institut an der Universität Wien) (Vienna), Band XXIII (1949), 1–124.

Güttenberger, Heinrich. "Der anthropogeographische Aufriss des Burgenlandes," *Mitteilungen der Geographischen Gesellschaft in Wien* (Vienna), Band 65, Heft 1–12 (1922), 47–55.

Haller, P. "Die Volksabstimmung von 1921," *Der Ungarndeutsche* (Munich), September 20, 1959.

Hartshorne, Richard, "Geographic and Political Boundaries in Upper Silesia," *Annals of the Association of American Geographers*, Vol. XXIII (Dec., 1933), 194–228.

Homma, Josef Karl. "Burgenlands Vereinigung mit Österreich," *Österreich in Geschichte und Literatur* (Vienna), Jg. 4, Sonderheft (1960), 18–27.

———. "Das Werden der Ostgrenze des Burgenlandes," *Burgenländische Heimatblätter* (Eisenstadt), 13/1 (1951), 39–41.

Karall, Lorenz. "Dreissig Jahre Burgenland, *ibid.*, 13/4 (1951), 213–14.

Kiszling, Rudolph. "Das Problem Ödenburg," *Österreich in Geschichte und Literatur* (Vienna), Jg. 4, Sonderheft (1960), 28–31.

Koller, Paul. "Wie Eisenstadt die Hauptstadt des Burgenlandes wurde," in *Eisenstadt. 300 Jahre Freiheit*. Vienna, 1948. Pp. 20–24.

Kunnert, Heinrich. "Vor Zehn Jahren," *Burgenland Vierteljahrshefte für Landeskunde, Heimatschutz und Denkmalpflege* (Eisennstadt), Band II, Heft 2 (1929), 125–31.

Lendl, Egon. "Die Siedlungslandschaft des Raabbeckens," *Mitteilungen der Geographischen Gesellschaft in Wien* (Vienna), Band 86, Heft 1–3 (1943), 104–18.

Lendl, Hubert. "Das Gesellschaftliche Gefüge des Landvolks im deutsch-madjarischen Grenzraum östlich des Neusiedler Sees," in Brackmann, Hassinger und Metz, *Deutsches Archiv für Landes- und Volksforschung*. Leipzig, 1938. Jg. 2, pp. 800–835.

Lukas, Georg A. "Das Burgenland," *Geographischen Zeitschrift* (Leipzig), Band XXXIV, Heft 9 (1928), 530–46.

Missuray-Krúg, Lajos. "Sopron nagy napjai" (Sopron's Day of Greatness), *A Sopronvármegye Népszavazási Emlékalbuma* (An Album in Rememberance of the Sopron Plebiscite). Sopron, 1932. Pp. 45–72. This is probably the best Hungarian work on the plebiscite.

"The New Boundaries of Austria," *Geographical Review* (New York), Vol. VIII (Dec., 1919), 345–49. Map with short text.

Nowak, Hans. "Das Erziehungswesen," in *Burgenland, Landeskunde*. Vienna, 1951. Pp. 538–46.

Oberhummer, E. "Der Name Burgenland," *Geographischen Zeitschrift* (Leipzig), Band XXXV, Heft 3 (1929), 162–63.

Patry, Josef. "Allerlei aus der Zeit vor zum Anschluss," *Der Freie Burgenländer* (Festnummer, *Drei Jahre bei Deutschösterreich*), Sauerbrunn, November 16, 1924.

———. "Westungarn zu Deutschösterreich," *Alldeutsches Tagblatt*, Vienna, June 17, 1906.

Rausnitz, Alfred. "Die Gendarmerie im Burgenlande," in Franz Neubauer, *Die Gendarmerie in Österreich 1849–1924*. Vienna, 1925. Pp. 231–63.

Reisner, J. "Alte und Neue Verwaltung," *Reichspost*, Vienna, August 28, 1921.

Renner, Karl. "Wie es zur Befreiung des Burgenlandes kam," in *Die Gendarmerie. 10 Jahre Österreichische Gendarmerie in Burgenland*. Vienna, 1931. Pp. 1–11.

Sieger, Robert. "Natürliche Räume und Lebensräume," *Petermanns Geographischen Mitteilungen* (Gotha), Band LXIX, Heft 11/12 (1923), 252–56.

———. "Zur politisch-geographischen Terminologie, II. Natürliche und politische Grenzen," *Zeitschrift der Gesellschaft für Erdkunde zu Berlin* (Berlin), 1/2 (1918), 48–69.

Sinowatz, Fred. "Zur Geschichte des Landesnamens," manuscript of article that will probably appear shortly in the *Burgenländische Heimatblätter* (Eisenstadt).

Temperley, Harold. "How the Hungarian Frontiers Were Drawn," *Foreign Affairs*, Vol. 6 (April, 1928), 432–47.

Traeger, Ernö. "A Soproni népszavazás" (The Sopron Plebiscite), in Gusztáv Thirring, *Sopron: Civitas Fidelissima*. Sopron, 1925. This has also appeared in translation as: Ernst Traeger. *Die Volksabstimmung in Sopron*, Sopron, 1928. In either version this is little more than a sentimental paean to the city.

Vancsa, Max. "Zur Geschichte des Burgenlandes," in Eduard Stepan, *Burgenland Festschrift*. Vienna, 1920. Pp. 12–17.

Walheim, Alfred. "Also doch um Oedenburg," *Deutschösterreichische Tages-Zeitung*, Vienna, September 22, 1921.

———. "Der Ausschuss für Auswärtiges und das Burgenland," *ibid.*, August 25, 1921.

———. "Das gefährdete Burgenland," *Wiener Mittag*, October 17, 1921.

———. "Heinzenland, Burgenland," *Burgenland, Vierteljahrshefte für Landeskunde, Heimatschutz und Denkmalpflege* (Eisenstadt), Band I, Heft 1–2 (1927), 1–2.

———. "Ist das Burgenland lebensfähig?" *Österreichische Volkszeitung*, Vienna, June 1, 1924.

———. "Die italienische Vermittlung und die österreichischen Sozialdemokraten," *Deutschösterreichische Tages-Zeitung*, Vienna, October 8, 1921.

———. "Die Kommunistenfurcht im Heinzenland," *Ostdeutsche Rundschau*, Vienna, January 16, 1920.

———. "Oedenburg den Oedenburgen!" *Deutschösterreichische Tages-Zeitung*, Vienna, August 27, 1921.

———. "Ohne Oedenburg Kein Burgenland," *ibid.*, September 22 and 29, 1921; *Reichspost*, Vienna, September 26, 1921; and *Wiener Mittag*, September 5, 26, 28, and October 3, 1921.

———. "Österreich und die Entente," *Deutschösterreichische Tages-Zeitung*, Vienna, October 1, 1921.

———. "Die Stimmung der Heinzen," *ibid.*, November 6, 1921.

———. "Die Übernahme des Burgenlandes durch Deutschösterreich," *ibid.*, August 19, 1921.

———. "Von der Christlichsoziale Partei des Burgenlandes," *ibid.*, August 23, 1921.

———. "Wer weiss eine Hauptstadt?" *Österreichische Volkszeitung*, Vienna, February 24, 1924.

———, "Wie das Burgenland zu seinem Wappen gekommen ist," *ibid.*, February 10, 1924.

Weinberger, Otto. "Das Eherecht nach der Vereinigung," *Reichspost*, Vienna, August 28, 1921.

Governmental Publications

Adressenbuch des Burgenlandes, 1924. Sauerbrunn, 1924.

Adressenbuch vom Burgenland für Industrie, Handel und Gewerbe. Vienna, 1948, 1950, 1954.

Allied and Associated Powers. *The Conditions of Peace with Austria. Treaty of Peace between the Principal Allied and Associated Powers and Austria*. (Treaty of St. Germain.) Washington, 1919.

Allied Commission for Austria. *Gazette of the Allied Commission for Austria I, December 1945—January 1946*. Vienna, 1946.

Amt der Burgenländischen Landesregierung. Landesstelle für Statistik. *Burgenländische Statistiken*. Eisenstadt, 1959.

Amtsblatt des Deutschen Hauses in Oedenburg. Hauptamt für Deutsch-Westungarn. Ödenburg (Sopron), 1920.

Amtsblatt für den Gau Deutsch-Westungarn. Ödenburg (Sopron), May–December, 1919.

Amtsblatt für das Gouvernement Deutsch-Westungarn. Ödenburg (Sopron), March–May, 1919.

Amtskalender für das Jahr 1949, 1950, 1954. Vienna, 1949, 1950, 1954.

Anschluss Archiv, Landesarchiv, Eisenstadt. This consists of 44 "Kartonen" containing the "Akten," that is, all the available papers concerning the events in Burgenland 1918–22. I made special use of "Kartonen" 1, 7, and 26.

Bericht über die Tätigkeit der deutschösterreichischen Friedensdelegation in St. Germain en Laye. Vienna, 1919.

Bundesamt für Eich und Vermessungswesen. *Karte des Burgenlandes 1:200,000.* Vienna, 1956.

———. *Provisorische Ausgabe der österreichischen Karte 1:50,000.* (Sheets 60, 61, 76, 77, 78, 79, 80, 106, 107, 108, 109, 136, 137, 138, 139, 167, 168, 192, 193). Vienna, 1946–56.

Bundesamt für Statistik. *Die Ergebnisse der österreichischen Volkszählung vom 22. März 1934.* Vienna, 1935.

———. *Die Ergebnisse der Volkszählung vom 7. März 1923.* Vienna, 1924.

———. *Statistische Nachrichten. Sonderheft: Wahlstatistik, Nationalratswahlen vom 24. April 1927.* Vienna, 1927.

———. *Statistische Nachrichten. Sonderheft: Nationalratswahlen vom 9. November 1930.* Vienna, 1931.

Bundesgesetzblatt für die Republik Österreich. 12. Dez., 1952. Vienna, 1952.

Bundesgesetzblatt für die Republik Österreich. 30. Juli, 1955. Vienna, 1955.

Bundesministerium für Verkehr und Elektrizitätswirtschaft. *Amtliches Eisenbahn- und Strassenbahnstatistik der Republik Österreich, Berichtsjahr 1955.* Vienna, 1956.

———. *Amtliches Österreichisches Kursbuch. Winter 1956–57, Winter 1960–61.* Vienna, 1956, 1960.

———. *Übersichtsplan der Postautolinien im Bereich der Post- und Telegraphendirektion. Für Wien, Niederösterreich und Burgenland in Wien. Stand von 23 V 1954.* Vienna, 1954.

Burgenländisches Landesarchiv. *Der Verwaltungsbezirk Neusiedl am See.* Eisenstadt, 1956.

Burgenländisches Adressenbuch, Samt Amtskalender, 1928, 1931, 1937. Sauerbrunn, 1928; Eisenstadt, 1931, 1937.

Federal Information Service. *Austria, Facts and Figures.* Vienna, 1959.

Jahrbuch und Adressbuch der Land- und Forstwirtschaft, Ergänzungsband 1930/1931, 1931/1932. Vienna, 1930, 1931.

Kammer für Arbeiter und Angestellte. *Wirtschaftsbericht über das Jahr 1928.* Sauerbrunn, 1929.

Központi Statisztikai Hivatal. *Az 1941 Évi Népszámlálás.* (1941 Census.) Budapest, 1947.

———. *1960 Évi Népszámlálás. 1 Előzetes Adatok.* (Preliminary Report of the 1960 Census.) Budapest, 1960.

Landesamtsblatt für das Burgenland 1921, 1922, 1923, 1924. Sauerbrunn, 1921, 1922, 1923, 1924.

Landesgesetzblatt für das Burgenland, Jahrgang 1922. Sauerbrunn, 1922.

Magyar Statisztikai Közlemények. *Az 1930 Évi Népszámlálás.* (1930 Census.) Budapest, 1932.

Österreichischer Amtskalender für das Jahr 1956. Vienna, 1956.

Österreichischen Statistischen Zentralamt. *Die Ergebnisse der Volkszählung vom 1. Juni 1951.* Vienna, 1952.

———. *Die Nationalratswahlen vom 25. November 1945, 9. Oktober 1949, 22. Februar 1953, 13. Mai 1956, 10. Mai 1959.* Vienna, 1946, 1950, 1953, 1956, 1959.

———. *Statistisches Handbuch für die Republik Österreich VI. Jahrgang. Neue Folge.* Vienna, 1955.

Oesterreichisches Verkehrsbureau. *Austria Verkehr—Kursbuch.* Vienna, 1932, 1933.

Staatsgesetzblatt für die Republik Österreich, Jahrgang 1919, 1920, 1945. Vienna, 1919, 1920, 1945.

Stenographisches Protokoll. 28. Sitzung der II Wahlperiode des Burgenländischen Landtages, Donnerstag den 30. April 1925. Sauerbrunn, 1925.

Volksbildungswerk für das Burgenland. *Mein Heimatvolk—Mein Heimatland.* Eisenstadt, 1951.

Vorlage der Staatsvertrag von St. Germain mit den allierten und assozierten Mächten, samt drei Annexen. Vienna, 1919.

Books

Adamovich, Ludwig, and Froehlich, Georg. *Die österreichischen Verfassungsgesetze des Bundes und der Länder.* Vienna, 1925.

———. *Die Novellen zur Bundesverfassung.* Vienna, 1926.

Aull, Otto. *Eisenstadt. Ein Führer durch seine Geschichte und Kunst.* Eisenstadt, 1931.

Benedikt, Heinrich. *Geschichte der Republik Österreich.* Munich, 1954.

Beneš, Edward. *Der Aufstand der Nationen.* Berlin, 1928.

Berka, Günther. *Die tschechische Irredenta in Deutschösterreich.* Graz, 1928.

Bodo, Fritz. *Burgenland Atlas.* Vienna, 1940.

Cvijić, Jovan. *Frontière Septentrionale des Yougoslaves.* Paris, 1919.

Erdödy, Tamás, *Habsburgs Weg von Wilhelm zu Briand. Memoiren des Grafen Tamás von Erdödy*, edited by Paul Szemere and Erich Czech. Zürich, Leipzig, Vienna, 1931.

Haromy, Franz. *Das Burgenland-Buch.* Vienna, 1950.

Héjjas, Jenö. *A Nyugatmagyarországi Felkelés, Kecskemétiek az 1921. Évi Nyugatmagyarországi Harcokban.* (The West Hungarian Uprising; the Kecskemét-ites in the 1921 Battles in West Hungary.) Kecskemét, 1929. This gives a detailed description locale by locale of the activities of these troops.

Hellbling, Ernst C. *Österreichische Verfassungs- und Verwaltungsgeschichte*. Vienna, 1956.

Knobloch, Johann. *Romāni-Texte aus dem Burgenland*. Eisenstadt, 1953.

Lendl, Hubert, "Die Sozialökonomische Struktur der Burgenländischen Wirtschaft." Unpublished Doctoral dissertation, Hochschule der Bodenkultur, Vienna, 1937.

Masaryk, Thomas. *Die Welt Revolution*. Berlin, 1927.

Miller, David Hunter. *My Diary at the Conference of Paris. With Documents*. Volumes XIV, XVI, XVII, XIX, New York, 1924.

Miltschinsky, Viktor. *Das Verbrechen von Ödenburg*. Vienna, Zürich, 1922.

Missuray-Krúg, Lajos. *A Nyugatmagyarországi Felkelés*. (The West Hungarian Uprising.) Sopron, 1938. Although obviously pro-Hungarian, this is probably the best work available on the clashes in Burgenland between the Austrian gendarmerie and the Hungarian bands.

Nicolson, Harold. *Peacemaking, 1919*. London, 1933.

Nowak, K. Friedrich. *Chaos*. Munich, 1923.

Paschinger, Herbert. *Entwicklung und Wesen der Hauptstädte der österreichischen Bundesländer*. Innsbruck, 1954.

Rottensteiner, Rupert. *Das Burgenland Buch*. Vienna, 1937.

Seipel, Ignaz. *Der Kampf um die österreichische Verfassung*. Vienna, 1930.

Szmudits, Friedrich. "Geschichte der Angliederung des Burgenlandes an Österreich." Unpublished Doctoral dissertation, University of Vienna, 1937. A thorough coverage but strongly pro-Austrian/German.

Tschida, Josef. "Die Stellungnahme der Wiener Presse zum Anschluss und zur Einrichtung des Burgenlandes." Unpublished Doctoral dissertation, University of Vienna, 1947. A good summation of the attitudes of the Vienna newspapers towards the events in Burgenland 1918–22.

Vondracek, Felix J. *The Foreign Policy of Czechoslovakia 1918–1935*. New York, 1937.

Wambaugh, Sarah. *Plebiscites Since the World War*. 2 vols. Washington, 1933.

INDEX